Energy, Environmental and Economic Sustainability in East Asia

This book looks at institutional reforms for the use of energy, water and resources toward a sustainable future in East Asia.

The book argues that developments in the East Asian region are critical to global sustainability and acknowledges that there is an increasing degree of mutual reliance among countries in East Asia – primarily China, Japan, Korea and Taiwan. It analyzes environmental impacts stemming from the use of energy, water and mineral resources via economic development in East Asia in the medium to long term (through 2050) through theoretical and empirical modelling. The book also evaluates the ripple effects of environmental and resource policies on each country's economy and clarifies the direction of institutional reform in energy systems, resources and water use for a sustainable future.

Soocheol Lee is Professor of Faculty of Economics, Meijo University in Japan. He graduated from Seoul National University and received his PhD at the Graduate School of Kyoto University. He had worked for the Federation of Korean Industry as a team leader of Economic Research Department. He has written many books and papers on energy and environmental policy design and cooperation for sustainable low-carbon economy in East Asia.

Hector Pollitt is Director and Head of Modelling at Cambridge Econometrics, with extensive expertise in the development and application of macroeconomic modelling approaches for policy assessment. He has made significant contributions to several official assessments of energy and climate policy in the European Union and is responsible for development of the global E3ME simulation model.

Kiyoshi Fujikawa is Professor of Applied Social System Institute of Asia, Nagoya University in Japan. He graduated from Kobe University in Japan and received his PhD there. He had worked at the Department of Economics and Social Affairs in the United Nations as a statistician before teaching in Japan. He has made significant contributions to application of input-output analysis on environmental economics.

Routledge Studies in Sustainability

The Politics of Sustainability in the Arctic
Reconfiguring Identity, Space, and Time
Edited by Ulrik Pram Gad and Jeppe Strandsbjerg

Global Planning Innovations for Urban Sustainability
Edited by Sébastien Darchen and Glen Searle

The Question of Limits
A Historical Perspective on the Environmental Crisis
Christian Marouby

Urban Social Sustainability
Theory, Practice and Policy
Edited by Ramin Keivani and M. Reza Shirazi

Holistic Sustainability through Craft-design Collaboration
Rebecca Reubens

Sustainable Development Teaching
Ethical and Political Challenges
Katrien Van Poeck, Leif Östman and Johan Öhman

Utopia in the Anthropocene
A Change Plan for a Sustainable and Equitable World
Michael Harvey

Sustainability Governance and Hierarchy
Philippe Hamman

Energy, Environmental and Economic Sustainability in East Asia
Policies and Institutional Reforms
Edited by Soocheol Lee, Hector Pollitt and Kiyoshi Fujikawa

For more information on this series, please visit www.routledge.com/Routledge-Studies-in-Sustainability/book-series/RSSTY

Energy, Environmental and Economic Sustainability in East Asia

Policies and Institutional Reforms

Edited by Soocheol Lee,
Hector Pollitt and
Kiyoshi Fujikawa

LONDON AND NEW YORK

First published 2020
by Routledge
2 Park Square, Milton Park, Abingdon, Oxon OX14 4RN

and by Routledge
605 Third Avenue, New York, NY 10017

First issued in paperback 2021

Routledge is an imprint of the Taylor & Francis Group, an informa business

© 2020 selection and editorial matter, Soocheol Lee, Hector Pollitt and Kiyoshi Fujikawa; individual chapters, the contributors

The right of Soocheol Lee, Hector Pollitt and Kiyoshi Fujikawa to be identified as the authors of the editorial material, and of the authors for their individual chapters, has been asserted in accordance with sections 77 and 78 of the Copyright, Designs and Patents Act 1988.

All rights reserved. No part of this book may be reprinted or reproduced or utilised in any form or by any electronic, mechanical, or other means, now known or hereafter invented, including photocopying and recording, or in any information storage or retrieval system, without permission in writing from the publishers.

Trademark notice: Product or corporate names may be trademarks or registered trademarks, and are used only for identification and explanation without intent to infringe.

Publisher's Note
The publisher has gone to great lengths to ensure the quality of this reprint but points out that some imperfections in the original copies may be apparent.

British Library Cataloguing-in-Publication Data
A catalogue record for this book is available from the British Library

Library of Congress Cataloging-in-Publication Data
A catalog record for this book has been requested

Typeset in Galliard
by Apex CoVantage, LLC

ISBN 13: 978-1-03-209064-1 (pbk)
ISBN 13: 978-1-138-50006-8 (hbk)

Contents

Figures

Tables

Contributors

Aiko Azuma is Associate Professor of Shokei Gakuin University, Japan.

Li-Chun Chen is Professor at Yamaguchi University, Japan.

Unnada Chewpreecha is Principal Economic Modeler at Cambridge Econometrics, United Kingdom.

Akihiro Chiashi is Associate Professor at Ferris University, Japan.

Yongsung Cho is Professor at Korea University, South Korea.

Kiyoshi Fujikawa is Professor at Nagoya University, Japan.

Mary Goldman is Economist at Cambridge Econometrics, United Kingdom.

Yanmin He is Lecturer at Otemon Gakuin University, Japan.

Hector Pollitt is Director at Cambridge Econometrics, United Kingdom.

Seonghee Kim is Senior Researcher at The Institute of Energy Economics, Japan.

Florian Knobloch is Researcher at Radboud University, The Netherlands.

Aileen Lam is Lecturer at the University of Macao, China.

Soocheol Lee is Professor at Meijo University, Japan.

Tae-Yeoun Lee is Professor at Ryukoku University, Japan.

Chun-Hsu Lin is Research Fellow at Chung-Hua Institute for Economic Research, Taiwan.

Ken'ichi Matsumoto is Associate Professor at Nagasaki University, Japan.

Jean-François Mercure is Senior Lecturer at the University of Exeter, United Kingdom.

Sung-In Na is Professor at Hiroshima Shudo University, Japan.

Park Seung-Joon is Professor at Kwansei-Gakuin University, Japan.

Sunhee Suk is Associate Professor at Nagasaki University, Japan.

Pim Vercoulen is Economist at Cambridge Econometrics, United Kingdom.

Bin Xu is a doctoral student at Meijo University, Japan.

Zuoyi Ye is Associate Professor at Shanghai University of International Business and Economics, China.

Introduction

Soocheol Lee, Hector Pollitt and Kiyoshi Fujikawa

Overview

If the world is to move towards a sustainable future, developments in the East Asian region are crucial. The region currently accounts for about 35% of global CO_2 emissions and includes three of the top ten global emitter countries, including the one with the highest emissions levels: China. The region accounts for a substantial and, in many cases, growing share of global material consumption; for example, China, Japan and South Korea (Korea, hereafter) remain as four of the world's top five producers of steel. Pressures on freshwater resources have been illustrated by the South-North Water Transfer Project in China. Air pollution in China is estimated to kill up to more than one million people per year.[1]

The aim of this book is to demonstrate the necessary direction of an institutional reform for the use of energy and resources towards a sustainable future in East Asia. We consider four countries in the region (China, Japan, Korea and Taiwan),[2] each of which sets its own national policy. However, all of them also show a growing degree of mutual reliance in both economic terms and environmental sustainability.

In this book, we analyze the impact of different policies that can be used to address climate change and sustainability in East Asia. Through theoretical and empirical modelling, we estimate quantitatively the environmental and economic impacts from the introduction of such policies. In the field of climate policy, we consider a range of policies – including carbon taxes, energy-efficiency mandates, measures to promote renewable energy forms and many more – with the aim of achieving long-term targets of emission reduction in East Asia that are consistent with the global target of a less than 2°C rise in temperature.

We then consider how climate policy might interact with other areas of sustainability in East Asia, including impacts on air quality, material use and fresh water consumption. We show that interactions are complex and there might be a need for further policies to alleviate different environmental pressures.

Throughout this book we also evaluate the ripple effects of environmental and resource policies on each East Asian country's economy. We conclude with a set of recommendations on the direction of institutional reforms regarding energy systems and natural resource management in East Asia, and a desirable policy cooperation for a sustainable future.

The main analytical tool used in our analysis is the state-of-the-art E3ME-FTT model (see Chapter 1). The E3ME model is one of the largest macroeconomic models in the world and is able to divide each East Asian economy into 43 sectors. It integrates the economy, labor market and different aspects of sustainability – for example, energy and material consumption. E3ME is well established in the analysis of climate policy and resource efficiency, and is used frequently by the European Commission for its 'Impact Assessment' of new policy measures. The model is also used by national governments to assess proposed new policies. As described in Chapter 1, E3ME is highly empirical and based on theory that is different to that in the standard Computable General Equilibrium (CGE) model typically used for environmental policy analysis.

The E3ME model is linked to four bottom-up models of technology diffusion (Future Technology Transformation, FTT) for power generation, the steel industry, road transport and household heating. These models, which were originally developed by Jean-François Mercure (Exeter and Cambridge University, UK), simulate the diffusion of technology, which is crucial in any ambitious climate scenario. They are linked to E3ME to provide a micro-level technology representation.

The complete integrated modelling framework is able to provide a wide range of policy analyses that are potentially of high interest to other researchers as well as policy makers. Throughout this book we also refer frequently to the underlying post-Keynesian and Schumpeterian theory that underpins the modelling, which is designed to provide educational value.

Background and aim of the book

This book builds on previous work by the same team, also published as a book, *Low-carbon, Sustainable Future in East Asia: Improving energy systems, taxation and policy cooperation* (Lee, Pollitt and Park (2015). The previous book assessed how mid-term CO_2 emissions targets in 2030 could be met in East Asia through reform of the power generation sector and national taxation systems. The current book assesses how, in light of the acceptance of the long-term emissions targets by 2050 under the Paris climate agreement, East Asia can develop in a way such that emissions are reduced without putting pressure on other environmental resources such as mineral resources and water, while at the same time promoting economic prosperity. It therefore adds a long-term perspective to the previous analysis and also considers use of energy and material resources in the context of a broader sustainable development strategy.

As already noted, it is recognized that environmental problems are already emerging in the East Asia region. These are due to mass consumption, rising energy demand, resource depletion and uneven allocation of water usage (including virtual water transfers in trade) – major threats to sustainability in East Asia that could give rise to resource nationalism. Addressing them at a cross-border regional level is, therefore, an urgent matter. Furthermore, greenhouse gases, and pollutants generated through energy, water, mineral resource and land use

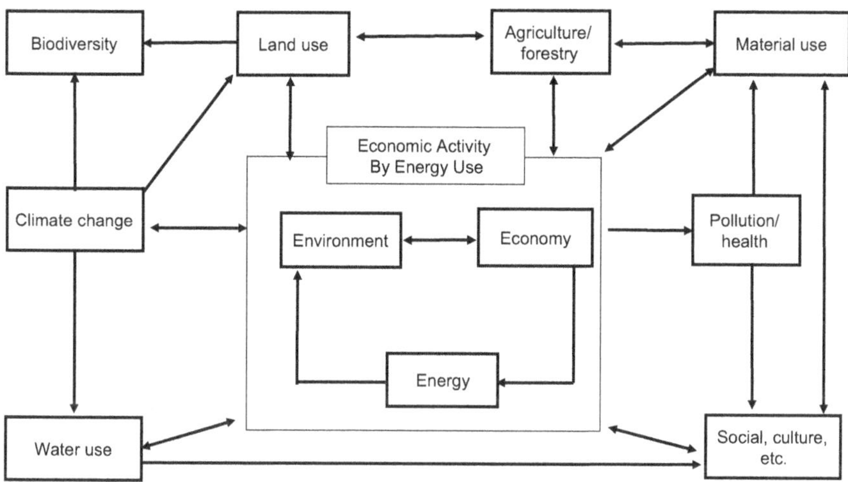

Figure 0.1 Nexus among economy, energy, resources and pollution

are having harmful impacts on the climate, agricultural output and health. The effects extend to biodiversity, society and culture (Figure 0.1).

These issues are closely interwoven; for example, there is reciprocity among energy, water and resource consumption, and competition between agricultural production and biomass resources. It is essential to understand problems relating to all these resources from a comprehensive perspective. A great deal of previous research has tackled these individual issues at the country level. However, there are few examples of comprehensive investigations based on the situation as it pertains to the East Asian region.

The analysis in this book is the result of a long-standing collaboration between researchers in East Asia and the UK. Over the past eight years, the Research Group for East Asia Environmental Policy Studies (REEPS) and Cambridge Econometrics developed a version of the E3ME-FTT model to specifically analyze the East Asian region (E3ME-FTT-Asia). The scenarios presented in this book are the results of that effort.

Significance and summary of this book

This book consists of three parts, providing answers to the following key questions:

- How to build a sustainable, low-carbon power generation sector that is not dependent on nuclear power and that is economically viable?
- How to promote innovation in low-carbon technologies in final energy use, so as to keep East Asia consistent with the Paris climate agreement?
- How to promote efficient use of other natural resources to reduce environmental pressures across the region?

We hope that this book will contribute to the development of policy packages to boost renewable energy, innovation in low-carbon technologies and resource efficiency in East Asia, thereby putting the region on a path towards a sustainable future. We test a variety of different policies, including market-based instruments, regulatory policies and measures to boost the adoption of key technologies. Policy simulations that use a large-scale macro-econometric model facilitate the provision of persuasive analysis in areas such as provision of low-carbon, resource-efficient social infrastructure; investment in technological development; and deployment and more efficient use of water and material resources.

As already noted, East Asian countries are increasingly interdependent, not just in economic terms but also in terms of energy, resources and the environment. We aim for this research to contribute to a close energy and environmental cooperation in East Asia and, ultimately, the establishment of an East Asian community, thereby, contributing to peace in the region.

The book is financially supported by Grants-in-Aid for Scientific Research of the Japanese Society for the Promotion of Science.

We would like to take this opportunity to deeply thank the Society for their support.

Soocheol Lee, Hector Pollitt and Kiyoshi Fujikawa
On the behalf of authors of this book
September 2019

Notes

1 www.scmp.com/news/china/science/article/2166542/air-pollution-killing-1-million-people-and-costing-chinese
2 For convenience, we regard Taiwan as a country in this book but do not make a judgment on its political status.

1 Introduction to the E3ME and FTT models

Hector Pollitt, Soocheol Lee and Unnada Chewpreecha

Introduction

Throughout this book, computer modeling is used to illustrate the effectiveness of different public policies. Specifically, we draw upon results from the E3ME macro-econometric model and the FTT energy technology models that are linked to E3ME. This chapter describes these models.

Before getting to the details of the modeling tools we have applied, it is important to be aware of the more general context in which modeling is often carried out. Macroeconomic modeling is playing an ever-increasing role in the policy-making process, but the strengths and limitations of modeling remain a rather niche topic. While it is well known that economists frequently disagree with one another, it is less well known that the models they develop reflect these disagreements.

The various assumptions that economists apply in economic analysis are carried through to other areas in which the models are applied. For example, assumptions about optimizing behavior in the economic system are typically applied in the energy system as well. The users of model results (e.g. policy makers) are rarely aware of the underlying assumptions in the models or how they relate to the conclusions from the analysis.

In the area of climate policy, a notable example is the use of different policy instruments to meet CO_2 reduction targets. Many economists have applied Computable General Equilibrium (CGE) modeling approaches that are based on neoclassical economics to answer the question about what the best policy instruments should be. They find that a carbon-pricing measure (i.e. tax or an emission trading scheme) outperforms all other policy instruments in terms of 'efficiency' to reduce emissions. However, this finding simply reflects the assumptions of the model, that 'perfect' markets are best suited to the efficient allocation of scarce resources and, therefore, a carbon market will automatically outperform any regulatory measures.

To agree with the conclusion that carbon markets produce the best outcome, one would have to accept the assumptions of the modeling applied. To name a few:

- Markets are always 'perfect', with prices adjusting freely to balance supply and demand. No firms have monopoly positions or can set product prices beyond what the market dictates. Wage rates are also fully flexible and move to rates at which there is no unemployment.
- All individuals and companies have 'perfect' knowledge about all the potential ways that they can spend their money.
- All individuals are identical and behave in the same way. All individuals and companies act in a fully 'rational' manner, and spend their money in the way that optimizes their welfare or profit.
- There is a limited amount of money in the economic system.
- Technology develops independently from what is going on in the wider economy.

All these assumptions have been contested by researchers in other fields. As we describe in the next section, none of them are applied in the E3ME model. The outcome is that E3ME can produce opposite results to those obtained using a standard CGE model. For example, measures to support specific renewable technologies may turn out to be better than a carbon tax, both in terms of CO_2 reduction and economic impact.

The award of the 2018 Nobel Prize for economics to the US economist William Nordhaus has raised a similar debate among economists about the role of modeling and assumptions in policy analysis. The Dynamic Integrated Climate-Economy (DICE) model built by Nordhaus was pioneering in the way it forms linkages between the economic and natural environments, that is, forming an 'Integrated Assessment Model'. The model is used to estimate values of the 'social cost of carbon', a value the US government uses to price CO_2 emissions in all its policies (most recent estimates from DICE are in Nordhaus, 2017). The DICE model is fully transparent and available for researchers to use in their own analysis. Despite its widespread use, the DICE model has come in for substantial criticism (Pindyck, 2013; Stern, 2013). The paper by Pindyck may be summarized by its title and the opening of its abstract: *Climate Change Policy: What Do the Models Tell Us? Very little.*

DICE may be criticized for being overly simplistic (e.g. Ackerman et al., 2010). However, more substantial concerns arise from the underlying philosophy of the DICE model and, more generally, the social cost of carbon. The model is based on optimization principles that are solved by finding the point at which human economic welfare is maximized. It currently predicts that the optimal limit of global warming is much above the target level of 2°C set out in the Paris Agreement and, based on its assumption of 'perfect knowledge', ignores the risk of catastrophic climate-related events.

In summary, model results should always be considered in the context of the assumptions that the model is based on. The purpose of this chapter is to present our key assumptions in an accessible manner. We do not present equations but provide external references for more technical-minded readers who are interested in exploring the key relationships in the modeling further.

The E3ME macro-econometric model

E3ME is a computer-based model of the world's economic and energy systems, and the environment. It was originally developed through the European Commission's research framework programs in the 1990s, and is now widely used in Europe and beyond for policy assessment, forecasting and research purposes.

The model breaks the world down into 59 regions, which include an explicit representation of all G20 countries, all European Union countries and other regional groupings to match global totals. East Asia is represented by four regions of the model: China, Japan, Korea and Taiwan. However, we do not limit the analysis to these four regions; interactions with the rest of the world may be important, for example, through international trade.

Within each region of the model, the economy is split into 43 economic production sectors. These sectors include primary production (e.g. agriculture, mining), manufacturing, construction and a range of services sectors. Each of these sectors interacts with the other sectors (modeled through input-output tables that determine purchases between sectors) and uses natural resources in different amounts and in different ways. When considering sustainability policy, the sectoral disaggregation is, therefore, important.

The modeling approach is highly empirical. Data for the four East Asian regions are taken from national statistical agencies as annual time series that cover the time period back to 1970 (where available). These data are used in econometric equations to estimate behavioral parameters in the model; for example, the response in demand to a change in prices. There are ~35 sets of econometric equations, each one disaggregated by sector and region.

Figure 1.1 presents the different modules of the E3ME model. The figure shows how the model links the economic system to the consumption of natural resources (energy and materials) but also the feedbacks to the economy (e.g. through the economic performance of the extraction sectors). Similarly to the approach used in systems dynamics modeling, each module uses its own units – with physical quantities used where possible. These linkages are crucial for addressing the issues of sustainable development that are posed throughout this book.

The economic modeling is based on the standard system of national accounting, as originally developed by Richard Stone in Cambridge, UK. Many of the identity relationships in the model (e.g. that GDP is equal to private and public consumption plus investment plus net trade) reflect the balances in the

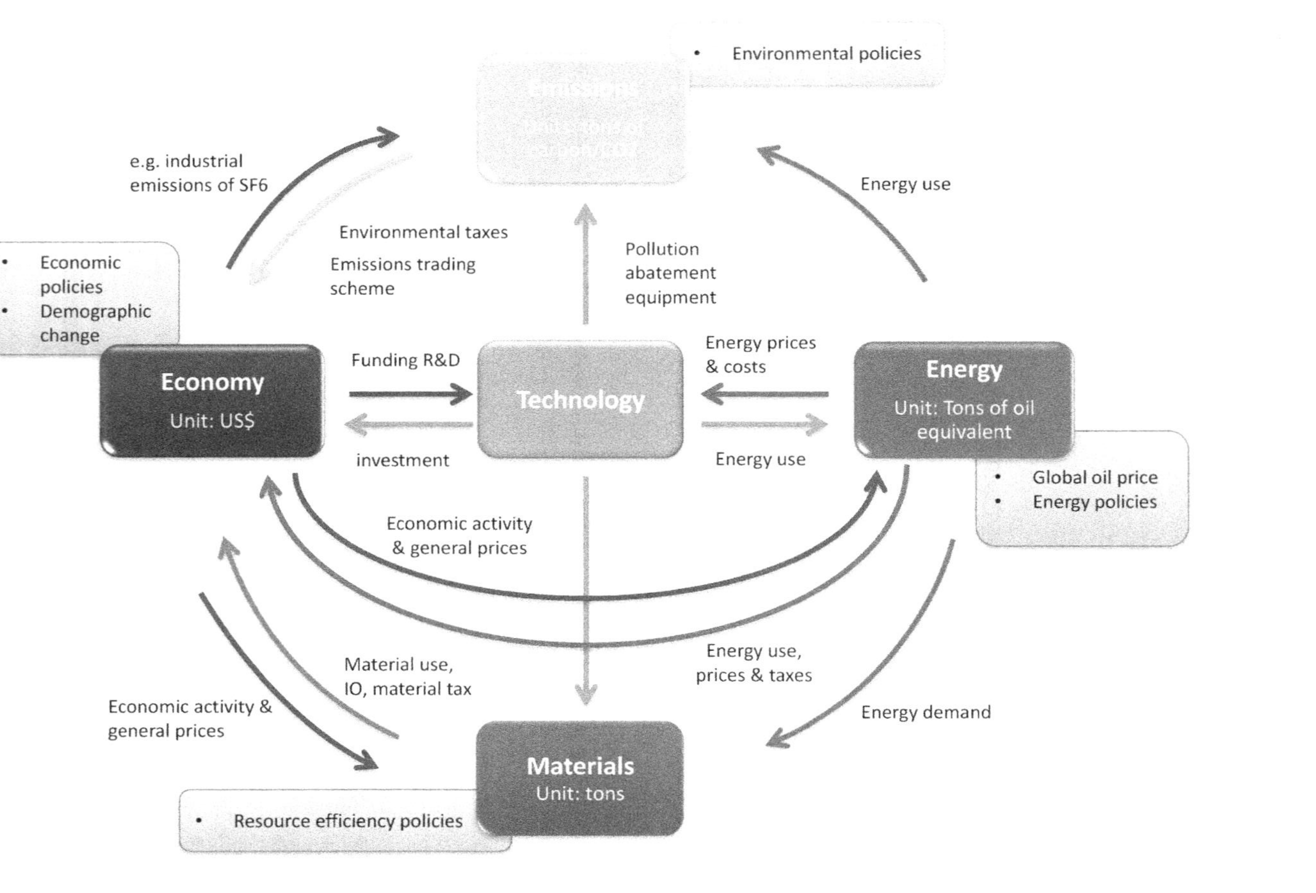

Figure 1.1 The different modules in the E3ME model

national accounts and provide the overall framework for the economic analysis. The econometric equations then add behavioral relationships to the accounting structure.

The E3ME model is typically referred to as a macro-econometric model, reflecting the method used to estimate its parameters. However, many of its most important properties are derived from its representation of post-Keynesian macroeconomic theory. Post-Keynesian economics builds on the original work of Keynes in the mid-20th century to reflect the structure of the modern economy, particularly the importance of finance. Most of the core principles, however, are consistent with the original work of Keynes, for example, that the economy is 'demand-driven' and unemployment is an important feature of the economy. An introduction to post-Keynesian economics is provided in King (2015) and a more-complete description in Lavoie (2015).

In the modeling, the starting point is fundamental uncertainty, as described in Keynes' Treatise on Probability (Keynes, 1921). The assumption of perfect knowledge that was described in the introduction to this chapter is, therefore, not adopted in post-Keynesian economics. The even more extreme assumption of 'perfect foresight', which requires full knowledge of the future, is clearly not applicable either.

A lack of knowledge means that it is not possible to optimize decision making. An alternative way of modeling human behavior is, therefore, required – which is where the econometrics comes in; the assumption is instead that behavior is based on that which may be observed in the historical data. The use of econometrics has in the past been criticized (e.g. Lucas, 1976), and uncertainty around future behavior must be acknowledged. However, the econometric parameters provide our best unbiased guess and the Lucas Critique is applicable to alternative modeling approaches as well (Haldane and Turrell, 2018).

Leaving aside questions of model parameterization, the relaxation of the assumption of optimal behavior changes the modeling paradigm. If the system does not optimize, then there may be spare resources in the economy (e.g. unemployed workers). The result is that, in line with the writing of Keynes, the level of output in the economy is determined by the level of aggregate demand for resources, not the maximum potential supply. Whereas constraints on the availability of resources are respected in the modeling, output is typically below its potential level.

One of the most important findings in Keynes' *General Theory* (Keynes, 1936) was that unemployment is a natural outcome of the economy. Contrary to the beliefs of many economists, this finding is not only due to the 'stickiness' of wages that is described in the foregoing example, but also reflects the role of money and the financial system in the modern economy. The representation of the financial system in E3ME reflects these findings (Pollitt and Mercure, 2017), and we discuss this further in Chapter 10. Crucially, central banks now recognize that the modern financial system works as depicted in E3ME and not as in standard CGE models (McLeay et al., 2014).

While discussion about optimal behavior and how the financial system works may sound overly technical in nature, it has a strong bearing on the model results. For example, consider the following three statements:

- If decision making is not optimal, then there is a role for policy making to improve outcomes.
- If individuals' optimal decisions do not lead to the best outcome for society as a whole, then there is a role for policy making to improve outcomes.
- If not all available economic resources are used, then it is possible to increase output by finding policies that use them.

Under a standard CGE model that is based on neoclassical economics, none of these statements is relevant as the conditions are not met. Under the post-Keynesian modeling framework offered by E3ME, however, each one may be true, although the final outcome of the modeling depends on the policies that are being suggested. The important point is that the potential positive net impacts of policy making (including both price-based measures and regulation) are not ruled out by assumption.

Results from the E3ME model are often compared with those from CGE models. Examples of such exercises include Lee et al. (2015), European Commission (2015) and Jansen and Klaassen (2000). Increasingly, the model is used alongside CGE models for policy analysis, so as to provide a range of possible different outcomes (e.g. European Commission, 2015).

Previously, the E3ME model was applied to assess a wide range of sustainability policies in East Asia, in Lee et al. (2015). It has also been applied to specific assessments of carbon taxation (Lee et al., 2012) and nuclear energy (Pollitt et al., 2014) in East Asia. At global level, recent high-profile applications of the model have been presented in New Climate Economy (2018), which suggests a portfolio of policies that could benefit both the environment and the economy. Mercure et al. (2018a) suggests that more than $1 trillion of value could be lost from fossil fuel assets under existing technological trends.

Further information about the E3ME model can be found in the model manual (Cambridge Econometrics, 2019), which is available on the model website www.e3me.com. Further discussion of the modeling approach in the context of sustainability is provided in Mercure et al. (2016). A full list of equations is provided in the appendix to Mercure et al. (2018b).

Modeling the power generation sector – Part 1

The success of a low-carbon sustainable transition will be determined by the technologies that are adopted both in East Asia and the rest of the world. Any attempt to model this transition, therefore, requires a detailed treatment of technology development and adoption.

The basic E3ME model is not well equipped to provide such a treatment, for several reasons. First, the sectoral disaggregation of the model is not detailed enough to incorporate a high level of technological detail. Second, the econometric approach requires a complete set of historical data, which is, by definition, unavailable for new technologies. Third, the process of technology development and deployment is highly non-linear and, therefore, difficult to fit into an econometric structure.

We, thus, require a different approach but one that is broadly compatible with the assumptions that underpin E3ME. This is provided by the Future Technology Transformation (FTT) family of models. Like E3ME, FTT follows a simulation-based approach and does not make assumptions about companies and individuals optimizing their behavior.

FTT uses a decision-making core for investors in key energy sectors that face several different options (Mercure, 2012). For example, an electricity utility investing in new capacity can choose among a range of different conventional and renewable technologies. The decision-making core takes place by pairwise 'levelized' cost comparisons that include up-front investment and lifetime running costs. The approach is conceptually equivalent to a binary logit model, parameterized by measured technology cost distributions.

Investment costs decrease over time, following a path that is determined by a set of learning curves. The diffusion of technology follows a set of coupled non-linear differential equations, sometimes called 'Lotka-Volterra' or 'replicator dynamics', which represent the better ability of larger or well-established industries to capture the market and the life expectancy of technologies. Owing to learning-by-doing and increasing returns to adoption, it results in path-dependent technology scenarios that arise from electricity sector policies.

FTT:Power (Mercure, 2012; Mercure et al., 2014) was the first FTT model to be constructed. It takes electricity demand from the E3ME model and estimates the technology mix used to generate the required power. Feedbacks to E3ME include electricity, energy consumption and investment made by the power sector. FTT:Power includes restrictions on the share of intermittent technologies in the electricity grid.

Modeling energy demand in the steel, transport and household heating sectors – Part 2

Aside from the power sector, the version of E3ME that is applied in this book is linked to three other FTT models. The sectors covered by these models include the passenger transport sector (Mercure et al., 2018c) and the household heating sector (Knobloch et al., 2018). The fourth FTT model, of the steel sector, is new and has not yet been formally published in any peer-reviewed journal.

These models are described in their respective chapters in Part 2 of this book. In summary, the approach is similar to that of the FTT:Power model, with the diffusion of various technologies estimated by using a set of differential equations on the basis of levelized costs. The different technologies include different types of vehicle, household heating systems and ways of manufacturing steel.

In most countries these sectors when combined account for a large proportion of total energy consumption. For the remaining sectors, econometric equations, including income and price elasticities, are used to estimate energy demand. These equations do not account for specific technological options but provide a representation of energy demand that responds to taxation and efficiency policies.

Total energy consumption in the model is constrained by a global database of renewable and non-renewable resources (Mercure and Salas, 2012, 2013). This database provides a set of cost curves that place capacity constraints on fuel consumption; as rates of consumption increase, the cheapest sources of energy are used up and prices, therefore, rise.

Modeling resource consumption – Part 3

In Part 3 of this book we extend the modeling into other areas of sustainable use of resources and water that have not been covered previously. This is an important development that is meant to identify potential 'problem shifting' and possible bottlenecks that might prevent the decarbonization targets from being met. For example, the interaction between energy and material consumption is not well understood. The availability of fresh water is becoming a key issue of sustainability in many parts of the world but is also linked to energy consumption, for example through energy-intensive desalination plants, hydro power and cooling for thermal power plants. Air pollution, and its associated health effects, is now recognized as an important issue across much of Asia.

Food production and land use are also closely linked to energy and water consumption, forming what is sometimes referred to as the 'Energy-Water-Food' nexus. There is a particular concern over the use of bioenergy to meet decarbonization targets, and the land requirements to produce this bioenergy. This remains work in development but is an issue that is touched upon in several places in this book.

Conclusions

There is an ongoing debate among economists about whether it is possible to transition to a sustainable global economy while economic growth continues. This debate has been framed as 'green growth' vs 'degrowth'. Support for degrowth has grown recently, following the vision laid out by Jackson (2009). The terms of the debate vary across the different areas of environmental sustainability. For example, in terms of decarbonization, there is no theoretical reason that economic growth could not continue based on renewable energy, so the debate focuses on whether continued economic growth is an insurmountable barrier to decarbonizing fast enough. For biological resources, the question relates to how intensively food can be produced and what the side effects of intensive agriculture are. On mineral resources, finite stocks mean that, eventually, there will be limits on consumption.

The chapters in this book aim to explore paths in which East Asia's economies can continue to grow without breaching environmental limits, that is, where green growth is possible. The modeling shows that, in many ways, a reduction in environmental pressures becomes a driver of growth, for example through new investments in clean technologies. These pathways are always linked to specific policies that are available to national policy makers. Although it is never possible to say for sure that the outcomes are fully sustainable (because it is not possible to track every resource type in our analysis), the results of the modeling provide support for future green growth patterns.

In summary, the modeling in this book departs from the standard equilibrium analysis that is usually used by economists to estimate the costs of climate policy. Our approach is highly empirical and dynamic in nature, and has a strong emphasis on capturing the trends in technology development and diffusion that are required in a low-carbon transition. There are no assumptions about optimizing behavior in the modeling.

In Part 3, we further attempt to link the analysis of low-carbon development to other areas of sustainability, so as to present a future in East Asia in which economic growth may continue in a way that limits environmental degradation.

Finally, it must be recognized that all models are abstractions of reality and, therefore, face limitations. E3ME is no different, and at various points throughout this book we discuss some of the key assumptions that must be made and the resulting limitations in the analysis. The overall aim of our research is to use the modeling to help better understand the problems that East Asia faces, as well as providing quantitative estimates of the impacts of policies aimed at moving toward a sustainable future in East Asia.

References

Ackerman, F, EA Stanton and R Bueno (2010) 'Fat tails, exponents, extreme uncertainty: Simulating catastrophe in DICE', *Ecological Economics*, Volume 69, Issue 8, pp 1657–1665.

Cambridge Econometrics (2019) *E3ME manual: Version 7*, available at www.e3me.com

European Commission (2015) 'Assessing the employment and social impact of energy efficiency', *Final Report for European Commission, DG ENER*, available at https://ec.europa.eu/energy/sites/ener/files/documents/CE_EE_Jobs_appendices%2018Nov2015.pdf

Haldane, AG and AE Turrell (2018) 'An interdisciplinary model for macroeconomics', *Oxford Review of Economic Policy*, Volume 34, Issue 1–2, pp 219–251.

Jackson, T (2009) *Prosperity Without Growth*, New York: Routledge.

Jansen, H and G Klaassen (2000) 'Economic impacts of the 1997 EU energy tax: simulations with three EU-wide models', *Environmental and Resource Economics*, Volume 15, Issue 2, pp 179–197.

Keynes, JM (1921) *Treatise on Probability*, London: Macmillan & Co.

Keynes, JM (1936) *The General Theory of Employment, Interest and Money*, New York: Palgrave Macmillan.

King, JE (2015) *Advanced Introduction to Post Keynesian Economics*, Cheltenham, UK and Northampton, MA: Edward Elgar.

Knobloch, F, H Pollitt, U Chewpreecha, V Daioglou and J-F Mercure (2018) 'Simulating the deep decarbonisation of residential heating for limiting global warming to 1.5°C', *Energy Efficiency*, Volume 12, Issue 2, pp 521–550, available at https://link.springer.com/article/10.1007/s12053-018-9710-0

Lavoie, M (2015) *Post-Keynesian Economics: New Foundations*, Cheltenham, UK and Northampton, MA: Edward Elgar.

Lee, S, H Pollitt and SJ Park (2015) *Low-Carbon, Sustainable Future in East Asia*, New York: Routledge.

Lee, S, H Pollitt and K Ueta (2012) 'A model-based econometric assessment of Japanese environmental tax reform', *The Scientific World Journal*, Volume 2012 (2012), Article ID 835917.

Lucas, R (1976) 'Econometric policy evaluation: A critique', in Brunner, K and A Meltzer (Eds.), *The Phillips Curve and Labor Markets*, Carnegie-Rochester Conference Series on Public Policy, New York: American Elsevier, pp 19–46.

McLeay, M, A Radia and R Thomas (2014) 'Money creation in the modern economy', *Bank of England Quarterly Bulletin*, Q1.

Mercure, J-F (2012) 'FTT:Power: A global model of the power sector with induced technological change and natural resource depletion', *Energy Policy*, Volume 48, pp 799–811.

Mercure, J-F, S Lam, S Billington and H Pollitt (2018c) 'Integrated assessment modelling as a positive science: Private passenger road transport policies to meet a climate target well below 2°C', *Climatic Change*, Volume 151, Issue 2, pp 109–129.

Mercure, J-F, H Pollitt, AM Bassi, JE Viñuales and NR Edwards (2016) 'Modelling complex systems of heterogeneous agents to better design sustainability transitions policy', *Global Environmental Change*, Volume 37, pp 102–115.

Mercure, J-F, H Pollitt, NR Edwards, PB Holden, U Chewpreecha, P Salas, A Lam, F Knobloch and JE Viñuales (2018b) 'Environmental impact assessment for climate change policy with the simulation-based integrated assessment model E3ME-FTT-GENIE', *Energy Strategy Reviews*, Volume 20, pp 195–208.

Mercure, J-F, H Pollitt, JE Viñuales, NR Edwards, PB Holden, U Chewpreecha, P Salas, I Sognnaes, A Lam and F Knobloch, (2018a) 'Macroeconomic impact of stranded fossil fuel assets', *Nature Climate Change*, Volume 8, pp 588–593.

Mercure, J-F and P Salas (2012) 'An assessment of global energy resource economic potentials', *Energy*, Volume 46, Issue 1, pp 322–336.

Mercure, J-F and P Salas (2013) 'On the global economic potentials and marginal costs of non-renewable resources and the price of energy commodities', *Energy Policy*, Volume 63, pp 469–483.

Mercure, J-F, P Salas, A Foley, U Chewpreecha, H Pollitt, PB Holden and NR Edwards (2014) 'The dynamics of technology diffusion and the impacts of climate policy instruments in the decarbonisation of the global electricity sector', *Energy Policy*, Volume 73, pp 686–700.

New Climate Economy (2018) *Unlocking the Inclusive Growth Story of the 21st Century*, Washington, DC: New Climate Economy.

Nordhaus, WD (2017) 'Revisiting the social cost of carbon', *PNAS*, Volume 114, Issue 7, pp 1518–1523.

Pindyck, RS (2013) *Climate Change Policy: What Do the Models Tell Us?*, NBER Working Paper No. 19244.

Pollitt, H, S Lee, SJ Park and K Ueta (2014) 'An economic and environmental assessment of future electricity generation mixes in Japan – An assessment using the E3MG macro-econometric model', *Energy Policy*, Volume 67, pp 243–254.

Pollitt, H and J-F Mercure (2017) 'The role of money and the financial sector in energy-economy models used for assessing climate and energy policy', *Climate Policy*, Volume 18, Issue 2, pp 184–197.

Stern, N (2013) 'The structure of economic modeling of the potential impacts of climate change: Grafting gross underestimation of risk onto already narrow science models', *Journal of Economic Literature*, Volume 51, Number 3, pp 833–859.

Part I

Building low-carbon power generation while simultaneously reducing the role of nuclear

2 Regulatory policies to reduce the amount of nuclear and coal-fired power generation in East Asia

Aiko Azuma, Unnada Chewpreecha, Sung-In Na, Li-Chun Chen, Yanmin He, Ken'ichi Matsumoto and Soocheol Lee

Introduction

This chapter investigates the effects of nuclear and coal power regulations on the power sector fuel mix CO_2 emissions out to 2050 in the four East Asian countries. The analysis was carried out using the E3ME model, linked to the FTT:Power model (Mercure, 2012). The analysis builds on Ogawa et al. (2015) but assesses more sophisticated scenarios and considers a longer time horizon.

By having extended the period to 2050, we assume further evolvement of renewable energy technology and a reduction regarding the costs of renewable energy generation. In general, research forecasts infer that the cost of renewable energy generation – that is, solar power, primarily – might decrease compared with that for nuclear and coal power, as solar reaches grid parity (see, e.g. IEA, 2016). Moreover, coal-fired thermal generation facilities in East Asia will have recouped capital costs, that is, eliminated the capital stock lock-in effect, by 2050. This timeframe in this chapter is, therefore, long enough to ensure an easy transition to the generation of renewable energy.

Our reference scenario is based on actual data and the assumption of the Asia/World Energy Outlook (AEO)'s reference scenario, produced by the Institute of Energy Economics, Japan (IEEJ) in 2017.

In our first scenario, we analyze nuclear regulations. In the second scenario, we analyze coal-fired power plant regulations. The third and final scenario analyzes the restriction on both nuclear and coal-fired power simultaneously. The focus of this chapter is on how regulations on coal and nuclear power affect the power mix and power sector emissions. The economic impacts of these same scenarios are explored in Chapter 3.

The following section provides an overview of the current power sector situation and the related policies in each of the four countries, and the next section describes the E3ME-FTT modeling methodology that was applied. After that, the next two sections describe the scenarios that were assessed and show the corresponding energy mixes in each case. The final section outlines policy implications from our analysis.

Overview of the power sector in East Asia

China

Since initiating market reforms in 1978, China's rapid economic development has brought about a growing demand for electricity. In 2014, it had the world's largest installed electricity generation capacity with 1505 GW, and generated 5679 TWh (IEA, 2016). As China has substantial domestic fossil fuel resources (mainly coal), most of its electricity is generated from fossil sources. In 2014, 74.7% of electricity was provided by thermal power generation (excluding Hong Kong) (IEA, 2016). Coal is still the main source of electricity generation, providing 72.3% of electricity. The use of coal in power generation accounts for 47% of energy-related CO_2 emissions in the country (IEA, 2016). Hydropower is the largest among non-fossil fuel energy sources, accounting for 18% of electricity supply in China (IEA, 2016).

Public concerns over local air pollution and increasing greenhouse gas (GHG) emissions from coal combustion were triggered because of extremely high levels of atmospheric particulate matter with a diameter <2.5 μm (PM2.5) in key regions. To tackle this problem, air quality policies, including coal consumption caps in some Chinese provinces, were implemented from 2013 onwards. Strategies regarding the development of other energy sources and moving away from coal dependency have become important. In recent history, China's renewable energy industry has been characterized by fast growth and an enormous installed base. As a result of this, it has the largest capacity of renewable energy in the world (199 GW, excluding hydropower); however, challenges include lack of transmission infrastructure, and curtailment of wind and solar photovoltaic (PV) generation (REN21, 2016).

The Energy Development Strategy Action Plan (2014–2020), published by the state council in 2014, aims to reduce China's high energy consumption per unit of GDP through a set of measures and mandatory targets, promoting a more efficient, self-sufficient, green and innovative energy production and consumption. The targets include a cap on annual primary energy consumption, set at 4.8 billion tons of standard coal equivalent (bn tce) until 2020. Annual coal consumption should be held below 4.2 bn tce until 2020. The share of non-fossil fuels in the total primary energy mix is to rise from 9.8% in 2013 to 15% by 2020.

In addition, the national policy on nuclear power has moved from 'moderate development' of nuclear power to 'positive development' in 2004 and, after the 2011 Fukushima accident, to 'steady development with safety' in 2011–2012. The national nuclear capacity target for 2020 became 58 GW in operation and 30 GW under construction, increasing to 150 GW by 2030 and at least 200 GW by 2050 and 1400 GW by 2100.[1] China's 13th Five-Year Plan (FYP) on National Economy and Social Development (National 13FYP; 2016–2020), unveiled in March 2016, outlines an energy consumption cap and a target goal for the share of non-fossil–based energy in total primary energy consumption by 15%. Furthermore, China's 13th FYP for Energy Development (Energy 13FYP; 2016–2020)

Table 2.1 Power generation mix plan by the NDRC

Power source	*2015 achievements*	*Targets by 2020*		*Targets by 2050*
		Energy Development Strategy Action Plan	*Electricity 13FYP*	*2050 Road Map*
Hydro	320 GW	350 GW	380 GW (incl. 40 GW of PSP[1])	554 GW
Nuclear	27 GW	58 GW	58 GW	100 GW
Wind	131 GW	230 GW	210 GW	2396 GW
Solar PV	43 GW	100 GW	110 GW[2]	2,696 GW[3]
Bioenergy	10.3 GW	30 GW	15 GW	133 GW[4]
Geothermal	0.03 GW	0.1 GW	N/A	11 GW
Coal	900 GW	N/A	<1,100 GW	886 GW
Gas	66 GW	N/A	110 GW	220 GW

Source: NDRC (2016), ERI (2015)

Notes:
1 Pumped-storage hydropower plants
2 Including distributed solar energy systems
3 Including distributed solar energy systems
4 Including biomass pellets, straw and stalks and biogas

and the 13th FYP for Electricity Development (Electricity 13FYP; 2016–2020) issued by the Chinese National Development and Reform Commission (NDRC) in the same year announced more specific goals of power-installed capacity (Table 2.1). Electricity 13FYP also outlined the main direction of development for China's electricity sector and includes technology-specific targets and goals for grid expansion, as well as projections regarding the growth in electricity demand.

The China 2050 High Renewable Energy Penetration Scenario and Roadmap Study (2050 Road Map) by the Energy Research Institute (ERI) of the NDRC analyzes how China can gradually phase out fossil energy – especially coal – in the scenario of High Renewable Energy Penetration. The results of the study show that it is both technically and economically feasible for renewable energy to satisfy >60% of China's primary energy consumption and 85% of its electricity consumption by 2050.

Japan

The accident in the Fukushima nuclear power plant on 11 March 2011, caused by the Great East Japan Earthquake, completely changed the basis of Japanese energy and climate policy. Nuclear power had, until then, been regarded as the main source of electricity generation. Before the accident, there had been 54 commercial nuclear power plants in Japan, and electricity output from nuclear power had accounted for 25–30% of total electricity supply (Figure 2.1).

Until then, energy and climate policy in Japan relied heavily on the expansion of nuclear power capacity, and the Japanese government had planned to build 14

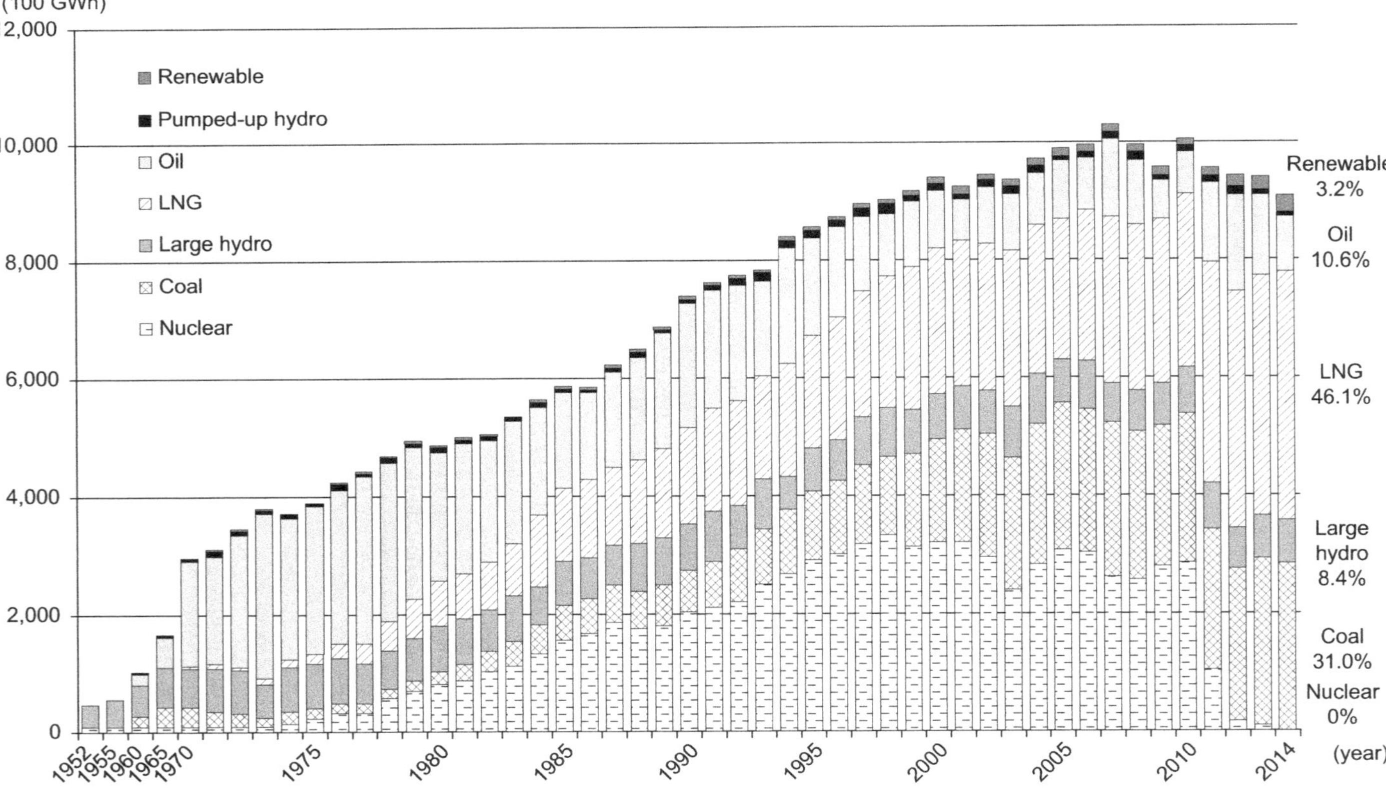

Figure 2.1 Trend of power generation mix in Japan

Source: Agency for Natural Resources and Energy, Japan (2016) new nuclear plants by 2030. However, immediately after the crisis, most nuclear power plants were temporarily shut down to examine the official safety analysis. To date – owing to strong public aversion to nuclear power – it seems unlikely that new nuclear power plants will be built.

In response to the Fukushima accident, the Japanese Ministry of the Environment established a new regulatory agency for nuclear power plants – the Secretariat of the Nuclear Regulation Authority (NRA). The NRA brought in a new regulation regarding nuclear power plants: at their reopening, all plants have to pass every safety criterion under the new law. The NRA also introduced a lifetime regulation, such that nuclear power plants in Japan cannot operate for longer than 40 years. It has already been decided to decommission the Fukushima No.1 nuclear power plant, which comprised six reactors. The remaining 48 nuclear power plants were temporarily shut from 15 September 2013[2] until 14 August 2015.[3]

Twelve nuclear power plants passed the official safety test (Kashiwazaki unit Nos. 6 and 7, Mihama unit No. 3, Takahama unit Nos. 1–4, Ikata unit No. 3, Genkai unit Nos. 3 and 4 and Sendai unit Nos. 1 and 2). Five plants had restarted production by December 2017 (Takahama unit Nos. 3 and 4, Ikata unit No. 3 and Sendai unit Nos. 1 and 2), and seven plants are currently still (first quarter of 2019) under investigation, waiting to restart. In total, 14 nuclear power plants, including Fukushima No.1, had been decommissioned by December 2017 because they had been in operation for almost 40 years; any implementation of additional improvements, such that official safety tests under the new law could be passed, would not have been cost effective. Table 2.2 summarizes the condition of nuclear power plants in Japan as of December 2017.

Table 2.2 Reoperation of Japanese nuclear power plants (as of December 2017)

<table>
<tr><td colspan="3" rowspan="2">Application for reactor reoperation was submitted</td><td colspan="3">(Unit: Number of reactors)</td></tr>
<tr><td>Application for reactor reoperation not yet submitted</td><td>Decommissioning was decided after 2011</td><td>Total</td></tr>
<tr><td colspan="3">25</td><td rowspan="5">15</td><td rowspan="5">14</td><td rowspan="5">54</td></tr>
<tr><td colspan="2">Application for reactor reoperation was permitted by NRA</td><td>Application for reactor reoperation is under review</td></tr>
<tr><td colspan="2">12</td><td rowspan="3">13</td></tr>
<tr><td>Operating</td><td>Not yet operating</td></tr>
<tr><td>5</td><td>7</td></tr>
</table>

Source: Website from the Federation of Electric Power Companies of Japan www.fepc.or.jp/theme/re-operation/

The reduction in the generation of nuclear power has led to increases in the use of thermal generation. This has resulted in increased costs of electricity generation, as well as in increased emissions of CO_2. In 2014, fossil fuels provided 87.6% of the electricity supply in Japan (see Figure 2.1). The import bill for fossil fuels went up by 2.4 trillion JPY from 2010 to 2013 (Agency for Natural Resource and Energy, 2014). At the same time, CO_2 emissions from the power generation sector increased by 110 Mt-CO_2 in 2013 compared with 2010 (Agency for Natural Resource and Energy, 2014).

Japanese utilities were bidding for 10 GW of new thermal power plants in 2014 and for all new capacities to switch to coal power by 2020, because the generation cost of a coal power plant is less than that of a gas power plant. In addition, the Japanese government accelerated the deregulation of the electricity retail market in 2016. This encouraged independent power producers to construct 5 GW of new coal plants because they intended to enter the electricity market, taking advantage of the cheap coal-derived power. As a result, new investments in coal power plants amounting to ~15 GW were under plan in Japan in 2017.

Before the accident at the Fukushima nuclear power plant, Japan's GHG emission reduction target was to reduce emissions by 25% from the 1990 level. To achieve this goal, low-carbon sources of power supply were drastically increased and, in Japan's Third Energy Plan issued in 2010, the share of nuclear power in the power mix anticipated for 2030 was 53%. After the Fukushima

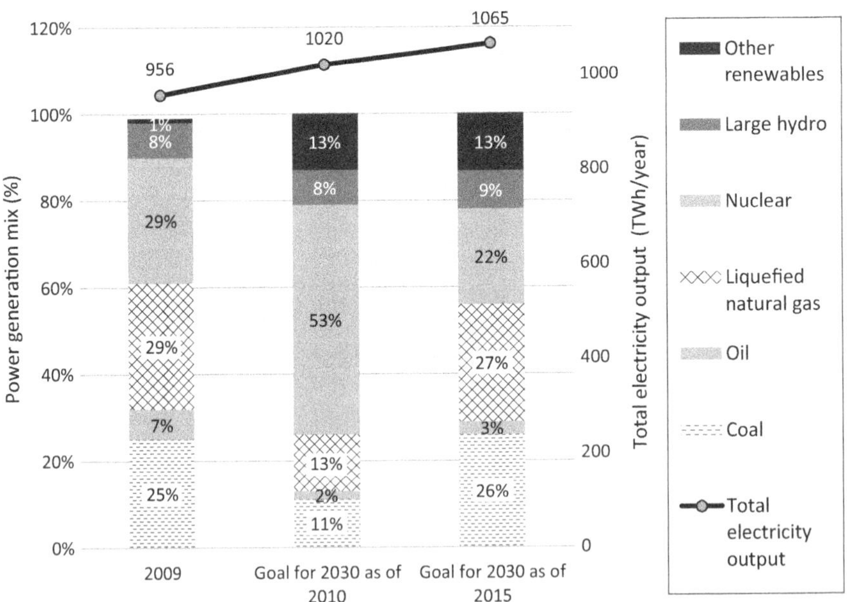

Figure 2.2 Composition of future power generation in Japan

Source: Agency for Natural Resources and Energy, Japan (2015)

Nuclear Power Plant accident, however, it became difficult to restart nuclear power plants and to construct new ones. Therefore, the composition of power supply for 2030 was greatly revised in 2015, with the share of nuclear power now being reduced to 22% for 2030 (Figure 2.2). When comparing the change of the current target with that for 2010, the share of renewable energy has not changed. However, generation from coal and gas-fired thermal power has overtaken that of nuclear power. In the Paris Agreement of 2015, Japan set the goal of reducing GHG emissions by 26% compared with levels in 2013. To achieve this climate change target, it is necessary to suppress carbon-intensive power generation and extend that of renewable energy by far more than currently planned.

Korea

Total power generation in Korea in 2015 was more than 528 TWh, according to the Korea Electric Power Corporation (KEPCO). Korea's power generation has increased annually by an average of 4% since 2005 although, in the past two years, growth rates of electricity consumption have slowed down by ~1%. This recent deceleration of electricity consumption is attributed to a decline in economic demand and export growth rates, to more temperate weather and to demand-side management.

The 7th Basic Plan for Long-term Electricity Supply and Demand published in 2015 by the Korean government showed a 2.2% decrease in the anticipated annual growth of electricity demand until 2029. The government intends to cut its GHG emissions through energy conservation measures and through the use of cleaner energy from nuclear and renewable energy sources.

Fossil fuel sources accounted for 64% of Korea's total electricity generation in 2015, whereas the share of nuclear-derived electricity was 31%; that of renewable sources, including hydroelectricity was 5%. Coal – used as a baseload source – was the fossil fuel mostly used to generate electricity, and natural gas was the second-most used. Oil contributed only a little to power generation. Although fossil fuel–fired capacity was dominant in Korea, in 2015, nuclear power was also a baseload power source. In 2015, ~55% of electricity was consumed by industry, 25% by commercial and service enterprises, 13% by the residential sector and 6% by other sectors, such as transportation and agriculture.

The goal of the Korean government is to reduce its GHG emission levels by 37% from business-as-usual projected levels by 2030. However, the government of Moon Jae-in embarked early in 2017 on its aims to abolish nuclear power generation in the long term. On 19 June 2017, the government shut down Korea's oldest nuclear power plant, Gori-1. However, this policy will lead to increases of CO_2 emissions because nuclear power will be substituted by coal and gas.

The government has also declared its goal to reduce PM2.5 emissions by 30% by 2022. This will be achieved by shutting down old coal-fired power plants and by reducing the number of diesel cars on the streets. This policy will therefore decrease CO_2 emissions from coal plants.

Table 2.3 Power generation capacity in Korea (2014–2029) (in %)

Source	*Share in 2014*	*Target for 2029*
Nuclear	22.2	23.7
Coal	28.2	26.7
LNG	28.7	20.5
NRE	6.7	20.0
Others	14.2	9.1

Source: Korean Ministry of Trade, Industry and Energy (2016)

Note: LNG (liquefied natural gas); NRE (new and renewable energy)

Renewable sources (primarily solar, wind, biomass and waste) accounted for 5% of electricity generation in 2015 in Korea. The country used to have a Feed-in Tariff (FIT) system that was replaced by the Renewable Portfolio Standard (RPS) in 2012 to promote renewable energies. The 4th Basic Plan for New and Renewable energies (2014–2035) in Korea includes a New and Renewable Energy (NRE) target of 5.0% in the primary energy supply by 2020, and of 11.0% by 2035. The generation target is to achieve 13.4% of total power generation using NRE sources by 2035 – with a focus on solar and wind energy – while scaling down energy-from-waste (EfW).

Moon Jae-in's government announced that by 2020 it would expand the share of NRE generation to 20%. However, the government did not propose concrete policies to achieve this target. The 8th Basic Plan for Long-term Electricity Supply and Demand was published in 2018. It includes policies and measures to achieve targets on nuclear, coal and renewables power generations (Table 2.3).

Before that, in 2014, the previous Korean government announced the 4th Basic Plan for New and Renewable Energies. In that plan, 11.0% of the total primary energy supply should have come from NRE sources by 2035. As shown in Table 2.4, it also suggested a reduction in the relative importance of waste, while developing solar and wind power as main energy sources, so that 13.4% of total electric energy would be supplied by new and renewable energies by 2035.

Taiwan

Total power generated in Taiwan in 2016 amounted to 264 TWh, an increase compared with that of 2015 (258 TWh) of 2.3%. Of this, pumped-storage hydropower contributed 1.3%, thermal power 82%, nuclear power 12%, and conventional hydropower, geothermal, solar and wind power, biogas, biomass and waste constituted 4.8%. The total fuel consumption by thermal power stations of the Taiwan Power Company in 2016 was 30 million kiloliters of oil-equivalent (KLOE), which was 2.4% more than the 29.3 million KLOE in 2015. Of this consumption, coal comprised 50.4%, diesel oil 0.4%, fuel oil 8.4% and liquefied natural gas (LNG) 40.9%. In 2016, the amount of electricity consumed was 7.4% by the energy sector's own use; 53.1% by industry; 0.5% by transportation; 1.1%

Table 2.4 NRE supply composition proportion (2014–2035) (in %)

	2014	*2025*	*2035*	*Mean annual growth rate*
Solar (thermal)	0.5	3.7	7.9	21.2
Solar (PV)	4.9	12.9	14.1	11.7
Wind	2.6	15.6	18.2	16.5
Biomass	13.3	19.0	18.0	7.7
Hydraulic	9.7	4.1	2.9	0.3
Geothermal	0.9	4.4	8.5	18.0
Marine	1.1	1.6	1.3	6.7
Waste	67.0	38.8	29.2	2.0
Proportion of total primary energy supply	**3.6**	7.7	**9.7**	**11.0**

Source: Hwang In-Ha (2014)

Note: NRE (new and renewable energy)

by agriculture, forestry and fishery; 19.3% by services and 18.5% by the residential sector. When compared with 2015, the energy sector's own use of electricity decreased by 0.5%; increases of electricity use were seen for industry (1.6%); transportation (1.0%); agriculture, forestry and fishery (0.2%); services (1.7%) and the residential sector (5.5%). In 2016, electricity consumption per capita was 10,928 kWh – an increase of 1.9% compared with 10,720.7 kWh in 2015 (Bureau of Energy, Taiwan, 2017).

In Taiwan, the Bureau of Energy, Ministry of Economic Affairs (MOEA) is the authority responsible for drafting and carrying out national energy policies, laws and regulations. To cope with the internationalized and liberalized trend of economic development, energy policies have changed substantially in recent years. On the one hand, they now actively encourage energy enterprises to become liberalized and private, and open private power plants and refineries. They also regulate domestic oil and electricity prices and make them more transparent, and strengthen the management of energy demands. On the other hand, they emphasize energy and environmental issues and countermeasures, with the expectations of achieving economic growth, environmental protection and a balance of energy demands (Chen, 2014).

All these developments indicate that Taiwan's energy industry is becoming more liberalized through new laws and regulations. However, since there are still many social factors that need to be taken into consideration when it comes to these liberalization policies, legislation does not always take effect as expected.

Taiwan is now on the path towards its own energy transformation. The administration of the Democratic Progressive Party (DPP), starting in May 2016, vowed to eliminate nuclear power in Taiwan,[4] while simultaneously slashing GHG emissions by 20% from 2005 levels, in line with both domestic law and international commitments. At the same time, the administration pledged to maintain an

Table 2.5 Targets of renewable energy production in Taiwan (in MW)

	2015	*2020*	*2025*	*2030*
Hydro	2,089	2,100	2,150	2,200
Wind	737	1,720	3,200	5,200
Solar	842	3,615	6,200	8,700
Biomass	741	768	813	950
Geothermal		100	150	200
Total	4,409	8,303	12,513	17,250

Source: Bureau of Energy, Taiwan (2017)

adequate, reliable and affordable electricity supply to power Taiwan's industrialized economy. In addition to replacing the 16% of electricity currently generated by nuclear power, the government aims to see a 20% increase of power generated from renewables. This is on the basis of planned solar power capacity delivering 20 GW and offshore wind power delivering 3 GW. The administration also expects energy conservation efforts to save the energy equivalent of power generated from two nuclear power plants, and envisions investments in renewable energy to spark new global business opportunities for Taiwan's industrial sector. All of this is to be achieved in less than a decade, by 2025 (Table 2.5).

Modeling method

In this section, we describe the tools used to model the power technology mix in East Asia. We use the E3ME model, complemented by a simulation model of power technology diffusion, FTT:Power (Mercure and Salas, 2012).[5] E3ME provides the demand for electricity-providing industrial activity, household income and electricity prices in 59 world regions, including China, Japan, Korea and Taiwan. FTT:Power takes this electricity demand as an input, determines the technology mix with given electricity sector policies, such as carbon taxes or technology support mechanisms, and calculates electricity prices, power sector investment, power sector fuel demand and power sector GHG emissions. These FTT outputs are fed back into E3ME to obtain feedback on electricity demand and other economic impacts. The combined E3ME-FTT model was first used to analyze the impact of climate policy instruments to reduce emissions worldwide (Mercure et al., 2014).

The dynamical equation

FTT:Power is composed of two parts: the choice of investors and the diffusion of technology. The choice of investors is represented by using a method that is related to discrete choice theory, a binary logit (see the appendix in Mercure et al., 2014), involving sets of distributed diverse agents that make cost comparisons between available options. These choices are used to drive the diffusion of technology options according to the rate of replacement (using life expectancies) and the rate of construction. Technical constraints, such as those related to the predictability and/or flexibility of power sources, may not allow particular compositions to arise, because of grid stability problems (e.g. 100% wind power); it is assumed that investors, seeking to avoid stranded assets, have the foresight to avoid making such investment errors. By representing technology choice and by using a matrix of preferences between every possible pair of options F_{ij}, a matrix of timescales of technological change A_{ij} and technical constraints G_{ij}, the central equation that drives FTT:Power is a set of non-linear finite differences equations:

$$\Delta S_i = \sum_j S_i S_j \left(A_{ij} F_{ij} G_{ij} - A_{ji} F_{ji} G_{ji} \right) \frac{1}{\tau} \Delta t. \tag{1}$$

where S_i is the generation capacity, t is time and τ_j is life expectancy.

This equation generates, for two competing technologies, slow diffusion at low penetration, followed by fast diffusion at intermediate stages before saturating at high penetration. It represents, however, the competition between 24 possible technology options (for a full list of technology options, see Mercure and Salas, 2012) that can produce more complex patterns – including, for instance, the technology ladder where series of intermediate technologies may diffuse in and out of the system.

Timescales of technology diffusion

The diffusion of technologies in FTT:Power, expressed by Eq. (1), follows simple population dynamics. Eq. (1) can either be called 'Replicator Dynamics' (as in evolutionary game theory) or 'Lotka-Volterra' (as in population biology). As is commonly done in survival analysis (and demography), one may define survival functions for technologies that correspond to the probability of survival over years. By also determining a differential rate of upscaling for these technologies, one may derive dynamics of technological change that respect (1) the statistical lifetime of technologies and (2) the rate at which they can be replaced, beyond what is related to investor choices. This theory is explained in detail in Mercure and Salas (2013) and leads to Eq. (1).

Natural resource use

The diversification of renewable power technologies in FTT:Power is limited by the availability of natural resources by using cost-supply curves. In this framework, extraction costs – which increase with increasing levels of development – are fed into the costs that influence investor choices, limiting adjustments when costs become prohibitive. For this purpose, an extensive assessment of renewable energy resources was carried out on the basis of both literature – with some of the results taken from land-use models – and calculations by Mercure and Salas (2012). This is included in the terms for investor choices F_{ij}.

In the case of non-renewable resources (fossil and nuclear fuels), a more complex depletion algorithm is used that generates path-dependent scenarios of depletion when given the price history (Mercure and Salas, 2013). In this calculation, the cost distribution of non-renewable resources consumed and the cost distribution left for future consumption depend on the price history of the commodity; thus, the price is determined as that generating the required supply. However, this methodology can reproduce depletion dynamics that are consistent with classic peak oil theory depletion profiles – including both conventional and unconventional resources, as well as some of the dynamics of the global market. Fuel costs are included in the calculation of levelized costs carried out by investors.

Peak demand, energy storage and grid stability

Grid flexibility issues, peak demand and energy storage are understood in FTT:Power as simple limits to the shares of every technology beyond which the system becomes unstable. Broadly speaking, three types of electricity generation exist: (1) *baseload* systems, which we define as having an output that cannot be changed rapidly (in several hours or days, e.g. nuclear and coal), (2) *flexible* systems, which can change their output rapidly enough to compensate for rapid changes in demand or variable supply (in minutes, e.g. gas turbines, oil generators or hydro) and (3) *variable* systems, renewables systems that have an uncontrollable variable output (e.g. wind, solar and wave). To maintain stability and supply demand, a grid cannot be uniquely composed of variable or baseload systems; the difference between the supply of baseload together with variable systems and the demand must be buffered by flexible systems, which can switch on and off at the right times. An additional constraint arises related to the profile of daily demand, which requires further flexibility. However, flexibility can also be provided by storage of electricity, which can displace the time profile of the demand – that is, variable supply – profile and loosen the constraint.

$$S_{flex}CF_{flex} + S_{var}CF_{var} + S_{base}CF_{base} = \overline{CF} \leq \overline{CF}_{rated}, \tag{2}$$

$$S_{flex}CF_{flex} + S_{var}CF_{var} \geq \overline{CF}\left(\frac{\Delta D}{D} + \frac{U_{var}T_D}{D} + \frac{E_s}{D}\right), \tag{3}$$

$$S_{flex} - S_{var} \geq \left(\frac{\Delta U_D}{U_{tot}} - \frac{U_s}{U_{tot}}\right), \tag{4}$$

$$S_{base} + S_{var} \leq \left(\overline{CF} - \frac{1}{2}\frac{\Delta U_D}{U_{tot}} + \frac{U_s}{U_{tot}}\right), \tag{5}$$

These limits are compactly expressed as inequalities for different types of shares, also shown schematically in Figure 2.3, where S_{flex}, S_{base} and S_{var} are the total shares of flexible, baseload and variable systems, respectively. $\frac{\Delta U_D}{U_{tot}}$ is the peak load to total capacity ratio, and $\frac{U_s}{U_{tot}}$ is the ratio of electricity storage production capacity to total capacity. $\overline{CF}$ is the weighted average capacity factor and $\frac{\Delta D}{D}$ is the peak to average electricity demand ratio. $\frac{U_{var}T_D}{D}$ is the total generation that would be produced by variable sources were they to have 100% capacity factors, and $\frac{E_s}{D}$ is the total energy storage to total demand ratio. $\overline{CF}_{rated}$ is the weighted average capacity factor.

Because operating flexible generators to back up variable renewables leads to lower capacity factors – as they run only a fraction of the time every day – these inequalities also determine the maximum capacity factors that can be used for flexible technologies.

Thus, because of the share limits, as long as flexibility exists in ample supply, no restrictions constrain the development of any technologies. However, when a system ventures near one or the other of its share limits, some types of share exchange become prohibited in eq. (1).

This can lead to several possibilities. For instance, the variable renewables market may separate from the baseload market, where variable technologies compete for the amount of shares allowed by the amount of flexibility available; and this can take place at a different price level compared with baseload technologies. Similarly, the market for flexible generation can also form a

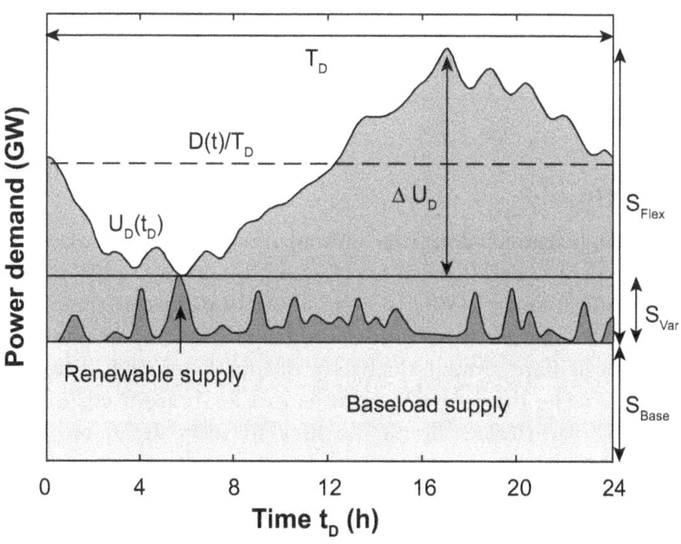

Figure 2.3 Simple representation of the share limits for grid stability, associated to equations 2–5

Source: Mercure and Salas (2012)

sub-market at a different price level to accommodate the amount of renewables or peak demand. It is often the case that increases in renewable energy are limited by the degree of flexibility and storage. A focus on renewable energy needs to be combined with increases in its storage capacity, demanding management to enable further growth.[6]

Linkages between FTT:Power and E3ME

The two models, FTT:Power and E3ME, are fully integrated within a single framework. While E3ME iterates within a year, it estimates the electricity demand for each region; FTT:Power estimates how the demand will be met. Prices of different fuels are also passed from E3ME to FTT:Power to calculate the cost of electricity generated through technologies that use fuels. Given this information, FTT:Power determines how electricity demand can be met by 24 technology options. The electricity price, investment cost for new plants and fuel use are then passed from FTT:Power to E3ME. The electricity price affects demand, and the demand is fed back into the iteration process. Investment costs outline the intermediate demand from the power sector to other industries through an input-output relationship. Fuel use is used to calculate emissions rates.

The scenarios

We investigate the effects of nuclear and coal power regulation on the power generation mix and CO_2 emissions out to 2050 in the four East Asian countries. The scenarios are based on different nuclear and coal power plant capacity assumptions.

Baseline scenario

On the basis of historical data, the annual operational rate of coal power plants in Japan, Korea and Taiwan is set at 0.70. China's operational rate of coal power plants is set at 0.60, and the annual operational rate of nuclear power plants is set at 0.85 for all four countries. These operational rates are used when we calculate annual electricity output from each power generation technology.[7] The original assumptions in E3ME are used for the other inputs, including historical economic statistics (for more detail, see Cambridge Econometrics, 2019).

Taking account of the current nuclear power situation of Japan, we assume that 16 GW of nuclear power capacity restarts in 2020 (based on the official safety analysis by NRA).[8] Installed capacity of nuclear power plants in Japan is interpolated between 2017 and 2020, and between 2020 and 2030. In addition, we extrapolate trends to 2050, by using growth rates between 2030 and 2040 as the baseline (Table 2.6).

Table 2.6 Baseline assumption of the installed capacity of nuclear and coal power plants (in GW)

Year		*2017*	*2020*	*2030*	*2040*	*2050*
China	Nuclear	35.8	–	94.2	131.3	168.4
	Coal	906.4	–	979.3	1,091.9	1,204.5
Japan	Nuclear	4.4	16.0	22.3	18.8	15.4
	Coal	45.8	–	53.0	50.2	47.5
Korea	Nuclear	23.1	–	41.5	41.5	41.5
	Coal	25.7	–	43.5	46.5	49.4
Taiwan	Nuclear	5.1	–	4.4	4.4	4.4
	Coal	14.5	–	19.2	18.4	17.6

Source: The Institute of Energy Economics, Japan (2016)

Policy scenarios

Scenario 1 – limiting the capacity of nuclear power

Scenario 1 (S1) investigates the effects of nuclear power regulation in each country. In this scenario, the capacity of nuclear power plants is either greatly reduced or phased out entirely.

- **China, Japan and Korea**
  The NRA in Japan introduced a lifetime regulation after the Fukushima accident and, in principal, nuclear power plants in Japan cannot operate for longer than 40 years. In this analysis, we assume that all reactors stop operating when they reach the end of their 40-year lifetime, except for three Japanese power plants.[9] In addition, new nuclear power plants are not allowed to be built after 2020. Therefore, in S1, the nuclear capacity between 2017 and 2020 is consistent with that of the reference scenario, with a gradual decrease during the lifetime of each nuclear power plant from 2020 to 2050 (Figure 2.4).
- **Taiwan**
  Although the denuclearization policy of the Taiwanese government was rejected in the referendum in 2018, we assume Taiwan to phase out nuclear power plants by 2025. Therefore, the three nuclear power plants currently in operation are assumed to shut down according to their 40-year lifetime from 2018 to 2025 (see Figure 2.4).

Scenario 2 – limiting the capacity of coal-fired power

In Scenario 2 (S2; restrictions of coal), it is assumed that the installed capacity of coal-fired thermal power is greatly reduced in East Asia. S2 aims to reduce CO_2 emissions to address climate change. In all four countries, we assume no further construction of coal-fired power plants between 2020 and 2030, and we further assume that the installed capacity of coal power plants will decrease linearly to zero from 2030 to 2050 (Figure 2.5). In China, the National Development and

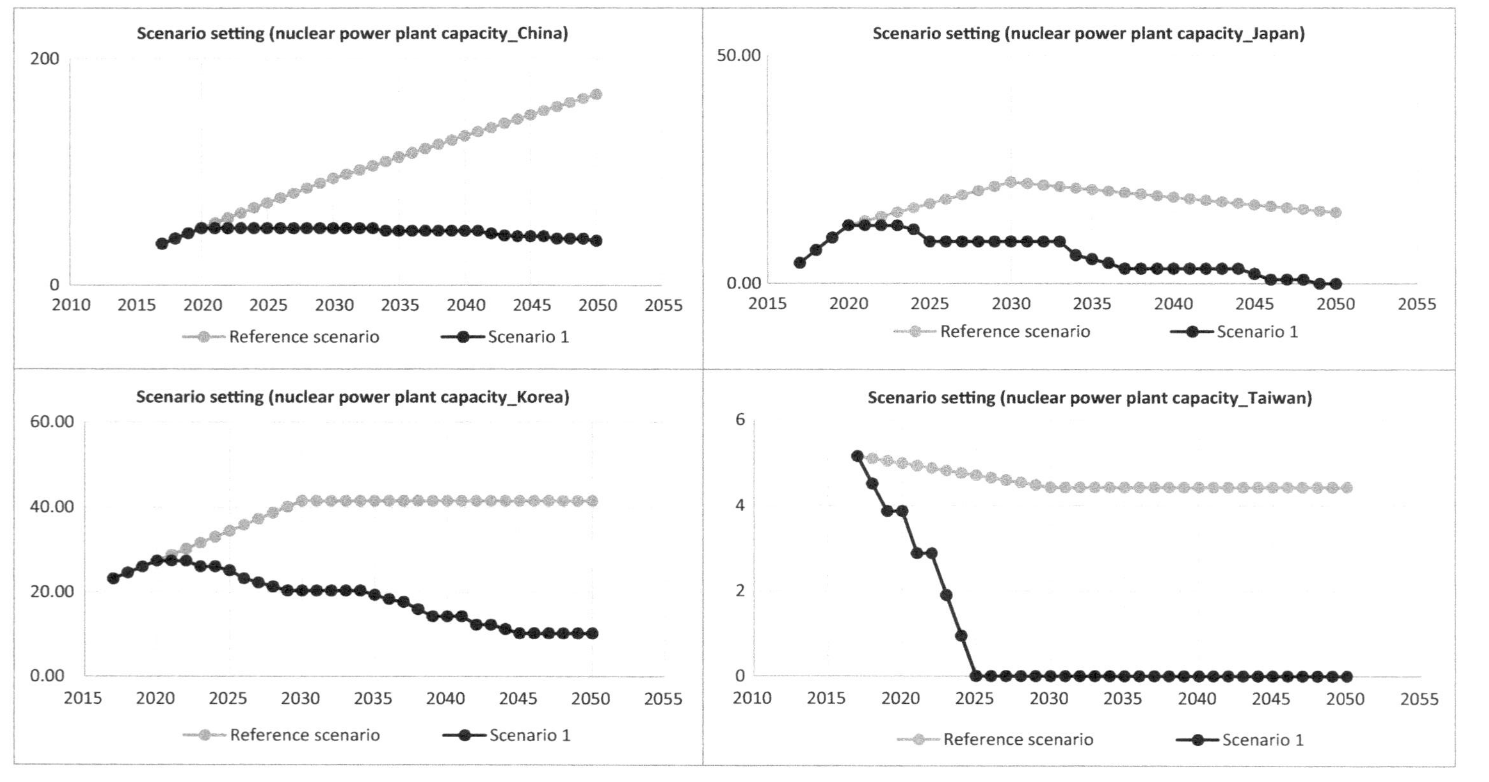

Figure 2.4 Comparison of nuclear power capacity between reference scenario and Scenario 1

Source: Original

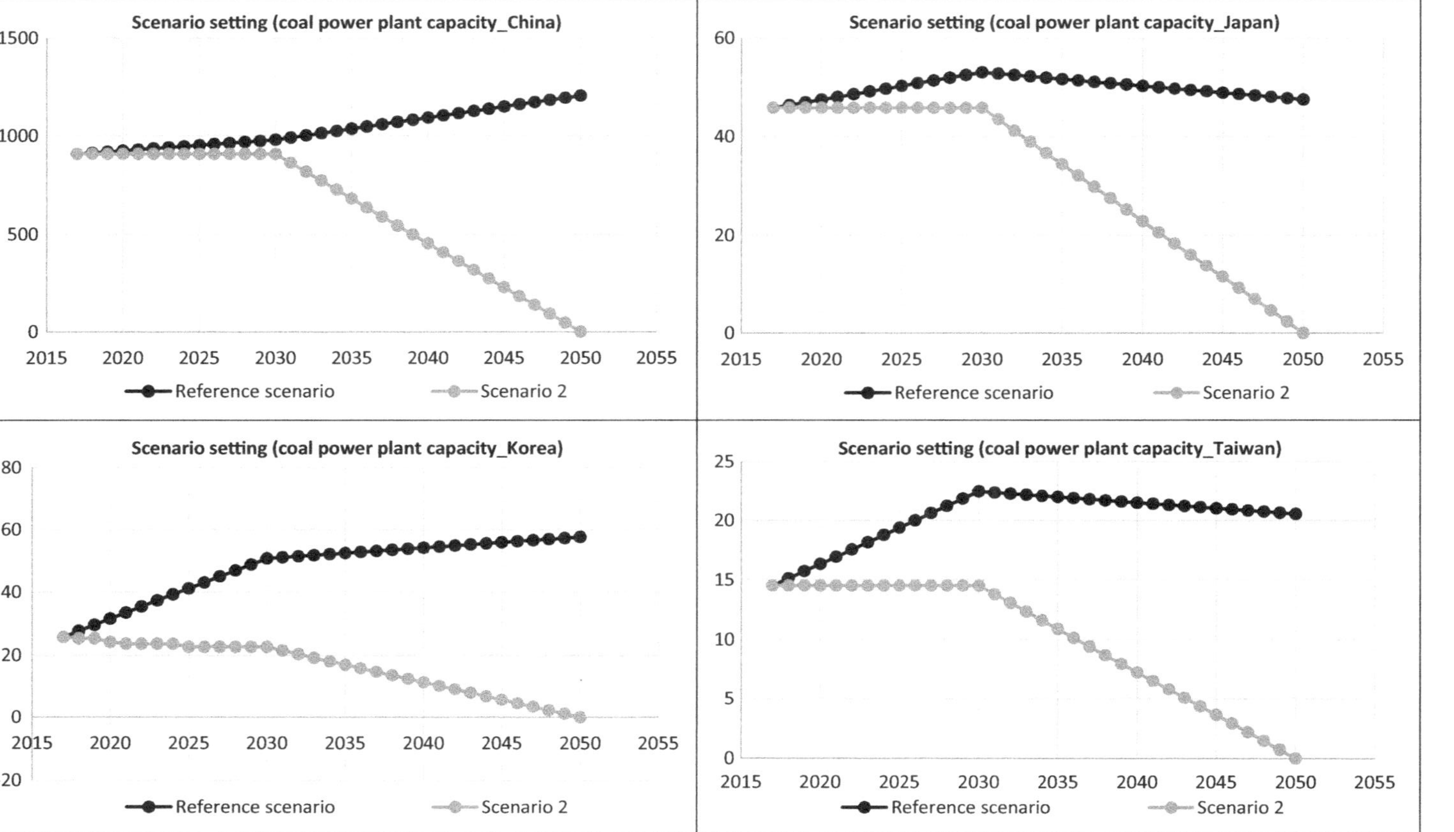

Figure 2.5 Comparison of coal power capacity between reference scenario and Scenario 2

Source: Original

Reform Committee (NRDC) plans to reduce the share of coal power generation from 67.5% in 2015 to 6.8% in 2050, according to their Power Generation mix under the High Penetration Scenario in 2015. In Korea, it is planned to shut down four coal power plants between 2018 and 2025.[10] Therefore, in S2, the installed capacity of coal power plants is gradually reduced from 2018 to 2025 in Korea. It should be noticed that our regulation assumptions regarding coal power in this scenario are not unrealistic, when considering the current trend of coal power reduction policies in East Asia.

Scenario 3 – limiting the capacity of both nuclear and coal-fired power

Scenario 3 (S3; simultaneous restrictions on both nuclear and coal-fired generation) assumes the simultaneous application of S1 and S2. That is, restrictions on nuclear power as in S1 and restrictions on coal-fired thermal power as in S2 are implemented at the same time.

Modeling results

China

Figure 2.6 shows the model results of changes in the power generation supply sorted by technology in China. In the baseline scenario, the share of renewable energy does not increase significantly from up to 2050. The reason behind this is that – although renewable energy increases in absolute terms – coal energy, which is the baseload technology dominating China's power sector, grows even faster in supplying the rapidly increasing electricity demand. This condition makes further diffusion of technologies regarding renewable energy comparatively difficult.

The results for S1 (nuclear regulation), show that limitation of nuclear power without having other policies in place leads to a shift back to coal power. In addition, we also see an increase of only 1.2% in renewable technologies compared with the baseline, as coal becomes the main source of power generation. The reasons given for this slight increase include (1) an avalanche effect resulting from economies of scale from coal generation, (2) no coal restrictions in S1 and (3) no incentive to invest in other technologies as coal is the cheapest. However, our estimation shows that electricity prices fall by almost 1.6% compared with the baseline by 2050, as cheap coal dominates power supply. Electricity demand increases by almost 0.3%.

In S2, the model results show big increases in all other technologies to compensate for the reduction of coal-generated power. Particularly, nuclear, IGCC (Integrated Gasification Combined Cycle), and onshore wind and solar power are technologies that see the biggest increase in the share of total power generation. In addition, not only wind and solar increase, but other less mainstream renewable technologies, for example, geothermal and tidal, as well as Carbon Capture and Storage (CCS) technologies also take off in this scenario. However, electricity

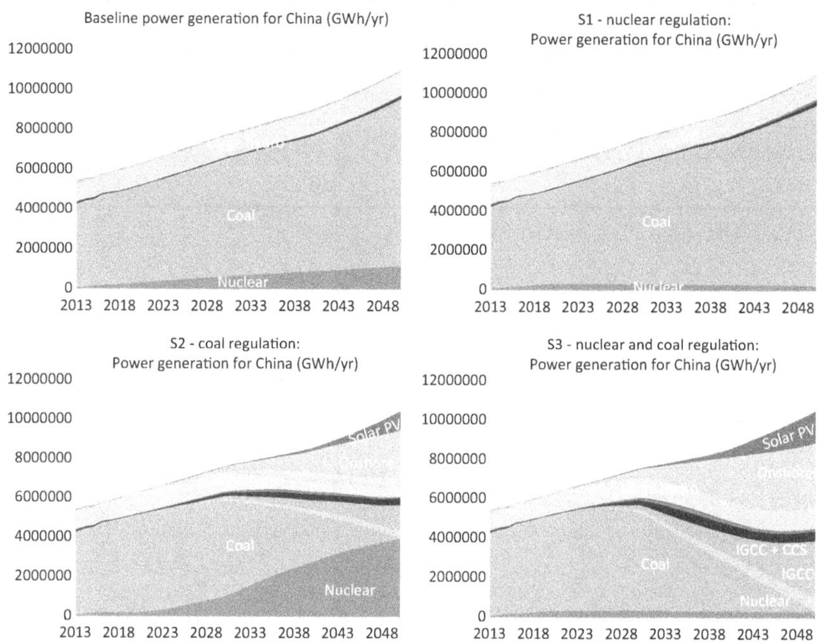

Figure 2.6 Power generation supply by technology, China

Source: E3ME-FTT Power simulation results

prices increase by 32.6% compared with the baseline in 2050 because the option to use cheap coal to produce electricity is no longer available. As a result of the higher electricity prices, total electricity demand reduces by 5%. CO_2 emissions, therefore, decrease by 88.5% compared with those in the baseline by 2050, making this policy very effective in decarbonizing the power sector.

In S3 (nuclear and coal regulation), the results are dominated by the restrictions on coal. This is because the nuclear share in the power generation mix in the baseline is much smaller than that of coal in China (74% coal compared with 10% nuclear in 2040). The power generation mix is similar to that seen in the results in S2, but without nuclear in the mix. The price of electricity in S3 increases by almost 30% because both nuclear (relatively cheap) and coal are no longer part of the generation mix, and, as a result, the demand for electricity decreases by 4.5%.

The share of renewables in power generation in 2050, in China, is shown in Table 2.7. The share of nuclear decreases in S1 and S3 compared with that in the baseline, whereas renewable technologies are pushed up in S2 and, especially, in S3. The share of renewable technology in S3 (78.7%) approaches the 2050 High Renewable Penetration target of the NDRC of China (2015). However,

Table 2.7 Share of renewables in power generation in 2050, in China (in %)

	Baseline	*S1*	*S2*	*S3*
Nuclear	10.8	2.5	38.0	2.6
Fossil fuels	76.2	83.4	9.6	18.7
Renewables (incl. CCS)	13.0	14.2	52.3	78.7
Total	100.0	100.0	100.0	100.0

Source: E3ME-FTT Power simulation results

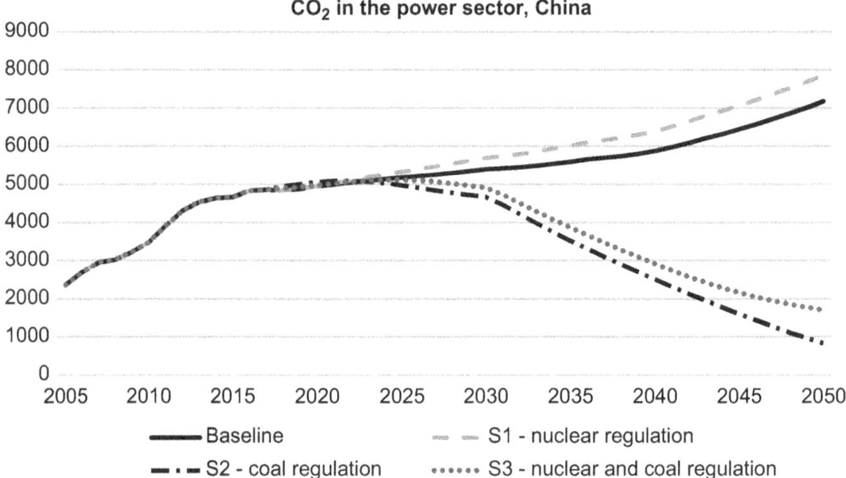

Figure 2.7 CO_2 emissions in the power sector, China (in Mt-CO_2)

Source: E3ME-FTT Power simulation results

the percentage of fossil fuel technologies, including gas and oil, increases in S3 compared with S2.

To reduce carbon emissions from the power sector, the Chinese government could aim to work out a comprehensive policy package that includes the promotion of renewable energy by expanding power sector Feed-in Tariffs, developing a carbon emission trading market at the national level, or introducing carbon taxes and other measures.

Figure 2.7 shows CO_2 emissions in the power sector for each model scenario in China. In S1 (nuclear regulation), overall CO_2 emissions from the power generation sector are 8,352 Mt-CO_2, which is slightly higher than in the baseline because of the increase in coal. In S2 (coal regulation), CO_2 emissions generated by coal power are reduced substantially compared with those for the baseline in 2050. This policy is, therefore, very effective for decarbonizing the power sector because all other technologies increase substantially to compensate for the reduction in coal power generation. In S3 (nuclear and coal regulation), the net CO_2 reduction is a bit less than in S2 because nuclear is no longer an available low-carbon option and power generation from gas and oil increase to compensate.

Japan

Figure 2.8 and Table 2.8 show the power sector technology mix in Japan. In the baseline, where the amount of electricity generation from nuclear and coal power is set according to the AEO 2016 assumption, nuclear power generation increases from 3% of total power generation to 9%, and coal-fired power generation drastically increases from 28% to 54% between 2017 and 2050. However, since the cost of gas-fired generation is assumed high, generation of electricity from gas-fired power decreases from 42% to 14% over the same period. The output from large hydro power is nearly flat. Renewable energy rises from 5% to 11% owing to increased solar and onshore wind power generation. This means that renewable energy gradually increases as the cost of renewable power generation decreases over time, because of innovative technologies, even without a policy in place that supports renewable energy.

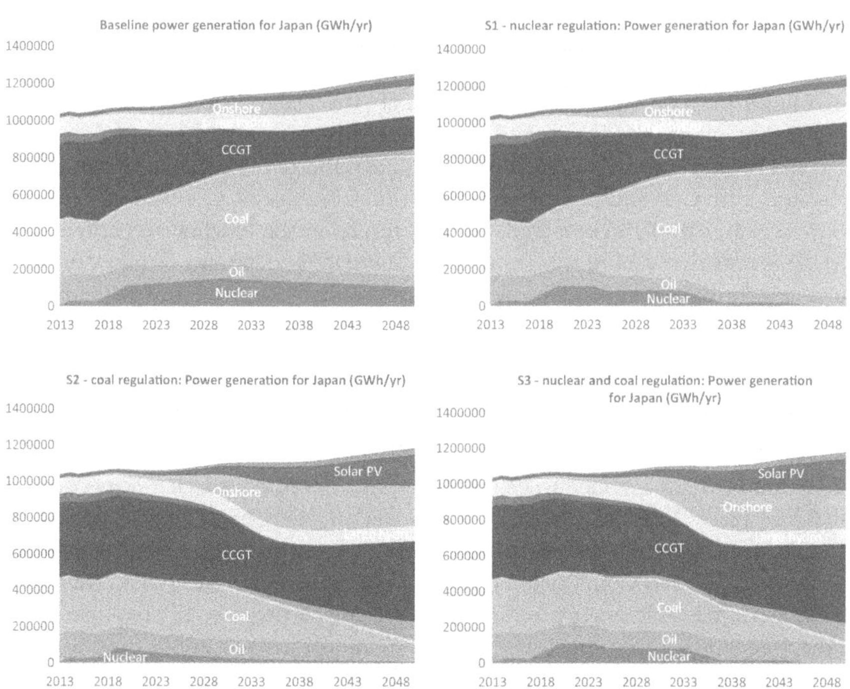

Figure 2.8 Power generation supply by technology, Japan

Source: E3ME-FTT Power simulation results

Table 2.8 Share of power generation by technology in 2050, in Japan (in %)

	Baseline		*S1*	*S2*	*S3*
	2017	*2050*	*2050*	*2050*	*2050*
Nuclear	3%	9%	0%	1%	0%
Oil	13%	5%	4%	8%	9%
Coal thermal + IGCC (incl. CCS)	28%	54%	59%	10%	10%
Gas thermal (CCGT) (incl. CCS)	42%	14%	16%	37%	37%
Large hydro	9%	7%	7%	7%	7%
Renewable	5%	11%	14%	36%	36%

Source: E3ME-FTT Power simulation results

The model results in S1 show that restrictions on nuclear power without an additional climate policy or Feed-in-Tariff for renewable energy increases coal power generation without CCS, because the generation cost for coal power is the lowest among all power-generating technologies. The share of coal increases from 28% in 2017 to 59% in 2050. Electricity generation from renewable technologies and gas-fired power slightly increases compared with that in the baseline. Because the share of coal-fired power generation is large, electricity prices fall by 3.8% and electricity demand increases by 1% in 2050 compared with the baseline.

In S2, the limit of coal-powered electricity generation to zero without implementing CCS results in replacement of coal power generation – not by nuclear power but by gas-fired power (37%) and renewable energy (36%, mainly solar PV and onshore wind) in 2050 (see Table 2.8). Electricity generation from coal, together with CCS and Integrated Gasification Combined Cycle (IGCC) technology, increases by 10% compared with the results in the baseline scenario and in S1. It means that coal power restrictions stimulate investments in other thermal power technologies and renewable energy substantially. In addition, generation of nuclear power does not increase, even when generation of coal power is restricted, because the cost of solar PV, onshore wind and other thermal power generation technologies becomes less than that of nuclear power generation. The share of nuclear power generation decreases to 1% by 2050. Electricity prices in 2050 increase by 24% compared with those in baseline because the generation cost for CCS and IGCC is assumed to be more than that of coal. Total electricity demand in S2 decreases by 5% as a result of higher electricity prices compared with S1.

In S3, nuclear- and coal-power regulation, the shares of other fossil fuel power technology, such as Combined Cycle Gas Turbine (CCGT) and IGCC technologies, and renewable energy are almost the same as those in S2, because in S2 power generation from nuclear decreases to almost zero in 2050, even without nuclear regulation (Figure 2.8).

Figure 2.9 shows CO_2 emissions in the power sector in each scenario in Japan. Because of the increase of coal power generation in S1 as a result of nuclear regulation, CO_2 emissions increase by 10%, compared with the baseline by 2050.

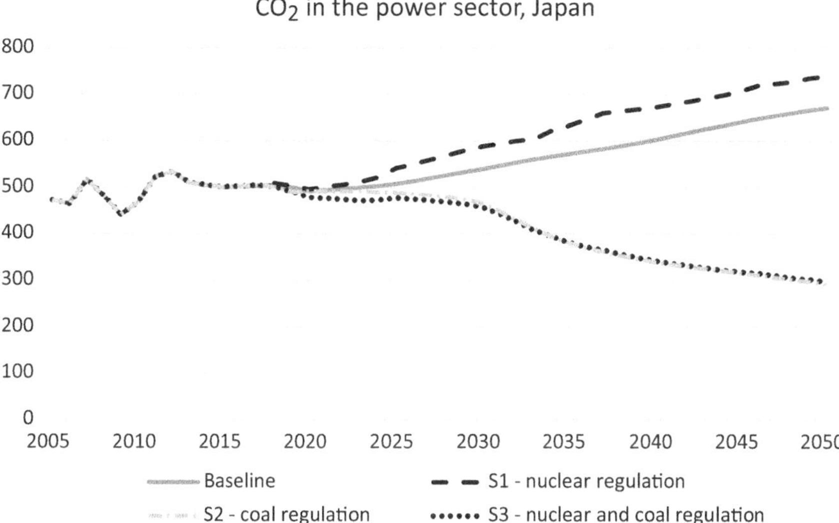

Figure 2.9 CO_2 emissions in the power sector, Japan (in Mt-CO_2)

Source: E3ME-FTT Power simulation results

However, in S2 (coal regulation), CO_2 emissions in the power sector are reduced by 56% compared with the baseline in 2050. The expansion of CCGT and renewable energy in 2050 contributes to the big reduction of CO_2 emissions. In S3, similarly to S2, most of the power supply comes from CCGT and renewable energy. Therefore, CO_2 emissions in the power sector are reduced by 56% in 2050 compared with those in the baseline.

Korea

Figure 2.10 shows the power generation technology mix in Korea. The model results for S1 show that limiting nuclear power without implementing other policy means a shift back to coal-powered electricity generation. They also show a big reduction in natural gas and smaller reductions in renewable technologies compared with those in the baseline scenario, as coal becomes the main source of power generation. Electricity prices fall as we no longer have as many expensive renewables in the power mix. As a result, electricity demand increases by almost 4% in S1, which is met by further power generation from coal.

In S2, a zero limit of coal-powered electricity generation has implications in Korea similar to a limit of nuclear-powered energy generation, because both types of power generation account for around a third of the total power generation in the baseline (remaining mostly from gas). The model results show increases in all other technologies to compensate for the reduction in

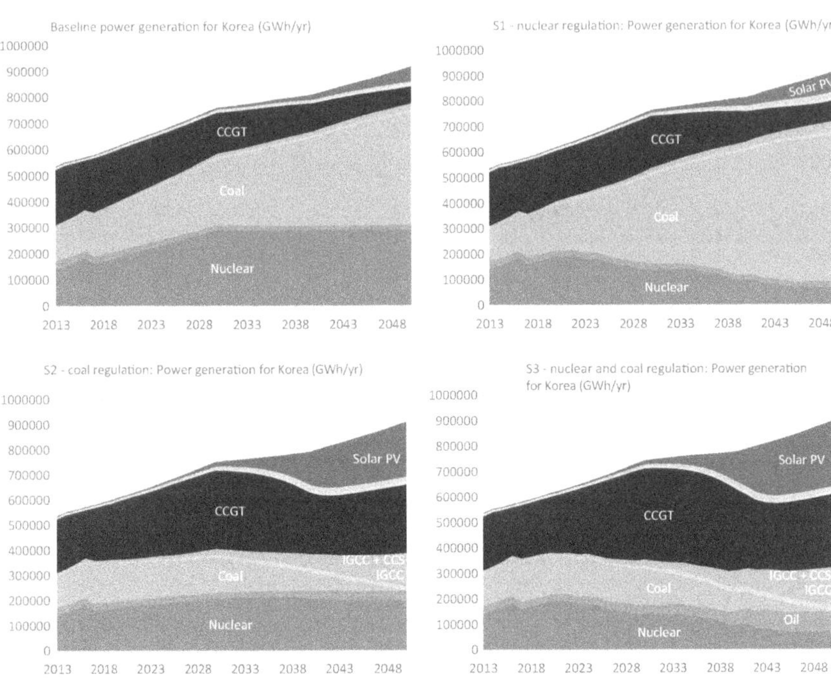

Figure 2.10 Power generation supply by technology, Korea

Source: E3ME-FTT Power simulation results

coal-powered electricity generation. IGCC sees the biggest increase in the share of total generation; interestingly, in Korea, coal is mostly replaced with gas and less with nuclear power. The share of solar increases substantially in this scenario but, with some exceptions, the use of other renewables declines, with gas-fired technology taking over. Electricity prices increase (11% from baseline by 2050) as the use of cheap coal for electricity production is no longer an option in S2. Total electricity demand falls by 1.6% because of the higher electricity prices. S2 has less of an effect in Korea because a substantial amount of electricity is still generated from gas.

In S3 (nuclear and coal regulation), the power generation mix is similar to that in S2, but without the presence of nuclear. Other technologies must, therefore, increase to compensate, increasing further the use of renewable technologies. However, gas and oil technologies also increase in this scenario. Electricity prices increase by 14% because both nuclear (relatively cheap) and coal (very cheap) are no longer part of the power generation mix. As a result, electricity demand decreases by 3%.

Table 2.9 summarizes the share of renewables in 2050. The share of nuclear power decreases in S1 and S3, but the share of fossil fuels increases dramatically

Table 2.9 Share of renewables in power generation in 2050, in Korea (in %)

	Baseline	*S1*	*S2*	*S3*
Nuclear	31.9	7.8	22.2	8.0
Fossil fuels	57.5	75.9	41.7	49.4
Renewables (incl. CCS)	10.6	16.3	36.1	42.6
Total	100.0	100.0	100.0	100.0

Source: E3ME-FTT Power simulation results

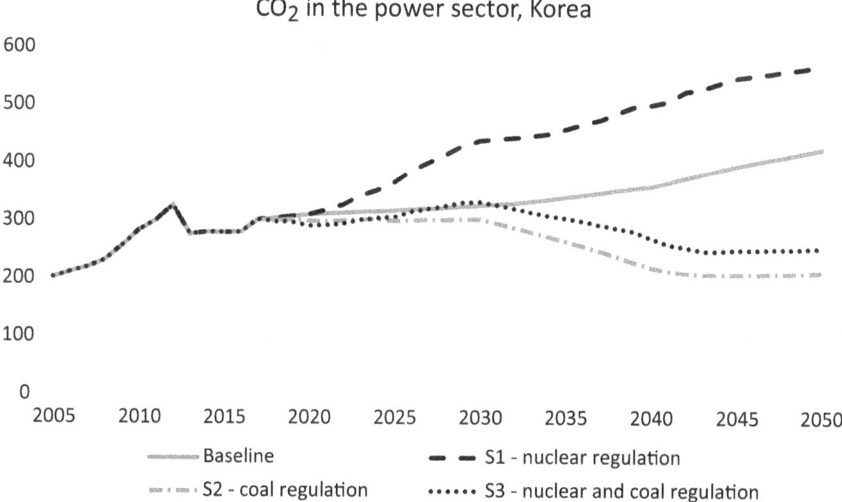

Figure 2.11 CO_2 emissions in the power sector, Korea (in Mt-CO_2)

Source: E3ME-FTT Power simulation results

in S1. The share of renewables increases by the most in S3 but, overall, the mix is still dominated by fossil fuels (natural gas) despite regulating the use of coal.

Therefore, to meet a CO_2 reduction target that is consistent with global targets, the Korean government needs to introduce further policy, such as an effective carbon price mechanism in the form of an emission trading market or carbon taxes at the national level. This will help to promote renewable energy to replace nuclear and coal power generation.

Figure 2.11 shows CO_2 emissions in the power sector for each scenario in Korea. In S1 (nuclear regulation), overall CO_2 emissions increase by almost 75% compared with those in the baseline by 2050, because nuclear is no longer a low-carbon option. The additional power generation comes from coal, which does generate CO_2 emissions. In S2 (coal regulation), CO_2 emissions fall by 26% compared with those in the baseline by 2050, because all other technologies that replace coal produce less CO_2. In S3 (nuclear and coal regulation), the net CO_2 reduction is very small (2%) because nuclear is no longer a low-carbon option and, despite coal being limited to zero, all additional power generation comes from gas, which also generates CO_2.

Taiwan

Figure 2.12 shows that the power generation technology mix in Taiwan follows a similar path to those in Japan and Korea. Renewables have the biggest share in S2 in Taiwan. Because Taiwan has decided to phase out nuclear power by 2025, a reduction of coal-fired power is replaced by gas and renewables. Regarding the national targets, the capacity of renewable energy totals 7,239 MW in 2025, not meeting the target of 9,952 MW. However, in 2030 it increases to 23,678 MW – twice the 12,502 MW target for that year. This is because, after going through slow technology diffusion at low penetration, fast technology diffusion at intermediate stages is realized. In S2, this intermediate stage starts even earlier and the total capacity of renewable energies reaches 35,977 MW in 2025, a level much higher than the national target. The high share of renewable energy is supported by the diffusion of flexible gas-fired power, also replacing coal-fired power.

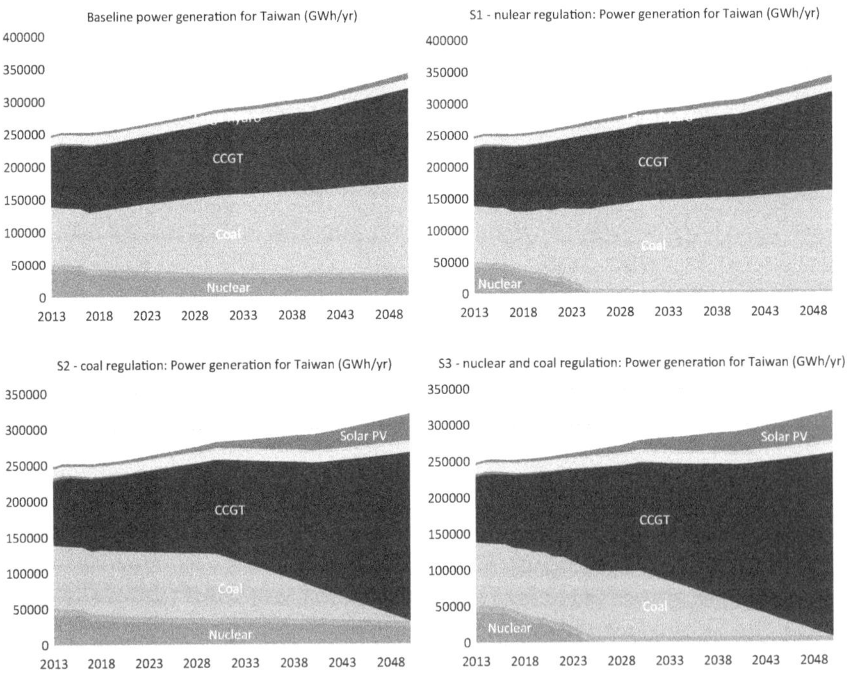

Figure 2.12 Power generation supply by technology, Taiwan

Source: E3ME-FTT Power simulation results

Table 2.10 Share of renewables in power generation in 2050, in Taiwan (in %)

	Baseline	*S1*	*S2*	*S3*
Nuclear	9.1	0.0	7.8	0.0
Fossil fuels (incl. gas and IGCC technologies)	84.1	92.5	75.7	81.6
Renewables (incl. CCS)	6.8	7.5	16.7	18.4
Total	100.0	100.0	100.0	100.0

Source: E3ME-FTT Power simulation results

Table 2.10 summarizes the share of renewables in 2050, in Taiwan. The share of nuclear power is zero in S1 and S3, but fossil fuel shares increase in S1 and S3. The power generation mix is similar to that in S2 but includes nuclear power. This means that other technologies must increase to compensate, which increases the renewable technologies further, although gas and IGCC technologies (including in fossil fuels) also increase in this scenario.

In S1, the limit of nuclear-powered energy generation without other policies in place means that power generation shifts back to coal. This does not only result in coal replacing nuclear, but also in a significant reduction in the use of gas and less substantial reductions in the use of renewable technologies compared with the baseline. In this case, coal becomes the main source of power generation. In S2, a limit of coal-powered electricity generation to zero has bigger implications than a limit of nuclear because power generation from coal accounts for around one third of the total power generation in the baseline. The model results show increases in all other technologies to compensate for the reduction in coal-powered generation. Gas, IGCC and nuclear are technologies that see the biggest increase in the share of power generation in total. Solar power increases the most among renewables, but CCS technologies also increase in this scenario.

In S3 (nuclear and coal regulation), the share of renewables increases by the most but, overall and despite the regulation of coal-powered energy generation, the mix is still dominated by fossil fuels (natural gas). Therefore, it is difficult to meet the CO_2 reduction target in the power sector, even though the regulation of coal effectively reduces CO_2 emissions. Moreover, some replacements are with natural gas, also emitting CO_2. Nuclear regulation, without other policies in place that promote the use of renewables or that limit fossil fuels, results in increased CO_2 emissions because the main nuclear replacements, for example, coal or gas, result in higher CO_2 emissions.

Figure 2.13 shows CO_2 emissions in the power sector for each scenario. In S1 (nuclear regulation), power sector CO_2 emissions increase by almost 36% compared with the baseline by 2050. This is because nuclear is no longer a low-carbon option and all additional power generation comes from coal. In S2 (coal regulation), power sector CO_2 emissions fall by 16% compared with the baseline. This is because coal power is replaced by technologies that are less

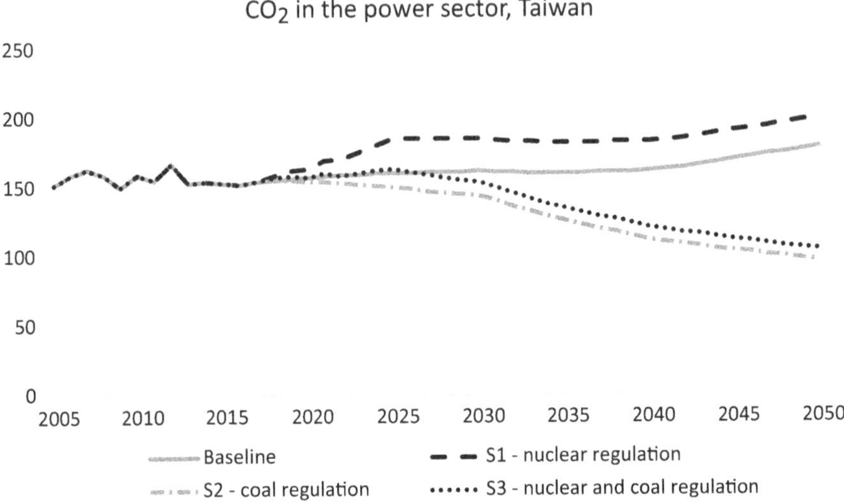

Figure 2.13 CO_2 emissions in the power sector in Taiwan (in Mt-CO_2)

Source: E3ME-FTT Power simulation results

carbon intensive. In S3 (nuclear and coal regulation), the net reduction in CO_2 emission is zero (0%) because the low-carbon nuclear option is no longer available. Moreover, despite coal-powered energy generation in S3 also being limited to zero, all additional power generation is replaced by natural gas, which yields increased CO_2 emissions.

Conclusions

By using the FTT:Power and E3ME models, our analyses indicate that, if the use of nuclear power within the power sector is phased out (as described for S1, nuclear regulation), the use of coal is likely to increase drastically. Renewable energy gradually increases owing to the reduced cost of energy generation up to 2050. In this chapter, however, we did not analyze additional renewable energy support policies, such as Feed-in-Tariffs, carbon taxes or renewable subsidies. Therefore, a limit of nuclear-powered electricity generation alone does not contribute much to a diffusion of renewable energy because carbon-intensive coal power is still the most cost-effective technology with which to generate power.

However, renewable energy increases by more in Scenario 2 (coal regulation). Here, coal power generation is replaced not by nuclear power but gas-fired power and renewable energy (mainly solar PV and onshore wind) by 2050.

Nuclear-powered electricity generation will, therefore, no longer be the most cost-effective technology in 2050, because new technologies that use renewable energy will proceed quickly, rapidly decreasing their unit costs. It is, therefore, important to regulate the share of coal-fired power generation within the power sector to promote sources of renewable energy.

Our research faces two challenges; one of which is the economic impact of the different power mixes in our policy scenarios. To evaluate which power mix is desirable from a social perspective, it is necessary to assess the effects that a different power mix has on the economy, including indicators such as GDP, competitiveness, employment and household incomes. We discuss this detail in the next chapter. The second challenge is how to promote the use of renewables – essential power sources leading to a sustainable low-carbon society in East Asia. In this chapter, we have shown that power mixes will diversify in Scenario 3 (nuclear and coal regulation), but also that this will mainly promote gas power and fewer technologies using renewables, especially in Japan and Korea. In Chapter 4, we discuss how to support the use of renewables through the introduction of Feed-in-Tariffs, as well as carbon taxes.

Notes

1 For more details, see 'Nuclear Power in China' (World Nuclear Association, http://world-nuclear.org/information-library/country-profiles/countries-a-f/china-nuclear-power.aspx, Access day: 2019.02.06)

2 The Ohi No. 4 nuclear power plant of Kansai Electric Power Company temporarily ceased to operate for inspection and maintenance on 15 September 2013.

3 The Sendai No. 1 nuclear power plant of Kyushu Electric Power Company restarted operation under the new law on 14 August 2015.

4 However, as mentioned in the Introduction, the denuclearization policy of the Taiwanese government was rejected in the referendum, in December 2018, by its people.

5 For details on the E3ME model, see Chapter 1 and www.e3me.com

6 Notice that the parameters for storage also implicitly represent the flexibility that is obtained through international trade of flexible generation. In this assumption, the amount of electricity traded sums to zero through the day. Since international trade of electricity is not covered in this version of the model, it is taken as an exogenous assumption.

7 Annual electricity output (kWh) = installed capacity (kW) × 8,760 hours × annual operational rate.

8 This number includes ten nuclear power plants (total of 9.25 GW) with permission for reactor installation by NRA as of June 2017, and the six newest plants (total of 6.77 GW) that will be able to operate after 2035 but had not yet applied for reactor installation.

9 Three nuclear power plants in Japan (Mihama unit No. 3, and Takahama unit Nos.1 and 2) were granted 60 years of operation by the NRA in Japan, in 2016. Therefore, in this analysis, these three plants operate for 60 years.

10 Seocheon unit Nos. 1 and 2 (400 MW) are planned to shut down in 2018, Samchonpo unit Nos. 1 and 2 (1,120 MW) in 2020, Honam unit Nos. 1 and 2 (500 MW) in 2021, and Boryeong unit Nos. 1 and 2 (1,000 MW) in 2025.

References

Agency for Natural Resources and Energy, Japan (2014) General Energy Statistics 2014, Agency for Natural Resources and Energy, Japan.

Agency for Natural Resources and Energy, Japan (2015) Long-term Energy Supply and Demand Outlook, available at www.meti.go.jp/english/press/2015/pdf/0716_01a.pdf

Agency for Natural Resources and Energy, Japan (2016) Energy White Paper 2016, Agency for Natural Resources and Energy, Japan, available at https://www.meti.go.jp/english/press/2016/pdf/0517_01.pdf

Bureau of Energy, Taiwan (2017) Energy Statistics Handbook 2016, Bureau of Energy, Taiwan.

Bureau of Energy, Taiwan (2013) Energy Statistics Hand Book 2012, Bureau of Energy, Taiwan.

Cambridge Econometrics (2019) E3ME Manual, available at www.e3me.com.

Energy Research Institute (ERI) (2015) China 2050 High Renewable Energy Penetration Scenario and Roadmap Study, available at www.efchina.org/Attachments/Report/report-20150420/China-2050-High-Renewable-Energy-Penetration-Scenario-and-Roadmap-Study-Brochure.pdf.

Hwang, I.-H. (2014) South Korea's National Basic Plan for New and Renewable Energies, IEEJ Report 2014 December, The Institute of Energy Economics, Japan.

IEA (2016) RED Renewable Policy Updated, Issue 11, 17, available at www.iea.org/media/topics/renewables/repolicyupdate/REDRenewablePolicyUpdateNo1220161222.pdf.

The Institute of Energy Economics, Japan (2017) Asia/World Energy Outlook 2017, The Institute of Energy Economics, Japan.

Ju-Yin, C. (2014) 'Current policy and challenges of energy utilities in Taiwan', *IPCBEE*, vol. 66, 146–150, Singapore: IACSIT Press, available at http://ipcbee.com/vol66/030-IEEA2014-A2015.pdf

Mercure, J.-F. (2012) 'FTT:Power A global model of the power sector with induced technological change and natural resource depletion', *Energy Policy*, 48, 799–811.

Mercure, J.-F. and Salas, P. (2012) 'An assessment of global energy resource economic potentials', *Energy*, 46(1), 322–336, available at http://dx.doi.org/10.1016/j.energy.2012.08.018

Mercure, J.-F. and Salas, P. (2013) 'On the global economic potentials and marginal costs of non-renewable resources and the price of energy commodities', *Energy Policy*, 63, 469–483, available at http://dx.doi.org/10.1016/j.enpol.2013.08.040

Mercure, J.-F., Salas, P., Foley, A., Chewpreecha, U., Pollitt, H., Holden, P. B. and Edwards, N. R. (2014) 'The dynamics of technology diffusion and the impacts of climate policy instruments in the decarbonisation of the global electricity sector', *Energy Policy*, available at http://dx.doi.org/10.1016/j.enpol.2014.06.029

The Ministry of Trade, Industry and Energy (2016) The 7th Basic Plan for Long-Term Electricity Supply and Demand (2015–2029), Sejeong, Korea.

NDRC (2016) 13th Five-Year Plan for Electricity Development (2016–2020), National Development Reform Committee.

Ogawa, Y., Mercure, J-F., Lee, S., Pollitt, H., Matsumoto, K. and Chiashi, A. (2015) 'Chapter 3: Modeling the power sectors in East Asia – The choice of power sources', in Soocheol Lee et al. (Eds.), *Low-Carbon, Sustainable Future in East Asia:*

Improving Energy Systems, Taxation and Policy Cooperation. New York: Routledge, pp. 1–28.

Pollitt, H., Park, S.-J., Lee, S. and Ueta, K. (2014) 'An economic and environmental assessment of future electricity generation mixes in Japan – An assessment using the E3MG macro-econometric model', *Energy Policy*, 67, 243–254.

REN21 (2016) Renewables 2016 Global Status Report, available at www.ren21.net/wp-content/uploads/2016/10/REN21_GSR2016_FullReport_en_11.pdf

3 The economic impacts of reduced reliance on coal and nuclear power in East Asia

Soocheol Lee, Unnada Chewpreecha, Aileen Lam, Akihiro Chiashi, Bin Xu, Aiko Azuma, Pim Vercoulen, Florian Knobloch and Hector Pollitt

Introduction

In Chapter 2, we used the E3ME and FTT:Power sub-models to predict changes in the power generation mix in the four East Asian countries (China, Japan, Korea and Taiwan) under three different scenarios of nuclear and/or coal regulation until 2050. The scenario results were compared with a baseline that contains trends from the Asia/World Energy Outlook (AEO) reference case (IEEJ, 2017). AEO is the only report providing detailed long-term assumptions regarding the power generation mix in each of the four countries.

In this chapter, we apply the power generation mix results under the three policy scenarios described in Chapter 2, to estimate the impacts on the economy (GDP, employment, etc.). By using E3ME-FTT modeling, we can understand which power generation mix is most desirable from an economic and environmental perspective.

In Chapter 3 of our previous book, Ogawa et al. (2015) conducted a similar analysis by using the E3ME-FTT model (Lee et al., 2015). Their results suggest that restricting nuclear and coal-fired thermal power in East Asia would increase power generation costs, thereby exerting a negative influence on the economy (particularly on GDP). Still, the effect of investment demand into alternative power sources – that is, the construction of power plants using renewable energy – and a reduction in imports of fossil energy, would eliminate the negative impacts over time. Regarding CO_2 emissions, the study highlighted reductions of ~10~–30%, although the amount differed among countries. However, Ogawa's research focused on a choice of power mix in the medium term, until 2030. We extended this analysis to 2050, with more sophisticated policy scenarios on coal and nuclear power regulations.

In this chapter, taking the foregoing concepts as a starting point, we use the E3ME-FTT model to estimate the impact that regulations regarding nuclear and coal power generation have on the four East Asian economies up to 2050. As mentioned in Chapter 2, by having a longer modeling period renewable energy technologies are very likely to have developed further. Generally, it has been forecast that the costs of renewable energy generation – primarily solar power, will be less than that of nuclear and coal, as solar power reaches grid parity (Center for

Low Carbon Society Strategy, 2015). By 2050, most existing coal-fired thermal generation facilities in East Asia will have recouped capital costs (eliminating the lock-in effect of capital), and this time frame is long enough to ensure an easier transition to renewable energy generation. In this chapter, FTT – as a bottom-up technology choice model – reflects this mechanism very well.

In the next section, we give an overview of the economic linkages that exist between the FTT:Power sector model and the economy in the E3ME model. The section after that presents the economic impacts of each of the scenarios defined in Chapter 2. In the final section, we discuss our findings and provide conclusions.

Linkage between the electricity sector described by the FTT:Power model and the macro-economy represented in the E3ME model

In this chapter, we model the choice and diffusion of power technology in East Asia by using the E3ME model,[1] complemented by the simulation model of power technology diffusion, FTT:Power.[2] E3ME provides the demand for electricity-given industrial activity, household income and electricity prices in each country. FTT:Power takes this demand as an input and – with given electricity sector policies, such as regulations, carbon taxes or technology support mechanisms – determines the technology mix and calculates GHG emissions. The combined model system is now well established and has been applied previously in several published sources, including Mercure et al. (2014) and Lee et al. (2015).[3]

The two models, FTT:Power and E3ME, are fully integrated within a single framework as mentioned in Chapter 2. E3ME iterates within a year and estimates the electricity demand for each region, whereas FTT:Power estimates how this demand will be met. Prices of different fuels are also passed from E3ME to FTT:Power to calculate the cost of electricity generated through technologies using these fuels. Given this information, FTT:Power determines how electricity demands can be met by applying 24 power technology options. The electricity price, investment cost for new power plants and fuel use are then passed from FTT:Power to E3ME. The electricity price affects demand, and the demand is fed back into the iteration process. Investment costs outline the intermediate demand from the power sector to other industries through an input-output relationship. Fuel use is used to calculate emissions. We describe the interaction between E3ME and FTT:Power (E3ME-FTT), that is, between the power generation sector and the economy as a whole, in more detail in the following three sections.

The price-demand interaction

The demand for electricity is calculated in E3ME by using a set of econometric equations that takes into account various explanatory factors. It reads as follows (Cambridge Econometrics, 2019):

$$\Delta \log D_{ij}{}^{4} = \beta_{ij}^{0} + \beta_{ij}^{1} \Delta \log \Upsilon_{ij} + \beta_{ij}^{2} \Delta \log P_{ij} \,/\, \Delta \log OP_{ij} + \beta_{ij}^{3} \Delta \log TPI_{ij} + \varepsilon_{ij}.$$

There is a demand for electricity, D_{ij} by energy user i in region j. Y_{ij} is the level of economic activity of the energy users, P_{ij} is the price of electricity relative to the price of other energy OP_{ij}, and TPI_{ij} is a measure of technological progress. β_{ij}^{k} are the parameters estimated from historical data. In general, the demand for electricity increases with higher economic output and/or lower electricity prices. However, unlike GDP, technological progress can only increase and, when it does, energy demand decreases. The factor TPI_{ij} cumulates increases in technology investments that, in part, involve systems with ever-improving energy efficiency, spilling over into the energy sector in the form of reduced demand. It is, thus, assumed that the world does not adopt again models of technology that have previously been abandoned; hence, the equation is asymmetric and, therefore, path dependent

The price of electricity comprises the cost of operating the electricity sector. When demand changes, the power sector model FTT:Power determines the technology mix (or energy mix) that supplies the demand, thereby generating the total cost of supplying electricity (see Mercure, 2012). This cost itself influences the price of electricity, which, again, changes demand. The convergence between the two models of supply and price constitutes the price-demand interaction. A policy that influences the technology mix, thus, also influences the price and the demand. In particular, when renewables that cost more are introduced into the grid, electricity consumption will be reduced, providing a double contribution to reducing emissions. Furthermore, increases in electricity demand may also generate higher operating costs because of the depletion of renewable and non-renewable resources, therefore also influencing the price. These interactions are complicated but crucial in order to correctly simulate the behavior of the system.

In our nuclear and/or coal power regulation scenarios, the key impacts in E3ME-FTT on the economy come from electricity prices and electricity investment feedbacks. The different power mix as a result of coal- and nuclear-powered energy regulation means the levelized cost of electricity (LCOE) will be different. This, in turn, will affect average electricity prices that are passed on to final consumers (Figure 3.1).

Restrictions on nuclear and coal-fired power would lead to an increase of power tariffs, at least in the short term. Equally, restrictions on both would lead to increased power generation from alternative sources, such as renewables and liquid natural gas (LNG), but these are costlier than nuclear or coal. For example, in 2013 in Japan, solar power generation (PV) unit costs were about 80% higher than nuclear and about 110% higher than coal-fired thermal power (Table 3.1). Accordingly, such changes in the power mix would lead to higher electricity tariffs and, at the same time, to increased inflation. This would negatively affect economic activity by reducing consumption and would hinder international competitiveness.

Changes in the power mix would also lead to changes in CO_2 emissions. Note that a restriction of nuclear power alone would increase a reliance on coal-fired

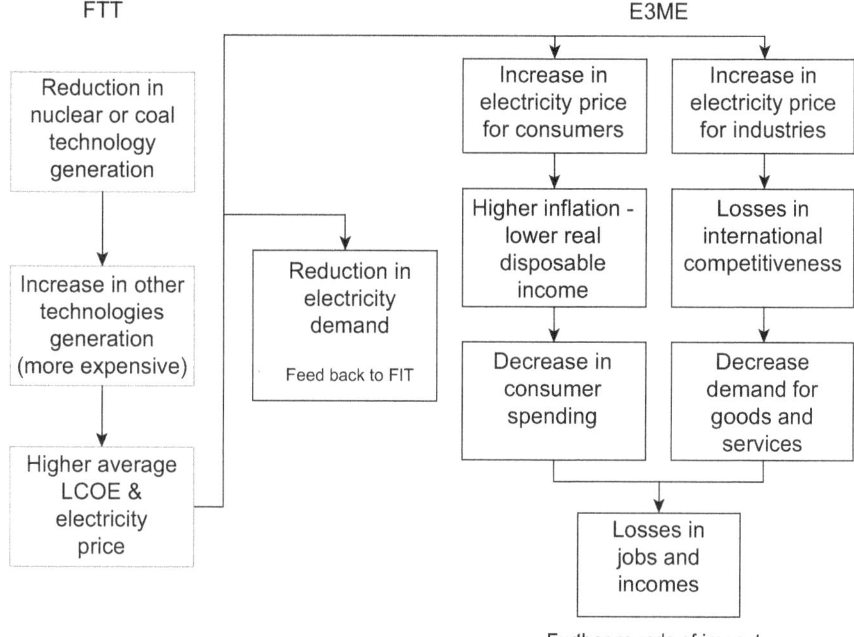

Figure 3.1 Price feedback in E3ME-FTT:Power

Source: Cambridge Econometrics (2019)

Table 3.1 Generation cost and CO_2 unit emission outlook in Japan (in Yen/kWh)

	2013	*2030*	*2050*
Nuclear	8.8	8.8	8.8
Hydro	10.8	10.8	10.8
Coal	7.7	7.8	7.8
LNG	10.8	11.4	11.8
Petroleum	16.7	17.9	18.9
PV	16.0	9.5	5.7
Wind power	14.1	10.2	10.2
Geothermal	12.5	12.5	8.0
Biomass	33.6	10.9	10.9

Source: Center for Low Carbon Society Strategy (2015)

thermal power – which is cheaper than renewables – and, thereby, increase CO_2 emissions (see Chapter 2). However, simultaneous limits on nuclear and coal-fired power would increase the energy output of renewables and constrain CO_2 emissions. Further, an increased share for renewable energy would see a reduction in fossil-fuel energy imports of and in fuel costs, with a positive impact on the economy.

The share of nuclear and coal-powered electricity generation is exogenously determined until 2050 in the different scenarios described in Chapter 2. Power sources other than nuclear or coal are endogenously determined within the FTT:Power model – depending on factors, such as their respective costs – to fulfill the demand for energy as calculated by E3ME. In FTT:Power, total power costs reflect the costs of the power sources selected within the model, and these are fed back into power tariffs for individual entities (industry, households, etc.) within E3ME. The increase in power tariffs paid by economic entities leads to reduced electricity demand.

Investment feedback

As mentioned previously, simultaneous restrictions on nuclear- and coal-powered electricity generation can negatively affect the economy because of a shift to more expensive power sources. This mechanism is apparent in E3ME and is commonly seen in virtually all other E3 models. However, E3ME is a demand-driven, non-equilibrium (Keynesian) model, and there is the potential to utilize spare capacity in an economy. The increase in power generated by renewables leads to an increase in related investment demand, which is effective demand that has a positive impact on the economy (via multipliers and increased employment). Investing new capital into the electricity sector has a multiplier effect across other sectors of the economy. It employs additional labor in sectors, such as construction, engineering, cement and mining; and output from these sectors stimulates further multipliers on other sectors (Figure 3.2). However, nuclear power is also a capital-intensive technology. A phase-out will lead to a decrease in investment demand, which may counteract the positive effects on the economy because of an increase of renewable technology uptake.

By contrast, Computable General Equilibrium (CGE) modeling is structured so that, even if this investment demand is generated, it is difficult for it to become an effective demand within the economy owing to the crowding-out effect (an increase in demand in one sector having the effect of eliminating demand in another sector). However, because E3ME allows for spare capacity in the economy, new investment demand stimulates economic activity because it is considered as additional demand. Pollitt et al. (2014) found that, if the share of nuclear power reached 0% in Japan, this would generate renewable energy investment demand worth 29.4 trillion JPY (of which 5.2 trillion JPY would be for grid connection) by 2030.

The FTT investment is characterized by a highly front-loaded pattern. For example, when there is a sudden requirement for power generation technology

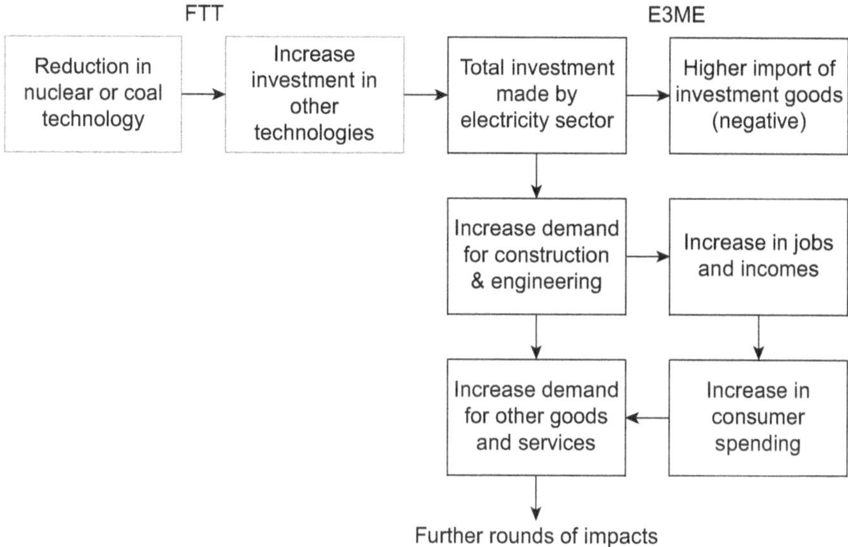

Figure 3.2 Investment feedback in E3ME-FTT:Power

Source: Cambridge Econometrics (2019)

caused by a reduction in coal use, investments for other technologies will have to be made in that year for the plants to come online to compensate for the loss of coal power plants. The model results show a very volatile impact on GDP because of investment made by the power sector.

GDP and fuel-use feedback

To summarize, restrictions on nuclear and coal power could have a negative impact on the economy because of higher electricity prices at least in short- or mid-term, but greater investment in renewables could have a positive effect. Both effects are likely to become smaller in the longer term because capital costs for renewables will fall. This mechanism is endogenous in FTT:Power and, over the medium to long term, renewable energy costs begin to reach grid parity. It should be noted that the speed of reaching grid parity differs according to the power generation technology.

There is a further important economic feedback: that increased demand for renewable energy reduces imports of fossil fuel energy and contributes to an increase in GDP via an improvement to the trade balance. Economies in East Asia – particularly Japan, Korea and Taiwan – import virtually all of the fossil fuel energy they consume. A reduction in the demand for fossil fuel energy, thus, directly flows through to an improvement in the trade balance in these countries. Accompanying increased energy demand because of economic growth in recent years, China has also turned into a fossil-fuel energy importer. For all countries an improved trade balance boosts GDP. A reduction in imports of fossil-fuel energy imports also improves energy security for the countries in East Asia.

In our modelling, FTT:Power estimates fossil fuel demands in physical terms by the power sector. E3ME then calculates the monetary value of reduced fossil fuel imports (on the basis of share of domestic supply to imports), which it sends to the trade balance. Impacts on trade are therefore fully captured in our results.

Scenarios and modeling results up to 2050

The scenarios in this chapter are identical to those described in Chapter 2. But the focus of this chapter is the effects that the regulation of nuclear and coal power have on the four East Asian economies. The scenarios are set on the basis of different nuclear and coal power plant capacity assumptions.

Baseline scenario

To investigate the effect of energy policy on the power generation mix up to 2050, installed capacity of nuclear and coal power plants was set at the 2017 level[5] and projected forward to 2050 by using data from AEO2017. These data assume the power generation mix in 2030 and 2050, in each of the four countries. On the basis of historical data, the annual operational rate of coal power plants in Japan, Korea and Taiwan was set at 0.70; China's operational rate of coal power plants was set at 0.60; and the annual operational rate of nuclear power plants was set at 0.85 in all four countries. These rates were used to calculate annual electricity output from each power generation technology.[6] The original assumptions in E3ME were used for the other inputs, including historical economic statistics (for more detail, see Cambridge Econometrics, 2019). These assumptions and the installed capacity of coal and nuclear are the same as those outlined in Chapter 2.

Policy scenarios

The policy scenarios are described in more detail in Chapter 2. A short summary is provided here.

Scenario 1 – limiting the capacity of nuclear power

In this scenario (S1), the capacity of nuclear power plants is either greatly reduced or phased out entirely. We assumed that all reactors stop operating when reaching the end of their lifetime of 40 years and no new nuclear plants may be constructed after 2020. Taiwan phases out nuclear altogether by 2025.

Scenario 2 – limiting the capacity of coal-fired power

In S2 it is assumed that the installed capacity of coal-fired thermal power is greatly reduced in East Asia. This reflects current policy ambition in East Asia.

Scenario 3 – limiting the capacity of both nuclear and coal-fired power

Scenario 3 (S3) assumes simultaneous application of S1 and S2. That is, restrictions on nuclear power as in S1 and restrictions on coal-fired thermal power as in S2 are implemented at the same time.

Economic results and analysis

In this section, we look into the economic impacts resulting from a phase-out of nuclear power (S1), a phase-out of coal power (S2) and the simultaneous phase-out of nuclear and coal power (S3) in each of the four East Asian countries.

China

China's economic results in S1 (nuclear regulation) show small and negative impacts on GDP, mainly because of reduced nuclear technology investments in the power sector under the conditions determined by the scenario. As nuclear power is taken offline, coal becomes the main source of power generation. As a result, investments that would have otherwise been received by nuclear power plants are no longer happening. Coal power plants have spare capacity and, therefore, need no or only little further investments to produce additional electricity. At the same time, the impact on electricity prices beneficial to electricity users is small because nuclear energy is only marginally more expensive than that of coal. Thus, by shifting from nuclear to coal only a small reduction in the price of electricity is achieved.

China's economic results in S2 (restriction of coal) show large increases in GDP by 2050. This result follows our own assumption on the coal regulation pattern (inputs to the scenario), that is, a large reduction in coal capacity after 2030. This causes a sharp increase of investment in other technologies because coal has a substantial role in power generation in China. By limiting coal power, big investment programs have to be put in place to meet the same level of electricity demand. The positive effect of investment outweighs the negative effect of increased electricity prices in this scenario. Although consumer spending decreases by 0.2% and imports increase by 0.2%, total investment increases by 0.8% and the net positive impact on Chinese GDP is 0.3% compared with the baseline in 2050.

Under the nuclear and coal regulation scenario (S3), investment demand in 2050 increases further as a result of nuclear and coal-powered capacity phase-out, which requires investments in replacement capital. Yet, in 2030, the investment demand does not increase by as much as in S2. Nuclear power is more capital intensive than coal power, so a phase-out of both technologies leads to a greater drop in investment demand than a phase-out of solely coal power (S2). However, the combined phase-out does lead to a larger capacity gap to fill by relatively capital-intensive technologies, and this leads to an increased investment demand by the power generation sector. Although the electricity price is higher, similarly to S2, the impacts on consumer spending are no longer negative under this scenario as higher investment creates jobs, and therefore increases incomes and consumer demand in the Chinese economy. The overall GDP impact in 2050 is 0.5% in China. Employment results follow the GDP results but to a lesser magnitude. The economic results in detail for China are summarized in Table 3.2, Figure 3.3 and Figure 3.4.

Japan

The economic results for Japan are volatile. This volatility is due to investment by the power sector, which is a result of our modeling input assumptions regarding the changes in capacity of nuclear power plants in response to nuclear power regulation.

In S1, the economic results for Japan, in response to nuclear power regulation, show the most positive impacts on GDP because of higher consumer spending and a reduction in imports (mainly a reduction of gas imports). Although investment results increase in the medium term, the long-term increase is not significant. In this scenario, coal-powered energy generation becomes the main

Table 3.2 Economic impact of nuclear and coal power regulation in China (2030, 2050)

Scenarios	*Differences from baseline (%) in 2030*		
	S1	*S2*	*S3*
GDP	-0.1	0.3	0.3
Consumer spending	0.0	0.3	0.3
Exports	0.0	0.0	0.0
Imports	0.0	0.1	0.0
Investment	-0.3	0.5	0.4
Employment	0.0	0.0	0.0
Inflation (consumer price)	0.0	0.1	0.1
Scenarios	*Differences from baseline (%) in 2050*		
	S1	*S2*	*S3*
GDP	-0.1	0.3	0.5
Consumer spending	-0.2	-0.2	0.0
Exports	0.1	0.0	0.1
Imports	0.0	0.2	0.3
Investment	-0.1	0.8	1.2
Employment	0.0	0.0	0.2
Inflation (consumer price)	-0.1	0.2	0.2

Source: E3ME-FTT Power simulation results

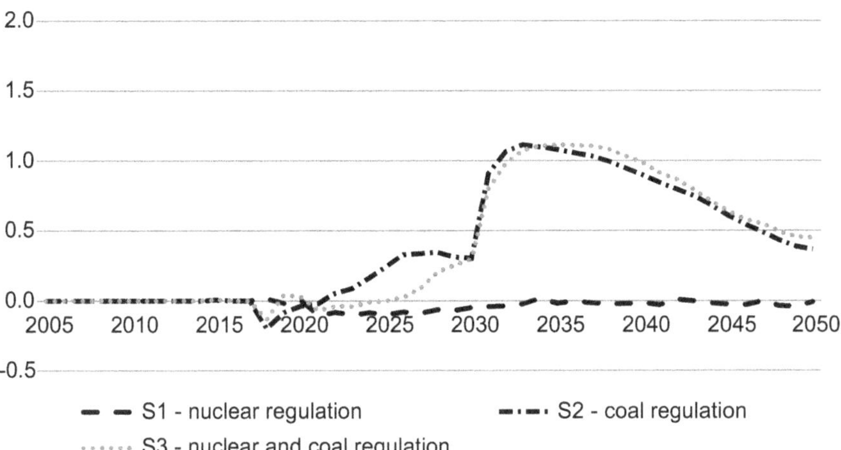

Figure 3.3 Impact on GDP in response to nuclear and coal power regulation in China (2015–2050)

Difference from baseline (%)

Source: E3ME-FTT Power simulation results

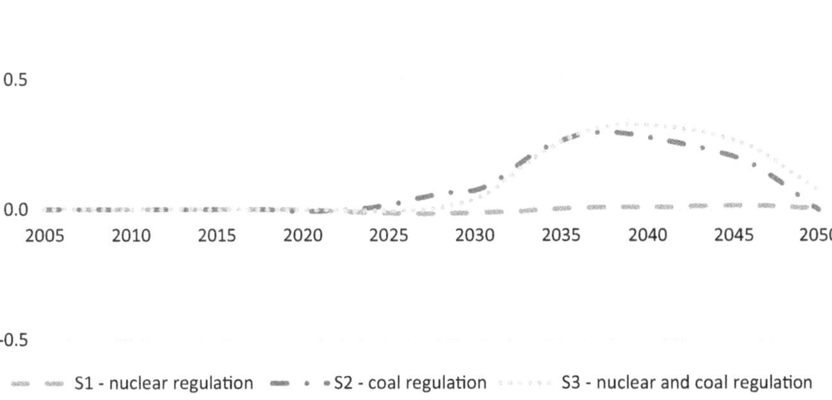

Figure 3.4 Impact on employment in response to nuclear and coal power regulation in China (2015–2050)

Difference from baseline (%)

Source: E3ME-FTT Power simulation results

technology, resulting in a lower electricity price, lower inflation and increased real disposable incomes to households. As coal expands its market share and is also substituted for gas in the baseline, we see a reduction in gas imports. There is very little change to electricity investment in the long term because coal power plants already have the potential to run at higher efficiency.

However, as CO_2 emissions in this scenario are the highest, it is important to bear in mind that, here, the positive outcome for the economy yields a negative outcome for the environment. In S2, restrictions on coal have a negative impact on the GDP in the short term because of a higher electricity price, as power generation moves away from cheap coal to other expensive technologies. In the long run, however, the investment impacts outweigh the negative effect on the electricity price and we see an ~0.3% increase on the GDP in Japan.

S3, coal and nuclear regulation, produces the most negative outcome in 2030 and the least positive outcome in 2050, mainly because of higher electricity prices. Nuclear and coal are relatively cheap sources of electricity in Japan, so moving away from these two technologies will increase the costs of electricity generation in Japan. This increase is passed down to the electricity price that consumers and businesses have to pay. Employment results in Japan follow those for GDP but to a lesser magnitude. The economic results in detail for Japan are summarized in Table 3.3, Figure 3.5 and Figure 3.6.

Table 3.3 Economic impact of nuclear and coal power regulation in Japan (2030, 2050)

	Differences from baseline (%) in 2030		
	S1	*S2*	*S3*
GDP	0.2	-0.1	-0.2
Consumer spending	0.2	-0.1	-0.1
Exports	0.0	0.0	0.0
Imports	-0.3	0.1	0.2
Investment	0.3	-0.1	-0.4
Employment	0.1	0.0	0.0
Inflation (consumer price)	-0.1	0.1	0.2
	Differences from baseline (%) in 2050		
	S1	*S2*	*S3*
GDP	0.4	0.3	0.1
Consumer spending	0.5	0.0	-0.1
Exports	0.0	0.0	0.1
Imports	-0.8	-0.3	0.3
Investment	0.1	1.1	1.0
Employment	0.1	0.1	0.1
Inflation (consumer price)	-0.4	0.1	0.2

Source: E3ME-FTT Power simulation results

Figure 3.5 Impact on GDP in response to nuclear and coal power regulation in Japan (2015–2050)

Difference from baseline (%)

Source: E3ME-FTT Power simulation results

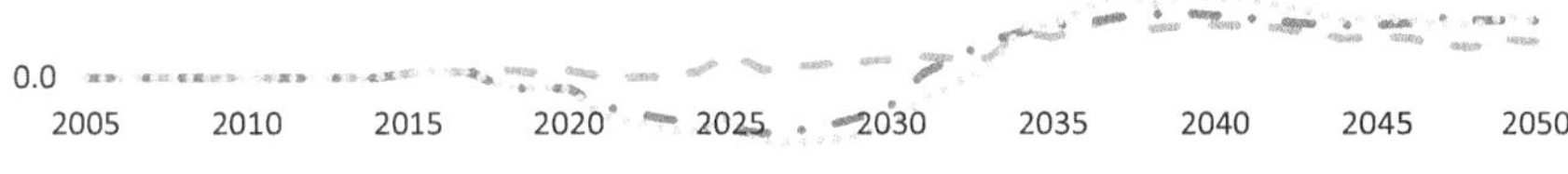

Figure 3.6 Impact on employment in response to nuclear and coal power regulation in Japan (2015–2050)

Difference from baseline (%)

Source: E3ME-FTT Power simulation results

Korea

The economic results for Korea follow the same pattern in each of the scenarios. Initially there is a reduction in investment for technologies that are being regulated, that is, nuclear in S1 and coal in S2. The fall in investment lasts up to 2030, following a steep decline in capacity until this point; after 2030 the reduction becomes steadier.

In S1, the initial negative impact on GDP comes from a reduction in nuclear investment that would otherwise have happened at baseline. The shift is to coal and gas, which can accommodate extra electricity demand without additional investment in the short run. After 2030, additional investment is made towards coal power plants, as nuclear generation is regulated further. This additional investment is needed to accommodate for additional capacity and to replace existing coal power plants that reach the end of their lifetime.

In S1, the results for Korea show that, in the medium term up to 2030, the displacement in power capacity from regulated nuclear also shifts to alternative technologies, not just to coal or gas, making average electricity price in the scenario higher than in the baseline. This results in higher inflation and a reduction in (real) consumer demand. After 2030, by replacing nuclear, coal becomes the main source of power generation. This results in lower average electricity prices that benefit consumers.

In S2 (coal regulation), although there is a reduction in coal power plant investment, the reduction is smaller than that in nuclear investment in S1, because investment costs towards coal power plants are generally cheaper than those towards nuclear power plants. At the same time, there are increases in investment in all other technologies, including nuclear. After 2030, these additional investments, especially driven by investment in gas-fired plants, outweigh reductions in coal investment and become positive. In this scenario, although we see higher electricity prices, the benefits of additional investment that creates jobs and increases incomes offset the inflationary effect.

In S3 (nuclear and coal regulation), the results combine the effects of those shown in S1 and S2. The negative impact on GDP initially is much bigger because of reduced investment to both coal and nuclear power generation. In the longer term, however, much stronger investment demand for alternative technologies leads to a small positive impact in Korea in S3. The investment offsets higher electricity prices and inflationary effects in the scenario. The economic results for Korea are summarized in Table 3.4, Figure 3.7 and Figure 3.8.

Taiwan

The economic results for Taiwan are summarized in Table 3.5, Figure 3.9 and Figure 3.10. Similarly to some of the results presented previously, we see that the economic impacts for Taiwan are volatile because of our input assumptions about the regulated coal and nuclear capacities. The volatility is more notable in the

Table 3.4 Economic impact of nuclear and coal power regulation in Korea (2030, 2050)

	Differences from baseline (%) in 2030		
	S1	*S2*	*S3*
GDP	−0.5	−0.3	-1.1
Consumer spending	−0.6	−0.3	-1.2
Exports	−0.1	0.0	0.0
Imports	−0.1	0.2	0.3
Investment	−0.8	−0.2	-1.6
Employment	−0.3	−0.2	-0.8
Inflation (consumer price)	0.2	0.3	0.6
	Differences from baseline (%) in 2050		
	S1	*S2*	*S3*
GDP	0.5	0.1	0.1
Consumer spending	1.2	0.4	0.2
Exports	0.0	0.2	0.3
Imports	0.1	0.6	0.9
Investment	0.7	1.2	1.9
Employment	0.7	0.3	0.4
Inflation (consumer price)	−0.6	0.4	0.5

Source: E3ME-FTT Power simulation results

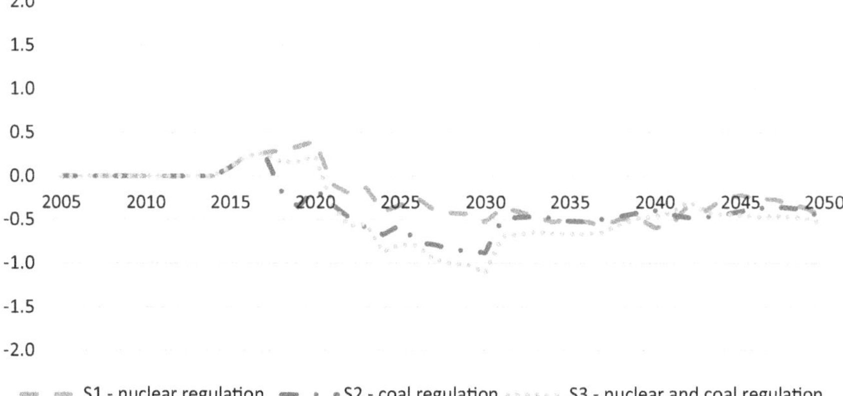

Figure 3.7 Impact on GDP in response to nuclear and coal power regulation in Korea (2015–2050)

Difference from baseline (%)

Source: E3ME-FTT Power simulation results

Figure 3.8 Impact on employment in response to nuclear and coal power regulation in Korea (2015–2050)

Difference from baseline (%)

Source: E3ME-FTT Power simulation results

Table 3.5 Economic impact of nuclear and coal power regulation in Taiwan (2030, 2050)

	Differences from baseline (%) in 2030		
	S1	*S2*	*S3*
GDP	0.1	−0.1	−0.2
Consumer spending	0.2	−0.1	0.0
Exports	0.0	0.0	0.1
Imports	−0.1	0.1	0.2
Investment	0.0	−0.4	−0.3
Employment	0.0	0.0	0.0
Inflation (consumer price)	−0.1	0.1	0.2
	Differences from baseline (%) in 2050		
	S1	*S2*	*S3*
GDP	0.1	0.1	0.2
Consumer spending	0.1	0.4	0.5
Exports	0.0	0.1	0.2
Imports	−0.1	0.3	0.4
Investment	0.0	2.4	2.8
Employment	0.0	0.1	0.1
Inflation (consumer price)	−0.2	0.2	0.1

Source: E3ME-FTT Power simulation results

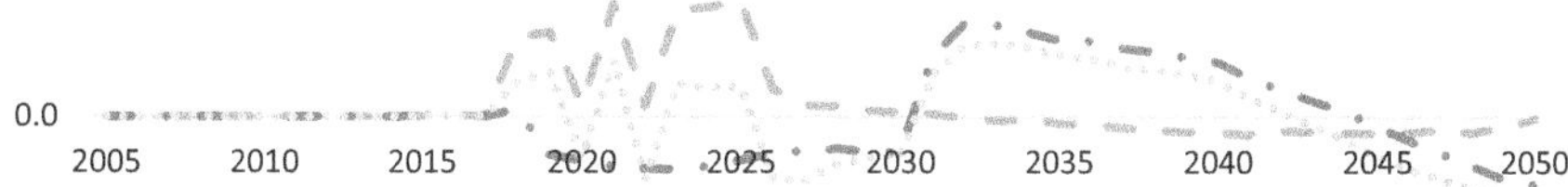

Figure 3.9 Impact on GDP in response to nuclear and coal power regulation in Taiwan (2015–2050)

Difference from baseline (%)

Source: E3ME-FTT Power simulation results

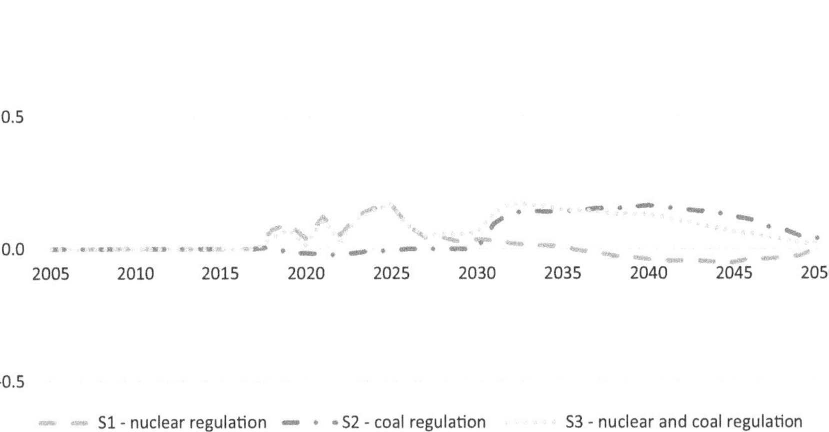

Figure 3.10 Impact on employment in response to nuclear and coal power regulation in Taiwan (2015–2050)

Difference from baseline (%)

Source: E3ME-FTT Power simulation results

results for Taiwan because of the step-change reduction in the nuclear capacity in our scenario assumptions (see Chapter 2).

In S1, GDP impacts in the short term follow power generation sector investment as a result of the changes in nuclear power capacity. The decrease in investment demand for nuclear power capacity is more than negated by diffusion of alternative power generation technologies which require substantial investments. In the long run, households benefit from using cheaper electricity generated from coal, resulting in higher real incomes and higher levels of consumer spending.

In S2 (coal regulation), the initial negative impact on GDP comes from reduction in coal investment but, in the long term, investment in other technologies increases, mainly IGCC and nuclear. This additional investment offsets the reduction of investment into coal, and creates positive effects throughout the Taiwanese economy. The price of electricity increases only slightly in S2 since replacement technologies are from nuclear and gas, which are not much more expensive than coal.

In S3 (coal and nuclear regulation), we see a combination of impacts from S1 and S2 but both investment and price effects are amplified because nuclear and coal are regulated simultaneously. As a result, higher investment is required for alternative technologies and the increased electricity prices reflect the new power generation mix. Employment results follow the GDP results, albeit to a lesser magnitude.

Conclusions

In this chapter, we have looked at the economic impacts of coal and nuclear regulations on the four East Asian economies. The scenarios and modeling approach applied are the same as those in Chapter 2, with the three scenarios testing changes to nuclear regulation, coal regulation and a combination of nuclear and coal regulations.

Restrictions on nuclear power alone (S1) typically have a negative short-term impact on the economy because of a reduction in nuclear investment that would otherwise have taken place. However, these negative impacts are compensated for by the lower-cost power generation from coal that substitutes for nuclear. Although the impacts of nuclear regulation on the economy are small, CO_2 emissions increase significantly because of the shift to coal power generation, as shown in Chapter 2 (increase of 681, 68, 145 and 21 in Mt-CO_2 in China, Japan, Korea and Taiwan, respectively).

Under the coal regulation scenario (S2), power generation costs increase, resulting in higher electricity prices and a modest burden on the economy. However, there is a further shift to renewable energy, which results in additional power generation sector investment. In this scenario, there is also a substantial decrease of 6,349; 379; 213 and 82 Mt-CO_2 emissions in China, Japan, Korea and Taiwan, respectively.

Under a combination of nuclear and coal regulation (S3), there is a larger initial burden on the economy than in Scenario 2 because of higher power generation costs, but the impacts turn neutral or even positive over the medium and long terms, as the costs of renewable technologies fall. Additionally, there is a further benefit to the economy from a reduction in fossil-fuel energy imports. Impacts on CO_2 emission levels differ somewhat by country, but the results from Chapter 2 suggest that large reductions may be expected in some places. Emissions decreased by 5,476; 374; 171 and 74 Mt-CO_2 in China, Japan, Korea and Taiwan, respectively.

Our research shows that, despite severe restrictions on nuclear and coal power, the negative impact on the economy is limited. Moreover, it is possible to shift to a sustainable power mix while improving the economy. Further, if the restriction on coal-fired power plants is implemented in all four regions simultaneously, the negative effect on GDP will decrease in Japan and Korea, two countries that face strong international trade competition, with the price of electricity becoming a determinant of comparative competitiveness.

Finally, we conclude that the simultaneous restriction on nuclear and coal-fired thermal power generation is necessary to promote clean technologies. The economy also benefits from additional investment in renewable technologies, as it creates jobs and there are further multiplier effects. At the same time, the trade balance of the country improves because fossil fuel imports are reduced. Benefits from investments and reductions in imports offset increases in the price of electricity in the long run, especially as renewable technologies become cheaper. However, building on the results from Chapter 2, we must also conclude that the regulations alone are not enough to promote a significant increase in the use of renewables, even if there may be a modest long-term economic benefit. It is, therefore, necessary for policy makers to introduce complementary policies, such as Feed-in Tariffs or carbon taxes to promote a higher share of renewable energy. This is examined in Chapter 4.

Notes

1 See Chapter 1, Cambridge Econometrics (2019) and www.e3me.com for further details on E3ME model.
2 See Chapter 2 and Mercure (2012) for details on the FTT:Power model.
3 For more details on the interaction of the E3ME model with that of FTT:Power, see Chapter 2 of Lee et al. (2015).
4 Δlog indicates differences of the logarithms of the quantities.
5 Installed capacity of nuclear power plants in Japan reflects the capacity at restart as of June 2017.
6 Annual electricity output (kWh) = installed capacity (kW) × 8760 hours × annual operational rate.

References

Cambridge Econometrics (2019) E3ME Manual, version 7.0, available at www.e3me.com

Center for Low Carbon Society Strategy (2015). *Future Power Costs and CO_2 Emissions*. Center for Low Carbon Society Strategy.

Institute of Energy Economics, Japan (2016). Asia/World Energy Outlook 2016, available at https://eneken.ieej.or.jp/data/7199.pdf

Lee, S., Pollitt, H. and Park, S.-J. (Eds.) (2015) *Low-Carbon, Sustainable Future in East Asia: Improving Energy Systems, Taxation and Policy Cooperation*. New York: Routledge.

Mercure, J.-F. (2012) 'FTT:Power: A global model of the power sector with induced technological change and natural resource depletion', *Energy Policy*, 48, 799–811.

Mercure, J.-F., Salas, P., Foley, A., Chewpreecha, U., Pollitt, H., Holden, P. B. and Edwards, N. R. (2014). 'The dynamics of technology diffusion and the impacts of climate policy instruments in the decarbonisation of the global electricity sector', *Energy Policy*, 73, 686–700. doi:10.1016/j.enpol.2014.06.029.

Ogawa, Y., Mercure, J.-F., Lee, S., Pollitt, H., Matsumoto, K. and Chiashi, A. (2015). 'Modeling the power sector in East Asia – Economic and environmental impacts of the choices of power sources', in S. Lee, H. Pollitt and S.-J. Park (Eds.), *Low-Carbon, Sustainable Future in East Asia: Improving Energy Systems, Taxation and Policy Cooperation*. New York: Routledge, pp. 63–72.

Pollitt, H., Park, S.-J., Lee, S., and Ueta, K. (2014) 'An economic and environmental assessment of future electricity generation mixes in Japan – An assessment using the E3MG macro-econometric model', *Energy Policy*, 67, 243–254.

4 The impacts of combined policies to promote sustainable low-carbon power generation in East Asia

Tae-Yeoun Lee, Unnada Chewpreecha, Sung-In Na, Yanmin He, Li-Chun Chen, Ken'ichi Matsumoto and Soocheol Lee

Introduction

The countries in East Asia have committed to meeting their NDCs (Nationally Determined Contributions) that were agreed upon under the Paris Agreement. They must also work towards a global long-term 2°C target.[1] The measures that were introduced in Chapters 2 and 3 started to move towards these goals, with power generation sectors in East Asia targeted by the regulation policies. However, they were found to be insufficient for the region to meet the specified targets.

In this chapter, we introduce carbon taxes in the four countries. We compare the carbon tax rates between a situation in which carbon taxes are uniformly introduced in all sectors of the economy, and one with specific measures only placed on the power sector. In East Asian countries, the power sector is responsible for 40–60% of total emissions (IEA, 2015).[2]

As we found in the previous chapters, choosing energy sources in the power sector can have a substantial impact on not only CO_2 emissions but also the wider economy. Therefore, in this chapter we test the environmental and economic impacts of various rates of carbon taxes in the power sector to meet the NDC and 2°C targets. To meet the CO_2 targets through only applying carbon taxes and Feed-in-Tariffs (FITs) would require very high carbon prices; this is politically not easy because of the potential burden on certain businesses. We expect that the carbon tax rates that are required to meet the NDCs and 2°C targets could be reduced if sectors implement other policies to contribute towards meeting the targets. Concretely, we focus on the power sector and will see how power mixes of East Asian countries might be influenced by FITs and regulations on the use of coal by 2050. If these measures can reduce emissions levels substantially, then the carbon tax rates required to meet the specified targets could be lower.

In the following section, we give an overview of the current renewable energy support systems in East Asian countries. After that we define and describe the four policy scenarios used in this chapter, and the metholodgy that was used for the model-based analysis. We draw on the coal regulation policy scenario that was used in Chapter 2. The next section provides the energy, environment and economic impacts from the modelling for each scenario in the power sector. The final section discusses the findings and concludes.

Overview of renewable support systems in East Asia

In this section, we focus on additional efforts to cut CO_2 emissions in the power sector by promoting renewables through policy support. In Chapter 2 (and also Azuma et al., 2017), we found that, when coal and other polluting power plants are regulated in Japan, Korea and Taiwan, the use of gas and coal, and Carbon Capture and Storage (CCS) grew, so that the share of renewable energy did not increase much. This suggests that it is necessary to explicitly support renewable energy introduction – for example, through FITs –to boost the use of renewables in East Asia. We, therefore, assess renewable support systems in this section.

China

Throughout the East Asian countries, FITs have been introduced in the power sector. In China, according to the 'Renewable Energy Law' (order of the President of the People's Republic of China, No. 33), which was enacted in 2005, grid companies are required to purchase renewable energy output. In 2009, the Chinese National Development and Reform Commission (NDRC) introduced a national FIT to support the deployment of electricity from wind power (Fa Gai Jia Ge 2009: No.1909). The initial benchmark purchase price setting is divided into four categories based on different resource areas (for the details, see Li et al., 2010). Tariffs vary among the categories:

- Category 1: 0.51CNY/kWh
- Category 2: 0.54CNY/kWh
- Category 3: 0.58CNY/kWh
- Category 4: 0.61CNY/kWh

In 2011, the NDRC announced the country's first nationwide solar photovoltaics (PVs) FIT policy (Fa Gai Jia Ge 2011: No.1594). In this notice, solar PV projects approved before July 1, 2011, and put in operation by December 31 of the same year, could receive a benchmark price of 1.15 CNY/kWh. This price also applied to solar PV projects situated in Tibet approved on July 1, 2011, or afterwards and approved before July 1 but not in operation by December 31, 2011. For solar PV projects in other regions, a price of 1 CNY/kWh was applied.

For biomass, the Renewable Energy Law introduced a 0.25CNY/kWh feed-in premium for biomass-generated electricity. This capital premium is added to province-specific prices of coal-generated power, and is applicable over a 15-year period. In 2010, the Notice on Improving the Pricing Policy for Biomass Power

Prices provided a new national unified FIT for biomass of 0.75 CNY/kWh (Fa Gai Jia Ge 2010: No.1579).

For hydropower, the NDRC issued the Notice on Improving the Pricing Mechanism for Hydropower Prices in January 2014 (Fa Gai Jia Ge 2014: No.61) and unveiled a new hydropower on-grid tariff pricing mechanism, in which prices would be decided through negotiations between hydropower operators and the receiving provinces. The new hydropower tariff is based on the average on-grid tariff of all power sources in the receiving province.

In 2014, the NDRC published a notice to set the FIT for offshore wind. The intertidal projects enjoyed a tariff of 0.75 CNY/kWh while the nearshore tariff was set at 0.85 CNY/kWh. The FIT applied to wind power projects that were commissioned before 2017. For projects that were commissioned during or after 2017, the NDRC determines the tariff in the future, in accordance with the construction costs and the bidding situation at that time (Fa Gai Jia Ge 2014: No.1216).

The tariff scheme and benchmark prices have been revised almost every year by the NDRC, in accordance with changes of investment cost and technological advancement. Recently, rates have been gradually adjusted. For example, the FIT for wind power existed initially only for onshore wind projects. More recently the FIT for offshore wind was added (Table 4.1), but the prices for wind power and solar are declining.[3] Document 2554, (Pilots for Local Consumption of

Table 4.1 Overview of FIT in China (2017)

Item	*Category*	*Price (unit: CNY/kwh)*
Solar	Category 1	0.65
	Category 2	0.75
	Category 3	0.85
	Tibet	1.05
Wind (land)	Category 1	0.40
	Category 2	0.45
	Category 3	0.49
	Category 4	0.57
Wind (offshore)	Intertidal	0.75
	Nearshore	0.85
Biomass	Waste materials	0.65
	Others	0.75

Source: The Notice on Adjusting the Pricing Policy for Solar Power and Offshore Wind Power Prices (Fa Gai Jia Ge, 2016: No.2729), The Notice on Improving the Pricing Policy for Biomass Power Prices (Fa Gai Jia Ge, 2010: No.1579), The Notice on Improving the Pricing Policy for Waste Materials Incineration Power Prices (Fa Gai Jia Ge, 2012: No.801)

Note: Prices as announced by the government.

Renewable Energy [Fa Gai Ban Yun Xing, 2015]), calls for the creation of a system of generation priority rights for renewable generators and a compensation mechanism that balances renewable energy. In March 2016, the NDRC issued a main policy (Fa Gai Neng Yuan, 2016: No.625) on a purchase-all program of renewable energy, again emphasizing generation priority rights for renewable generators, and outlined new compensation for coal-fired generators' curtailment (see RAP [Regulatory Assistance Project]).[4]

Japan

In Japan, the FIT was started in 2012 to promote use of renewable energy. It forces electric utilities to purchase electricity generated from renewable energy sources at a fixed purchase price (13.65–57.75 JPY/kW in 2012; see Agency for Natural Resources and Energy [ANRE])[5] for a fixed period (usually 10–20 years) determined by the Japanese government (see Table 4.2); for further details of the FIT scheme in Japan, see Morita and Matsumoto (2014), Matsumoto et al. (2017).

This scheme regulates the procedures on deciding purchase prices and periods, the certification of facilities, collection and adjustment of surcharges related to purchase costs and terms by which electric utilities can reject the contracts. It is expected to reduce uncertainty around investment in renewable electricity facilities, and will encourage additional investment in renewable energy sources (Kitamura, 2013). The Japanese FIT covers solar PV, wind, small- and medium-scale hydro, geothermal and biomass power (see Table 4.2; see Ministry of Economy, Trade and Industry [METI]).[6]

Prices and periods are set according to classification, installation mode and scale of facilities. The purchase prices, periods and classifications are discussed and reviewed every year by the Procurement Price Calculation Committee; the METI makes final decisions. Costs to purchase the generated electricity are shared by all electricity consumers in proportion to the volume of electricity they use. The surcharge is also determined by the METI based on the work by the Surcharge Adjustment Organization. The surcharge was 0.22 JPY/kWh in FY2012 and has increased to 0.35 JPY/kWh in FY2013; 2.64 JPY/kWh in FY2017 and 2.9 JPY/kWh in FY2018. However, purchase prices and surcharge rates for large-scale solar and wind power are being lowered.[7]

With this FIT scheme, the volume of power generated from renewable sources has increased substantially. The share of renewable energy (excluding large hydropower) in power generation was 1.4% in 2011 but increased to 8% in 2017 (of which 5.7% was PV derived).[8,9] PV facilities are popular because environmental assessment is not required and installation of facilities is easier than for other forms of electricity generation that use renewables (Kitamura, 2013). FIT rates for solar PV systems have decreased year by year, and PV systems generating more than 2 MW are subject to a bidding procedure to decide tariffs from 2017 (Table 4.2). Developers who propose higher discount rates receive priority to meet the quota.

Table 4.2 Overview of FIT in Japan

Category	*Capacity (kW)*		*FY2014 (JPY/kWh)*	*FY2016 (JPY/kWh)*	*FY2018 (JPY/kWh)*	*Purchase period (no. of years)*
Photovoltaic (PV) power	≥2,000		32	24	bidding	20
	10 <2,000		32	24	18	
	<10 kW	Generators not required to install output-control equipment	37	31	26	10
		Generators required to install output-control equipment		33	28	
Land-based wind power	≥20		22	22	22	20
	<20		55	55	55	
Offshore wind power	≥20		36	36	36	
Geothermal power	≥15,000		26	26	26	15
	<15,000		40	40	40	
Small and medium hydropower	≥1,000 to <30,000	Installing fully new facilities	24	24	24	20
		Utilizing existing headrace channels	14	14	14	
	≥200 to <1,000	Installing fully new facilities	29	29	29	
		Utilizing existing headrace channels	21	21	21	
	<200	Installing fully new facilities alone	34	34	34	
		Utilizing existing headrace channels	25	25	25	
Biomass	Wood (unused)	≥2,000 kW	32	32	32	
		<2,000 kW		40	40	
	Wood (general)		24	24	24	
	Wood (waste materials of buildings)		13	13	13	
	Waste materials (sewage sludge etc.)		17	17	17	
	Methane fermentation		39	39	39	

Source: ANRE (December 30, 2018)

Korea

Until 2011, Korea had a FIT system; but it was replaced by the Renewable Portfolio Standard (RPS) in 2012. The government maintains a FIT only for existing recipients, who may have options to either continue their FIT or exchange it for a Renewable Energy Certificate (REC) that enables transactions under the RPS. The RPS program requires that the 13 largest power companies (with installed power capacity of more than 500 MW) steadily increase their share of renewables in total power generation in the period 2012–24 (Table 4.3). For power companies to meet their RPS targets they can invest in renewable energy installations themselves or purchase RECs.

The government introduced long-term fixed-price contracts for solar and wind power in 2017. The system aims to deal with the volatility of the System Marginal Price (SMP) and the price of the REC. SMP refers to an electric power market price (in KRW/kWh) for the amount of power applied per dealing time, and is determined as the highest price for effective power generation for all generators to which outputs are allocated per time slot. The REC certifies that power generators produce and supply power by using new and renewable energy facilities. RECs are issued per MWh and enable transactions under the RPS. Table 4.4 shows the trends of the SMP and REC prices. The price of the SMP showed a sharp decline up to 2015. The price of the REC has been increasing, but the sum of SMP and REC prices has been decreasing.

Table 4.3 Annual RPS targets (in % of renewable energy power generation)

	2012	*2013*	*2014*	*2015*	*2016*	*2017*	*2018*	*2019*	*2020*	*2021*	*2022 after*
Target	2.0	2.5	3.0	3.5	4.0	5.0	6.0	7.0	8.0	9.0	10.0

Source: MTIE (2015)

Table 4.4 Price trends of SMP and REC in Korea (unit: KRW/kwh)

	2012		*2013*		*2014*		*2015*	
	Q1	*Q2*	*Q1*	*Q2*	*Q1*	*Q2*	*Q1*	*Q2*
SMP	166	156	155	150	147	135	111	92
REC	32	32	57	57	62	62	85	85
SMP + REC	198	188	212	207	209	197	196	177

Source: Korea New and Renewable Energy Center (July 19, 2017)

Note: Q1, 1st quarter of the year; Q2, 2nd quarter of the year.

Taiwan

In Taiwan, the government approved the 'Renewable Energy Development Act' on June 12, 2009, which promotes the use of renewable energy, thereby boosting energy diversification and helping to reduce greenhouse gas (GHG) emissions. The Act caps the subsidies for renewable energy up to 10 GW within 20 years. The core strategy of the Act is a FIT system. It authorizes the government to enhance incentives for the development of renewable energy technologies (RETs) through a variety of methods, including the acquisition mechanisms, incentives for demonstration projects and loosening of regulatory restrictions. According to the subsidies of the statute, the share of renewables in total power generation will triple by 2030 (Hwang, 2010). The initially targeted capacity for renewable power generation by 2030 was raised in 2015 to 17.25 GW.

A committee was formed to decide the formula for FITs. Tariffs and formulas should be reviewed annually, referring to technical advancement, cost variation, goal achievement status and other factors (Table 4.5). Tariffs should not be below the average cost for fossil-fired power of domestic power utilities. Currently, only solar PV tariff rates are set on the date when generating equipment installations are completed. Other technologies have tariff rates that are set on the Power

Table 4.5 FIT for renewable energy in Taiwan (2015)

Category	*Type*	*Capacity (kW)*	*Period 1 US ¢/kWh)*	*Period 2 US ¢/kWh)*
Solar PV	Roof type	≥1 to <20	22.14	21.52
		≥20 to <100	18.51	17.99
		≥100 to <500	17.30	16.82
		≥500	16.75	16.30
	Ground type	≥1	15.76	15.33
Wind Power	Onshore	≥1 to <10	27.12	
		≥10	8.78	
	Offshore		18.52	
Hydropower	Stream-type		8.50	
Geothermal			15.91	
Biomass	Without biogas equipment		8.50	
	With biogas equipment		10.90	
RDF	Refuse-derived fuel (RDF)		9.11	
Others			8.50	

Sources: BOE (2015)

Notes:

1 Exchange rate: US$ 1 = NT$ 31.

2 For those who are exempt from bidding, the equipment completed from every year's January 1 to June 30 will be subject to period 1; from July 1 to December 31 will be subject to period 2.

Purchasing Agreement (PPA) signing date. The tariffs are applied for 20 years, and the PPA is a very important credit for banks to provide project financing. The Bureau of Energy (BOE) announces a PV capacity quota every year. PV systems that are greater than 50 kW in size are subject to a bidding procedure to decide tariffs. Developers that propose higher discount rates receive priority to get the quota. The installed capacity of PV systems increased by more than 60 times in the five years after FITs were implemented (BOE, 2015).

Scenarios and methodology

Scenarios

In this section, we analyze the impacts of additional policy efforts in the power sector, including the introduction of FITs, coal power regulations and carbon taxes, to meet the NDCs (2030) and 2°C (2050) targets. The policies are applied to China, Japan, Korea and Taiwan, and the emission reduction targets are met in each country.

The intuition of the baseline scenario is the same throughout this book, that is, there are no additional climate policies to existing ones. However, in this chapter, we use a baseline that incorporates specific power sector information (notably on the share of nuclear generation). The path of future emissions in the baseline is thus different to that used in Part 2 of this book.

In total there are four policy scenarios:

- S1 – FIT only in the power sector
- S2 – FIT plus coal regulation in the power sector
- S3 – FIT, coal regulation plus carbon tax in all sectors, to meet the 2°C target
- S4 – Decarbonization scenario with carbon tax only in all sectors, to meet the 2°C target

No new nuclear plants may be built beyond those in the baseline, although the share of nuclear energy in power generation may increase if there are reductions in capacity elsewhere. In S1, S2 and S3, we assumed no additional climate action in the rest of the world regions for the baseline scenario. In S4, we assumed that all world regions also take action to meet the 2°C target. We used the E3ME model and, while the policies here are applicable to China, Japan, Korea and Taiwan, the model can be used for all 59 world regions simultaneously. Further explanations for each scenario are given later (see Cambridge Econometrics, 2014).

In S1, we consider the impact of a FIT policy. As described in the previous section, FITs have been introduced in the power sector to increase penetration rates of renewable energy by guaranteeing to purchase electricity generated from renewable energy sources. The FIT is given as a fixed rate of US$10/MWh and is applied to biomass (including CCS), wind and solar technologies.

In S2, we apply the FITs again but also add coal regulation as described in Chapter 2. The logic here goes beyond GHG emissions. In East Asian countries,

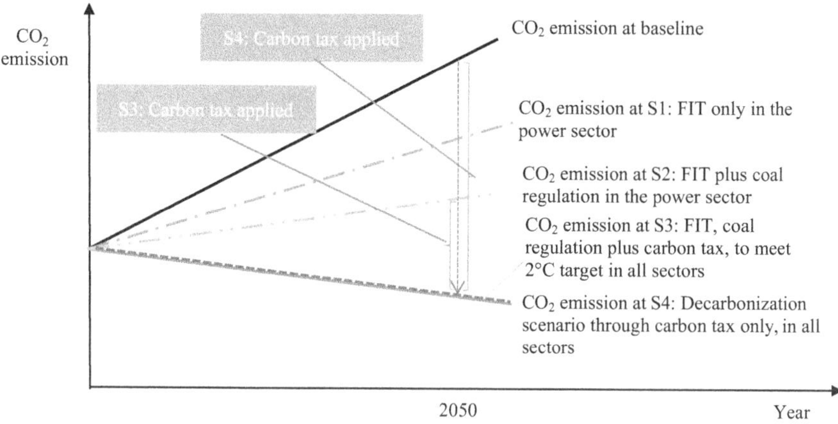

Figure 4.1 Total CO_2 emissions, schematic of business as usual (BAU), target and scenarios

the proportion of coal used is high and is causing serious air pollution (see Chapter 13). Therefore, we assume that coal regulation occurs in the power sector as a separate measure to FITs.

In S3, we add a carbon tax in addition to FITs and regulations. A carbon tax is added, so that emission reduction targets are met in each country. We assume that the carbon tax revenues collected by the national government are not recycled back to the economy. S4 is a decarbonization scenario that is achieved through a carbon tax alone. The emission reduction target in S4 and S3 are the same.

In S4, we additionally assume that other world regions are also taking action to meet the long-term emission reduction target. Figure 4.1 illustrates the expected impacts on CO_2 emissions in each scenario relative to those of baseline according to the Institute of Energy Economics, Japan (IEEJ), 2017.

Key interactions in the modelling

Figure 4.2 summarizes the key macroeconomic impacts of a FIT in S1. Generally, FITs will result in higher electricity prices for end users because of additional costs. These result from charges that must be paid to small generators to 'reward' them for the renewable electricity they add to the grid. This increases the cost of supply, which is then passed on to customers in the form of additional surcharges. At the same time, a FIT scheme should encourage the uptake of RETs, as it makes expensive renewables more attractive. Thus, there will be an increase in investment by organizations and individuals who participate in the FIT scheme.

The impact of coal regulations in S2 is omitted here, as it is described in Chapters 2 and 3. Figure 4.3 summarizes the key macroeconomic impacts of a carbon tax like those imposed in S3 and S4. Energy price increases will be passed on to more general increases in prices throughout the economy, which will cause

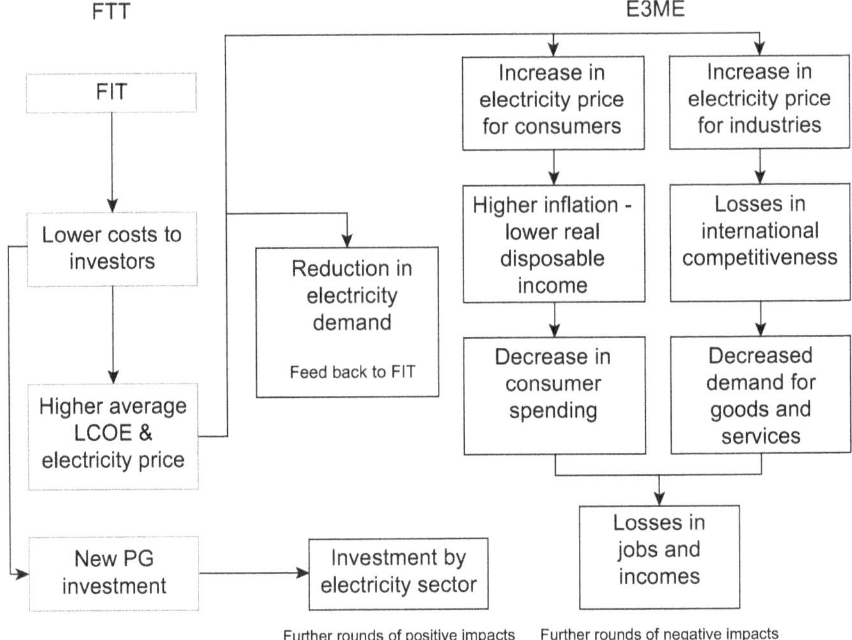

Figure 4.2 Economic impacts of a FIT in S1

Note: LCOE, levelized cost of electricity; PG, power generation.

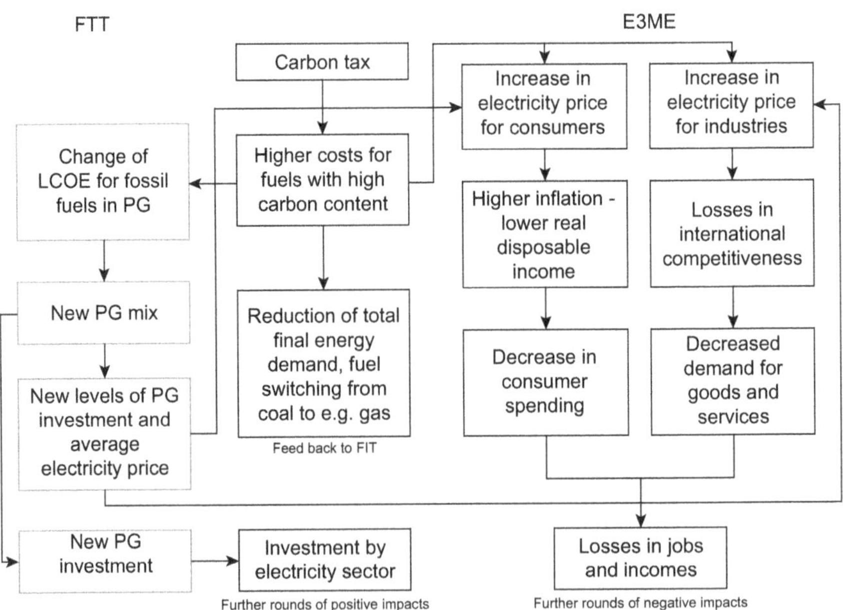

Figure 4.3 Potential economic impacts of a carbon tax in S3 or S4

Note: LCOE, levelized cost of electricity; PG, power generation.

substitution in consumers' expenditure, in exports, and between imports and domestic production. There will be a reduction in product demand across the economy because of higher prices. However, there are some positive impacts too. A carbon tax could encourage investors to invest in low-carbon technologies and, in the longer term, could reduce demand for energy imports, thereby boosting the trade balance and GDP. These impacts are discussed further in Chapter 5.

Results and policy implications

China

Energy and environmental impacts

First, we look at the total CO_2 emissions (Figure 4.4 and Table 4.6). FITs only (S1) have a small effect on the levels of economy-wide CO_2 emissions, a reduction of 2.6% compared with the baseline by 2050. However, a combination of FITs plus coal regulation (S2) leads to a reduction of 48.6% in CO_2 emissions by 2050 (and 82.1% in the power sector). We also find that, by 2050, emission reductions in S3 (with a very small rate of carbon tax of US\$7.3/tCO_2) are almost identical to those in S4 (high carbon tax of US\$960.6/tCO_2, applied to all sectors). This means that, in China, there are two very effective options to achieve the emissions reduction target, both of which could have different economic impacts.

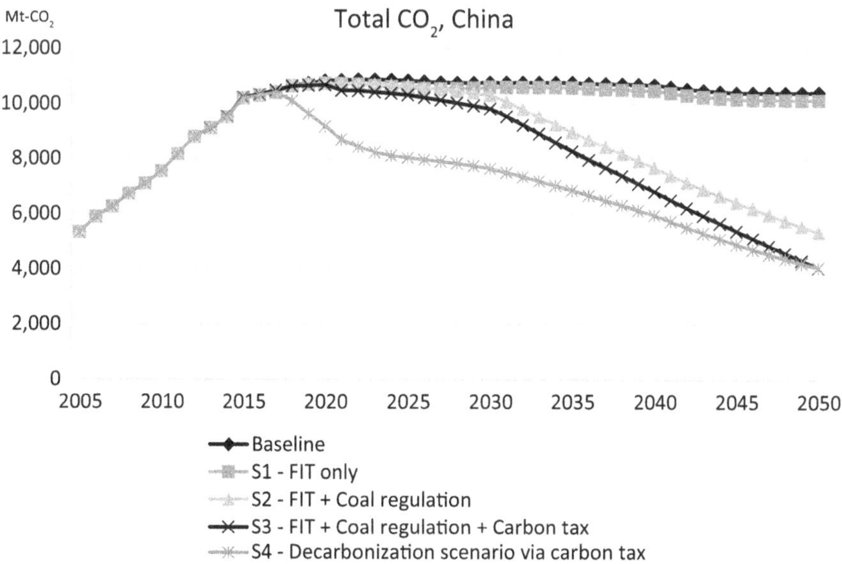

Figure 4.4 Total CO_2 emissions (Mt-CO_2), China

Table 4.6 CO_2 emissions and economic impacts relative to baseline in S1–S4, in 2030 and 2050, China (difference from baseline, %)

China	*2030*				*2050*			
	S1	*S2*	*S3*	*S4*	*S1*	*S2*	*S3*	*S4*
Power sector CO_2 emissions	-3.3	-9.1	-9.4	-33.0	-4.5	-82.1	-87.6	-67.7
Total CO_2 emissions	-1.6	-4.3	-8.8	-29.0	-2.6	-48.6	-61.0	-61.0
GDP	0.0	0.3	0.1	0.2	0.0	0.2	0.2	-1.1
Employment	0.0	0.1	0.0	-0.1	0.0	0.0	0.0	-0.8
Consumer spending	0.0	0.2	-0.2	-1.8	0.0	-0.8	-0.2	-2.2
Exports	0.0	0.1	0.0	0.1	0.0	0.1	0.0	-0.5
Imports	0.0	0.1	-0.1	-0.3	0.0	0.1	0.2	-0.7
Investment	0.0	0.4	0.2	1.3	0.0	1.1	0.9	-1.1
Inflation (consumer price)	0.0	0.0	0.1	1.6	0.0	0.3	0.2	1.2
Electricity price	0.8	7.1	7.2	18.4	1.1	27.3	27.3	30.8
Carbon tax ($US\$_{2010}/tCO_2$)			1.9	248.2			7.3	960.6

Source: Estimated by Cambridge Econometrics for this study

The FITs in S1 have only a small impact on rates of renewables uptake (Figure 4.5; see also Table 4.10), but this was partly because the FIT rates used were small. S2 further promotes the uptake of renewables because energy generation from coal is no longer an option, and the power sector must find alternative power sources. The largest increases are in Integrated Gasification Combined Cycle (IGCC), IGCC with CCS, nuclear, large hydro, onshore wind and solar PVs. The renewable energy share is about 75.9% in S2 by 2050. In S3, large hydro has the biggest increase because the carbon tax pushes towards low-carbon options, without necessarily favoring renewables. Onshore wind and solar PV also increase in both S2 and S3. Renewable energy increases to about 79.1% of total electricity generation in S3 by 2050, and this increased share of renewables contributes most to the decarbonization in this scenario.

If we consider the carbon tax alone (and across all sectors), results are a bit different. In S4, the share of nuclear power generation increases slightly (compared with baseline) to 12.4% by 2050, while renewable energy's share is only 57.6% (see Table 4.10).

Economic impacts

The impact of FITs on the Chinese economy is small in S1, S2 and S3. FITs increase the price of electricity and, as discussed in Chapter 3, this has a negative effect on consumer spending and presents higher costs to businesses (see Table 4.6). However, the overall economy is slightly positive, primarily because of higher investment in RETs when coal is phased out. In S3, where a low carbon

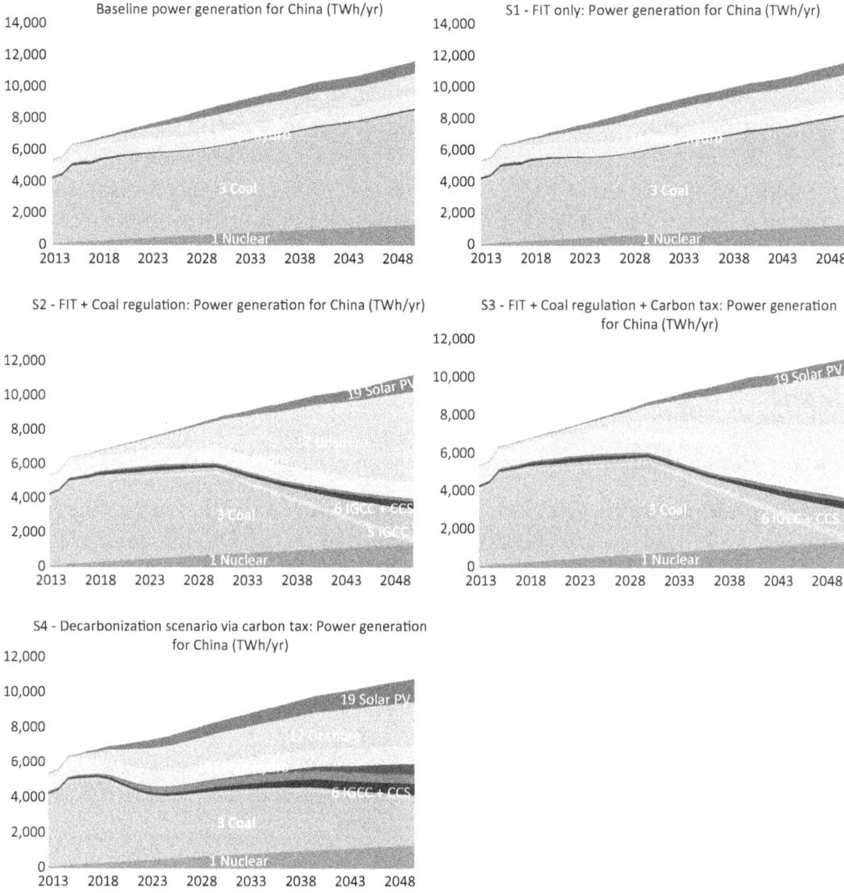

Figure 4.5 Power generation mix, China (TWh/yr)

tax (approximately US\$7.3/tCO_2) is introduced on top of regulations and FITs, the impact on GDP is still positive.

In S4, a high carbon tax (approximately US\$960.6/tCO_2) is applied to all sectors, so price increases are not limited to the electricity price but also cover, for example, road transport uses of gasoline or industry uses of coal. A carbon tax causes an inflationary effect, which affects real incomes and expenditures (see results later) as well as reductions in international competitiveness. All of these things have a negative impact on GDP.

As mentioned previously, the carbon tax rates are much lower in S3 than in S4. This is because coal regulation is very effective in China, making the power sector's carbon reduction target easier to achieve than relying on carbon taxes alone. This means only a small additional effort in CO_2 reduction is required to meet the 2°C target and, hence, a much lower carbon tax is required.

Policy implications

Under the current and assumed FIT system, there are only small impacts on CO_2 reduction because the rate is too small to promote the development of RETs. By contrast, coal regulation is very effective at reducing CO_2 emissions without damaging the economy. It, therefore, appears that to increase the regulation of coal is the top priority. Therefore, the FIT rate should be raised gradually, to promote the installation of RETs. An effective carbon taxing mechanism, such as a national-level carbon emission trading market and carbon taxes could accelerate the transition to a clean energy economy and will promote green growth in the future. As shown in Table 4.6, scenarios without a carbon tax or with low carbon taxation generate better results in terms of GDP, employment and investment.

Japan

Energy and environmental impacts

Japan's results regarding total CO_2 emissions are given in Figure 4.6 and Table 4.7. The FIT in S1 leads to a small (2.5% reduction in total CO_2 emissions by 2050, compared with those in the baseline. FIT plus coal regulation in S2 reduces CO_2 emissions further (by 17.9%) compared with the baseline. By contrast, S3 and S4, which include carbon taxes, show large (66.9%) reductions in CO_2 emissions by 2050, compared with the baseline. This means that, in Japan, a policy mix including FITs, coal regulation and carbon taxes is effective in achieving the CO_2

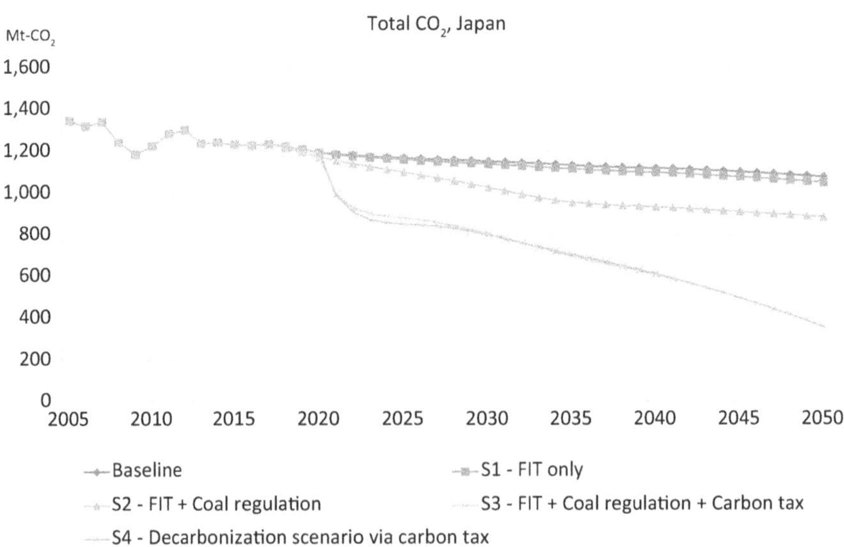

Figure 4.6 Total CO_2 emissions (Mt-CO_2), Japan

Table 4.7 CO_2 emissions and economic impacts relative to baseline in S1–S4, in 2030 and 2050, Japan (differences from baseline, %)

Japan	*2030*				*2050*			
From baseline (%)	*S1*	*S2*	*S3*	*S4*	*S1*	*S2*	*S3*	*S4*
Power sector CO_2 emissions	-2.7	-25.9	-40.6	-39.1	-4.8	-34.4	-76.4	-74.8
Total CO_2 emissions	-1.1	-10.8	-30.2	-30.7	-2.5	-17.9	-66.9	-66.9
GDP	0.0	0.0	-0.9	-1.5	0.0	-0.2	-0.4	-1.2
Employment	0.0	0.0	-0.5	-0.7	0.0	-0.1	-0.2	-0.5
Consumer spending	0.0	-0.2	-2.4	-3.3	0.0	-0.3	-1.9	-3.2
Exports	0.0	0.1	-0.3	-0.2	0.0	0.1	-0.1	-0.3
Imports	0.0	0.6	-4.4	-5.3	0.0	0.4	-7.9	-9.0
Investment	-0.1	0.9	-0.6	-1.6	0.0	-0.2	-1.4	-2.5
Inflation (consumer price)	0.0	0.3	3.1	4.3	0.1	0.3	2.0	3.2
Electricity price	1.1	12.2	19.5	13.4	1.6	14.0	28.9	22.8
Carbon tax ($US\$_{2010}/tCO_2$)			188.0	248.2			727.6	960.6

Source: Estimated by Cambridge Econometrics for this study

emission targets. The carbon tax on its own achieves the same target but at a larger cost to GDP (see Table 4.7).

Next, we look at the impacts on energy sources in Japan (see Table 4.10), which, overall, follow a similar pattern compared with those for China. The FITs in S1 only have a small impact on promoting the uptake of renewables in Japan. Again, this is partly due to the fact that FIT rates are insufficiently high. S2 further promotes uptake of renewables because power generation from coal is no longer an option, and the power sector must find alternative power sources. The results show that Japan increases its shares of onshore wind and solar PV from the baseline.

In S3, there is an increase in use of CCS, followed by onshore wind and solar PVs; the share of renewable energies in power generation increases to 44.1% and contributes most to decarbonization in this scenario. In S4, a similar pattern is observed. Nevertheless, in Japan an additional very high carbon tax (US\$727.6/ tCO_2; see Table 4.7) is needed in S3 to reach the 2°C target by 2050.

Economic impacts

The impact of FITs alone in the power sector (S1) on the Japanese economy is initially close to zero (see Table 4.7). In the longer term, however, there is a small negative effect, as FITs increase electricity prices, and this has a negative effect on real incomes for consumers and higher costs for business. FITs plus coal regulation (S2) also has almost no economic impact in the short run (2030) but

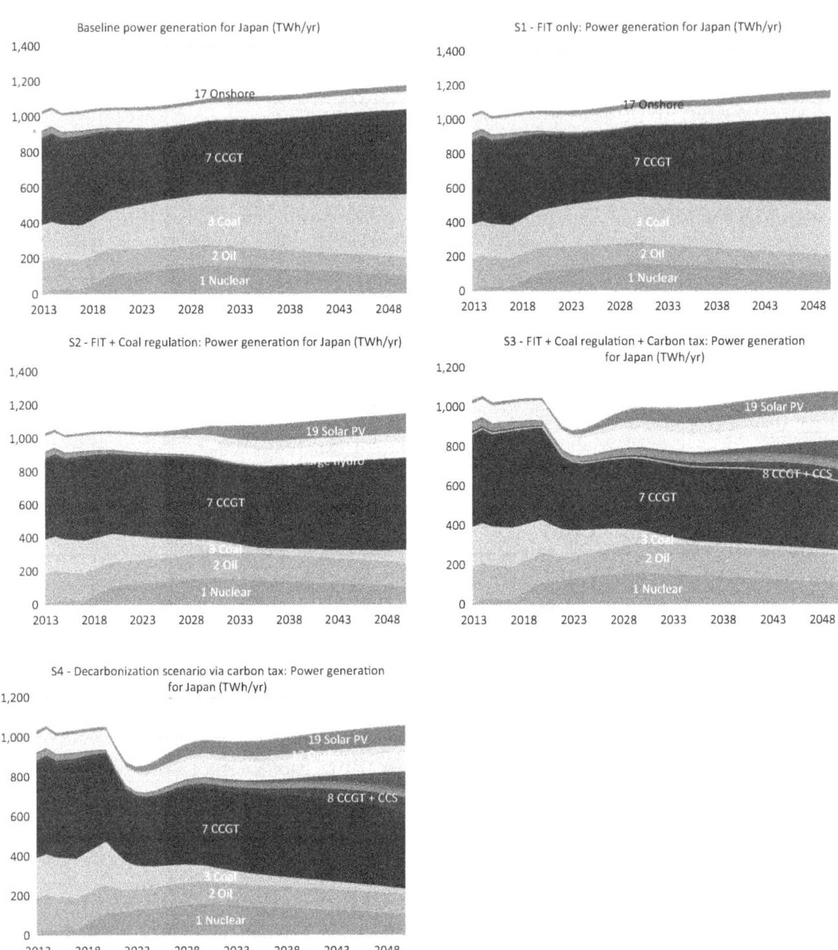

Figure 4.7 Power generation mix, Japan (TWh/yr)

again there are small negative effects in the long run because of reduced use of cheap coal.

In S3, with a carbon tax added, the impact on GDP in Japan is negative in the short and long runs. In S4, GDP and employment are – as in S3 – negative in 2050, although the impact is larger in S4 than in S3 (with virtually the same reductions in CO_2 emissions). Therefore, the policy mix scenario (S3) could achieve the same CO_2 emission reduction but with less of an economic impact when compared with the carbon tax–only scenario (S4).

Policy implications

In Japan, the policy mix in S3 (FITs, coal regulations plus carbon taxes) could reduce total CO_2 emissions to the same level as the carbon tax–only scenario, S4. In addition, the 2°C target could be met without much of a negative impact on the economy. The effects of a carbon tax alone are negative (and larger), so it would be beneficial to explore wider policy options for the power sector.

Korea

Energy and environmental impacts

Figure 4.8 and Table 4.8 show CO_2 emissions in each scenario. The model results for S1 (FIT only) show reductions of total CO_2 emission by 2.7% from baseline in 2050. In S2 (FIT plus coal regulation), total CO_2 emissions are reduced by 25.6% compared with the baseline in 2050. In Korea, the reduction in CO_2 emissions from FITs and coal regulation is not as large as in China and Japan, and other policy measures are needed. In S3 (added carbon tax to S2), total CO_2 emissions can be reduced by 59% from baseline, with a carbon tax rate of US\$873.2/tCO_2 in 2050. However, in S4 (carbon tax only), it is necessary to impose an even higher carbon tax of 960.6 US\$/tCO_2, to achieve a reduction similar to that

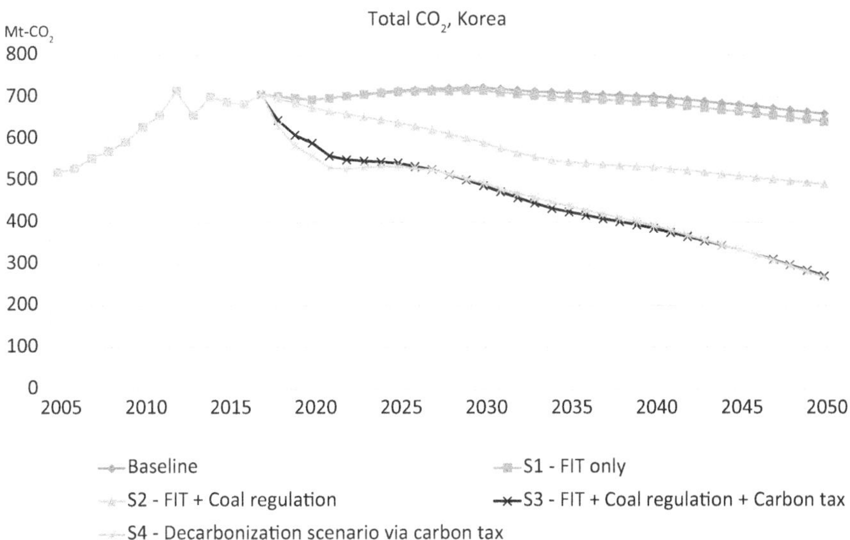

Figure 4.8 Total CO_2 emissions (Mt-CO_2), Korea

Table 4.8 CO_2 emissions and economic impacts relative to baseline in S1–S4, in 2030 and 2050, Korea (differences from baseline, %)

Korea	*2030*				*2050*			
	S1	*S2*	*S3*	*S4*	*S1*	*S2*	*S3*	*S4*
Power sector CO_2 emissions	-2.1	-35.3	-48.4	-46.3	-4.3	-38.9	65.4	-66.1
Total CO_2 emissions	-1.1	-18.4	-32.6	-31.6	-2.7	-25.6	-58.8	-59.4
GDP	0.0	0.3	-1.8	-1.8	0.0	0.0	-0.3	-0.7
Employment	0.0	0.2	-0.9	-0.7	0.0	0.0	-0.8	-1.0
Consumer spending	0.0	0.0	-3.6	-3.6	0.0	0.3	-0.5	-0.9
Exports	0.0	0.3	-0.2	-0.1	0.0	0.2	-0.1	-0.7
Imports	0.0	1.3	-1.6	-1.7	0.1	0.9	-0.1	-0.6
Investment	-0.1	2.6	0.7	-0.1	0.0	0.4	0.4	0.2
Inflation (consumer price)	0.0	0.6	8.5	8.9	0.0	0.7	10.1	10.9
Electricity price	0.9	19.5	29.6	20.9	1.9	22.1	41.7	34.9
Carbon tax ($US\$_{2010}/tCO_2$)			225.6	248.2			873.2	960.6

Source: Estimated by Cambridge Econometrics for this study

seen in S3. The largest single reduction in power sector emissions comes from the coal regulations.

In S1, FITs promote uptake of renewables, especially in large hydro and onshore wind (Figure 4.9; see also Table 4.10). This leads to an increase in electricity costs.

In S2, we add coal regulation in S1. The model results show increases in all other technologies to compensate for reductions in coal power generation. CCGT and IGCC gas-fired power generation see the biggest increases in the share of total power generation. The substitution from coal is mostly to gas. A combination of FITs and coal regulation in Korea provides further uptake of onshore wind.

In S3, a carbon tax in the power sector is added to S2. The impacts of the carbon tax on CO_2 emissions in the long term are negative because of additional investment in CCS and solar technologies. CO_2 emissions are reduced by 59% compared with the baseline in 2050 (see Table 4.8). Although the share of solar PV is less than in S2, the overall share of renewable energy is increased from 22.6% (S2) to 37.6% (S3) in 2050 (see Table 4.10). However, S3 is not as effective in Korea as in other countries because a lot of electricity is still being generated from gas. The combination of FITs, coal regulation and carbon taxes in Korea means there is further uptake of solar technologies. S4 shows a tendency similar to that in S3. Overall, Korea has the lowest share of renewable energy in the power sector among the four countries.

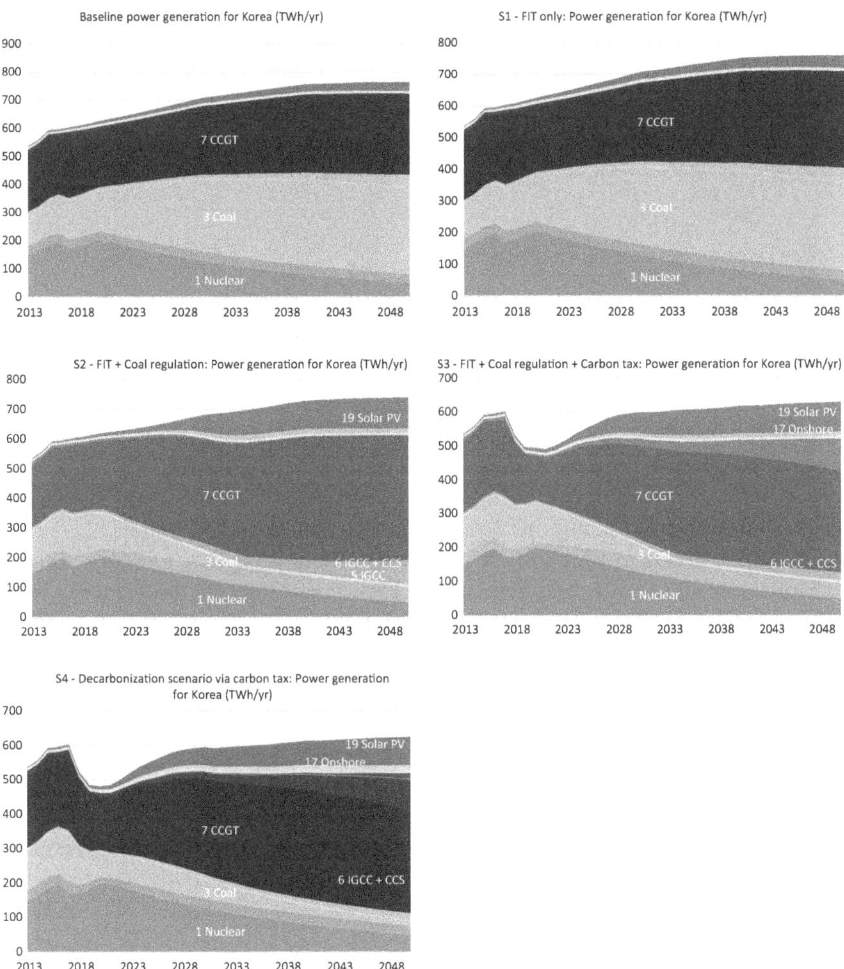

Figure 4.9 Power generation mix, Korea (TWh/yr)

Economic impacts

The impacts of FITs in Korea (S1) in the short run are minor, although electricity prices rise slightly (see Table 4.8). In S2, the negative GDP effects of higher electricity prices (once cheap coal is excluded from the system) are roughly balanced by additional investment in renewables. However, GDP and employment are negative in S3 and S4, when the carbon taxes are introduced.

The negative impacts on GDP in S3 and S4 are greater in 2030 than in 2050 because, by 2050, some of the effects of higher electricity prices are offset by investment in renewables. We see a larger negative impact in S4 because the carbon tax policy is less focused on promoting investment-intensive renewables.

Overall, in Korea, there are negative effects on the economy while reducing CO_2 emissions in all four scenarios. The policy mix in S3 achieves the emissions reduction target with the lower negative impact than in S4 on GDP.

Policy implications

Korea used to have a FIT system that was replaced with the RPS in 2012. The government introduced long-term fixed-price contracts for solar and wind power from 2017. Our model results show that FITs have impacts on promoting onshore wind power generation. Coal regulation in Korea is important for improving air quality (see Chapter 13) as well as for reducing CO_2 emissions. The move came as President Moon Jae-in pledged to reduce domestic fine-dust emissions by 30% by the end of his term, by shutting down old coal-fired power plants and reducing the number of diesel cars on the streets.

The introduction of FITs and coal regulation in our modelling in Korea leads to a shift from coal to gas power generation. This is consistent with the energy policies in Moon's government, aimed at Liquefied Natural Gas (LNG) to become the top energy source for electricity generation by 2030. LNG should replace the nation's high dependency on coal and nuclear power, which between them accounted for nearly 70% of electricity generation in 2016.

Looking at the share of renewables in the power generation mix in 2050, the shares remain lower than for the other countries in all our scenarios. Therefore, to meet the required CO_2 reduction target, the Korean government must consider a range of power sector policies, in addition to the current carbon emissions trading.

Taiwan

Energy and environmental impacts

Figure 4.10 and Table 4.9 show CO_2 emissions for each scenario. The FITs in S1 lead to a 2.6% reduction of total CO_2 emissions compared with baseline in 2050. FITs plus coal regulation in S2 reduce CO_2 emissions by 32.5% relative to the baseline. In S3 and S4, both of which have carbon taxes, total CO_2 emissions see very large reductions of 77% below the baseline.

These emission reductions are achieved through uptake of CCS (attached to gas plants) and increased use of biomass (Figure 4.11). Including CCS, Taiwan has the potential to be the largest user of renewables out of the four countries (see Table 4.10).

The FITs in S1 are found to boost the uptake of renewables in Taiwan but only slightly (see Figure 4.11 and Table 4.10). In S2, our model results show

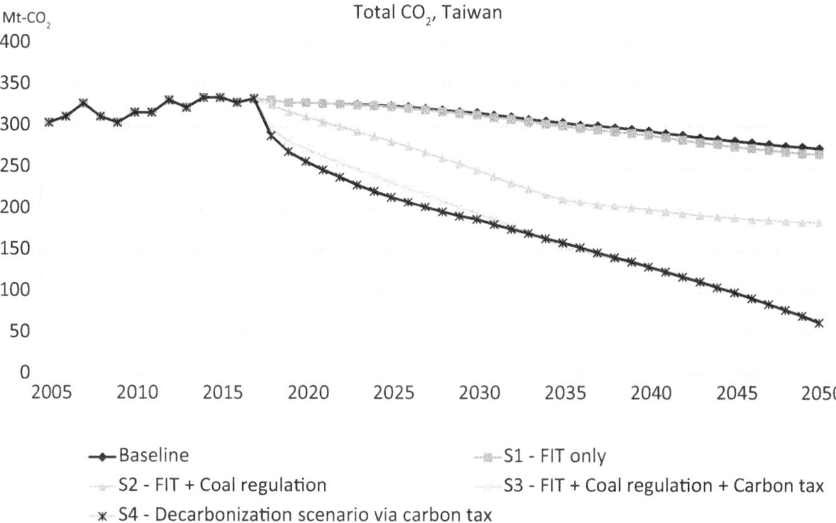

Figure 4.10 Total CO_2 emissions (Mt-CO_2), Taiwan

Table 4.9 CO_2 emissions and economic impacts relative to baseline in S1–S4, in 2030 and 2050, Taiwan (differences from baseline, %)

Taiwan	*2030*				*2050*			
	S1	*S2*	*S3*	*S4*	*S1*	*S2*	*S3*	*S4*
Power sector CO_2 emissions	−1.2	−41.4	−58.6	−64.5	−4.5	−49.7	−107.9	−107.9
Total CO_2 emissions	−0.9	−21.8	−38.5	−40.7	−2.6	−32.5	−77.0	−76.6
GDP	0.0	0.2	−2.1	−2.5	0.0	0.1	−2.8	−3.6
Employment	0.0	0.3	−0.3	−0.4	0.0	0.0	−0.6	−0.8
Consumer spending	0.0	0.2	−5.1	−5.9	0.0	0.2	−6.6	−8.1
Exports	0.0	0.2	−0.2	0.0	0.0	0.2	0.0	−0.4
Imports	0.0	1.4	0.3	0.1	0.1	0.8	0.2	−0.1
Investment	0.0	5.8	4.4	2.1	0.1	2.5	2.2	1.6
Inflation (consumer price)	0.0	0.8	7.9	9.5	0.0	0.6	9.8	11.9
Electricity price	0.7	26.3	39.1	44.9	2.2	29.4	85.3	89.9
Carbon tax (US$$_{2010}$/t$CO_2$)			200.6	248.2			776.1	960.6

Source: Estimated by Cambridge Econometrics for this study

increases in all other technologies to compensate for the reduced power generation using coal. As seen for the other three countries, gas-based CCGT and IGCC technologies are also used to replace coal but without much of a shift to nuclear power generation (which is restricted). S2 in Taiwan leads to further uptake of onshore wind.

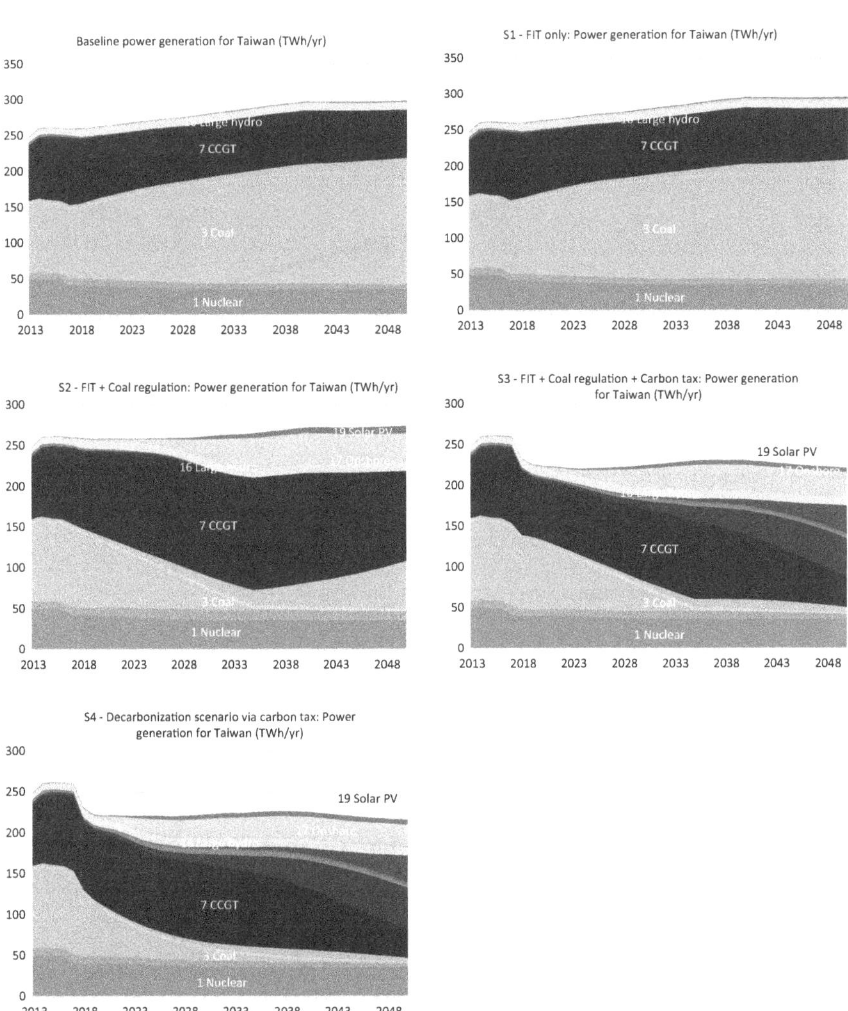

Figure 4.11 Power generation mix, Taiwan (TWh/yr)

In S3, the carbon tax leads to increased use of CCS in gas plants and increased use of biomass in the power sector. The share of renewable energy (plus CCS) in S3 and S4 doubles compared with S2, and becomes 63.8% and 64.9%, respectively.

Economic impacts

The impact of FITs only (S1) on Taiwan is close to zero in both 2030 and 2050 (see Table 4.9). The impact of having additional coal regulation (S2) in Taiwan follows the pattern of the coal regulation scenario in Chapter 2. The initial reduction is from coal investment because of coal regulation policy, but between 2030 and 2040 the investment from other technologies creates positive effects throughout the Taiwanese economy. By 2050, however, despite a price increase because of increased uptake of renewables and continuous FITs, they contribute to an increase in real income and in Taiwanese exports, thereby causing an overall increase in GDP of 0.1% compared with the baseline.

In comparison, S3 – where a carbon tax is introduced in addition to coal regulation and FITs – impact to GDP is negative in 2030 as higher costs are passed on through an increase in electricity prices, with secondary impacts throughout the economy.

In S4, GDP and employment are negative in 2050, similar to S3 (GDP: -2.8% from baseline). The impact is larger in S4 (GDP: −3.6% from baseline) than in S3 with the same CO_2 emission reduction, because the increase in investment is lower. Therefore, the policy mix scenario (S3) could achieve the same CO_2 emission reduction with a smaller negative economic impact than the carbon tax–only scenario (S4).

Policy implications

The results suggest a policy mix would be the best way to reduce emissions. Thus, to support the development of sustainable energy, reduce CO_2 emissions and increase Taiwan's own internal energy supply, development of RETs and adjustment of the industrial structure should be a crucial strategy for the country. To encourage the development of renewable energy, combined policies of regulations, taxes and subsidies should be proposed by the central and local governments to promote the development of wind, solar, hydropower and biomass generation. Low electricity prices have an adverse effect on energy-saving and carbon reduction schemes because there is a lack of incentives to invest in energy-saving equipment by manufacturers and users of energy. Therefore, the government should establish an appropriate energy price policy that reflects internal and external costs, to ensure that energy prices are rationally determined.

Findings and suggestions

In the modelling of the power generation sectors we have seen many consistencies, but also differences, among the East Asian countries. In this final section we draw some general conclusions from the analysis.

First, we consider the results of different power mixes. Table 4.10 summaries the power mixes in the different scenarios for the four countries. The results show that China contributes most to the uptake of renewables in the decarbonization scenario, S4. There are three reasons for this:

- The existing Chinese power mix is heavily reliant on coal (60% compared with around a third in the other three countries), meaning that there is more space for renewables to move into when coal is regulated.

- The scale of the Chinese electricity market makes it attractive for investors to invest in alternative technologies.
- Current energy prices in China are relatively low compared with those in Japan and Korea; consequently, China would respond more to price increases because of a carbon tax.

Second, a single decarbonization target for China, Japan, Korea and Taiwan, with a single carbon tax among the four countries would mean that the other countries do not have to make as large an effort because China's effort alone is enough to meet this target.

Table 4.10 Share of renewables in power generation in 2050 in East Asian countries

China (%)					
	Baseline	*S1*	*S2*	*S3*	*S4*
Nuclear	11.5	11.5	11.9	12.2	12.4
Fossil fuels	61.4	58.9	12.1	8.7	30.0
Renewables (incl. CCS)	27.0	29.6	75.9	79.1	57.6
Total	100.0	100.0	100.0	100.0	100.0
Japan (%)					
	Baseline	*S1*	*S2*	*S3*	*S4*
Nuclear	9.7	9.8	10.0	10.6	10.8
Fossil fuels	76.8	75.2	64.2	45.3	46.1
Renewables (incl. CCS)	13.4	15.0	25.8	44.1	43.1
Total	100.0	100.0	100.0	100.0	100.0
Korea (%)					
	Baseline	*S1*	*S2*	*S3*	*S4*
Nuclear	6.7	6.7	6.9	8.1	8.2
Fossil fuels	85.2	83.9	70.5	54.3	53.2
Renewables (incl. CCS)	8.1	9.4	22.6	37.6	38.6
Total	100.0	100.0	100.0	100.0	100.0
Taiwan (%)					
	Baseline	*S1*	*S2*	*S3*	*S4*
Nuclear	12.3	12.4	13.4	16.5	17.0
Fossil fuels	81.2	79.8	59.4	19.6	18.1
Renewables (incl. CCS)	6.5	7.8	27.1	63.8	64.9
Total	100.0	100.0	100.0	100.0	100.0

Source: Estimated by Cambridge Econometrics for this study

Third, the FIT in S1 has, in general, only a small impact on promoting the uptake of RETs in our modelling. This is partly because the FIT rates were set quite low. It also shows that applying FITs to different types of renewable energy can be counterproductive, as it might promote one type of renewable at the expense of other RETs (e.g. solar vs onshore wind), if the FIT rates applied cause different levels of price competitiveness among technologies.

Fourth, FITs plus coal regulations in S2 further promote uptake of renewables because generation from coal is no longer an option, and the power sector must find alternative generation sources. The results show that China has the highest increase in renewable shares, whereas in other countries the impacts on renewables are limited because a reduction in coal power generation is replaced by gas (as discussed in Chapter 2).

Last, in S3, FITs, coal regulation plus carbon taxes, we meet the same CO_2 reduction target as in a 2°C scenario (approximately –80% from 1990), where we try to meet the target alone from a carbon price which is applied as a single carbon price for these countries in S4. As the result in S3 shows, renewable shares in the power sector become the highest in China and Taiwan. A policy mix of FITs, coal regulation and carbon taxes in S3 is the most effective method to increase renewable energy in the two countries. However, in Japan and Korea the proportion of fossil fuel is still the highest, and there is a need for further policy measures to promote fuel switching to renewable energy.

The impacts of the policies in S3 and S4 are summarized in Table 4.11. In the case of S3, the GDP impact for China is positive and for the other countries is

Table 4.11 CO_2 emissions and economic impacts relative to baseline in S3 and S4 in 2050 (China, Japan, Korea and Taiwan; differences from baseline in 2050, %)

	China		*Japan*		*Korea*		*Taiwan*	
	S3	*S4*	*S3*	*S4*	*S3*	*S4*	*S3*	*S4*
Power sector CO_2 emissions	-87.6	-67.7	-76.4	-74.8	-65.4	-66.1	-107.9	-107.9
Total CO_2 emissions	-61.0	-61.0	-66.9	-66.9	-58.8	-59.4	-77.0	-76.6
GDP	0.2	-1.1	-0.4	-1.2	-0.3	-0.7	-2.8	-3.6
Employment	0.0	-0.8	-0.2	-0.5	-0.8	-1.0	-0.6	-0.8
Consumer spending	-0.2	-2.2	-1.9	-3.2	-0.5	-0.9	-6.6	-8.1
Exports	0.0	-0.5	-0.1	-0.3	-0.1	-0.7	0.0	-0.4
Imports	0.2	-0.7	-7.9	-9.0	-0.1	-0.6	0.2	-0.1
Investment	0.9	-1.1	-1.4	-2.5	0.4	0.2	2.2	1.6
Inflation (consumer price)	0.2	1.2	2.0	3.2	10.1	10.9	9.8	11.9
Electricity price	27.3	30.8	28.9	22.8	41.7	34.9	85.3	89.9
Carbon tax ($US\$_{2010}/tCO_2$)	7.3	960.6	727.6	960.6	873.2	960.6	776.1	960.6

Source: Estimated by Cambridge Econometrics for this study

negative in 2050. For S4, GDP is negative in all countries. Employment is negatively affected in all countries in both scenarios.

We also see that, by imposing a carbon tax, consumer prices and electricity prices rise and consumption expenditure decreases in all countries. The investment impacts may be positive or negative, depending on the individual national characteristics of each country.

Overall, the GDP results for S3 are always better than for S4. The results suggest that a policy mix is a more effective way of meeting the CO_2 reduction targets.

Conclusion

In this chapter, we have shown the energy, environmental and economic impacts of different policies aimed at the power sector, with the aim of meeting national NDCs and the 2°C target. We show that carbon taxes – which are required to meet NDCs and the 2°C target – will be lower if additional policies are implemented for the power sector.

Our results regarding CO_2 emission levels show that FITs cause a small reduction from baseline, but that additional coal regulation is very effective at further reducing CO_2 levels. Therefore, only selected changes, including less-high carbon taxes, are required to reduce CO_2 emissions and meet the 2°C target. This is an option because in the four East Asian countries, and especially in China, coal power regulation can be effectively used to achieve the CO_2 reduction target, and is easier than relying on a high carbon tax alone.

Looking at the power mix, FITs have small impacts in promoting the uptake of renewables in our modelling results. Partly, this is because the FIT rates were small. It also shows that, if FIT rates create competitiveness between technologies when applied to different types of renewables, it could have a disadvantageous effect, that is, by creating a bias towards certain RETs and neglecting others.

However, FITs and coal regulations promote renewables uptake further as coal power generation is no longer an option, and the power sector must find alternative sources of generation. Impacts on renewable energies are limited because the reduction in coal power generation is simply being replaced by gas. Our modelling results show that, in the policy mix scenario S3, the share of renewables becomes highest in all four East Asian countries. Therefore, the policy mix comprising FITs, coal regulation and carbon taxes is the most effective way to increase renewable shares in all four countries and to achieve sustainable low-carbon power generation. In conclusion, the message to policy makers from this chapter is that a mix of policies will be required to meet CO_2 reduction targets effectively, while minimizing economic cost.

Having assessed power sector policies in some detail, we now turn attention to the rest of the economy. Part 2 of this book focuses on a range of sector-specific policies that can contribute to meeting East Asia's aggregate CO_2 reduction targets.

Notes

1 WRI, 'What Is INDCs?' (www.wri.org/indc-definition, Access day: March 1, 2017).
2 See IEA, 'Energy and CO_2 Emissions in the OECD', with detailed data up to 2016. (www.iea.org/media/statistics/Energy_and_CO_2_Emissions_in_the_OECD.pdf).
3 For more details, see the Notice on Adjusting the Pricing Policy for Offshore Wind Power Prices (Fa Gai Jia Ge 2014: No.3008); the Notice on Adjusting the Pricing Policy for Offshore Wind Power and Solar Power Prices (Fa Gai Jia Ge 2015: No.3044); the Notice on Adjusting the Pricing Policy for Solar Power and Offshore Wind Power Prices (Fa Gai Jia Ge 2016: No.2729) and the Notice on the Pricing Policy for CSP (Fa Gai Jia Ge 2016: No.1881).
4 RAP, 'China's String of New Policies Addressing Renewable Energy Curtailment: An Update' (www.renewableenergyworld.com/articles/2016/04/china-s-string-of-new-policies-addressing-renewable-energy-curtailment-an-update.html, Access day: April 3, 2019).
5 ANRE, 'Skim of Feed-in-Tariff?' (www.enecho.meti.go.jp/category/saving_and_new/saiene/kaitori/kakaku.html, Access day: December 30, 2018).
6 See news releases of METI, 'Present Status and Promotion Measures for the Introduction of Renewable Energy in Japan' (www.meti.go.jp/english/policy/energy_environment/renewable/index.html, Access day: September 20, 2017).
7 Ibid.
8 METI, 'Current Status and Issues of Institution for Promoting the Introduction of Renewable Energy' (www.meti.go.jp/committee/sougouenergy/shoene_shinene/shin_ene/pdf/012_02_00.pdf, Access day: March 9, 2017).
9 ISEP, 'Status of Renewable Energies in Japan' (www.isep.or.jp/en/statistics, Access day: September 20, 2017).

References

ANRE (Agency for Natural Resources and Energy). (2018) 'Skim of Feed-in-Tariff', available at www.enecho.meti.go.jp/category/saving_and_new/saiene/kaitori/ (Access day: December 30, 2018) (in Japanese).

Azuma, A., Chewpreecha, U., Na, S., Chen, L. C., He, Y., Matsumoto, K. and Lee, S. (2017) 'Modelling the power sectors of East Asia in 2050 – The choice of power sources by nuclear and coal power regulation', Paper submitted to EAAERE2017.

BOE (Bureau of Energy, Ministry of Economic Affairs). (2015) 'Renewable Energy Promotion Policies in Taiwan', available at www.eclareon.com/sites/default/files/5_dr.ho_taiwanembassy.pdf

Cambridge Econometrics (2014) 'E3ME Manual', available at www.camecon.com/Libraries/Downloadable_Files/E3ME_Manual_V6.sflb.ashx

Hwang J. J. (2010) 'Promotional policy for renewable energy development in Taiwan', *Renewable and Sustainable Energy Reviews*, 14, 1079–1087. Elsevier.

IEA (International Energy Agency). (2018) 'Energy and CO_2 Emissions in the OECD', with detailed data up to 2016, available at www.iea.org/media/statistics/Energy_and_CO_2_Emissions_in_the_OECD.pdf

IEEJ (The Institute of Energy Economics, Japan). (2017) 'Asia/World Energy Outlook 2016'.

ISEP (Institute for Sustainable Energy Policies). (2017) 'Status of Renewable Energies in Japan', available at www.isep.or.jp/en/statistics (Access day: September 20, 2017).

Kitamura, T. (2013) 'Situation of the FIT scheme and challenge toward substantial expansion of renewable energy', *Energy and Resources*, 34, 129–133 (in Japanese).

Korea New and Renewable Energy Center. (2017) 'RPS', available at www.knrec.or.kr/business/rps_guide.aspx (Access day: July 19, 2017).

Li, J. F., Shi, P. f. and Gao, H. (2010) 'China Wind Power Outlook 2010', available at http://large.stanford.edu/courses/2010/ph240/jin1/docs/wind-power-report-english-2010.pdf (Access day: April 13, 2017).

Matsumoto, K., Morita, K., Mavrakis, D., and Konidari, P. (2017) 'Evaluating Japanese policy instruments for the promotion of renewable energy sources', *International Journal of Green Energy*, 14(8), 724–736. doi:10.1080/15435075.2017.1326050

METI (Ministry of Economy, Trade and Industry: Japan). (2017) 'Current Status and Issues of Institution for Promoting the Introduction of Renewable Energy' 再生可能エネルギーの導入促進に向けた制度の現状と課題 (in Japanese), available at www.meti.go.jp/committee/sougouenergy/shoene_shinene/shin_ene/pdf/012_02_00.pdf (Access day: March 09, 2017).

METI. (2017, July 17) 'Feed-in Tariff Scheme in Japan', available at www.meti.go.jp/english/policy/energy_environment/renewable/pdf/summary201207.pdf (Access day: July 20, 2017).

METI. (2017) 'Present Status and Promotion Measures for the introduction of Renewable Energy in Japan', available at www.meti.go.jp/english/policy/energy_environment/renewable/index.html (Access day: September 20, 2017).

Morita, K. and Matsumoto K. (2014) 'Renewable energy-related policies and institutions in Japan: Before and after the Fukushima nuclear accident and the Feed-In Tariff introduction', in *Legal Issues of Renewable Electricity in Asia Region: Recent Development at a Post-Fukushima and Post-Kyoto Protocol Era*, eds. A. M. Z. Gao and C. T. Fan. Alphen aan den Rijn: Kluwer Law International, 3–28.

MTIE (Ministry of Trade, Industry and Energy: Korea). (2015) 'Obligation Rate of Renewables in RPS', available at http://english.motie.go.kr/www/main.do (Access day: December 30, 2017).

RAP (Regulatory Assistance Project). (2016) 'China's String of New Policies Addressing Renewable Energy Curtailment: An Update', available at www.renewableenergyworld.com/articles/2016/04/china-s-string-of-new-policies-addressing-renewable-energy-curtailment-an-update.html (Access day: April 13, 2017)

UNFCCC (United Nations Framework Convention on Climate Change). (2015) 'Nationally Determined Contributions (NDCs)', available at http://unfccc.int/focus/ndc_registry/items/9433.php (Access day: March 1, 2017)

WRI (World Resource Institute). (2015) 'What Is INDCs?', available at www.wri.org/indc-definition (Access day: March 1, 2017).

Part II

Innovating to reduce CO_2 emissions in industry, transport and buildings

5 Policy mixes to meet CO_2 emission reduction targets in all sectors of the economy in East Asia

Hector Pollitt, Unnada Chewpreecha, Soocheol Lee, Tae-Yeoun Lee and Jean-François Mercure

Introduction

In Part 2 of this book we turn our attention to the wider economy. While it is clear that the power sector will play an instrumental role in meeting climate targets, the rest of the economy will need to contribute as well. Our focus, therefore, becomes the whole-economy targets that were set in the Nationally Determined Contributions (NDCs) submitted as part of the Paris Agreement and the long-term 2°C temperature target that is set at global level.

East Asia will undoubtedly play a major role in determining the eventual success of limiting global warming to substantially less than 2°C. China is the world's largest emitter but is increasingly being seen as a global leader in building renewable power sources. The other economies in East Asia each face their own unique challenges in meeting emission reduction goals.

Policy makers in East Asia and other countries now face several challenges:

- How to determine the policies to meet their NDC commitments
- How much to 'ratchet' up NDC ambition levels
- How to determine long-term targets for emission reductions (i.e. after 2030)
- How to decarbonize economies while still expanding prosperity across the region

Much of the focus on how to meet climate goals, including in East Asia, has been on carbon taxes and other instruments to price the use of carbon (e.g. emissions trading schemes). In Chapter 4, we presented one such scenario of our own (S4) but showed that there may be alternative policy options available that are preferable. From a policy maker's perspective, carbon pricing through taxation or a trading scheme may not be the most attractive or, even, a feasible option. We showed in Chapter 4 that other policy options exist in the power sector. Is this also the case for other sectors?

In this chapter, we present more scenarios from the E3ME-FTT modelling framework that covers a much broader range of policy options. We apply the modelling framework to a set of CO_2 reduction targets for East Asia and show that subsidies, and/or regulatory policies can work alongside carbon taxes to achieve larger emission reductions; and can also mean that lower carbon tax rates are needed to meet a fixed target. Ultimately, any potential negative impacts on national economies could be reduced by adopting a broad portfolio of policies.

The following section describes the modelling framework. After that, the next two sections present the scenarios, and the impacts on emissions and national economies, before the final section concludes.

Modelling approach

The analysis again uses the combined E3ME-FTT model. The E3ME model is introduced in Chapter 1, and we do not repeat the description here. The FTT models are also described in the relevant chapters of this book.

In Chapter 1, we provided an example of how Computable General Equilibrium (CGE) models had been used in the past to show that carbon taxes are the optimal way to reduce emissions. Here we expand on this discussion to put our results in this chapter (and in Chapter 4) into context.

In the E3ME model, the level of production is determined in a post-Keynesian framework. The starting point is the assumption that agents do not have perfect knowledge and, therefore, cannot optimize their behaviors. Similarly, markets may not adjust perfectly through movements in prices. In contrast, in a typical CGE framework, optimal behavior is assumed, output is determined by supply-side constraints and prices adjust fully so that all the available capacity is used.

As a result, in E3ME it is possible to have spare capacity in the economy. The model is more demand driven, and it is not assumed that prices always adjust to market-clearing levels. In addition, as described in Pollitt and Mercure (2017), there is not a fixed supply of money in E3ME, reflecting the real-world observations from central banks (e.g. McLeay et al., 2014). Effectively, any money that is spent adds to aggregate demand, whereas any money that is saved does not (see Chapter 10). For example, if an individual spends his/her savings on a new car; this will create demand for the products of all the companies that contribute to making the car. If he/she puts the money in a bank account instead, there is no stimulus effect.

The differences have important practical implications. They mean that, in E3ME, regulation and other policy may lead to increases in output if they are able to draw upon spare economic capacity in ways a simple carbon tax cannot. Many of the policies that we model in this chapter attempt to draw on this spare capacity. For example, as discussed in Chapter 3, additional investment in the power sector will pull in new financial resources, and need additional labor resources to build and install equipment. Subsidies of renewables may be more effective at encouraging investment than a carbon tax that leads only to a shift from coal to gas-fired generation.

In addition, although the carbon tax may attempt to stimulate investment, in these scenarios it also takes money out of the economy, and money that is spent paying taxes does not boost demand for products. In this chapter, we assume that the government does not spend the additional tax revenues; this is tested further in Chapter 9.

Scenarios

The baseline

The starting point for the modelling is a standard baseline scenario, based on the Asia/World Energy Outlook (IEEJ, 2017). This forms the reference case to which all the other results are compared. The baseline is a case in which existing policies remain in place but no additional policies are added in the period up to 2050.

For the rest of the world, we assume that policies are put in place that are consistent with a 2°C scenario. In the policy scenarios East Asia is, thus, decarbonizing in line with the rest of the world and would not be expected to suffer major losses of competitiveness because of implementing new policy. We use the same set of policies as applied in Mercure et al. (2018). Although in 2019 it is the case that certain large economies are currently not implementing the necessary policies, the assumption is that, by 2050, all economies take action.

Meeting the 2°C target

The remaining scenarios are based on policy inputs. In each case, the policies are designed to meet the 2°C target. We start off by trying to meet the target through just a carbon tax (as many neoclassical economists recommend) and then gradually introduce new policies to different sectors, resulting in a lower carbon tax rate to reach the same 2°C target.

In most cases, the countries in East Asia do not yet have formal targets for 2050 to be consistent with the 2°C target for limiting climate change, and so we provide our own values. Moreover, in this analysis we are combining developed and developing countries – as defined in the 'annex 1 list' of the United Nations Framework Convention on Climate Change (UNFCCC) – and differentiated targets would, therefore, be expected. For China we set a slightly less ambitious target than for the other countries when comparing with 1990; however, when comparing with 2015 emission levels, China's target is the most ambitious. The CO_2 reduction targets are given in Table 5.1.

These targets partly reflect the trends in the reference case, the results in Mercure et al. (2018) and the initial findings from our model runs. As we see in the results, the burden of CO_2 emission reduction is not shared evenly across East Asia. All the targets are defined in terms of energy CO_2, that is, emissions from fuel combustion, because the current version of the E3ME model does not have specific policy options for process emissions, and does not cover agriculture and land use in a high level of detail.

Table 5.1 CO_2 reduction targets for 2050 relative to levels in 2015 or 1990

	2015 level (%)	*1990 level (%)*
China	-94	-70
Japan	-82	-80
Korea	-91	-80
Taiwan	-91	-80

Note: The targets here may not exactly match existing long-term national targets as we have used a global scenario to guide the level of ambition (and national targets could be expected to change by 2050). The targets are applied to energy CO_2 emissions.

The scenarios aim to meet the targets by implementing:

- S0: Carbon taxes only
- S1: Power sector Feed-in-Tariffs, fuel taxes on transport and heating, a moderate energy efficiency plan in industry
- S2: S1 plus further renewable subsidies, phase-out of inefficient vehicles, subsidies for new household-heating technologies and further industrial energy efficiency
- S3: S2 plus a coal phase-out, biofuel mandates in transport, ambitious industrial energy efficiency programs and targeted public procurement to new technologies

Further details of the policy measures are given subsequently. In general, the policies that are applied in this chapter are similar to those applied in the chapters on individual sectors. However, some differences arise, as a greater level of detail is explored in the chapters that focus on specific sectors, and policy solutions that match the requirements of the individual sectors are found.

Carbon taxes are levied on all use of fossil fuels in relation to carbon content. They are additional to any carbon-pricing policies that are already included in the baseline and increase linearly up to 2050. There are no exemptions. In the current version of the analysis, the revenues are not recycled back into domestic economies, meaning that the taxes will likely have a negative effect on GDP. Even when we introduce policies to other sectors, the carbon taxes are still applied to those sectors, as the policy interactions are important.

The power sector policies entered into the FTT:Power model are:

- S1, S2 and S3: Feed-in-Tariffs – FITs are designed to close the gap between the strike price for electricity and the cost of generating with renewables.
- S2 and S3: Direct renewables subsidies – subsidies on initial capital investments may boost the uptake of renewable technologies.
- S3: Mandates to prevent new coal power plants being built.

Carbon taxes also apply to the power sector and feed into the levelized cost calculations, based on associated emissions with each generation technology.

The energy efficiency programs are modelled as mandates imposed by government. The values used in S3 match those in the IEA's 450PPM scenario (IEA, 2016). The energy savings in S1 are one third of the IEA values, and in S2 they are two thirds of the IEA values. The exogenous inputs to the model are:

- Energy savings (in tons of oil equivalent, split across sectors, energy carriers, on an annual basis).
- Investment required to build and install the equipment (in monetary terms).

The following policies are applied to the road transport sector:

- S1, S2 and S3: Taxes on fuels – this tax is paid on each unit of fuel consumed.
- S2 and S3: Registration taxes based on the fuel economy of the cars – the taxes are paid upfront when purchasing vehicles.
- S2 and S3: New vehicle efficiencies are assumed to be upgraded over time.
- S2 and S3: Some types of vehicle, for example, older petrol and diesel vehicles, are phased out and replaced with higher-efficiency versions or alternative propulsion vehicles (EV, CNG, etc.). Vehicles in use live to the end of their statistical lifetimes.
- S3: Public procurement measures – it is assumed that some new vehicle technologies are boosted through procurement schemes.
- S3: Biofuel mandates – it is assumed that by 2050 60–65% of liquid fuels are biofuels rather than conventional fuels.

The following policies are put in place on heating:

- S1, S2 and S3: Taxes on residential fossil fuel use – the tax is paid on fuel consumption, relative to the carbon content of the fuel.
- S2 and S3: Direct subsidies for renewables – the subsidies are defined as a share of the capital cost of new heating technologies; they feed into the levelized cost calculations and are funded by government.
- S3: Public procurement – new heating systems are adopted initially in public buildings.

In all the scenarios, a limit of US$1,500 is put in place on the carbon tax rates that may be applied. Although the limit is fairly arbitrary, it is unlikely that such a high carbon tax would ever be levied in reality and model results become too uncertain beyond this point. It is, therefore, possible for countries to miss their carbon reduction targets.

Results

Impacts on emissions

Table 5.2 shows the difference in CO_2 emission levels in 2050 in each scenario as a percentage relative to levels in 1990. The figures in the table show the different

Table 5.2 Percentage difference in CO_2 emissions (energy CO_2), in 2050 in each scenario from those in 1990

	China	*Japan*	*Korea*	*Taiwan*
Target	-70	-80	-80	-80
Baseline	126	-5	84	4
S0 (carbon tax)	100	-38	72	40
S1 (minimum)	-23	-80	-60	-80
S2 (medium)	-27	-80	-80	-80
S3 (ambitious)	-70	-80	-80	-80

Source: Estimated by Cambridge Econometrics for this study

Notes: The table shows the change in CO_2 emission levels in 2050 relative to their respective levels in 1990, in %. Positive numbers indicate higher CO_2 levels; for example, for the baseline scenario, CO_2 levels in China, in 2050, are 126% higher than those in 1990.

Table 5.3 Carbon tax rates[1] in each scenario in 2050 (in US$/t$CO_2$) in addition to baseline

	China	*Japan*	*Korea*	*Taiwan*
Baseline	0	0	0	0
S0 (carbon tax)	1,500	1,500	1,500	1,500
S1 (minimum)	1,500	1,500	1,500	182
S2 (medium)	1,500	482	1,179	161
S3 (ambitious)	321	178	279	131

Source: Estimated by Cambridge Econometrics for this study

Note:
1 Carbon tax rates are expressed in 2018 prices, and are in addition to any carbon pricing in the baseline.

baseline trajectories for each country in East Asia, and how each country responds to the carbon taxes and the other policies. The results for S0 show that the carbon taxes can substantially reduce CO_2 emissions in every country, but not by enough to meet the targets that we set (given the maximum carbon tax rates allowed; see Table 5.2). All four countries therefore miss their targets.

In S1, the additional policies allow the CO_2 reduction targets to be met in Japan and Taiwan, although still with a high carbon price in Japan (Tables 5.2 and 5.3). Korea and China do not meet their targets in S1. Korea meets its target in S2, but China only meets its target in S3.

Table 5.3 shows the carbon prices in each scenario. In cases where the CO_2 reduction targets are not met, a maximum value of US$1,500/t$CO_2$ is applied. In all the scenarios, a path of linear increases in carbon tax rates is applied over the projection period.

The table shows the role that non-pricing policies can play in reducing overall CO_2 emission levels. We see that the effects are not simply additive as there can be strong interaction between the different policies. For example, carbon taxes can alter the choice of technology used, but the technologies must be developed and commercially viable to begin with, which likely requires different policy.

The effects of adding new policies vary across the different East Asian countries, reflecting the different ways that each country uses energy. For example, in Taiwan, the results show that the limited policies in S1 are enough to meet the CO_2 reduction target with a modest carbon tax rate. Further policies have a relatively small impact on the carbon price needed to meet the targets. In China, the measures in S1 also have a big impact on emissions levels (see Table 5.2) but do not impact on the carbon tax rate as the CO_2 emission reduction target is not met. Adding the policies in S2 makes little difference but in S3 the CO_2 reduction target is met and the carbon tax rate is reduced substantially. Japan and Korea both see steady decreases in CO_2 emission levels and/or carbon tax rates across the scenarios.

In S3, it is noted that carbon prices are still high by today's standards but may not be unrealistic in the time frame to 2050.

Impacts on the economy

Table 5.4 shows the impact of the different policies on GDP in each country. It should be noted that the national policies are implemented simultaneously and, so, trade effects between the different countries are included in the impacts. For example, if GDP increases in China, demand for exports from the other countries in East Asia may be boosted.

It should also be remembered that we have not included any revenue-recycling measures in the analysis. The revenues from the carbon taxes are used to pay off government debt, rather than boosting demand elsewhere in the economy. However, some of the other measures – notably the energy efficiency investments – do require government expenditure and, therefore, provide economic stimulus. We come back to this topic in Chapter 9.

Table 5.4 Impacts of each scenario on GDP in 2050 (in %) relative to baseline scenario

	China	*Japan*	*Korea*	*Taiwan*
S0 (Carbon tax)	-0.7	-4.8	-1.7	-4.8
S1 (minimum)	-1.3	-4.0	-1.4	-0.9
S2 (medium)	-1.1	-0.5	-0.4	-0.6
S3 (ambitious)	-0.6	1.3	1.4	-0.4

Source: Estimated by Cambridge Econometrics for this study

Table 5.5 Change in government balance[1] as percentage of GDP in 2050 relative to baseline scenario

	China	*Japan*	*Korea*	*Taiwan*
S0 (Carbon tax)	12	7	15	13
S1 (minimum)	16	6	9	2
S2 (medium)	15	2	6	2
S3 (ambitious)	0	1	1	1

Source: Estimated by Cambridge Econometrics for this study

Note(s):
* Government balance only covers carbon tax revenues minus climate policy costs. Climate policy costs include funding of energy efficiency investment, technology subsidies and scrappage costs.

Table 5.5 shows the changes in government balances in 2050. These numbers are calculated from carbon tax revenues minus any climate policy costs that are introduced in the scenarios. The climate policy costs included in the calculation are:

- Funding for energy efficiency investment
- Subsidies for new technologies
- Early scrappage costs of plants and equipment

The government subsidies occur in the early years and are phased out by 2050, so the remaining expenditure is for energy efficiency investment, which is by far the largest direct cost to government. There are also indirect changes in government balances as a result of changing economic activities that are not reported here.

The results show that the carbon tax alone could raise 7–15% of national GDP in S0, which highlights that a carbon tax rate of US\$1,500/tCO_2 without other policy is rather unrealistic (see Table 5.5). Since there is no revenue recycling, these additional revenues are used to improve the government balance.

However, the results for other scenarios also show that all the climate policies introduced in our scenarios can be more or less self-funded if combined with the carbon tax. Some readers may be surprised to see positive GDP impacts in two of the four countries in S5. In part, the positive impacts are due to the stimulus from government expenditure but there may also be a private sector stimulus from additional investment in energy efficiency and renewable equipment. Finally, in all scenarios there is a reduction in imported fossil fuels; a shift from spending on imports to spending on domestically produced goods could provide further stimulus effects.

It should be noted that the magnitude of GDP impacts varies substantially between the different countries. Japan and Taiwan see much larger losses of GDP than China and Korea (see Table 5.4). This is despite China and Korea remaining more carbon intensive regarding production in 2050 than Japan and Taiwan (in both cases by 2.5–3 times).

The reason for this finding varies between the countries. In China, what happens to energy prices is important. China has such a large weight in global energy consumption that its policies affect global prices. So, while carbon tax rates increase the costs of production, falling coal and fuel prices (13% and 9%, respectively) offset higher costs to some extent. Although the model results show that electricity prices increase by almost 50% in S0, parts of Chinese industry are unable to pass on higher prices owing to global competition. Domestic action in China has, therefore, much less of an impact on prices faced by Chinese consumers.

In Korea, there is a large increase in prices, but this increase is matched by wage growth. While higher wage rates and unit costs have some negative competitiveness effects (although mitigated here because the rest of the world is also implementing climate measures), the loss of real incomes is reduced. In a previous analysis of Japan using the E3ME model (Park et al., 2016), we found that wages tended to be rigid so aggregate economic impacts are more negative. It should, however, be noted that the econometric equations in E3ME are based on time series covering an extended period of deflation in Japan and so may not reflect future labor market behavior.

Table 5.6 shows the impacts across the different economic sectors (aggregated from the 43 sectors in E3ME). The largest decreases are found in sectors associated with energy, and these losses are fairly consistent across the scenarios (albeit less in S0 because the CO_2 reduction targets are not met). Within the other sectors, results are less negative when the carbon tax rates are lower (see Table 5.6), which is in line with the aggregate GDP impacts. Construction and advanced manufacturing (including engineering) could gain most from the additional investment.

The results for employment follow to some extent from the GDP impacts (Table 5.7). As a general rule of thumb (Okun's law), the impacts on employment are half the size of the impacts on GDP. In the case of Japan and Taiwan, this is roughly what we observe (for both countries the ratios are slightly less than half). In China, impacts on employment may be larger than aggregate GDP impacts. This finding is not new and reflects the many jobs that are likely to be lost in the

Table 5.6 Impacts of each scenario on sectoral output in 2050 (in %) relative to baseline scenario

	S0	*S1*	*S2*	*S3*
Agriculture	-2.1	-2.3	-1.6	-0.8
Basic manufacturing	-1.2	-1.3	-0.7	0.1
Advanced manufacturing	-1.1	-1.1	-0.4	0.7
Energy extraction	-53.5	-44.8	-46.3	-66.1
Utilities	-7.4	-3.2	-3.5	-3.6
Construction	0.4	0.5	1.3	2.8
Services	-1.7	-1.9	-1.1	-0.3

Source: Estimated by Cambridge Econometrics for this study

Table 5.7 Impacts of each scenario on employment in 2050 (in %) relative to baseline scenario

	China	*Japan*	*Korea*	*Taiwan*
S0 (Carbon tax)	-0.8	-1.9	-1.8	-1.2
S1 (minimum)	-0.8	-1.7	-2.0	-0.3
S2 (medium)	-0.7	-0.4	-1.4	-0.3
S3 (ambitious)	-0.4	0.4	0.0	-0.3

Source: Estimated by Cambridge Econometrics for this study

Chinese coal sector. As the amount of value added per job is relatively low in the coal sector, it is possible – at aggregate level – to see larger impacts on employment than on GDP. In Korea, the same response in wages that reduces GDP costs leads to a larger reduction in employment. These results highlight how important it is to consider labor market responses in this type of analysis.

Conclusions

Many economists state that the optimal way to reduce CO_2 emissions is to put a tax on them. The carbon tax provides a price signal that can incentivize households and businesses to adapt their behavior accordingly. Any other policies that try to reduce emissions will lead to a misallocation of resources and sub-optimal outcomes. In the world that policy makers face, however, the picture is much less clear. Policies to develop and diffuse new technologies may be just as important as carbon pricing instruments – but carbon pricing alone may not be sufficient to meet an ambitious emission reduction target.

To understand the impacts that any implementation of a broader range of policies has, policy makers need modelling tools that can represent these policies within a broad, simulation-based framework. Unfortunately, not many options are available beyond the E3ME-FTT model that we apply in this book.

In this chapter, we tested four scenarios (S0–S3) that include carbon taxes and a set of policies that expands in each new scenario. The policies assessed cover the three 'pillars' that were described in Grubb (2014). Specifically, we address short-term easy wins through mandating energy efficiency standards. Policies to support the long-term development of new technologies are also added for each sector. The carbon tax ensures that there is sufficient incentive for new technologies to be adopted, once gaps in knowledge are considered.

For each of the four East Asian countries we have set ambitious decarbonization targets. Our scenarios show that carbon taxes alone (S0) will not be sufficient to meet the targets, unless the tax rates were to be unrealistically high (above US$1,500/t$CO_2$ in 2018 prices). As we add other low-carbon policies, not only do the CO_2 reduction targets become attainable but also the carbon tax rate required to meet the targets becomes lower. From a tax rate of US$1,500/t$CO_2$

that fails to reach the targets, we find a range of US$131–321/t$CO_2$ in S3 in line with the targets.

The economic impacts of the carbon taxes are also reduced when a lower carbon tax rate is applied. We do not apply revenue recycling in this analysis, so the carbon tax rates on their own are a burden to the East Asian economies. Reducing the tax rates allow some of the more-positive impacts – for example, through reduced fuel imports or increased investment stimuli – to have a larger role in the results. We find similar patterns in our results for employment.

It should be stressed that the analysis is not complete without an analysis of how the tax revenues might be used. We return to this topic in Chapter 9, after assessing the policies that are applied to the individual sectors.

However, it is clear that a lower carbon tax rate would reduce distributional impacts across sectors and, therefore, improve the political feasibility of the overall policy package. To summarize, this is the sort of analysis that policy makers are increasingly going to require as the world moves from setting emission reduction targets to asking how to meet the targets that have been set. We hope that our analysis provides a first step in this direction.

References

Grubb, M (2014), *Planetary Economics*, New York: Routledge.

IEA (2016), *World Energy Outlook*, Paris, France: IEA/OECD Publishing.

IEEJ (2017), 'Asia/World Energy Outlook 2016', the Institute of Energy Economics Japan.

McLeay, M, A Radia and R Thomas (2014), 'Money Creation in the Modern Economy', *Bank of England Quarterly Bulletin*, Volume Q1, pp 14–27. See www.bankofengland.co.uk/publications/Documents/quarterlybulletin/2014/qb14q102.pdf

Mercure, J-F, H Pollitt, JE Viñuales, NR Edwards, PB Holden, U Chewpreecha, P Salas, I Sognnaes, A Lam and F Knobloch (2018), 'Macroeconomic Impact of Stranded Fossil Fuel Assets', *Nature Climate Change*, Volume 8, pp 588–593.

Park, SJ, Y Ogawa, T Kawakatsu and H Pollitt (2016), 'The Double Dividend of an Environmental Tax Reform in East Asian Countries', in S Lee, H Pollitt and SJ Park (eds) *Low-Carbon, Sustainable Future in East Asia*, New York: Routledge.

Pollitt, H and J-F Mercure (2017), 'The Role of Money and the Financial Sector in Energy-Economy Models Used for Assessing Climate and Energy Policy', *Climate Policy*, Volume 18, Issue 2, pp 184–197.

6 Policies to decarbonize the steel industry in East Asia

Pim Vercoulen, Soocheol Lee, Sunhee Suk, Yanmin He, Kiyoshi Fujikawa and Jean-François Mercure

Introduction

We now turn our attention to industry. The industrial sector is a broad term that consists of many different types of industry, including both energy-intensive and non–energy-intensive sectors. The focus of climate mitigation is, naturally, on the heavy-emitting industrial sectors that are defined by Grubb (2014) as the 'Big 6' – that is, steel, non-ferrous metals, cement, paper and pulp, chemicals and refining. These sectors account for most industrial emissions. The steel sector alone accounts for 31% of all direct industrial emissions (IEA, 2015).

Steel production from virgin materials is a carbon-intensive process, producing 1.5–3.3 tCO_2 equivalent per ton of crude steel (tcs) (Morfeldt, Nijs and Silveira, 2015), because carbon-based materials are necessary to reduce iron ore to iron. Steel production is also an energy-intensive process (requiring 19.8–31.2 GJ/tcs; Morfeldt, Nijs and Silveira, 2015). Coal resources (either directly or in the form of coke) are used both as a reducing agent and as a combustible energy source.

Combined, China, Japan, Korea and Taiwan account for 74% of total emissions from the steel industry in the world (IEA, 2017), so our focus on production in East Asia has global implications. Of these emissions, around 40–50% come from manufacturing and 10–20% come from iron smelting. The introduction and diffusion of novel, low-carbon technologies could lead to large emission reductions in the steel industry (Köhler et al., 2006). However, it is difficult to predict the uptake of these technologies and policy makers require guidance on how to promote their use. The brand new FTT:Steel model is designed to provide such insights.

Like the other FTT models, FTT:Steel is a bottom-up, non-equilibrium evolutionary model that accounts for sector-specific conditions (Mercure et al., 2018). In the model, 26 integrated steelmaking technologies are included, in all the regions covered by the E3ME model over the period 2015 to 2050. At the start of modelling, the conventional Blast Furnace-Basic Oxygen Furnace (BF – BOF) route and the Scrap-Electric Arc Furnace (Scrap – EAF) routes have the greatest market shares. The model also includes radical new technologies that are currently still in research phase, such as Hydrogen Flash Smelt (HFS) coupled to EAF and Molten Oxide Electrolysis (MOE). When applicable, Bio-based (BB) and Carbon Capture and Storage (CCS) options are also added to the technologies. Technological diffusion is calculated according to the levelized cost of steel production (LCOS, see 'FTT Methodology') and how it changes over time. The technological changes lead to differences in annual emissions, sectoral investments and material consumption. Also, as in the other FTT models, FTT:Steel is connected to the E3ME model so that there are two-way feedbacks between the steel sector and the wider economy.

In this chapter, the iron and steel industries in East Asia are exposed to a range of carbon taxes and we evaluate the diffusion of new technologies in each case, and the resulting CO_2 emissions. Before starting the modelling, we first consider the current status of each East Asian country's economy and steel industry (see the next section). Following that, the modelling approach is presented in more detail. In the section after that, the results are presented, and they are discussed further in the subsequent section. In the final section, we briefly summarize the main conclusions

Country profiles of East Asia

East Asian countries account for 62% of global steel production (World Steel Association, 2017) and, as noted previously, 74% of global steel sector emissions. China, Japan, Korea and Taiwan are the first-, second-, sixth- and twelfth-largest steel producers in the world. China produced roughly 823 millions of tons (Mt) of crude steel in 2014. In the same year, Japan, Korea and Taiwan produced 111, 72 and 23 Mt of crude steel, respectively (World Steel Association, 2017) (Figure 6.1). China's current steel production is more than that of the rest of the world combined; mainly because of rapid 1,385% growth since 1990. In 1990, Japan was the world's largest steel producer, with an output of 110 Mt of crude steel, while China produced only half of that (World Steel Association, 2017). The increase in production in China can be explained by its rapid GDP growth over the same period, much of which was fueled by investment in buildings and infrastructure, with car purchases also increasing from the new middle class (National Bureau of Statistics of China, 2017). Japan, Korea and Taiwan had already reached economic maturity by this point; therefore, steel production increased much less (World Bank, 2018).

The bulk of all steel production in 2017 occurred in integrated steel mills, both globally and in East Asia. These mills consist of blast furnace (BF) units to reduce the iron ore to pig iron, which is subsequently refined in the basic oxygen furnace (BOF) to crude steel (World Steel Association, 2017). Almost all other steel was produced in an electric arc furnace (EAF) via two primary routes (World Steel Association, 2017). One route is connected to the direct reduction (DR) technology, of which two types exist: gas-based and the coal-based DR. Within a DR plant the fossil fuel (natural gas or coal) is reformed to produce a highly reductive syngas. Iron ore agglomerates are fed into the DR plant and reduced to iron without melting it (Midrex, 2017). The intermediate iron product is then

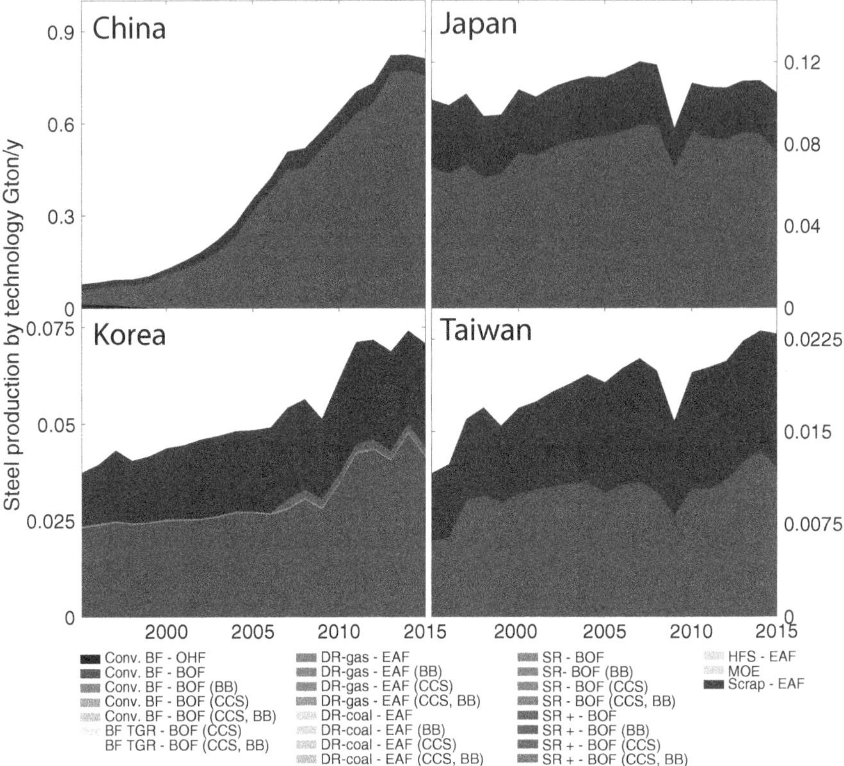

Figure 6.1 Historical production by technology

Source: Pictured by Cambridge Econometrics for this study

refined in the EAF. The other EAF route does not consume virgin materials but uses steel scrap instead.

The market share of the Scrap-EAF route has recently declined slightly in China because of a mismatch in steel demand and limited scrap availability (World Steel Association, 2017). For Japan, Korea and Taiwan the shares of EAF are greater because the amount of scrap steel relative to new production is higher. Korea also has integrated steelworks that utilize the COREX process and FINEX process coupled to BOF. Both are smelt reduction (SR) technologies, with the distinction that FINEX is a more advanced, hereafter referred to as SR^+, technology. Up to the year 2000, China used another route to produce steel. BF units coupled to Open Hearth Furnaces (BF – OHFs) produced significant amounts of steel during the previous century but have since been discontinued.

China

Before World War II, the Chinese steel industry was underdeveloped and of insignificant size. After the war, the Chinese government decided to develop industry in general, and the iron and steel industry in particular. As mentioned previously, Chinese crude steel output has grown rapidly since 1990. Between 1996 and 2003, steel production doubled from ~100 Mt to ~200 Mt. Production doubled again to ~400 Mt in 2006, and again to ~800 Mt in 2014 (World Steel Association, 2017). As well as rates of higher economic growth (World Bank, 2018), the sector benefitted from government incentives that increased steel demand because of the export-driven and investment-led nature of the Chinese economy (Primetals Technologies, 2017). Since 2014, steel production has stagnated owing to a slowdown in demand.

Apparent steel use[1] in China has grown considerably in recent years because of the government‘s stimulus package in 2017 (World Steel Association, 2017). However, soon steel consumption is expected to stagnate owing to a slowdown in industrial steel demand (National Bureau of Statistics of China, 2016). Looking further ahead, steel demand in China might decline because of a decrease in population (UN, 2017), a reduction in investment growth because of indebtedness (IMF, 2017) and a decline in the absolute consumption volumes caused by improvements in steel quality, meaning that final products that are made of steel require less of it (World Steel Association, 2012).

The Chinese steel industry is under pressure because of domestic overcapacity (OECD, 2015). China had a production capacity of more than 1.5 Gt of crude steel in 2015 (Primetals Technologies, 2017). With a steel output of roughly 0.8 Gt crude steel, the utilization factor of the integrated steelworks was ~53%. The government of China has, therefore, decided to decrease soon the production capacity. By 2020 it wants to reduce capacity by 10% (Primetals Technologies, 2017). It will do so mainly by closing down small, inefficient plants and by merging steel companies (Greenpeace East Asia and Beijing Custeel E-Commerce Co. Ltd., 2017).

According to the Chinese Nationally Determined Contribution (NDC), the country should lower its energy intensity per unit of GDP by 40–45% by 2020 compared with the level of 2005. It will reach peak emissions and initiate reduction by 2030. The country will invest in research and development (R&D) on CCS. Another important statement from the NDC is China's pledge to set up a national emission trading scheme (ETS) (National Development and Reform Commission of China, 2015). The ETS system should be implemented within two to three years (Tang et al., 2018), which will then act as a market pull mechanism to increase the production costs of emission-intensive processes, including steel production, thereby making less emission-intensive technologies more competitive.

In addition to the Chinese NDC, the 'Adjustment and Upgrading Plan of the Steel Industry' has been in operation since 2016. Its main goal is to 'implement green upgrading, circular economy, promote green consumption, and decrease the energy intensity up to 2020'. In other words, the Chinese government seeks to transform its steel industry from one that is unprepared for potential climate change mitigation policies to one that is more resilient to new policy.

Japan

The steel industry in Japan accounted for 7.2% of manufacturing value added in 2012. Crude steel production is ~110 Mt per year (World Steel Association, 2017). Steel is one of Japan's main export commodities, of which a large part can be attributed to Japanese car assembly in other countries (International Trade Administration, 2018). According to the Japan Iron and Steel Federation (JISF), in 2016, crude steel output in Japan has continued to decline because of low domestic demand. However, steel demand has since recovered because of a rebound in the construction and automobile sectors (JISF, 2017).

The Japanese steel industry focuses on developing technologies to supply high-grade steel that meets the diversifying and exacting requirements of companies that use steel products. At the same time, steelmakers are making productivity gains in all manufacturing processes. The fiscal year 2008 saw the beginning of a project called CO_2 Ultimate Reduction in Steelmaking Process by Innovative technology for cool Earth 50 (COURSE50). It aims to develop less carbon-intensive steelmaking technologies to meet a greenhouse gas (GHG) emission reduction target of 80% by 2050 (Tonomura, 2013). This program evaluates technologies that incorporate hydrogen or biomass, CCS and direct electrolysis. The latter involves electrolysis of iron ore (Allanore, Ortiz and Sadoway, 2011). These technologies are expected to be commercially introduced by 2030 and to increase in market share from then on.

Japan has formulated an NDC target of 26% GHG emission reduction by 2030 compared with 2013 levels (Ministry of Economy Trade and Industry, 2015). In addition, the NDC has explicitly formulated targets for the iron and steel industry, that is, efficiency improvements in electricity-consuming facilities, more chemical recycling of waste plastic at steel plants, introduction of next-generation coke making, improvement of power generation efficiency processes (SCOPE21), enhanced energy efficiency and conservation facilities, introduction of the innovative ironmaking process (Ferro Coke) and introduction of the environmentally harmonized steelmaking process (COURSE50).

In response to the Global Warming Countermeasures that the Japanese Cabinet approved in May 2016, the Japanese steel industry indicated the implementation of 'Commitment to a Low Carbon Society' and is already engaged in some efforts, coordinated by the Japan Iron and Steel Federation (JISF) (ISIJ, 2017). 'Commitment to a Low Carbon Society' is a voluntary initiative that started in the fiscal year 2013. It has four central components: eco-process, eco-product, eco-solution and the development of innovative technologies. One goal is to further improve the steel industry's energy efficiency in Japan, which is already the highest in the world. Another goal is to promote the use of Japan's higher-quality steel products and energy conservation technologies around the world (JISF, 2017).

Korea

The Korean government initiated the exponential growth of its steel industry in the 1960s, and the country has been ranked sixth in terms of total crude steel production since 1995. This growth went hand in hand with Korea's economic growth (World Bank, 2018). However, the Korean economy is not in rapid growth presently, and there has been a decline in steel demand from shipbuilders and car manufacturers (POSCO Research Institute (POSRI), 2016).

The Korean government has set GHG emission reduction targets of 30% below those of Business As Usual (BAU) by 2020 and 37% below those of BAU by 2030, as presented in its NDC (Republic of Korea, 2015). The national target for the steel industry is an emission reduction of 11.1% compared with that of BAU in 2030. Korea's ETS, which has been in operation since 2015, is also part of the NDC. The steel sector is included in the ETS.

In addition, the largest Korean steel company, POSCO, has set its own GHG emission reduction target. It aims to reduce the emission intensity of steel production by 9% by 2020 compared with the average emission level in the period 2007–2009. POSCO intends to achieve the target by reducing coal consumption, improving energy efficiency and developing new low-carbon technologies. The company's focus has shifted towards hydrogen-based steelmaking that is essentially zero-emission when only direct CO_2 emissions are considered (Sabat and Murphy, 2017).

Besides climate change, Korea also faces major air pollution issues (see Chapter 13). Fine dust (PM2.5) is one of the main problems. Korean steelmakers are also therefore interested in reducing PM2.5 pollution. That is why POSCO developed the FINEX process, which reduces formation of PM2.5 (Primetals Technologies/POSCO, 2015).

Taiwan

Although Taiwan is not officially a signatory to the Paris Agreement, it unilaterally announced its 'Greenhouse Gas Reduction and Management Act' (Republic of China [Taiwan], 2015). The Taiwanese GHG target is to reduce emissions by 50% by 2030 compared with BAU emissions. No specific actions were taken to promote reductions of GHG emissions of the iron and steel industry, other than reducing its emission intensity, that is, no quantitative target was announced.

The Taiwanese steel industry is mainly characterized by high production volumes through secondary steelmaking, ~50%. All other steel is produced through the Conv. BF – BOF route. Owing to its high consumption of scrap metal, many energy-intensive processes are averted, which results in a lower overall emission factor (~0.6 tCO_2/tcs in 2010).

Methods and materials

Integrated steelmaking technologies

For the development of the FTT:Steel model, a full review of relevant research papers, policy documents and institutional reports was carried out. In this section we present the model in more detail, drawing on the findings from that review.

It is important to note that, in this chapter, we consider only the pathways from raw materials and scrap to crude steel. The finishing processes of crude steel are excluded, since these processes do not consume raw materials and, therefore, have no direct emissions (Remus et al., 2013). An overview of all integrated steelmaking routes is provided in Figure 6.2.

Precursor plants

In some cases, the raw materials for steel production require pre-processing. For example, in a coke plant, hard coal is converted to coke to serve as a better reducing agent (AIST, 2015). At the same time, most ironmaking processes require high-quality iron ore, called lump ore, which is becoming increasingly rare. To circumvent using solely lump ore, many integrated steel plants have sinter plants or pelletizing plants available onsite to produce iron ore agglomerates that have a higher porosity and, therefore, increase the rate of reduction from iron oxides to metallic iron (Daniëls, 2002). Some integrated steelworks have an onsite lime kiln to produce burnt lime with limestone as input. This is used as fluxing agent in the iron ore reduction process to remove impurities. However, the overall use of limestone and lime is low, so this process does not account for a large share of costs associated with steel production. A similar argument applies for an oxygen plant (Hooey et al., 2013).

Ironmaking technologies

The conventional blast furnace (Conv. BF) route is currently the most commonly used process to reduce iron oxides to metallic iron (World Steel Association, 2017). Coke and iron ore agglomerates are required as feed materials (Van Wortswinkel et al., 2010). Another, currently used, process is the direct reduction (DR) by use of natural gas or coal (DR-gas or DR-coal, respectively), which does not require coke but iron ore agglomerates (Remus et al., 2013; Midrex, 2017). Smelt reduction (SR) has recently gained a market share in the iron and steel sector and, like the DR processes, it only requires agglomeration of iron ore to some degree (Primetals Technologies, 2015).

Many research and development programs around the world have put effort into ironmaking innovations (e.g. Meijer et al., 2009; Tonomura, 2013). For example, Top Gas Recycling Blast Furnace (BF TGR) should reduce the need for raw materials, as energy is recycled to some degree (Zuo and Hirsch, 2009). However, like Conv. BF, it requires precursor plants. An advanced version of the

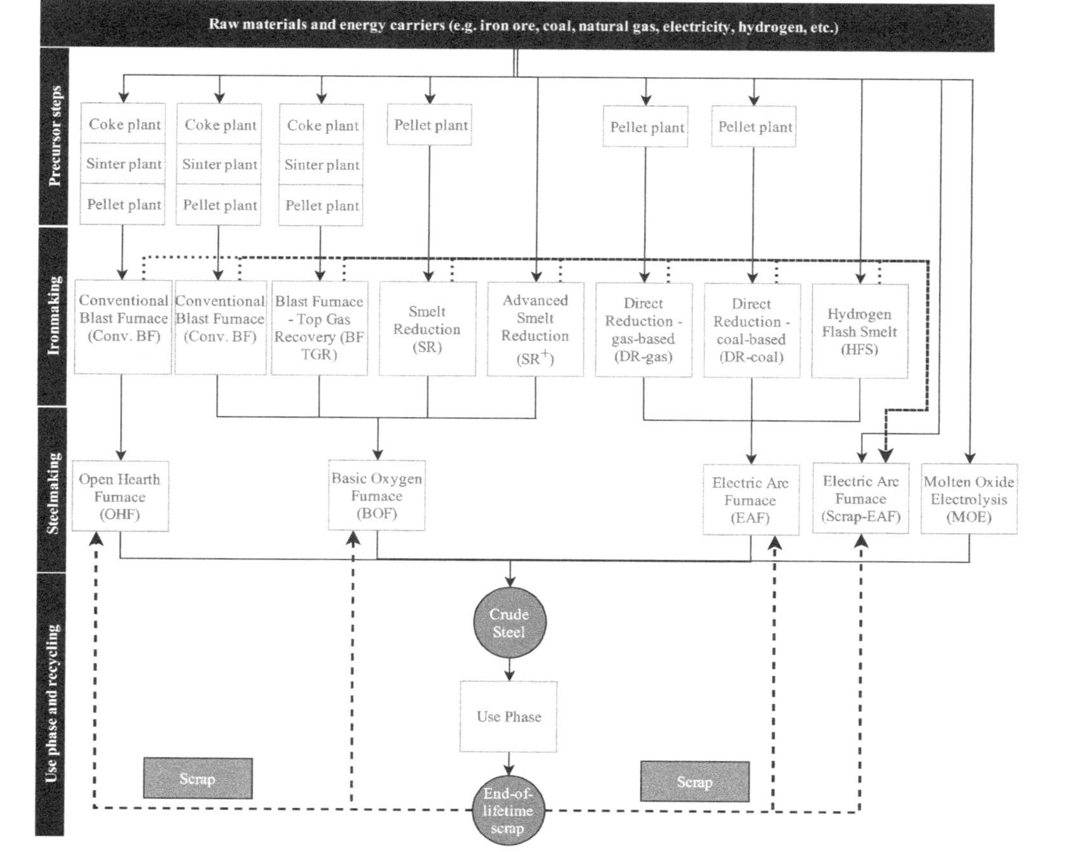

Figure 6.2 The different routes towards crude steel production

Source: Pictured by Cambridge Econometrics for this study

SR technology route (SR^+) does not require any precursor plants as it can use coal and iron ore of any quality as feed material (Primetals Technologies/POSCO, 2015; van Boggelen et al., 2016). To curb emissions, efforts have also been made to develop a process that uses hydrogen as the reducing agent instead of carbon. The most promising technology is called hydrogen flash smelt (HFS), which does not use precursor steps (Hiebler and Plaul, 2004; Pinegar, Moats and Sohn, 2011, 2012; Sohn et al., 2017).

Steelmaking technologies

The oldest technology still used in some countries, although now decreasing in market share, is the Open Hearth Furnace (OHF) (World Steel Association, 2017). Over time, other processes replaced OHF because these possess higher production volumes, fewer emissions and greater versatility (Daniëls, 2002).

The Basic Oxygen Furnace (BOF) is one of the steelmaking technologies replacing OHF (Grübler, Nakićenović and Victor, 1999). As its name suggests, oxygen is blown in the furnace, thereby oxidizing residual carbon and other impurities that end up in the slag layer. The BOF technology is highly versatile as it can be used to produce steel of different qualities and compositions (Daniëls, 2002). All remaining steel is produced in electric arc furnaces (EAFs) (World Steel Association, 2017). As its name suggests, EAFs consume mainly electricity (Van Wortswinkel et al., 2010) and, therefore, do not result in direct emissions.

The last steelmaking technology included in this chapter is molten oxide electrolysis (MOE). This novel technology electrolyzes iron oxide into metallic iron that is of crude steel quality (Allanore, Ortiz and Sadoway, 2011; Allanore, 2014; Wiencke et al., 2018). When not considering the emissions caused by electricity generation, MOE does not emit CO_2 during its production process.

Variations

Figure 6.2 shows the main integrated steelmaking technologies, but it excludes the use of biomass, CCS[2] and a combination of the two. Where applicable, we have included these options. For example, the Conv. BF – BOF route can consume biomass in the form of charcoal, partly as a reductant and partly as a fuel source (Babich, Senk and Fernandez, 2010). Table 6.1 shows all the technologies and variations thereof.

Table 6.2 shows the costs, that is, capital expenditure (CAPEX) and operating expenditure (OPEX), emission factors (EF) and energy intensities (EI) for the production of 1 tcs. Here, a scrap input of 15% for the primary production technologies and 100% for the secondary production technology was used to estimate the parameters. All BB technologies show high costs because of the expected high costs of charcoal or biogas. All CCS options show slightly higher costs than the default version of the steelmaking route. The CAPEX of the CCS options was increased by 50 $\$_{2008}/tCO_2$, avoided as a result of the installation of the necessary equipment, and the OPEX was increased by 5 $\$_{2008}/tCO_2$, avoided because of

Table 6.1 All technologies included in FTT:Steel and their variations

Ironmaking technology	*Steelmaking technology*	*Integrated steelmaking designation*	*No. of variations*
Conv. BF	OHF	Conv. BF – OHF	1 (D)
Conv. BF	BOF	Conv. BF – BOF	4 (D, BB, CCS, CCS+BB)
BF TGR	BOF	BF TGR – BOF	2 (CCS, CCS+BB)
DR-gas	EAF	DR (gas) – EAF	4 (D, BB, CCS, CCS+BB)
DR-coal	EAF	DR (coal) – EAF	4 (D, BB, CCS, CCS+BB)
SR	BOF	SR – BOF	4 (D, BB, CCS, CCS+BB)
SR^+	BOF	SR^+ – BOF	4 (D, BB, CCS, CCS+BB)
HFS	EAF	HFS-EAF	1 (D)
–	MOE	MOE	1 (D)
–	EAF	Scrap-EAF	1 (D)
Total no. of technologies in FTT:Steel			**26**

Source: Cambridge Econometrics for this study

Note: D, default; BB, Bio-based production; CCS, Carbon Capture and Storage; CCS+BB, Carbon Capture and Storage in combination with bio-based production.

transportation and storage. For the BB options only the material input changes, which increases the total cost of material consumption and CO_2 emissions (not shown in Table 6.2). Note that coke production cannot be fully BB (Babich, Senk and Fernandez, 2010).

The CAPEX for the SR^+ – BOF, HFS – EAF and Scrap – EAF routes was found to be lower than that of the other technologies. The main reason for this outcome is that none of these technologies requires installed capacity of precursor plants for raw material processing. MOE is an exception to this rule. Not only is MOE expensive in terms of CAPEX but also in terms of material costs. It consumes a lot of electrical energy; however, bear in mind that regional prices vary. The costs listed in Table 6.2 were calculated by using average prices. HFS-EAF, MOE and Scrap-EAF are the only non-carbothermic processes and, therefore, have the lowest emission factors. Furthermore, as Scrap-EAF does not require the reduction of iron ore, it has a much lower energy intensity than the other technology pathways.

FTT methodology

In FTT:Steel the diffusion of integrated steelmaking technologies is investigated for all of the E3ME model regions over the period 2015 to 2050. We use a mathematical framework that is similar to that described by Mercure (Mercure, 2012; Mercure et al., 2014), previously applied to the diffusion of power generation (see Chapters 2–4), road transport (see Chapter 7) and residential heating technologies (see Chapter 8). The framework is briefly repeated here.

Decision making behind the diffusion process is assumed to be based on cost. Within the mathematical framework, the discounted levelized cost to produce 1

Table 6.2 CAPEX, OPEX, EF and EI for the default variant of each technology group

Technology	*CAPEX* ($\$_{2008}$/*tcs capacity*)	*OPEX* ($\$_{2008}$/*tcs production*)	*EF*[1] (tCO_2/*tcs production*)	*EI*[2] (*GJ/tcs production*)	*Material/Energy cost*[3] ($\$_{2008}$/*tcs production*)			
					China	*Japan*	*Korea*	*Taiwan*
Conv. BF – OHF	490	60	2.104 (2.18–2.30)	22.74	213.7	264.4	241.2	281.5
Conv. BF – BOF	460	50	1.783 (1.87–1.98)	20.03	209.3	253	234.2	264.3
BF TGR – BOF	632	51	0.3569 (0.53–0.76)	19.35	223.8	282.1	260.7	280.7
DR-gas – EAF	450	55	0.691 (1.13–1.71)	14.98	305	445.5	440.2	386.1
DR-coal – EAF	450	55	2.677 (3.11–3.67)	31.99	277.6	413.8	343.6	392.8
SR – BOF	372	39	2.481 (2.54–2.61)	26.56	201.7	270.1	245.6	296.5
SR⁺ – BOF	285	35	1.235 (1.32–1.43)	13.82	195.9	239.8	220	244.5
HFS – EAF	367	57	0.0138 (0.54–1.23)	16.96	413.5	498.7	442.5	430.4
MOE	4,000	37	0.0058 (5.13–11.83)	39.7	539	1528	971.1	678.4
Scrap – EAF	81	37	0.0138 (0.40–0.91)	3.25	279.5	293.8	260.7	303.5

Source: Cambridge Econometrics for this study

Note: Estimates of emission factors and energy intensities were based on 15% scrap consumption per tcs for the primary steelmaking routes except for MOE, which produces crude steel directly from iron ore. The emission factors only entail direct emissions. Indirect emissions resulting from electricity consumption are presented in parentheses.

1 Emission factors (EFs) for each East Asian country were used to calculate the indirect CO_2 emissions resulting from electricity consumption; min-max ranges are shown. Emission factors caused by electricity consumption were taken from (Ecometrica, 2011).
2 Energy intensity (EI) was calculated by using energy density factors.
3 Material costs (calculated values) are presented for each of the four East Asian countries. Calc., calculated values.
4 Values shown for CAPEX, OPEX, EF and EI are based on estimates using data from the following sources: Conv. BF – OHF (Daniëls, 2002; Van Wortswinkel et al., 2010; Pardo and Moya, 2013); Conv. BF – BOF (Daniëls, 2002; Van Wortswinkel et al., 2010; Pardo and Moya, 2013); BF TGR – BOF(Zuo and Hirsch, 2009; Van Wortswinkel et al., 2010); DR-gas – EAF (Daniëls, 2002; Van Wortswinkel et al., 2010); DR-coal – EAF (Daniëls, 2002; Van Wortswinkel et al., 2010); SR – BOF (Daniëls, 2002; Siemens VIA, 2011; Primetals Technologies, 2015); SR⁺ – BOF (Meijer et al., 2013; Primetals Technologies/POSCO, 2015); HFS – EAF (Van Wortswinkel et al., 2010; Pinegar, Moats and Sohn, 2011, 2012); MOE (Rosenberg et al., 2012); Scrap – EAF(Van Wortswinkel et al., 2010).

tcs (*LCOS*) is calculated according to Equation 1. It constitutes the break-even cost of crude steel production, which is compared between competing technologies, guiding investment decisions by heterogeneous agents. The *LCOS* is calibrated by a value gamma (γ), which is based on the increment of market share changes for each technology over the past four historical years and the first four modelled years.

$$\text{LCOS} = \frac{\sum_0^{\tau} \frac{IC/_{CF} + OM + FC + CO_2C}{(1+r)^t}}{\sum_0^{\tau} \frac{1}{(1+r)^t}} + \gamma \tag{1}$$

In Equation 1, *IC* is the investment cost; it is divided by the capacity factor (*CF*). *OM* is the operation and maintenance costs, *FC* the costs of material consumption (e.g. coal, natural gas, iron ore, etc.) and CO_2C are the costs associated to a possible carbon tax. All of these are discounted by the rate r and sums are taken over the lifetime of the plant. Since costs are not strictly defined, a standard deviation of the *LCOS* was calculated. Different agents might perceive costs differently based on local conditions. The standard deviation represents the heterogeneity of investors. Using the LCOS and its standard deviation, investor preferences are calculated between all technology pairs (Equation 2).

$$\Sigma_j \Delta S_{j \to i} = \Delta S_i = \Sigma_j S_i S_j \cdot \left(F_{ij} A_{ij} - F_{ji} A_{ji} \right) \cdot \Delta t \tag{2}$$

Equation 2 represents the transitions in the same way as the other FTT models. *A* is the replacement rate from one technology to another. A uniform distribution is assumed for the decommission time of all the plants. So, for each year a share equal to 1/lifetime of the plants is decommissioned. Only decommissioned plants are eligible for replacement. Matrix A_{ij} contains the replacement rates between technologies i and j, according to the constraints of build-time of technology i and the lifetime of technology j.

Equation 2 can be split into three parts. First, the term $S_i\ S_j$ can be regarded as description of technological lock-in. This value can only be large when the market shares of both technologies are close to 0.5. Second, the F_{ij} and F_{ji} terms depict investor choices. And, third, the A_{ij} and A_{ji} terms depict the natural rate of replacement of one technology by another. This is dependent on the lifetime of the technology to be replaced and the build time of the technology replacing it.

Besides end-of-lifetime replacements, investors may also choose to scrap technology j and replace it with another technology i, if the production of an additional unit of crude steel by technology j appears to be more expensive than the lifetime costs of an alternative technology i. The calculation of before-end-of-lifetime replacements is shown in Equation 3.

$$\Sigma_j \Delta SE_{j \to i} = \Delta SE_i = \Sigma_j S_i S_j \cdot \left(FE_{ij} SR_i - FE_{ji} SR_j \right) \cdot \Delta t \tag{3}$$

In Equation 3, *SR* is the scrapping rate, which depends on the inverse payback period minus the share of integrated steelworks that naturally reach end of lifetime. *FE* is the investor preference, similar to that of Equation 2, except that now the marginal costs of one technology and the lifetime costs of another technology are compared, instead of using the LCOS.

To mimic incremental innovation within a technology group, a learning rate is applied to both the investment costs and material consumption. Over time the investment costs associated with building a new plant of the same type decrease because of learning-by-doing. In addition, a lesser amount of energy will be required to produce 1 tcs. The effect of the learning rate on the LCOS (with and without implementation of a carbon tax) is illustrated in Figure 6.3. The top panel illustrates how the LCOS would develop over time. The established technologies, such as Conv. BF – OHF and Conv. BF – BOF, show little decrease compared with the relative novel technology DR-gas – EAF, or the completely novel technologies SR^{+} – BOF and HFS – EAF. In this illustrative example, it was assumed that the established technology Scrap – EAF increases substantially in capacity and, therefore, reduces in cost. The bottom panel of Figure 6.3 illustrates the development of the LCOS when a linearly increasing carbon tax is implemented. The carbon-intensive technologies increase in costs, while learning still takes place if the installed capacities increase (see, e.g. DR – gas – EAF).

Many studies have stated that the inclusion of scrap in the steelmaking process is important to reduce the emission intensity of the iron and steel industry. Scrap can become available by recycling end-of-life cars and appliances, and by decommissioning buildings (Morfeldt, Nijs and Silveira, 2015). The lifetimes of steel within each product group play an important role in determining the availability of scrap, as this dictates when certain parts of the steel stock become available as scrap (Pauliuk, Wang and Müller, 2013). We take region-specific data on historical steel use, lifetimes and loss rates from Pauliuk et al. (Pauliuk, Wang and Müller, 2013). We then follow the assumptions made by Morfeldt et al. (Morfeldt, Nijs and Silveira, 2015) of increasing lifetimes and decreasing loss rates over time because of an anticipated increase in societal focus on recycling. As a result, the need for virgin materials can vary over time, which changes the costs of steel production and the amounts of CO_2 emitted.

Linkages to E3ME

FTT:Steel simulates innovation in the steel sector, whereas E3ME simulates the economic environment. The models are connected through a set of two-way feedbacks.

In FTT:Steel the technological mix for steel production is derived from total steel demand and the implementation of climate change mitigation policies that may affect the LCOS. E3ME calculates steel demand in terms of monetary units by aggregating intermediate demand, investment demand, consumer demand and net trade. The total demand in monetary units is compared with the total demand

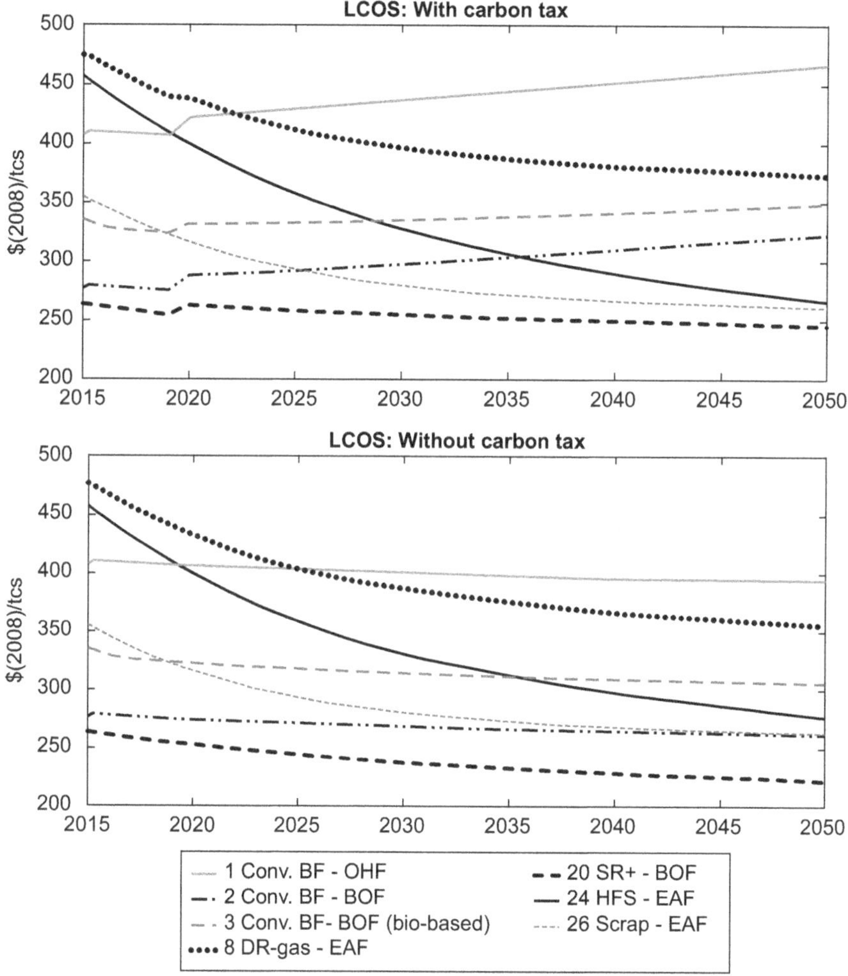

Figure 6.3 Conceptual illustration showing the effect of learning-by-doing on the LCOS, with (top panel) and without (bottom panel) a carbon tax

Source: Estimated by Cambridge Econometrics for this study

Note: Average material/energy costs were assumed. Carbon tax is applied from 2020 onwards, which is increasing linearly from 5 $\$_{2008}$ to 50 $\$_{2008}$.

of the year 2014, and this is applied to steel production of 2014 to estimate future steel production.

Once the technological mix is estimated, FTT:Steel provides feedbacks to E3ME in the form of levels of energy and resource consumption, the price of steel, and investment demands. Levels of resource consumption are used by E3ME to calculate the marginal resource costs that were affected by resource scarcity functions (Mercure and Salas, 2013). A change in steel prices changes total demand. Such changes all work through E3ME and may affect levels of imports, exports, GDP and employment, among other indicators.

Scenario definitions

The scenarios in this chapter differ from those in other chapters because the FTT:Steel model was still being developed while the other analyses were carried out. However, the basic intuition remains the same, with a focus on carbon taxation. The carbon tax rate used in S3 is fairly similar to the rate used in S3 in Chapter 5.

The rate of technological diffusion and impacts on CO_2 emissions are estimated for three policy scenarios and compared with the same baseline as that described in Chapter 5. In each policy scenario a different carbon tax rate is set (Table 6.3). The carbon taxes are implemented in 2020 at US$5 (2008 prices) and increase linearly to their respective end values in 2050. Carbon taxes were set to also apply to other sectors, as implementation of a carbon tax solely for the iron and steel industry is unlikely. In these scenarios, no carbon tax revenue is recycled (see Chapter 9).

Results

Technological diffusion

Under baseline conditions, no major changes in the technology mix are expected. In each country, the Conv. BF – BOF increases its market share at the expense of Scrap – EAF. However, we see different results when the carbon taxes are introduced.

The low carbon tax scenario (S1) shows two main changes compared with the baseline: first, there is a small decrease in total steel production because prices increase; second, although variants of the Conv. BF – BOF show a slight increase in market share (especially in Japan), the CCS and BB variants of the SR – BOF and SR$^+$ – BOF routes slightly increase their market share in Japan (Figure 6.4).

Under the medium carbon tax scenario (S2), total steel production decreases further. The technology mix also becomes more diverse, with increasing shares

Table 6.3 Policy scenarios

Scenario	*Policy*	*Carbon tax (2020–2050)*
Baseline (S0)	No policies	–
1 (S1)	Low carbon tax	$5 to $50
2 (S2)	Medium carbon tax	$5 to $100
3 (S3)	High carbon tax	$5 to $200

Note: Implementation of carbon taxes start in 2020 and increases linearly until its end value is reached in 2050. Carbon tax rates are given in US$ in 2008 prices per ton of CO_2.

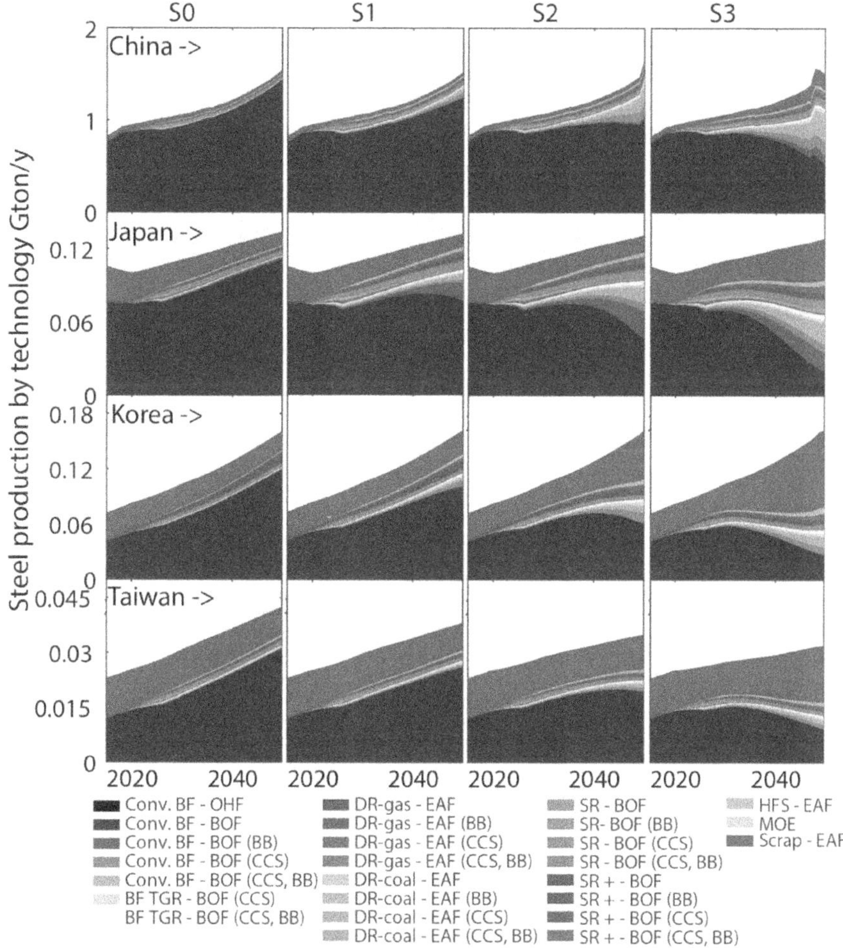

Figure 6.4 Technology diffusion in each country of interest, under each scenario (per row)

Source: Estimated by Cambridge Econometrics for this study

of BB and CCS variations of Conv. BF – BOF. For Japan, the trend in S1 is continued. Similar trends appear for China, Korea and Taiwan, although Korea and Taiwan also show an increase in the share of Scrap – EAF technology.

All these trends continue when the most stringent carbon tax is applied. In all countries, the default variant of the Conv. BF – BOF is largely replaced by low-carbon alternatives. Overall, the CCS variants of the SR – BOF route and SR^{+} – BOF show some diffusion in Japan and Korea, but less in China and Taiwan. In all countries, but especially in Korea, the share of Scrap – EAF grows at the expense of Conv. BF – BOF technologies. However, HFS – EAF is unable to penetrate the steel market quickly enough and, therefore, has limited diffusion, and MOE is unable to get a foothold. The market shares in 2050 under the baseline (S0) and the high carbon tax scenario (S3) are shown in Table 6.4.

The driving mechanism behind the differences of technology diffusion in FTT:Steel is the development of the LCOS. Carbon-intensive integrated steel-making routes face a large increase in LCOS under the carbon tax scenarios. The opposite is true for CCS in combination with BB processes because of its net negative emissions. The developments of the LCOS for each technology are illustrated in Table 6.5 for China and Japan, and Table 6.6 for Korea and Taiwan.

In the baseline, there is a decrease in LCOS because of learning-by-doing. In China, Conv. BF – BOF, SR – BOF and SR⁺ – BOF are the cheapest integrated

Table 6.4 Market shares of each technology (in %) in 2050 under S0 and S3 for China, Japan, Korea and Japan

Integrated steelmaking route	*China*		*Japan*		*Korea*		*Taiwan*	
	S0	*S3*	*S0*	*S3*	*S0*	*S3*	*S0*	*S3*
Conv. BF – OHF	0.0	0.0	0.0	0.0	0.0	0.0	0.0	0.0
Conv. BF – BOF	93.6	34.9	83.0	15.2	74.6	16.3	75.7	19.6
Conv. BF – BOF (bio-based)	0.0	6.7	1.5	12.0	0.0	0.4	0.0	0.3
Conv. BF – BOF (CCS)	0.2	9.1	0.2	5.2	0.4	4.9	0.2	4.7
Conv. BF – BOF (CCS, bio-based)	0.1	20.4	0.1	14.2	0.1	7.2	0.1	6.6
BF TGR – BOF (CCS)	0.3	2.0	0.3	1.7	0.4	1.9	0.5	2.1
BF TGR – BOF (CCS, bio-based)	0.1	2.1	0.3	3.2	0.3	2.6	0.3	2.5
DRI-gas – EAF	0.1	0.1	0.1	0.0	0.0	0.0	0.0	0.0
DRI-gas – EAF (bio-based)	0.1	0.2	0.1	0.2	0.0	0.0	0.0	0.0
DRI-gas – EAF (CCS)	0.1	0.2	0.1	0.1	0.0	0.0	0.0	0.0
DRI-gas – EAF (CCS, bio-based)	0.1	0.5	0.1	0.9	0.0	0.2	0.0	0.1
DRI-coal – EAF	0.1	0.1	0.2	0.0	0.1	0.0	0.1	0.0
DRI-coal – EAF (bio-based)	0.1	0.1	0.1	0.1	0.0	0.0	0.0	0.0
DRI-coal – EAF (CCS)	0.1	0.1	0.1	0.1	0.0	0.0	0.0	0.0
DRI-coal – EAF (CCS, bio-based)	0.1	1.2	0.1	2.9	0.0	0.7	0.0	0.2
SRI – BOF	0.2	0.0	0.9	0.2	1.6	0.2	0.9	0.2
SRI – BOF (bio-based)	0.2	0.9	0.5	1.8	0.2	0.3	0.1	0.3
SRI – BOF (CCS)	0.3	0.8	0.4	1.0	0.4	0.7	0.4	1.0
SRI – BOF (CCS, bio-based)	0.2	1.6	0.3	2.5	0.1	1.6	0.1	1.3
SRI⁺ – BOF	0.5	0.3	0.9	0.3	7.7	1.0	1.0	0.3
SRI⁺ – BOF (bio-based)	0.2	1.5	0.6	2.7	0.1	0.9	0.2	0.7
SRI⁺ – BOF (CCS)	0.3	1.3	0.5	1.4	0.4	1.8	0.6	2.1
SRI⁺ – BOF (CCS, bio-based)	0.2	2.9	0.4	4.6	0.1	3.5	0.1	2.6
HFS – EAF	0.4	1.7	0.7	3.0	0.7	4.2	0.9	4.2
MOE	0.1	0.2	0.1	0.2	0.1	0.1	0.1	0.1
Scrap – EAF	2.2	11.2	8.3	26.5	12.6	51.7	18.6	51.2

Source: Estimated by Cambridge Econometrics for this study

Table 6.5 Technology-specific levelized cost of steelmaking in $\$_{2008}$/tcs, for all scenarios in China and Japan

	China					*Japan*				
	2015 – S0	*2050 – S0*	*2050 – S1*	*2050 – S2*	*2050 – S3*	*2015 – S0*	*2050 – S0*	*2050 – S1*	*2050 – S2*	*2050 – S3*
Conv. BF – OHF	364	362	463	554	791	372	364	458	562	802
Conv. BF – BOF	208	196	281	357	564	231	212	289	376	584
Conv. BF – BOF (BB)	236	221	283	335	494	237	212	268	328	472
Conv. BF – BOF (CCS)	228	212	243	259	362	267	241	260	282	334
Conv. BF – BOF (CCS+BB)	249	230	234	223	271	278	246	241	233	214
BF TGR – BOF (CCS)	237	219	257	272	410	282	250	270	292	345
BF TGR – BOF (CCS+BB)	280	259	273	263	350	283	246	243	238	226
DR-gas – EAF	367	360	458	495	829	411	367	412	467	605
DR-gas – EAF (BB)	387	370	435	436	693	410	359	380	396	424
DR-gas – EAF (CCS)	388	378	450	455	737	434	385	405	428	475
DR-gas – EAF (CCS+BB)	408	388	427	396	602	434	377	373	358	296
DR-coal – EAF	340	330	520	655	1193	383	343	462	617	1040
DR-coal – EAF (BB)	444	420	485	489	745	438	368	393	414	452
DR-coal – EAF (CCS)	395	381	470	493	807	440	392	427	468	566
DR-coal – EAF (CCS+BB)	498	470	436	332	372	494	415	359	269	–5
SR – BOF	213	203	327	447	729	219	205	325	458	775
SR – BOF (BB)	306	286	296	299	341	269	234	247	253	265
SR – BOF (CCS)	268	252	295	317	457	282	256	284	314	385
SR – BOF (CCS+BB)	359	333	265	176	82	331	284	209	115	–109
SR + – BOF	225	212	311	400	641	242	221	311	412	653
SR + – BOF (BB)	295	274	287	289	349	279	242	253	258	270
SR + – BOF (CCS)	261	244	278	295	412	281	253	274	298	354
SR + – BOF (CCS+BB)	330	303	256	189	132	318	273	218	150	–15
HFS – EAF	242	231	302	297	587	292	252	268	279	293
MOE	1294	1321	2037	1963	4793	1780	1640	1806	1865	1902
Scrap – EAF	308	313	370	364	609	372	353	367	372	373

Source: Estimated by Cambridge Econometrics for this study

Table 6.6 Technology-specific levelized cost of steelmaking in $\$_{2008}$/tcs, for all scenarios in Korea and Taiwan

	Korea					*Taiwan*				
	2015 – S0	*2050 – S0*	*2050 – S1*	*2050 – S2*	*2050 – S3*	*2015 – S0*	*2050 – S0*	*2050 – S1*	*2050 – S2*	*2050 – S3*
Conv. BF – OHF	368	364	470	573	777	368	364	452	536	702
Conv. BF – BOF	224	210	300	386	560	224	210	285	355	497
Conv. BF – BOF (BB)	273	253	322	381	499	281	257	315	363	460
Conv. BF – BOF (CCS)	242	223	245	263	302	253	235	257	272	304
Conv. BF – BOF (CCS+BB)	282	256	255	242	219	287	259	260	251	233
BF TGR – BOF (CCS)	249	227	249	267	303	249	228	252	267	298
BF TGR – BOF (CCS+BB)	279	251	252	241	221	281	251	257	249	234
DR-gas – EAF	385	367	427	473	559	385	371	433	472	543
DR-gas – EAF (BB)	430	399	431	435	438	443	410	449	453	457
DR-gas – EAF (CCS)	407	386	410	419	432	407	390	424	433	445
DR-gas – EAF (CCS+BB)	452	417	414	381	314	465	428	440	415	361
DR-coal – EAF	358	337	509	668	976	357	339	492	622	873
DR-coal – EAF (BB)	523	482	541	544	547	557	509	563	567	570
DR-coal – EAF (CCS)	414	389	433	465	521	413	391	443	470	517
DR-coal – EAF (CCS+BB)	579	532	466	346	107	612	559	514	418	224
SR – BOF	216	203	341	477	747	216	203	316	426	646
SR – BOF (BB)	363	333	369	371	376	392	350	377	379	384
SR – BOF (CCS)	274	254	284	311	367	274	254	284	307	353
SR – BOF (CCS+BB)	419	381	313	211	9	449	398	345	263	101
SR + – BOF	229	214	317	418	620	229	214	300	382	547
SR + – BOF (BB)	340	310	337	338	340	363	323	345	346	349
SR + – BOF (CCS)	266	246	269	290	331	266	246	270	287	322
SR + – BOF (CCS+BB)	377	340	290	214	64	399	353	315	254	133
HFS – EAF	263	238	251	252	248	262	238	269	271	269
MOE	1495	1377	1480	1486	1456	1492	1364	1659	1683	1672
Scrap – EAF	335	323	330	326	323	331	314	339	341	340

Source: Estimated by Cambridge Econometrics for this study

steelmaking routes. For Japan, the cheapest options are the SR – BOF, Conv. BF – BOF and Conv. BF – BOF (BB) routes. In Korea and Taiwan, investors are most likely to choose the SR – BOF, SR^+ – BOF and Conv. BF – BOF routes.

When the carbon taxes are applied, the LCOS for DR-coal – EAF (default), SR – BOF (default), Conv. BF – OHF and Conv. BF – BOF (default) increase over time in line with the carbon taxes. Under S1, many CCS variants become viable alternatives. When a medium carbon tax is applied (S2), some BB variants also become viable alternatives. In China and Japan, the SR – BOF, (CCS+BB) and SR^+ – BOF (CCS+BB) routes become the cheapest alternatives, although this is not the case for Korea and Taiwan.

The high carbon tax scenario (S3) results in SR – BOF (CCS+BB), SR^+ – BOF (CCS+BB) and DR-coal – EAF (CCS+BB) becoming the cheapest alternatives in 2050 in all four countries. All steelmaking routes that require coke as an input material do not decrease much in LCOS, even with the application of CCS and the transition to BB production, for example Conv. BF – BOF (CCS+BB) and BF TGR – BOF (CCS+BB). Biomass can only replace a small amount of coal for the production of coke, and therefore considerable emissions remain. The LCOS of MOE increases in all countries, except Korea, under all carbon tax scenarios despite having close to zero emissions. This is due to the carbon tax also affecting the power sector, which results in higher prices for electricity and, thereby, increasing the LCOS of MOE. This emphasizes that sectoral interaction effects are important.

Environmental impact

Annual emissions from steelmaking change both because of changes in the quantity of steel produced and changes in the mix of technologies used (Figure 6.5; see also Table 6.4). In the baseline, all four countries show an increase of emissions because of higher levels of steel production. In all countries, there is a shift in relative market share towards more carbon-intensive production.

In all scenarios, the Conv. BF – BOF route contributes the most to total emissions. Under the carbon tax scenarios S1–S3, emissions decrease compared with those under baseline S0 (and in most cases also in absolute terms) because of a combination of less volume of steel production and a shift towards less carbon-intensive methods of production.

Table 6.7 compares CO_2 emission levels of the steel sector estimated for 2050 with 2005 levels. The table shows that China does not achieve emission reductions under any carbon tax scenario, whereas Japan reduces emissions under all scenarios. Korea and Taiwan only show a decrease if the carbon tax rate is high, that is, only under S3.

Increases in 2050 emissions levels compared with those in 2005 are mainly caused by increases in total steel production. When comparing emission levels under each carbon tax scenario to those of the baseline scenario in 2050, all countries show decreases under all scenarios.

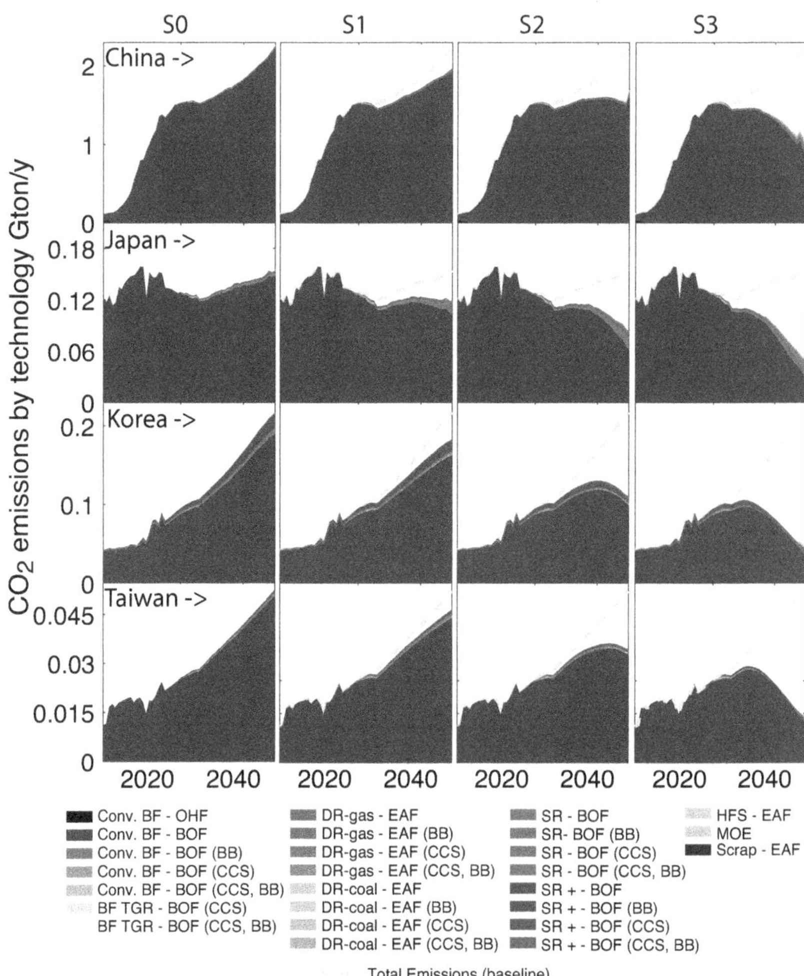

Figure 6.5 CO_2 emission levels of the entire iron and steel industry in each country of interest, under each scenario

Source: Estimated by Cambridge Econometrics for this study

Economic impact

Implementation of a carbon tax adds to the production cost of steel, which in turn leads to increased average domestic steel prices (Figure 6.6, bottom row). Steel prices increase most in China in 2050 (+38%, +63%, +100% for S1, S2, S3, respectively, compared with S0), but also considerably in the other three countries (ranging from +22% to + 82%).

Table 6.7 Comparison of CO_2 emission levels in 2050 under each carbon tax scenario with that under the baseline scenario in 2050 or 2005, and the cumulative CO_2 emissions averted

	China			*Japan*		
	S1	*S2*	*S3*	*S1*	*S2*	*S3*
2050 vs 2005 (%)	251	191	49	-23	-49	-62
2050 vs 2050 of baseline (%)	-13	-51	-63	-26	-51	-68
Total averted (Gt CO_2)	3.5	7	13.6	0.5	0.9	1.4
	Korea			*Taiwan*		
	S1	*S2*	*S3*	*S1*	*S2*	*S3*
2050 vs 2005 (%)	272	117	-27	160	91	-34
2050 vs 2050 of baseline (%)	-16	-51	-83	-11	-35	-77
Total averted (Gt CO_2)	0.4	1	2	<0.1	0.2	0.4

Source: Estimated by Cambridge Econometrics for this study

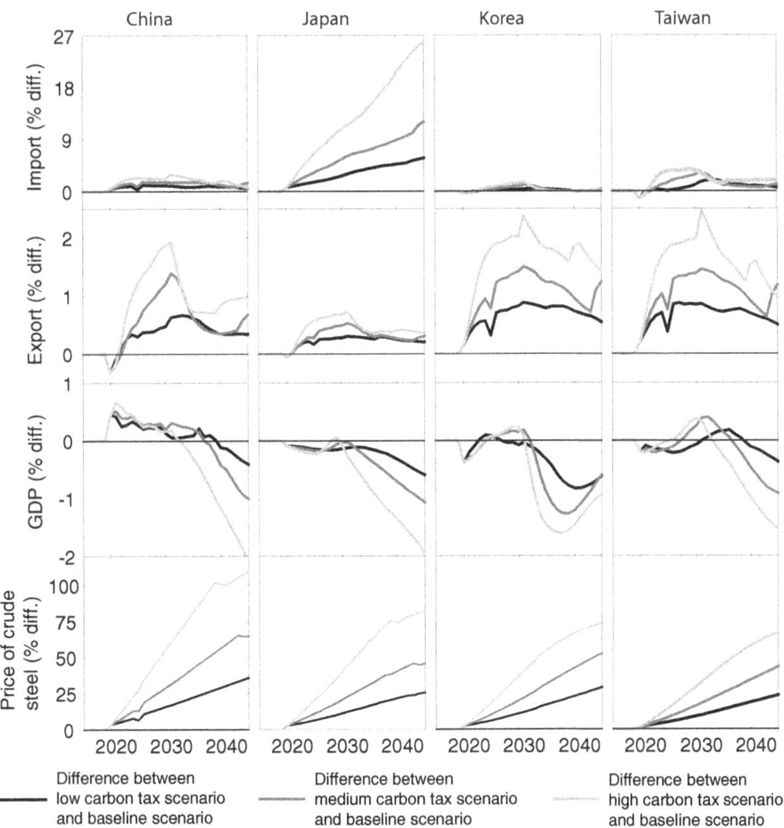

Figure 6.6 Comparison of carbon tax scenarios to baseline scenario with regard to import of steel, export of steel, GDP development and average price of crude steel

Source: Estimated by Cambridge Econometrics for this study

The increase in steel prices affects the competitiveness of the East Asian steel industries on the international market. Imports of steel increase in all the scenarios and, especially, for Japan; but less so for Korea. It should be remembered that the competitiveness effects in any single East Asian country would be higher if the carbon tax was not implemented simultaneously in all four countries.

Overall, without any revenue recycling (see Chapter 9), carbon taxes have a negative impact on GDP. Impacts are typically small, that is, until ~2030, but after 2030 the loss of GDP (compared with baseline) could be as high as 2%.

Discussion

Innovation

The coupling of FTT:Steel and E3ME allows us to assess how carbon taxes and other energy policies affect innovation within the iron and steel sector, and how this, in turn, affects the wider economy. Whereas the most stringent carbon tax scenario (S3) shows that SR – BOF (CCS+BB), SR$^+$ – BOF (CCS+BB) and DR-coal – EAF (CCS+BB) are the cheapest alternatives, they are limited in technological diffusion. These technologies are part of technology groups that do not yet have significant market share.

This is, of course, true for all novel technologies. Their limited market diffusion can be explained by technological lock-in of the Conv. BF – BOF and Scrap – EAF routes. In the steel sector, substitution rates are generally very low because of the substantial longevity of plants (25–40 years). However, implementation of CCS can occur faster than completely substituting a production method, so there might be a faster route to decarbonization. BB technologies in combination with CCS achieve greater reductions in LCOS production under carbon tax scenarios because of revenue generation as a result of negative emissions.

Under carbon tax scenarios, diffusion of the completely novel steelmaking routes (HFS – EAF and MOE) was shown to be limited. In addition, we found that a carbon tax could act against some low-carbon technologies because it was also applied to the power sector. This leads to an increased price of electricity and, in turn, the LCOS of the MOE and Scrap – EAF routes.

Climate change mitigation and economic impact

When carbon tax rates increase, we do see lower steel sector emissions. However, decarbonization is not necessarily promoted by diffusion between technology groups but, rather, within technology groups. To a lesser degree, emission reductions are also caused by a decrease in the total volume of steel production.

This last result could imply that production volume 'leaks' to countries in which no carbon tax is enacted, meaning that emissions are displaced rather than reduced overall. As the carbon tax also affects electricity prices and EAF technologies, steel prices will, inevitably, increase. The model results for trade suggest carbon leakage as a result. However, the point should not be overstated as most of the reduction in steel demand is absolute.

Besides the transfer of some production to other countries, the carbon taxes naturally affect the economy. Initially, impacts may be positive as the carbon taxes spur additional investment in new plants. In the longer term, however, in the absence of revenue recycling the effects become negative. In all three scenarios the four East Asian countries remain net exporters of steel. This result could change if the countries would not simultaneously introduce a carbon tax, that is, compete with one another. The present results, however, suggest that with cooperation, all four countries can maintain a steel industry.

Conclusion

This chapter presents the first application of the FTT:Steel model of technology diffusion within the steel sector. The model is the first of its kind for the steel sector and draws on the underlying methodology of the other FTT models described in this book. It provides a new tool for policy makers to assess a variety of policies that are aimed at decarbonizing the sector.

In this chapter, we have looked only at carbon taxes as a means to decarbonize steel production. We found that carbon taxes can reduce emissions from steel, but that taxes alone are not sufficient to introduce new technologies to the sector. This finding is similar to previous analyses of the sector (e.g. Nemet, 2009), and reflects both the long lifetimes of steel plants and the difficulties of new technologies in becoming established.

Despite being based on a separate analysis, the conclusions from this chapter are, thus, in line with those from other chapters. Carbon taxes are useful tools to reduce emission levels but must be complemented by other policies. These other policies promoting, for example, specific new technologies may also reduce some of the negative aspects of carbon taxes, notably the potential relocation of production to other countries, thereby, leading to carbon leakage. Further analysis of a broader set of policies is therefore needed to support policy makers in decarbonizing the steel sector.

Notes

1 In this context, apparent steel use is the total production minus export plus import. This is different from the true steel use, as steel may be imported and exported, for example, in the form of cars.

2 We include Carbon Capture and Utilization (CCU) in CCS here but do not further explore potential uses of the captured emissions.

References

AIST (2015) *Steel Wheel*. Available at: http://apps.aist.org/steelwheel/index.html (Accessed: 4 June 2018).

Allanore, A. (2014) 'Features and Challenges of Molten Oxide Electrolytes for Metal Extraction', *Journal of the Electrochemical Society*, 162(1), pp. E13–E22. doi:10.1149/2.0451501jes.

Allanore, A., Ortiz, L. A. and Sadoway, D. R. (2011) 'Molten Oxide Electrolysis for Iron Production: Identification of Key Process Parameters for Largescale Development', in *Energy Technology 2011*. Wiley-Blackwell, pp. 121–129. doi:10.1002/9781118061886.ch12.

Babich, A., Senk, D. and Fernandez, M. (2010) 'Charcoal Behaviour by Its Injection Into the Modern Blast Furnace', *ISIJ International*, 50(1), pp. 81–88. doi:10.2355/isijinternational.50.81.

Daniëls, B. W. (2002) *Transition Paths Towards CO_2 Emission Reduction in the Steel Industry*. Rijksuniversiteit Groningen/University of Groningen. Available at: www.rug.nl/research/portal/publications/transition-paths-towards-co$_2$-emission-reduction-in-the-steel-industry(b197f6bb-c53d-4e53-a1e5-97a4ba76c04c).html.

Ecometrica (2011, August) 'Electricity-Specific Emission Factors for Grid Electricity', pp. 1–22. doi:10.13044/j.sdewes.2014.02.0030.

Greenpeace East Asia and Beijing Custeel E-Commerce Co. Ltd. (2017) *Research Report on Overcapacity Reduction in China's Steel Industry*. Available at: www.greenpeace.org.cn/wp-content/uploads/2017/02/绿色和平报告：问诊2016钢铁去产能.pdf.

Grubb, M. (2014) *Planetary Economics: Energy, Climate Change and the Three Domains of Sustainable Development*. New York: Routledge.

Grübler, A., Nakićenović, N. and Victor, D. G. (1999) 'Dynamics of Energy Technologies and Global Change', *Energy Policy*, 27(5), pp. 247–280. doi:10.1016/S0301-4215(98)00067-6.

Hiebler, H. and Plaul, J. F. (2004) 'Hydrogen Plasma Smelting Reduction – An Option for Steelmaking in the Future', *Metalurgija*, 43(3), pp. 155–162.

Hooey, L. et al. (2013) 'Techno-Economic Study of an Integrated Steelworks Equipped With Oxygen Blast Furnace and CO_2 Capture', *Energy Procedia*, 37, pp. 7139–7151. doi:https://doi.org/10.1016/j.egypro.2013.06.651.

IEA (2015) *Energy Technology Perspectives 2015*. Paris, France: OECD/IEA. doi:10.1787/energy_tech-2015-en.

IEA (2017) *CO_2 Emissions From Fuel Combustion Highlights 2017*. Paris, France.

IMF (2017) *People's Republic of China 2017 Article Iv Consultation – Press Release; Staff Report; and Statement By the Executive Director for the People's Republic of China*. doi:9781484314654. Available at: https://www.imf.org/en/ublications/CR/Issues/2017/08/15/People-s-Republic-of-China-2017-Article-IV-Consultation-Press-Release-Staff-Report-and-45170

International Trade Administration (2018) *Steel Exports Report: Japan*. Washington, DC. Available at: www.trade.gov/steel/countries/pdfs/exports-japan.pdf.

ISIJ (2017) 'Production and Technology of Iron and Steel in Japan During 2016', *ISIJ International*, 57(6), pp. 957–969. doi:10.2355/isijinternational.57.957.

JISF (2017) *The Steel Industry of Japan*. Available at: www.jisf.or.jp/en/statistics/sij/documents/P2-3.pdf (Accessed: 16 July 2018).

Köhler, J. et al. (2006) 'The Transition to Endogenous Technical Change in Climate-Economy Models: A Technical Overview to the Innovation Modeling Comparison Project', *The Energy Journal*. Cleveland: International Association for Energy Economics, pp. 17–55, 279, 280. Available at: https://search.proquest.com/docview/222085669?accountid=12653.

Meijer, K. et al. (2009) 'ULCOS: Ultra-Low CO_2 Steelmaking', *Ironmaking & Steelmaking*. Taylor & Francis, 36(4), pp. 249–251. doi:10.1179/174328109X439298.

Meijer, K. et al. (2013) 'Developments in Alternative Ironmaking', *Transactions of the Indian Institute of Metals*, 66(5), pp. 475–481. doi:10.1007/s12666-013-0309-z.

Mercure, J.-F. (2012) 'FTT: Power: A Global Model of the Power Sector With Induced Technological Change and Natural Resource Depletion', *Energy Policy*, 48, pp. 799–811. doi:10.1016/j.enpol.2012.06.025.

Mercure, J.-F. and Salas, P. (2013) 'On the Global Economic Potentials and Marginal Costs of Non-Renewable Resources and the Price of Energy Commodities', *Energy Policy*, 63, pp. 469–483. doi:10.1016/j.enpol.2013.08.040.

Mercure, J.-F. et al. (2014) 'The Dynamics of Technology Diffusion and the Impacts of Climate Policy Instruments in the Decarbonisation of the Global Electricity Sector', *Energy Policy*. Elsevier, 73, pp. 686–700. doi:10.1016/j.enpol.2014.06.029.

Mercure, J.-F. et al. (2018) 'Environmental Impact Assessment for Climate Change Policy With the Simulation-Based Integrated Assessment Model E3ME-FTT-GENIE', *Energy Strategy Reviews*, 20, pp. 195–208. doi:https://doi.org/10.1016/j.esr.2018.03.003.

Midrex (2017) *World Direct Reduction Statistics, Midrex Technologies, Inc.* Charlotte. Available at: www.midrex.com/uploads/documents/MDXSTATS20127-3-13 Final.pdf.

Ministry of Economy Trade and Industry (2015) 'Submission of Japan's Intended Nationally Determined Contribution', *INDC*. Available at: www4.unfccc.int/Submissions/INDC/PublishedDocuments/Japan/1/20150717_Japan'sINDC.pdf.

Morfeldt, J., Nijs, W. and Silveira, S. (2015) 'The Impact of Climate Targets on Future Steel Production – An Analysis Based on a Global Energy System Model', *Journal of Cleaner Production*, 103, pp. 469–482. doi:https://doi.org/10.1016/j.jclepro.2014.04.045.

National Bureau of Statistics of China (2016) *China Statistical Yearbook 2016*. Available at: www.stats.gov.cn/tjsj/ndsj/2016/indexeh.htm (Accessed: 19 April 2018).

National Bureau of Statistics of China (2017) *China Statistical Yearbook*. Available at: www.stats.gov.cn/tjsj/ndsj/2017/indexeh.htm (Accessed: 10 July 2018).

National Development and Reform Commission of China (2015) 'Enhanced Actions on Climate Change: China's Intended Nationally Determined Contributions', *UNFCCC*, p. 36. Available at: www4.unfccc.int/submissions/INDC/Published%20Documents/China/1/China's%20INDC%20-%20on%2030%20June%202015.pdf.

Nemet, G. F. (2009) 'Demand-Pull, Technology-Push, and Government-led Incentives for Non-Incremental Technical Change', *Research Policy*, 38(5), pp. 700–709. doi:10.1016/j.respol.2009.01.004.

OECD. (2015) '*Excess Capacity in the Global Steel Industry: The Current Situation and Ways Forward*'. Directorate for Science, Technology and Industry. DSTI/SU/SC(2014)15/FINAL. OECD Publishing, Paris.

Pardo, N. and Moya, J. A. (2013) 'Prospective Scenarios on Energy Efficiency and CO_2 Emissions in the European Iron & Steel Industry', *Energy*, 54, pp. 113–128. doi:10.1016/j.energy.2013.03.015.

Pauliuk, S., Wang, T. and Müller, D. B. (2013) 'Steel All Over the World: Estimating In-use Stocks of Iron for 200 Countries', *Resources, Conservation and Recycling*, 71, pp. 22–30. doi:10.1016/j.resconrec.2012.11.008.

Pinegar, H. K., Moats, M. S. and Sohn, H. Y. (2011) 'Process Simulation and Economic Feasibility Analysis for a Hydrogen-Based Novel Suspension Ironmaking Technology', *Steel Research International*. WILEY-VCH Verlag, 82(8), pp. 951–963. doi:10.1002/srin.201000288.

Pinegar, H. K., Moats, M. S. and Sohn, H. Y. (2012) 'Flowsheet Development, Process Simulation and Economic Feasibility Analysis for Novel Suspension Ironmaking Technology Based on Natural Gas: Part 1 – Flowsheet and Simulation for Ironmaking With Reformerless Natural Gas', *Ironmaking & Steelmaking*. Taylor & Francis, 39(6), pp. 398–408. doi:10.1179/1743281211Y.0000000053.

POSCO Research Institute (POSRI) (2016) 'Asian Steel Market Outlook', *Asian Steel Watch*, pp. 102–119.

Primetals Technologies (2015) *Corex Efficient and Environmentally Friendly Smelting Reduction*. Linz. Brochure No.: T01-0-N063-L4-P-V2-EN.

Primetals Technologies (2017) *Steel in East Asia, Metals Magazine*. Available at: www.primetals.com/press-media/metals-magazine/issue-01-2017/steel-in-east-asia/.

Primetals Technologies/POSCO (2015) *The FINEX Process Economical and Environmentally Safe Ironmaking*. Linz. Available at: www.primetals.com.

Remus, R. et al. (2013) *JRC Reference Report. Best Available Techniques (BAT) Reference Document for Iron and Steel Production*. doi:10.2791/97469. Available at: https://publications.europa.eu/en/publication-detail/-/publication/eaa047e8-644c-4149-bdcb-9dde79c64a12/language-en

Republic of China (Taiwan) (2015) *Submission by Republic of China (Taiwan) Intended Nationally Determined Contribution (核定本)*. Taipei, Taiwan. Available at: https://enews.epa.gov.tw/enews/enews_ftp/104/1117/174044/SubmissionbyRepublicofChina(Taiwan)IntendedNationallyDeterminedContribution.pdf.

Republic of Korea (2015) 'Submission by the Republic of Korea Intended Nationally Determined Contribution', pp. 1–4. Available at: www4.unfccc.int/submissions/INDC/PublishedDocuments/RepublicofKorea/1/INDCSubmissionbytheRepublicofKoreaonJune30.pdf.

Rosenberg, E., Simbolotti, G. and Tosato, G. (2012) *Aluminum Production Process, Technology Brief I10*. Available at: www.iea-etsap.org/E-TechDS/PDF/I10_AlProduction_ER_March2012_FinalGSOK.pdf.

Sabat, K. and Murphy, A. (2017) 'Hydrogen Plasma Processing of Iron Ore', *Metallurgical and Materials Transactions B*, 48(3), pp. 1561–1594. doi:10.1007/s11663-017-0957-1.

Siemens VIA (2011) *SIMETAL Corex Technology Industrially and Commercially Proven Iron Making*. Linz. Available at: www.industry.siemens.com/datapool/industry/industrysolutions/metals/simetal/en/SIMETAL-Corex-technology-en.pdf.

Sohn, H. Y. et al. (2017) 'Status of the Development of Flash Ironmaking Technology', in Wang, S., Free M., Alam S., Zhang M., and Taylor P. (eds.), *Applications of Process Engineering Principles in Materials Processing, Energy and Environmental Technologies. The Minerals, Metals & Materials Series*. Springer, Cham, pp. 15–23.

Tang, R. et al. (2018) 'Key Challenges for the Establishment of the Monitoring, Reporting and Verification (MRV) System in China's National Carbon Emissions Trading Market', *Climate Policy*. Taylor & Francis, pp. 1–16. doi:10.1080/14693062.2018.1454882.

Tonomura, S. (2013) 'Outline of Course 50', *Energy Procedia*, 37, pp. 7160–7167. doi:10.1016/j.egypro.2013.06.653.

UN (2017) *World Population Prospects: The 2017 Revision*. POP/DB/WPP/Rev.2017/POP/F01-1.

van Boggelen, J. W. K. et al. (2016) *The Use of Hisarna Hot Metal in Steelmaking*, Scanmet V.

Van Wortswinkel, L. et al. (2010) *IEA ETSAP, Technology Brief I02-Iron and Steel*. Available at: https://iea-etsap.org/index.php/energy-technology-data/energy-demand-technologies-data

Wiencke, J. et al. (2018) 'Electrolysis of Iron in a Molten Oxide Electrolyte', *Journal of Applied Electrochemistry*, 48(1), pp. 115–126. doi:10.1007/s10800-017-1143-5.

World Bank (2018) *GDP Per Capita, PPP (Current International $)*. Available at: https://data.worldbank.org/indicator/NY.GDP.PCAP.PP.CD?locations=CN&view=chart (Accessed: 6 April 2018).

World Steel Association (2012) *Sustainable Steel: At the Core of a Green Economy*. Brussels. Available at: www.worldsteel.org/en/dam/jcr:5b246502-df29-4d8b-92bb-afb2dc27ed4f/Sustainable-steel-at-the-core-of-a-green-economy.pdf.

World Steel Association (2017) *Steel Statistical Yearbook 2017*. Available at: www.worldsteel.org/statistics/statistics-archive/yearbook-archive.html.

Zuo, G. and Hirsch, A. (2009, September 29) 'The Trial of the Top Gas Recycling Blast Furnace at LKAB's EBF and Scale-up', *Revue de Métallurgie*. EDP Sciences, 106(9), pp. 387–392. doi:10.1051/metal/2009067.

7 Policies to decarbonize passenger vehicles in East Asia

Aileen Lam, Soocheol Lee, Yongsung Cho, Chun-Hsu Lin, Florian Knobloch, Hector Pollitt, Unnada Chewpreecha and Jean-François Mercure

Introduction

As highlighted by the Intergovernmental Panel on Climate Change 5th Assessment Report (AR5), the transportation sector must play a key role in climate change mitigation but will face considerable challenges in doing so (IPCC, 2014). Demand for road transport in the four East Asian countries has increased rapidly over the past two decades. Vehicle emissions and increased oil demand have been driven primarily by an increased use of passenger cars. As of 2016, more than 250 million passenger cars were registered in China, Japan, Korea and Taiwan. The number of passenger cars in China increased by a factor of nine between 2006 and 2016, compared with a per capita GDP increase of four.

The demand for crude oil and petroleum by the road transport sector has increased by nearly 60% in China, Japan, Korea and Taiwan since 2004 (IEA Energy Statistics). Passenger cars accounted for more than 50% of the increase (Matsuhashi & Ariga, 2016) (Yan & Crookes, 2010) in demand. The dependence on fossil fuels has significant implications on energy security and greenhouse gas (GHG) emissions.

It is possible to reduce dependency on fossil fuels in the road transport sector by using existing technologies. The dynamics generated by the diffusion of new technologies into the marketplace and the improvement of existing technologies will determine the direction of technological progress, which will be critical for reducing future emissions from passenger vehicles (Kemp, Schot, & Hoogma, 1998). As stated in the IPCC report (IPCC, 2014), 'understanding how low-carbon transport and energy technologies will evolve (via experience curves and innovation processes) is not well developed, and assessing this gap remains challenging for the transportation sector'.

The successful implementation of policies to reduce GHG emissions from passenger cars is particularly challenging because of the dynamics of technological transition and consumer behavior. To design efficient policy instruments, knowledge of the mechanisms that facilitate the diffusion of new car technologies is needed. It is important to determine the relationship between policy instruments and the rate of adoption for low or zero-emission vehicles.

Previous studies that assessed the effectiveness of policy incentives in reducing emissions from passenger vehicles have typically focused on a single country or region in Asia (e.g. Ko, Myung, Park, & Kwon, 2014; Paltsev et al., 2016; Oshiro & Masui, 2015; Wang, Ou, & Zhang, 2017). These studies have looked at the effectiveness of taxation schemes (vehicle taxes and carbon taxes) and regulations (fuel economy standards) in shaping the diffusion of energy-efficient vehicles. We argue that there are two major gaps in the existing studies:

1 Most existing studies and Integrated Assessment Models (IAMs) feature only a small number of policy instruments for one particular East Asian country, for example, Ko et al., 2014; Fullerton, Gan, & Hattori, 2015. It was not possible for these studies to assess and compare the effectiveness of a range of policy instruments across countries.
2 The existing studies either took one particular car model or used a representative agent to examine the response of agents to a set of policy incentives. However, in reality, consumers are diverse and may respond to policy incentives in unexpected ways.

In this chapter, we use a model of technological diffusion, FTT:Transport (Mercure & Lam, 2015) linked to the E3ME macro-econometric model, to study possible future technological transitions in personal transport in East Asia. Our analysis covers a range of policy incentives. In contrast to most other modelling frameworks, the E3ME-FTT:Transport model considers consumer heterogeneity in the car market and enables the simulation of detailed climate policies in private road transportation. We consider four policy scenarios that include carbon taxes, electric vehicle (EV) subsidies and regulations – each with a layer of specific policy incentives for the four East Asian countries, to find a set of policy incentives that leads to the diffusion of new energy vehicles (NEVs) and significant emission reductions from private passenger vehicles.

The chapter is structured as follows: the first section following this introduction discusses the current policy framework to reduce emissions in the passenger car sector in China, Japan, Korea and Taiwan. The theoretical framework of the E3ME-FTT:Transport model is discussed next, and the policy assumptions are summarized after that. Then, a section is devoted to presenting the results from the scenario analysis and the policy implications for the four East Asian countries. The final section provides overall conclusions and discusses the limitations of the model, along with recommendations for future work.

Policy context

This section summarizes the main policies that have been implemented in East Asia to limit emissions from personal transport. First, Table 7.1 provides an overview of fuel economy standards around the world. The following sections then discuss each East Asian country individually.

Table 7.1 Overview of regulation specifications for passenger cars in major economies

Country or region	*Target year*	*Unadjusted fleet target/measure (liters of gasoline/100km)*	*Structure*	*Test cycle*
EU	2015	5.6	Weight-based average	NEDC
	2021	4.09		
China	2015	6.9	Weight-class based per vehicle and corporate average	NEDC
	2020 (proposed)	5		
US	2016	6.5	FP-based corporate average	US combined
	2025	4.19		
Japan	2015	5.95	Weight-class based corporate average	JC08
	2020	4.93		
Brazil	2017	5.32	Weight-based corporate average	US combined
India	2016	5.6	Weight-based corporate average	NEDC for low-powered vehicle
	2021	4.87		
Korea	2015	5.88	Weight-based corporate average	US combined
Mexico	2016	5.99	FP-based corporate average	US combined

Source: The International Council on Clean Transportation (ICCT, 2017)

Note: NECD, New European Driving Cycle; FP, Function Point; JC08.

China

Because of China's rapid economic growth, demand for private passenger vehicles has grown significantly in the past 25 years. From 1991 to 2015, total annual vehicle production grew from approximately 700,000 units to 24 million units. Annual sales of passenger cars have increased more than 20 times since 1990. By the end of 2015, there were more than 116 million cars on the road in China. However, in terms of passenger cars per 1000 people, China measured 154 cars in 2016,[1] which is still much less than the ratio in the US. The potential for future growth in vehicle ownership, therefore, remains substantial.

At the national level, to reduce its dependency on foreign oil and to encourage the development of more fuel-efficient vehicle technologies, the passenger vehicle market has been subject to fuel economy standards since 2004. Fuel economy limits for passenger cars are based on vehicle weight, divided into 16 categories. The Phase 1 and Phase 2 standards require each individual vehicle model to comply with fuel consumption regulations before entering the market. The standards are set based on weight classes. China continues to reduce the fuel consumption limit, and Phase 4 fuel consumption standards for passenger vehicles are currently under development. In 2014, the Chinese Ministry of Industry and Information Technology (MIIT) released a fuel consumption standard for passenger cars. Compared with the Phase 3 standard, the new consumption standard will fall to 5 liters/100km, representing an overall reduction in fuel consumption of 28% between 2015 and 2020. The proposed fuel economy standard is presented in Table 7.2.

Electric vehicles (EVs) offer opportunities to address simultaneously oil security, local pollution and GHG emissions; EV deployment is taken by the central government as an essential strategy to tackle local pollution. China launched the EV Subsidy Scheme (EVSS) in 2009, followed by an update in 2013. Under Phase 1 EVSS, subsidies for the private purchase of plug-in hybrid EVs (PHEVs) and battery EVs (BEVs) are based on battery capacity, with a subsidy rate of 3000 RMB/kWh (Hao, 2014). Under Phase 2, subsidies for the private purchase of PHEVs and BEVs are based on the electric range of the vehicle. Those with electric ranges of more than 250 km, 150–250 km or 80–150 km qualify for subsidies of 60,000 RMB (9520 USD), 50,000 RMB (7930 USD) or 35,000 RMB (5550 USD), respectively (Hao, 2014).

Environmentally friendly and energy-efficient vehicles, including PHEVs and BEVs, are exempt from vehicle excise duty and annual registration tax. Before 2010, car excise duty rates were based on engine size; small-engine cars enjoyed a lower tax rate. After 2010, the excise duty was 10% before value-added tax (17%), regardless of car engine sizes. Registration tax was paid annually based on engine size and as established by individual provinces or cities.

Table 7.2 China's Phase 1 and Phase 2 EV Subsidy Scheme (EVSS)

Criteria/phase		*Phase 1*	*Phase 2*
Target market		Private	Public/private
Subsidy duration		2010–2012	2013–2015
Subsidy scope		PHEVs BEVs	PHEVs BEVs FCEVs
Subsidy standard	HEV	–	–
	PHEV	3000 RMB/kWh	35,000 RMB (range of ≥ 50km)
	BEV	3000 RMB/kWh	35,000 RMB (range of 80–150 km) 50,000 RMB (range of 150–250 km) 60,000 RMB (range of ≥ 250 km)
Phase-out mechanism		Not specified	10% reduction in 2014
Pilot cities		Six cities	28 cities and regions

Source: China Association of Automobile Manufacturing (CAAM, 2017)

BEV, battery electric vehicle; FCEV, fuel cell electric vehicle; HEV, hybrid electric vehicle; PHEV, plug-in hybrid electric vehicle

Table 7.3 Market shares of EVs and PHEVs in China between 2011 and 2015 (in %)

Type/year	*2011*	*2012*	*2013*	*2014*	*2015*
EV	0.056	0.074	0.082	0.227	1.192
PHEV	0.006	0.006	0.017	0.152	0.374
Total	0.056	0.081	0.098	0.379	1.57

Source: China Association of Automobile Manufacturing (CAAM, 2017)

In 2009, the Chinese government initiated the Ten Cities, Thousand Vehicles Program to stimulate the development of EVs through large-scale pilots in ten cities. Initially, the program targeted the deployment of EVs in government fleets. The program has since expanded to 25 cities and includes consumer incentives in six cities: Beijing, Shanghai, Hangzhou, Hefei, Changchun and Shenzhen (Gong, Wang, & Wang, 2013). Under this program, local authorities must increase the number of EVs on the road by either purchasing EVs themselves or introducing a rebate/subsidy for EV purchases. The program aims to kick-start wider demand for EVs.

The sales of EVs and PHEVs increased from 8000 units in 2011 to 330,000 units in 2015 and growth has since continued. Table 7.3 shows the change in EV and PHEV shares in China over this period. China had the largest share of global EV and PHEV sales in the world (33%) in 2015. China is targeting a domestic share of 20% NEV sales (two million) by 2025.[2] The Chinese government has also announced that companies that sell cars in China have a duty to sell a certain share of NEVs. In 2017, China's MIIT proposed a production quota under which automakers will have to produce NEVs to earn credits and avoid penalties. According to MIIT, automakers that sell 30,000 cars or more annually must in 2019 earn points equivalent to a 10% share of NEVs, rising to 12% in 2020.

Japan

The transportation sector accounted for about 17% of GHG emissions in Japan in 2016. Its share decreased from 18.4% in 2005 because of an increasing number of energy-efficient vehicles, including hybrid cars.[3]

Japan is the third-largest auto manufacturing market in the world, and Japanese automakers account for the majority of sales of hybrid cars and electric cars worldwide.[4] Toyota is the largest Japanese car manufacturer, holding an approximate 43% market share; Nissan and Honda are the second and third largest, with shares of 17% and 15%, respectively. More than 90% of the cars sold in Japan are Japanese (Kitano, 2013).

Under the Paris Agreement, the Japanese government pledged to reduce its national GHG emissions by 26% from 2013 levels by 2030. Japan has one of the most energy-efficient economies in the world, and its road transportation sector is among the most efficient because of a large share of small and hybrid vehicles.

Table 7.4 Market shares of EVs, PHEVs and Fuel Cell Electric Vehicle (FCEVs) in Japan between 2011 and 2015 (in %)

Type/year	*2011*	*2012*	*2013*	*2014*	*2015*
EV	0.635	0.847	1.201	1.504	1.908
PHEV	0.118	0.378	0.662	0.936	1.354
FCEV	<0.001	<0.001	<0.001	0.003	0.015
Total	0.753	1.225	1.862	2.444	3.227

Source: Japan Automobile Manufacturers Association (JAMA, 2017)

Table 7.4 shows the market shares of next-generation vehicles in Japan. Sales of next-generation passenger cars have expanded to a more than 20% share of Japan's new passenger car market because of the Japanese government's tax incentives and purchasing subsidies programs on them. The share of NEVs in Japan's fleet remains relatively small but is growing quickly.

Japan was one of the first countries to engage in research and policies for energy-efficient products. In 1998, Japan initiated the Top Runner Approach to encourage energy efficiency in end-use products. The scope of the program has been reviewed every few years and, by 2012, 23 products were included. The program has set mandatory efficiency standards or target values for automobiles based on the most efficient products. All vehicles were required to exceed new target values for their weight class within 3–10 years.

As part of the Energy Conservation Law, the program identified the most fuel-efficient automobile in each weight class and designated it 'top runner'. Because of the top runner program, Japanese fuel economy for new vehicles has improved significantly over the past 20 years. Overall, fuel economy has improved by more than 80% since 1995, and averaged 6% annual improvement over the five-year period up to 2015 (Rutherford, 2015).

Nine different types of tax can be applied when owning a car in Japan. These are the acquisition tax, consumption tax, tonnage tax, automobile tax, mini-vehicle tax, gasoline tax, diesel tax, LPG tax and in-use consumption tax (Iino & Lim, 2010). Tax breaks are available for three of these taxes (acquisition, tonnage and ownership). Tax breaks are determined by the level of compliance with the 2015 Japan Fuel Economy Standards (FES). Zero-emissions vehicles are exempt from both acquisition tax and tonnage tax. Cars that are compliant with the 2015 FES enjoy a reduction of up to 80% in acquisition tax and up to 75% reduction in automobile tonnage tax (Iino & Lim, 2010).

Korea

The transportation sector accounts for about 20% of GHG emissions in Korea. It is the country's second-largest emitter, trailing only the industrial sector. Within the transportation sector, on-road transportation dominates, with an emissions share of more than 80%. Thus, reducing the impact transportation has on the environment requires transformation of the current automobile-based transport system into a more energy-efficient, low-carbon and eco-friendly one. Sustainable development in transportation has also been a main concern for Korea. Both vehicle ownership and transport demand have increased substantially during the past two decades. As a result, energy consumption has increased rapidly, and vehicles have become the main source of urban air and noise pollution in many Korean cities. Current growth rates show no sign of subsiding.

One characteristic of the Korean automobile sector is the increasing demand for diesel cars. Diesel vehicles, especially imported diesel cars, have dominated in the Green car (environmentally friendly car) market. The share of diesel in imported vehicles increased from 16.4% in 2007 to 68.2% in 2014. SUVs and MPVs (multipurpose vehicles) led the sales of domestically produced diesel vehicles. Sedan cars remain popular, but the demand for SUVs has also been increasing in the imported diesel market.

Meanwhile, sales of hybrid vehicles have also increased continuously. Hybrid vehicles are competing with diesel vehicles in the domestic market. However, the sales volume of imported hybrid cars remains low.

Regarding EVs, prices have been falling and government subsidies have been increasing. For example, the automobile company Kia has recently cut the price of its Ray EV from 45 million Won (US$41,850) to 35 million Won (US$32,550). Some local governments have provided subsidies to buyers of EVs, notably the Jeju special self-governing province has provided subsides of eight million Won (US$7,440) per vehicle. However, the lack of any purchasing subsidies from the central government has hindered EV sales in Korea. For EVs to achieve a larger market share, the charging infrastructure throughout Korea needs to expand.

The key challenges for a low-carbon transition within the transportation sector in Korea are summarized as follows:

1 Substitution of fossil fuel. Cars with EVs require a reduction in the cost of batteries (which depends on international technology actions) and development of nationwide charging infrastructure.
2 Development of Green cars. The current heavy dependence of transport on fossil fuel should be reduced by diversifying energy sources. NEVs promise an alternative to conventional vehicles for short-distance trips in urban areas. Wireless electricity technology could facilitate the introduction of EVs by solving their current battery limitations. Fuel cell technology could be a long-term option in future alternative-fuel vehicle developments. Legal support and economic incentives should be provided for the development of these types of Green vehicle.
3 Non-motorized transportation. Non-motorized forms of transport yield zero carbon emissions. Bicycles are used extensively in many European and Asian cities, but their modal share in Korean cities is minimal because of limited infrastructure and low public acceptance. Use of bicycles should be promoted for short-distance commuting by providing adequate infrastructure and implementing safety measures.

Taiwan

Despite not being a member of the United Nations, Taiwan proposed a CO_2 emission reduction target as its Intended Nationally Determined Contribution (INDC) after the United Nations Framework Convention on Climate Change (UNFCCC) Conference of the Parties (COP21) in Paris in 2015. Taiwan pledged a 50% reduction in emissions compared with the levels of 2005 by 2050. The transportation sector is a main contributor to GHG emissions in Taiwan (~15% of Taiwan's total emissions), and it is also a major source of local air pollution, such as of PM2.5.

In Taiwan, all vehicles must comply with energy consumption standards, which are categorized by vehicle engine size. In addition, all vehicles must declare their ranking in the energy labelling system, ranging from Class 1 to Class 5.

To encourage the purchase of low-carbon vehicles, different governmental agencies offer several incentives. Financial incentives include the exemption of excise tax on all EVs until the end of 2021 and exemption of registration tax on all EVs until the end of 2018. For hybrid cars, the excise tax was reduced by 50% between February 2009 and December 2014. There are also direct subsidies offered for purchasing electric motorcycles, electric-assisted bicycles and electric bicycles. The subsidies range from 1000–10,000 NTD (US$30–330).

In addition to direct incentives to reduce GHG emissions from vehicles, excise tax is deducted. Moreover, 50,000 NTD (~US$1700) is provided for each new passenger car that leads to the retirement of an old car owned by the same family – regardless of the fuel type of the new vehicle – after the excise tax is deducted. For motorcycles, the reduction in excise tax is 4000 NTD (~US$130) in this program. Additional subsidies of 3000–7000 NTD (US$100–230) are provided for new motorcycles that are purchased to replace old ones equipped with two-stroke engines.

In most cases, incentives have been extended beyond their scheduled deadlines. The exception was that for hybrid cars, which was terminated in 2014, and was a key factor in the drop in sales of hybrid cars (which are mostly imported) from 17,788 in 2014 to 8341 in 2015.

Data overview

We have collected car sales data (for each model) from the MarkLines database,[5] and have consolidated these data with the data of car prices and car engine size (available in 2012) taken from the car manufacturers' websites. Figures show the distribution of CO_2 emissions for all vehicles and for hybrid cars only (Figure 7.1), and the distribution of car price for all types of vehicles and for new energy vehicles (hybrid, electric) only (Figure 7.2), in China, Japan, Korea and Taiwan for 2012.

The distributions show the diversity of consumer choice in each country. Notice that the distribution of car prices in China is much broader than that in Japan, Korea and Taiwan. By contrast, the distributions of prices and emissions are much narrower for Korea and Taiwan. This implies that consumer choices are

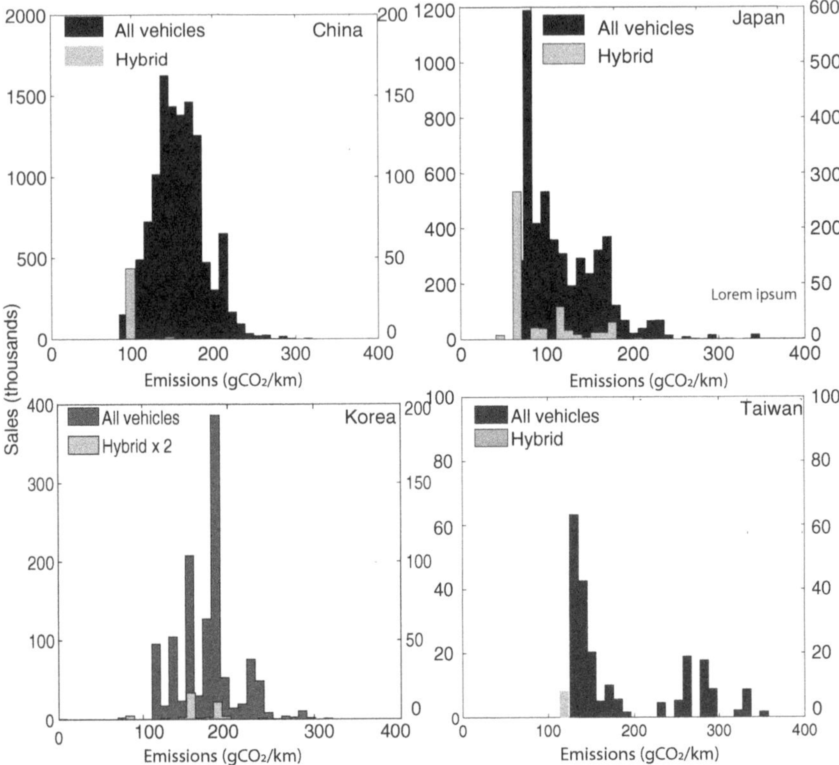

Figure 7.1 Emission distributions for the four East Asian countries.

Source: Cambridge Econometrics

more diverse in China, with most people showing preference for small/medium-size vehicles. Regarding emissions distributions, it is due to consumer choice with respect to car size and fuel efficiency that average CO_2 emissions are lower in China and Japan, with the standard distribution of CO_2 emissions being much larger in China than in Japan.

Left axis shows distribution of CO_2 emission for conventional cars; right axis shows distribution of CO_2 emission for hybrid cars.

The FTT:Transport model

Theoretical background

As a member of the FTT family of models, FTT:Transport aims to simulate technology diffusion dynamically in the transport sector, based on a decision-making module that represents the choices of a diverse group of agents that face restricted information and access to technology for consumers.

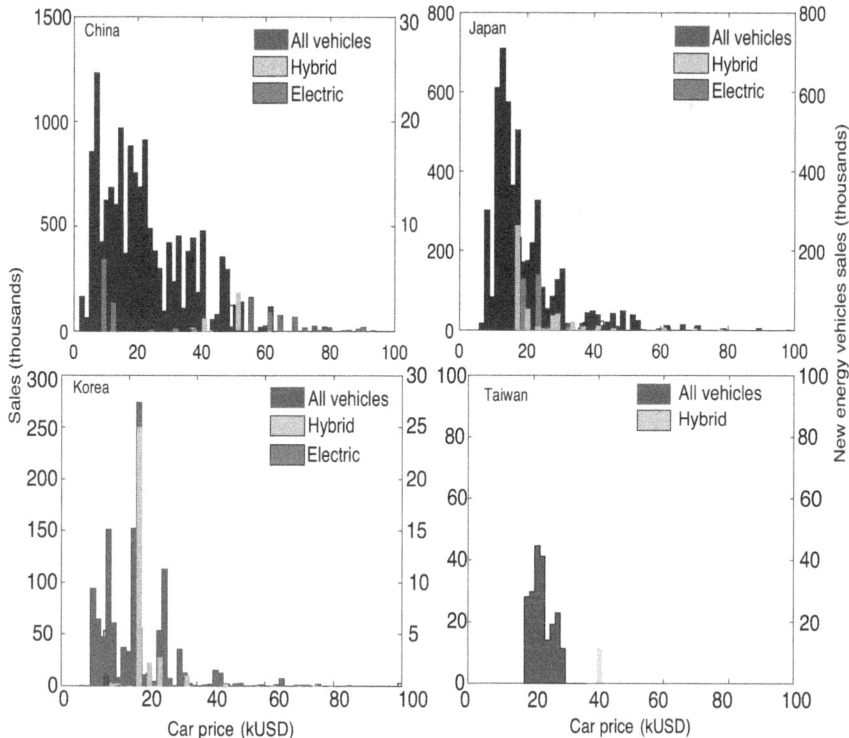

Figure 7.2 Price distributions in kUSD (thousand US$) of 2012 vehicle sales for the four East Asian countries. The left axis shows the car price distribution for conventional cars; the right axis shows the car price distribution for new energy vehicles, that is, hybrid and electric cars.

Source: Cambridge Econometrics

Similarly to the other FTT models, FTT:Transport assumes the presence of a diverse market with heterogeneous agents. This is done by using a probabilistic treatment of consumer decision making and by using a distribution of cost values. We assume that the cost distribution corresponds to the heterogeneity of consumer choices as a result of revealed preferences. The cost distributions are related to whether the consumers are early adopters, early majority, late majority or laggards, which drives the adoption and diffusion of technology as suggested by Rogers (2010). Agent heterogeneity and consumer choice are represented by introducing cost distributions over agent perspectives with the discrete choice theory.

As a result of increasing returns to adoption (Arthur, 1989), a technology can gain an increased market share as more consumers adopt and use it for the following reasons. First, people make choices according to what is fashionable or en vogue. For example, people like to behave in a 'socially desirable way' and may purchase low-emissions vehicles to boost their image within their own social groups (Liao, Molin, & van Wee, 2017). Second, many studies find that consumers have a 'wait and see' attitude (Chanaron, 1998) in choosing new technologies, in particular regarding new automobile technologies. This is because consumers are risk averse and new technologies, for example EVs, present uncertainty – for example, range anxiety, availability of charging stations – when users are inexperienced. Third, consumers may have a particular preference towards one range of car model (e.g. brand, engine size, style). If their preferences are not satisfied within the available EV models, the technology (e.g. EV) will not match the preference for this group of consumers. When new technologies become more popular with consumers, manufacturers are encouraged to boost the number of available models based on that technology, which will further boost sales of that technology. As we discuss in the next section, the FTT framework captures path dependence and effects of positive feedbacks in the diffusion process.

In summary, FTT:Transport shares many characteristics with the other FTT models. In FTT:Transport, however, the emphasis is on the range of preferences of different consumer groups. The following sections present an overview of the FTT:Transport model and its linkages to E3ME. The values for the initial parameters are presented in Appendix A.

Model structure and the Levelized Cost of Transport (LCOT)

Introduction

The basic equation structure in FTT:Transport is similar to that of the other FTT models. The technological diffusion rate is proportional to a comparison of cost distributions, equivalent to a binary logit model. In addition to quantifiable costs (e.g. capital cost, fuel tax), the model considers the non-quantifiable costs on consumer choices (e.g. comfort, luxury effect) by an arbitrary factor that is added to the quantifiable costs. A learning rate is incorporated to take into account the falling cost as production of the technology increases. Differences in cost distribution are important in facilitating future technological diffusion. The cost distributions correspond to population heterogeneity and drive technological diffusion.

The cost of the vehicle, as perceived by the investor purchasing a vehicle or unit of transport technology, must be taken into account, that is, must include all components relevant to decision making. Many of the components can be easily quantified by using available data. Others are not so straightforward, and we show later how this is done. When a vehicle is purchased, an initial investment is made, or a loan obtained, for the capital cost and, henceforth, fuel and maintenance costs are incurred for the lifetime of the technology, in addition to taxation.

Following this, the Levelized Cost of Transport (LCOT) after the introduction of policies is defined as:

$$LCOT_i = \sum_t \frac{I_i + VT_i + CT(\alpha_i) + FU_i(t)^* \, FT(\alpha_{i,}t) + MR_i + RT_i(t)}{(1+t)^t} \qquad (1)$$

where

- I_i is the capital cost of cars, in US\$/vehicle
- VT_i is a registration vehicle tax, in US\$/vehicle, paid at purchase time
- $CT\ (\alpha_i)$ is the carbon tax based on fuel economy α_i, in US\$/vehicle/(g CO_2/km)
- $FU_i\ (t)$ is the fuel consumption, in liter/vehicle
- $FT\ (\alpha_i,\ t)$ is a tax on fuel consumption, in US\$/liter
- MR_i is the vehicle maintenance costs in US\$/vehicle
- $RT_i\ (t)$ is a road tax in US\$/vehicle
- t is the time parameter, which is summed over the vehicle's lifetime

The generalized cost as a comparison measure

The costs of transportation are not the only elements of consumer decisions when purchasing a vehicle. Other aspects, such as infrastructure and car range, are valued by the consumer, but we cannot obtain this information without a large-scale survey We keep in mind that technologies have highly different pecuniary costs, particularly across engine-size classes. Despite this, higher costs can be compensated by higher benefits, such that higher-cost luxury vehicles maintain market shares.

Were we to simulate technology diffusion based on bare LCOT distribution comparisons, the lowest LCOT technologies would diffuse more successfully, which is not consistent with our historical data. Clearly, components would be missing in the LCOT – for instance, comfort, acceleration and style – that we may call the 'intangibles'. We define the intangibles for this model as the difference between the generalized cost, which leads to observed diffusion, and the LCOT as calculated from pecuniary vehicle properties, for which we have data. The value of the intangibles, denoted γ_i, is an empirical parameter that we obtain from making the FTT diffusion trajectory match the trajectory observed in our historical data, at the year of the start of the simulation.

Taking into account the intangibles, we assume that the choice of investors is made based on pairwise comparisons of general cost (C_i). For simplicity, we compare costs in lognormal space with a mean and a standard deviation with the following transformations:

$$C_i = \ln\left(\frac{LCOT_i^2}{\sqrt{LCOT_i^2 + \Delta LCOT_i^2}}\right) + \gamma_i \tag{2}$$

$$\Delta C_i = \sqrt{\ln\left(1 + \frac{\Delta LCOT_i^2}{LCOT_i^2}\right)} \tag{3}$$

The determination of intangibles (γ)

As just noted, the technological diffusion rate is proportional to a comparison of cost distributions, equivalent to a binary logit model. The parameter γ represents all unknown constant, non-pecuniary cost components (i.e. all costs and benefits not already explicitly included). This parameter has the unique value set that makes the diffusion rate continuous across the transition from historical data to simulated data at the start of the simulation (i.e. keeping the existing diffusion trends). To illustrate this, when $\gamma_i = 0$, we obtain a rate of diffusion that does not normally match historical diffusion (Figure 7.3). We conclude that realistic modelling requires a representation of the non-financial factors.

We perform an exercise that determines the sensitivity of our simulation results to the variation of γ (see the sensitivity analysis in Appendix B of this chapter).

Technology learning

As in the other FTT models, learning rates are applied based on cumulated production. The same caveats apply for new technologies (Anandarajah, McDowall, & Ekins, 2013; Weiss et al., 2012) and the potential for learning rates to change over

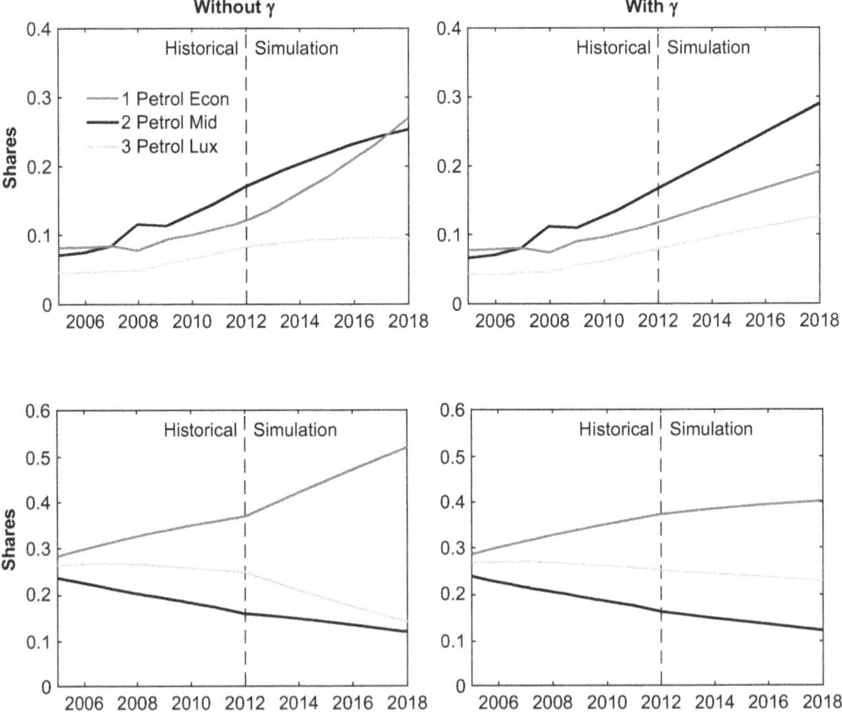

Figure 7.3 Graphical representation of γ

Source: Cambridge Econometrics

Note: The dashed line in each panel separates historical (left) and projected (right) market shares for petrol cars, without and with γ as indicated time (Sagar & van der Zwaan, 2006). This is particularly relevant for the personal transport sector, where a relatively new technology (EVs) will need to dominate if emissions are to be reduced substantially.

To account for the uncertainties regarding learning rates, a sensitivity analysis is presented in Appendix B. There we examine the extent to which the difference in learning rate creates uncertainties for the model (see also Lam et al., 2018).

Energy consumption and emissions

The total service generated by a particular technology is equal to the product of transport demand in passenger-kilometers (pkm) and the transport capacity of the technology, defined as the number of seats in cars. Thus, we have:

$$G_i = U_i * CF_i \tag{4}$$

$$G_i = U_i CF_i$$

where G_i is the service generated by a transport technology (in pkm/year).

Energy consumption is calculated from fuel consumption per kilometer and the services the vehicles provide, considering the filling factor FF_k,

$$J_{k,t} = G_{k,t} * EG_{k,t} / \left(FF_k * N_{seats}\right) \tag{5}$$

where N_{seats} is the number of seats in cars (i.e. N_{seats} = 4 in most cases), $J_{k,t}$ is energy consumption in Megajoules/year, $EG_{k,t}$ is the energy consumption factor in MJ/seat-km, calculated by a fuel economy factor multiplied by energy density for gasoline/diesel/ethanol. CO_2 emissions from passenger vehicles are closely related to energy consumption. Emissions are defined as:

$$E_{k,t} = G_{k,t} * CO_{2k,t} / (FF_k * N_{seats}) \tag{6}$$

where $E_{k,t}$ is the fleet emissions in Gt/yr and $CO_{2k,t}$ is the emissions factor.

Linkages between FTT:Transport and E3ME

The dynamic interactions between the FTT:Transport model and the E3ME model are shown in Figure 7.4. Vehicle purchase decisions are affected by four components, including consumer preference, government policies, market environment and the car model's availability. Each of the components leads to a dynamic change of market share in FTT:Transport.

Transport demand is calculated within the E3ME model by regressing total vehicle use (in km/year) with respect to fuel prices and income, and these values are projected to 2050, using fuel prices and income endogenously determined by E3ME. The number of cars is regressed against income and average vehicle prices, and constrained by population.

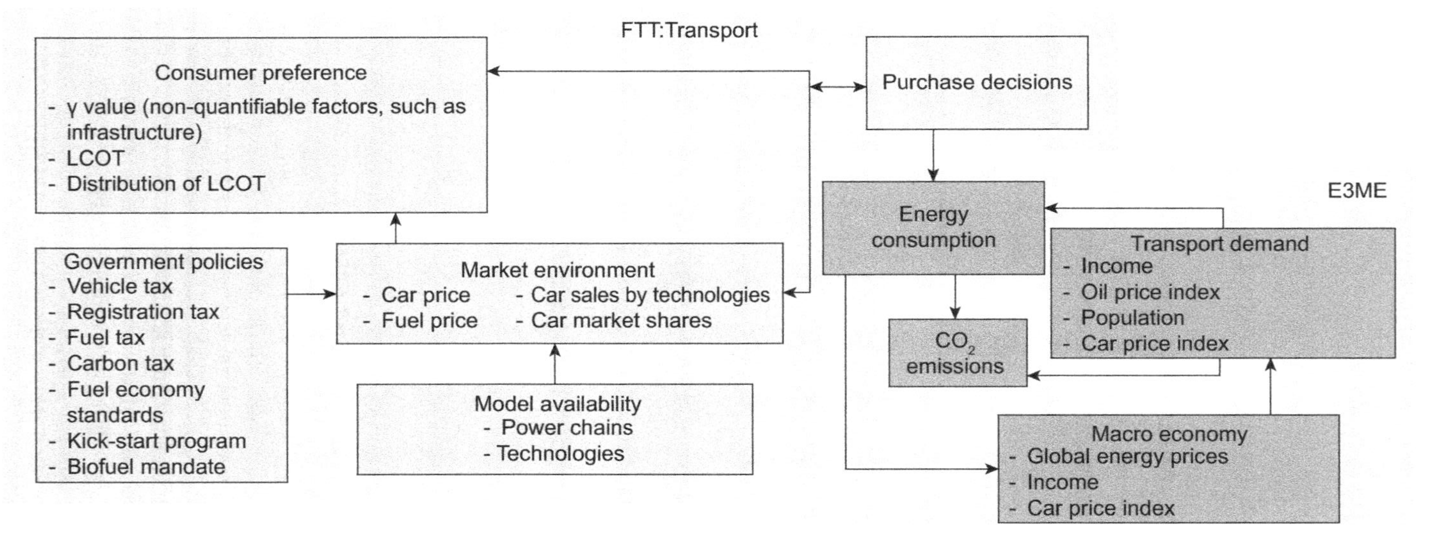

Figure 7.4 Structure of E3ME-FTT:Transport model

Source: Cambridge Econometrics

Policy assumptions

We have assessed four decarbonization scenarios that combine taxes and vehicle technology kick-start programs. The definitions of the policy incentives is provided in Table 7.5. The quantification of each policy is based on current or proposed policy in each country (see Table 7.6).

The baseline scenario makes projections based on the current policy framework. It is the benchmark scenario against which the other scenarios are compared. Scenario 2 assumes that tax incentives are combined with a more stringent kick-start program (assuming that 5% of car production is EVs). Scenario 3 assumes that a more stringent kick-start program (8% of car production is EVs) is added on top of the taxes. The scenario explores the effectiveness of the policy incentives to cut emissions from private passenger vehicles and demonstrates the extent to which different policy stringencies and kick-start programs will lead to significant emissions reductions.

Notice that the tax incentive assumptions and subsidies are higher than the level of existing policy incentives in East Asian countries. A kick-start program is assumed in every scenario to take into account current non-monetary programs (e.g. EV car sharing, EV license plate auctions) that have been introduced at a national level to encourage the diffusion of EVs.

Table 7.5 Definitions of policy incentives

Policy incentives	*Model representation*	*Examples of the real-world policy*
Registration tax	As a vehicle tax, this is a tax on expected (not yet emitted) CO_2 emissions. The tax is proportional to fuel economy in the unit of US\$/(g CO_2/km). It is added to the annual costs summed to get the LCOT.	Acquisition tax based on fuel economy road tax
Fuel tax	Added to the fuel cost. As a vehicle tax, this is a tax on expected (not yet emitted) CO_2 emissions. The tax is proportional to fuel economy in the unit of US\$/(g CO_2/km).	Fuel tax (e.g. petrol tax, diesel tax); acquisition tax based on fuel economy
Biofuel mandate	Biofuel as a certain percentage of liquid fuels is added to fuel cost.	Biofuel mandate
Fuel economy regulation	The sale of lower-efficiency liquid-fuel vehicles is banned.	Fuel economy standards
Kick-start program	A certain percentage of EVs are bought (e.g. by public or private institutions) as a policy or strategy.	Government-financed purchases
EV subsidies	EVs are financially subsidized by the public sector.	Variable taxation schemes

Table 7.6 Assumption of policy scenarios for China, Japan, Korea and Taiwan

	EV subsidies (USD)	*Fuel tax (USD/liter)*	*Carbon tax (USD/(t CO_2)*	*Kick-start program*	*Biofuel mandate*
Baseline scenario	Current subsidy of each country	Current fuel tax of each country	0	0	0
Scenario 1	+1000	+0.1	20	3%	0
Scenario 2	+2000	+0.2	50	5%	5%
Scenario 3	+3000	+0.3	100	8%	10%

Results

China

In the baseline scenario (S0), we find that the fleet share for EVs increases very slowly and does not reach 10% by 2050 (Figure 7.5). In Scenario 1 (S1), we assume that a carbon tax is increased by US\$20/tCO_2 and the fuel tax is increased by US\$0.1/liter. We assume that the subsidy for EVs is increased by up to US\$1,000.

To cut emissions significantly and to encourage the diffusion of EVs, we must impose both tax incentives, that is, regulations and a stronger kick-start program, to facilitate the diffusion of zero-emission vehicles. In Scenario 3 (S3), we assume that there are an additional one million EVs on the road by 2020 (fleet share = 0.8%), as a result of various kick-start programs (e.g. car-sharing programs, license plate auctions, public EV mandates). Scenario 3 shows a decrease in passenger car emissions as a result of a stronger kick start program. The share of EVs is more than 70% by 2050 and emissions peak around 2030, before falling to the level seen in 2005 by 2050 (see Figure 7.5).

Japan

We find that in the baseline scenario (S0) passenger car emissions in Japan fall by more than 40%, below the 2005 level, without any additional policy incentives. This is due to the diffusion of hybrid cars in Japan (see Figure 7.5).

In Scenario 2 (column 3), we assume that the carbon tax rate is increased by US\$20/tCO_2 and fuel tax by up to US\$0.1/liter. The EV rebate is increased by ~US\$1,000 per vehicle (for up to eight years). As a result of the tax incentives and EV subsidies, the share of EVs in Japan reaches 30% by 2050.

To cut passenger car emissions further (by more than 50% below the levels of 2005), we assume that, compared with the base year 2012, 450,000 EVs are on the road by 2020. This is the result of various kick-start programs (e.g. increasing

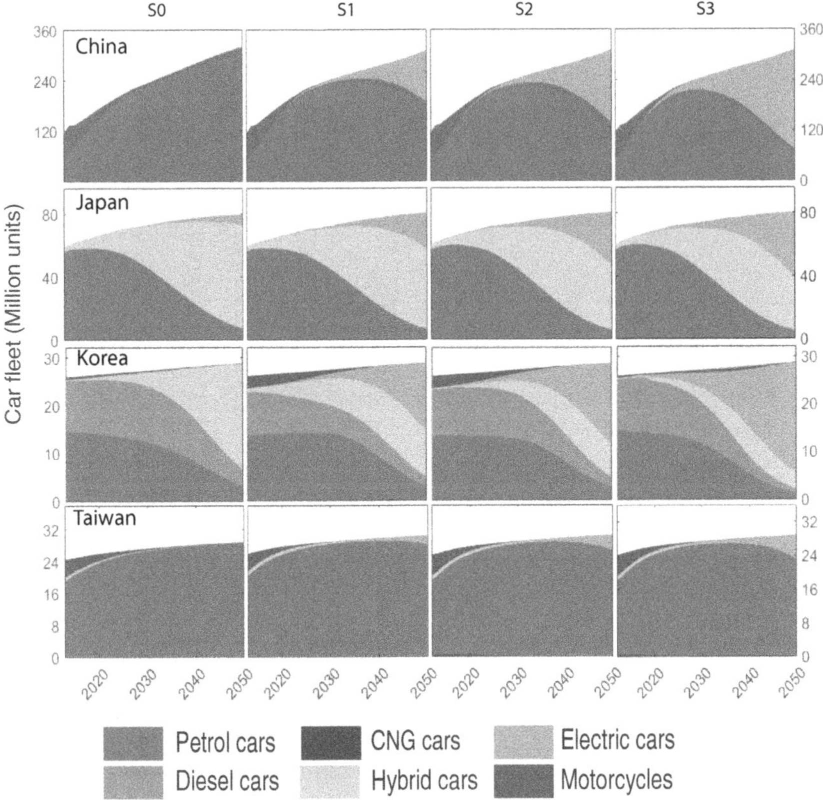

Figure 7.5 Demand of passenger transport (in Mpkm/year) according to different types of passenger vehicle in the four East Asian countries under the baseline (S0) and three policy scenarios (S1–3)

Source: Estimated by Cambridge Econometrics for this study

the number of charging stations, EV car-sharing). The fleet share for EVs increases by a further 10% by 2050, reaching 35%. Emissions are reduced by nearly 60% in Scenario 3, which is below the 2005 level (Figure 7.6).

Korea

In the baseline scenario (S0), luxury diesel cars and gasoline cars have a large market share until 2030 (see Figure 7.5). After 2030, luxury hybrid cars start to take off, and reach more than a 60% market share by 2050. Emissions continue to decrease in the baseline, as a result of the decreasing number of vehicles and the penetration of EVs in Korea (see Figure 7.6).

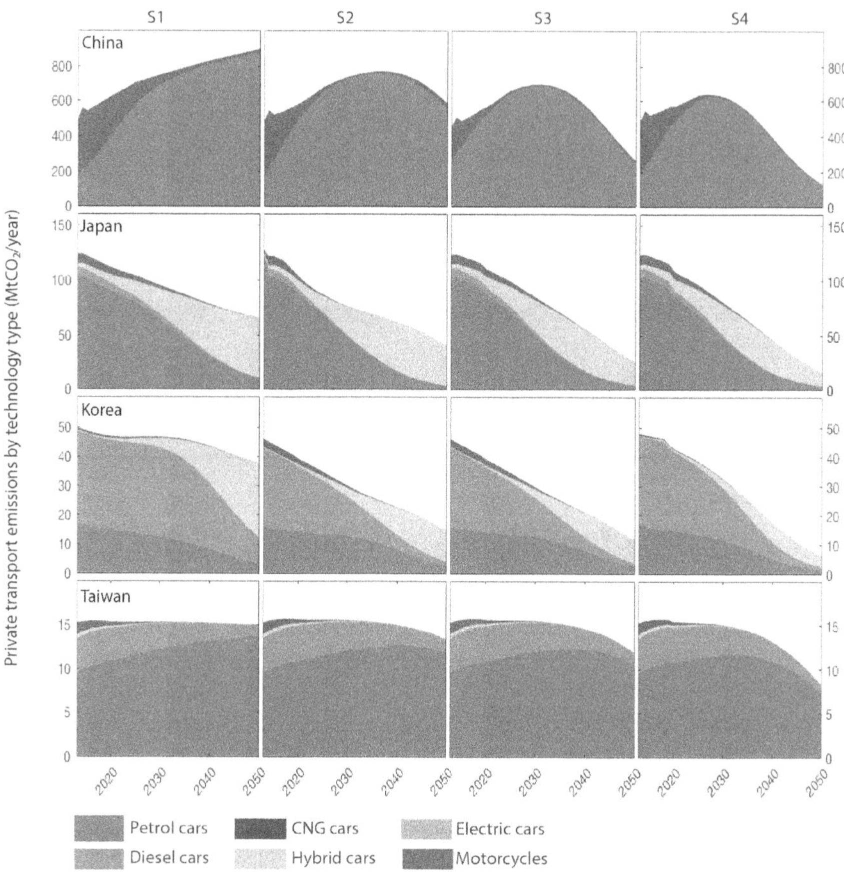

Figure 7.6 Emissions (in Mt CO_2/year) of private passenger vehicles in the four East Asian countries under the baseline (S0) and three policy scenarios (S1–3)

Source: Estimated by Cambridge Econometrics for this study

In Scenario 1 (S1), consistent with other countries, we assume an increase in the fuel tax of US\$0.1/liter and an increase in carbon tax by up to US\$100/tCO_2 for gasoline cars. We assume an additional subsidy that supports EVs, amounting to US\$2,000 for luxury EVs. As a result of the policy incentives, emissions are reduced by more than 60% below the 2005 level (see Figure 7.6).

To increase the rate of diffusion of EVs in Korea, we assume that the number of EVs increases by 190,000 in 2020 as a result of a kick-start program in S2. As shown in Figure 7.5, the share of EVs reaches nearly 50% by 2050. As a result, emissions fall by 80% below the levels of 2005 (see Figure 7.6). To cut emissions further, we assume that the kick-start program is stronger in Korea, reaching 8% by 2050. In Scenario 3, emissions fall by nearly 90% below the levels of 2005 (see Figure 7.6), as a result of strong policy incentives.

Taiwan

In contrast to Japan and Korea, the baseline shares for hybrid cars and EVs remain very small in Taiwan. The small shares in new energy technologies result in a very small fall in passenger vehicle emissions and energy consumption in the baseline (see Figure. 7.5).

When various tax incentives are taken into account (see Table 7.6, S1), we observe emissions falling slightly by ~5% below the levels of 2005 (see Figure 7.6). To cut emissions by 30% below those of 2005, it is necessary to introduce more zero-emission vehicles in Taiwan. In Scenario 2, we assume that there would be an additional 10,000 EVs (compared with 2012 levels) in Taiwan. To cut emissions a further 20% in Taiwan, in Scenario 3 we assume that 5% of the car fleet in Taiwan comprises EVs (Figure 7.6).

Policy implications and conclusions

The decarbonization of the private passenger vehicles sector plays an important role in increasing our chance of staying within the target level of 2°C set out in the Paris Agreement. In this chapter, we assessed a baseline and three scenarios that examine the interactive effect of transportation policy incentives on emissions from private passenger vehicles in East Asia. For all four countries, we find that an integrated approach of tax incentives, subsidies and kick-start programs yields the most significant emission reductions, primarily by allowing the diffusion of EVs. We can conclude that, in addition to taxes on conventional cars and subsidies for EVs, it is important to introduce non-monetary measures to increase the rate of diffusion for zero-emissions vehicles.

We have found that in the case of China, in the baseline case EVs do not gain a significant market share by 2050 without policy incentives. However, an integrated approach (i.e. a combination of tax incentives, subsidies and kick-start programs) will lead to a more than 50% share of EVs in China by 2050. We note that, in reality – in addition to EV subsidies and taxes on gasoline cars – some kick-start programs have already been introduced to increase the rate of EV diffusion in China.

For Japan, it is possible to achieve a reduction of more than 40% in emissions (compared with 2005 levels) without any new policy incentives. Emissions from passenger vehicles can be reduced further by increasing the EV rebate and by introducing kick-start programs. With 300,000 EVs on the road by 2021 (compared with their numbers at the 2012 level), it is possible to achieve a more than 80% reduction in emissions compared with the levels in 2005.

Similarly, for Korea we find that tax incentives are not sufficient to cut emissions significantly beyond the baseline. The diffusion of hybrid cars in Korea will not lead to significant emissions reductions because of an increase in the total number of cars. To cut emissions by more than 50% below the 2005 level, it is important to encourage the diffusion of EVs in Korea by a kick-start program that increases the number of EVs by ~120,000 (compared with that of 2012) by 2020. This is necessary, as there is a lack of policy incentives and charging infrastructure in Korea.

In the case of Taiwan, without a kick-start program and fuel economy regulation, emissions from passenger cars will not be reduced significantly. Owing to the existing small number of EVs and hybrid cars in Taiwan, we imply from the scenario analysis that a diffusion of new vehicle technology is slow compared with that in the other three Asian countries. To increase the rate of diffusion, it is necessary to introduce kick-start programs.

A main barrier to introducing taxes, regulations and the kick-start program is the cost of the policies to the government, the car manufacturers and car owners. The true cost/benefit of policy incentives is difficult to estimate, given that the disruptive impact of new energy vehicles on the economy and on the car manufacturers is unclear. For example, whereas the introduction of new energy vehicles potentially creates new employment, some car manufactures might be unable to compete in the new market conditions. Although we have not estimated the direct economic impact of the policy measures in this chapter, we cover them within the economy-wide modelling described in Chapter 5.

Like all modelling studies, we recognize the limitations to our approach to model future technological changes and emissions from cars. The three main limitations are:

1 In this chapter, we have identified currently available technologies, although new technologies will emerge in the future. However, it is impossible for the model to predict technologies that have not yet penetrated the market as, for example, fuel-cell vehicles.
2 The non-pecuniary cost is represented by the γ parameter, which is found by calculating the difference between the actual and predicted market shares. Our projections from 2012 to 2020 follow the trend from 2004 to 2012. However, γ parameters for EVs in Taiwan and Korea may carry a degree of uncertainty because our basis to determine the γ parameter is insufficient, as it is based on the fact that there is currently a limited number of EVs on the road.
3 Autonomous vehicles (AVs) represent a disruptive technology that will potentially affect vehicle size and transport demand for passenger cars.

In addition, there are several parametric uncertainties for the E3ME-FTT:Transport model. We take into consideration the possible consequences of these assumptions and perform a sensitivity analysis to determine the effects of any potential changes to the learning rate, the γ_i values, the discount rates used and the fuel prices, on the final results. The sensitivity analysis provides insight into the effects of uncertainties on our projections.

In Appendix B, we allow our chosen parameters to vary between 5% and 20%. The effect of the parametric uncertainties on the market shares and emissions projections depends on the scenario assumptions and the technology mix in each country. For example, the effect of the technology learning rate is more prominent as the share of EVs increase. We observe that certain parameters, such as fuel prices and discount rates, may have a larger effect on technology shares and emissions than other parameters, such as EV learning rates. This is because learning rates only impact on total emissions through variations in EV shares, whereas a rise or fall in oil prices dynamically affects the choice of vehicle. We find that the uncertainties in γ_i values have an overall small impact on the final results. Overall, the changes in market shares and emissions – as a result of the variations in parameters – are within 20%. Given our underlying assumptions, the results can, therefore, be considered robust.

Appendix A
Initial parameters

Tables A1, A2, A3 and A4 show the values of the parameters assumed in the model for China, Japan, Korea and Taiwan, respectively. Car prices, engine sizes and fuel economy data for each car model listed in MarkLines[6] were collected from various sources, including car manufacturers, car sales websites, car industry market reports and government institutions, matched to the car models listed in the MarkLines data. Notice that the prices obtained are the listed price of 2013, when the data were collected. Car fuel economy data were collected from the manufacturers' websites when available. In many cases, each car model has several car prices and fuel economy values, depending on vehicle options for one model. We usually took the mid-value for prices and engine sizes, unless it is known to us that a particular vehicle option/alternative is very popular. To ensure the reliability of the data outside the manufacturer's website, we checked prices, engine sizes and fuel economy data from these car sales, research websites and government institutions against the data obtained from the manufacturers.

The learning rate and the discount rate are subject to some degree of uncertainty. To account for the uncertainties regarding learning rates, a sensitivity analysis is presented in Appendix B, where we examine the extent to which the difference in learning rate creates uncertainties for the model.

Table A1 Initial parameters assumed for China

Technology	*Engine size*	*Prices of cars (USD/vehicle)*	*Standard deviation of price (USD/vehicle)*	*Fuel cost (USD/km)*	*Discount rate*	*Energy use (MJ/vkm)*	*Learning rate*
Petrol	Econ	9400.00	6249.00	0.07	0.15	2.05	1%
	Mid	21036.00	12005.00	0.08	0.15	2.26	1%
	Lux	40667.00	20083.00	0.10	0.15	2.74	1%
Adv Petrol	Econ	9400.00	6249.00	0.05	0.15	1.64	5%
	Mid	21036.00	12005.00	0.06	0.15	1.81	5%
	Lux	40667.00	20083.00	0.08	0.15	2.19	5%
Diesel	Econ	9400.00	1000.00	0.05	0.15	1.85	1%
	Mid	22000.00	5631.20	0.06	0.15	2.12	1%
	Lux	40300.00	4404.40	0.07	0.15	2.40	1%
Adv Diesel	Econ	9400.00	1000.00	0.04	0.15	2.95	5%
	Mid	22000.00	5631.20	0.05	0.15	1.70	5%
	Lux	40300.00	4404.40	0.06	0.15	1.92	5%
CNG	Econ	9635.00	1965.00	0.04	0.15	1.50	1%
	Mid	13953.00	2654.00	0.05	0.15	1.70	1%
	Lux	33710.00	2654.00	0.06	0.15	2.09	1%
Hybrid	Econ	31252.91	1654.00	0.02	0.15	0.68	5%
	Mid	41018.00	1654.00	0.02	0.15	0.85	5%
	Lux	47584.00	1571.00	0.02	0.15	0.92	5%
Electric	Econ	13250.00	3127.62	0.00	0.15	0.54	10%
	Mid	27072.75	4372.41	0.00	0.15	0.76	10%
	Lux	42423.52	1492.71	0.00	0.15	0.94	10%
Bikes	Econ	1373.00	1859.00	0.02	0.15	0.72	1%
	Lux	4989.00	3031.00	0.05	0.15	1.44	1%
Adv Bikes	Adv Econ	1373.00	1859.00	0.00	0.15	0.00	5%
	Adv Lux	4989.00	3031.00	0.00	0.15	0.00	5%

Note: 'Econ' denotes cars with engine sizes smaller or equal to 1400cc. 'Mid' denotes cars with engine sizes larger than 1400cc and smaller than 2000cc. 'Lux' denotes cars with engine sizes larger than 2000cc.

N/A indicates that data are not available or the car technology is not widely used in the country.
'Adv' indicates cars with advanced/more efficient engines.

Table A2 Initial parameters assumed for Japan

Technology	*Engine size*	*Prices of cars (USD/vehicle)*	*Standard deviation of price (USD/vehicle)*	*Fuel cost (USD/km)*	*Discount rate*	*Energy use (MJ/vkm)*	*Learning rate*
Petrol	Econ	12973.05	4044.80	0.064	0.150	2.052	1%
	Mid	22197.47	9597.81	0.068	0.150	2.260	1%
	Lux	31879.83	17485.23	0.077	0.150	2.740	1%
Adv Petrol	Econ	12973.05	4044.80	0.051	0.150	1.642	5%
	Mid	22197.47	9597.81	0.054	0.150	1.808	5%
	Lux	31879.83	17485.23	0.061	0.150	2.192	5%
Diesel	Econ	N/A	N/A	N/A	N/A	N/A	N/A
	Mid	N/A	N/A	N/A	N/A	N/A	N/A
	Lux	N/A	N/A	N/A	N/A	N/A	N/A
Adv Diesel	Econ	N/A	N/A	N/A	N/A	N/A	N/A
	Mid	N/A	N/A	N/A	N/A	N/A	N/A
	Lux	N/A	N/A	N/A	N/A	N/A	N/A
CNG	Econ	N/A	N/A	N/A	N/A	N/A	N/A
	Mid	N/A	N/A	N/A	N/A	N/A	N/A
	Lux	27472.00	0.00	0.070	0.150	2.093	1%
Hybrid	Econ	27547.72	836.16	0.023	0.150	0.684	5%
	Mid	31488.10	5548.62	0.028	0.150	0.848	5%
	Lux	40417.93	17197.10	0.031	0.150	0.923	5%
Electric	Econ	12448.00	1300.00	0.000	0.150	0.540	10%
	Mid	16841.40	2592.98	0.000	0.150	0.756	10%
	Lux	28407.61	2647.72	0.000	0.150	0.936	10%
Bikes	Econ	4516.00	2292.00	0.046	0.150	0.720	1%
	Lux	12357.00	4541.00	0.057	0.150	1.440	1%
Adv Bikes	Adv Econ	4516.00	2292.00	0.037	0.150	0.000	5%
	Adv Lux	12357.00	4541.00	0.046	0.150	0.000	5%

Note: 'Econ' denotes cars with engine sizes smaller or equal to 1400cc. 'Mid' denotes cars with engine sizes larger than 1400cc and smaller than 2000cc. 'Lux' denotes cars with engine sizes larger than 2000cc.

'N/A' indicates that data are not available or the car technology is not widely used in the country.
'Adv' indicates cars with advanced/more efficient engines.

Table A3 Initial parameters assumed for Korea

Technology	*Engine size*	*Prices of cars (USD/vehicle)*	*Standard deviation of price (USD/vehicle)*	*Fuel cost (USD/km)*	*Discount rate*	*Energy use (MJ/vkm)*	*Learning rate*
Petrol	Econ	17842.45	30920.21	0.079	0.15	2.05	1%
	Mid	19342.74	5601.90	0.103	0.15	2.26	1%
	Lux	38942.42	29216.44	0.139	0.15	2.74	1%
Adv Petrol	Econ	17842.45	30920.21	0.045	0.15	1.64	5%
	Mid	19342.74	5601.90	0.059	0.15	1.81	5%
	Lux	38942.42	29216.44	0.079	0.15	2.19	5%
Diesel	Econ	N/A	N/A	N/A	N/A	N/A	N/A
	Mid	22294.36	10372.06	0.078	0.15	2.12	1%
	Lux	29919.85	15199.82	0.093	0.15	2.40	1%
Adv Diesel	Econ	N/A	N/A	N/A	N/A	N/A	N/A
	Mid	22294.36	10372.06	0.042	0.15	1.70	5%
	Lux	29919.85	15199.82	0.050	0.15	1.92	5%
CNG	Econ	N/A	N/A	N/A	N/A	N/A	N/A
	Mid	N/A	N/A	N/A	N/A	N/A	N/A
	Lux	N/A	N/A	N/A	N/A	N/A	N/A
Hybrid	Econ	23080.00	1000.00	0.040	0.15	0.68	5%
	Mid	30655.62	3111.79	0.052	0.15	0.85	5%
	Lux	35031.11	10048.45	0.103	0.15	0.92	5%
Electric	Econ	10455.00	1000.00	0.004	0.15	0.67	10%
	Mid	12272.00	100.00	0.005	0.15	0.81	10%
	Lux	30460.00	1000.00	0.008	0.15	0.93	10%
Bikes	Econ	2071.00	831.00	0.026	0.15	0.72	1%
	Lux	6306.00	2366.00	0.032	0.15	1.44	1%
Adv Bikes	Adv Econ	2071.00	831.00	0.026	0.15	0.00	5%
	Adv Lux	6306.00	2366.00	0.032	0.15	0.00	5%

Note: ‘Econ’ denotes cars with engine sizes smaller or equal to 1400cc. ‘Mid’ denotes cars with engine sizes larger than 1400cc and smaller than 2000cc. ‘Lux’ denotes cars with engine sizes larger than 2000cc.

‘N/A’ indicates that data are not available or the car technology is not widely used in the country.
‘Adv’ indicates cars with advanced/more efficient engines.

Table A4 Initial parameters assumed for Taiwan

Technology	*Engine size*	*Prices of cars (USD/vehicle)*	*Standard deviation of price (USD/vehicle)*	*Fuel cost (USD/km)*	*Discount rate*	*Energy use (MJ/vkm)*	*Learning rate*
Petrol	Econ	12936.18	2872.35	0.068	0.15	1.98	0.01
	Mid	21320.53	3746.18	0.069	0.15	2.02	0.01
	Lux	27991.15	15787.11	0.095	0.15	2.77	0.01
Adv Petrol	Econ	15523.41	2872.35	0.061	0.15	1.59	0.05
	Mid	25584.64	3746.18	0.062	0.15	1.61	0.05
	Lux	33589.37	15787.11	0.085	0.15	2.22	0.05
Diesel	Econ	N/A	N/A	N/A	N/A	N/A	N/A
	Mid	N/A	N/A	N/A	N/A	N/A	N/A
	Lux	33589.37	15787.11	0.072	0.15	2.53	0.01
Adv Diesel	Econ	N/A	N/A	N/A	N/A	N/A	N/A
	Mid	N/A	N/A	N/A	N/A	N/A	N/A
	Lux	33589.37	15787.11	0.065	0.15	2.02	0.05
CNG	Econ	N/A	N/A	N/A	N/A	N/A	N/A
	Mid	N/A	N/A	N/A	N/A	N/A	N/A
	Lux	N/A	N/A	N/A	N/A	N/A	N/A
Hybrid	Econ	19513.46	2913.99	0.046	0.15	1.34	0.05
	Mid	22734.51	4844.60	0.057	0.15	1.67	0.05
	Lux	45303.10	13194.43	0.068	0.15	2.00	0.05
Electric	Econ	18984.94	190.13	0.000	0.15	0.21	0.1
	Mid	31287.74	1529.99	0.000	0.15	0.54	0.1
	Lux	40650.00	2080.00	0.000	0.15	0.58	0.1
Bikes	Econ	4516.00	2292.00	0.025	0.15	0.53	0.01
	Lux	12357.00	4541.00	0.026	0.15	0.77	0.01
Adv Bikes	Adv Econ	4516.00	2292.00	0.000	0.15	0.53	0.05
	Adv Lux	12357.00	4541.00	0.000	0.15	0.77	0.05

Note: 'Econ' denotes cars with engine sizes smaller or equal to 1400cc. 'Mid' denotes cars with engine sizes larger than 1400cc and smaller than 2000cc. 'Lux' denotes cars with engine sizes larger than 2000cc.

'N/A' indicates that data are not available or the car technology is not widely used in the country.
'Adv' indicates cars with advanced/more efficient engines.

Appendix B
Sensitivity analysis

In this section, we carry out a sensitivity analysis over most relevant technological parameters of FTT:Transport, including the discount rate, the learning rate, the γ factor and the fuel prices. These parameters were chosen because they would generate the most changes in emissions and technological shares.

The parameters varied are as follows:

1 Learning rates for the EVs. We did not vary the learning rate for conventional petrol and diesel cars because the learning for the mature technologies is insignificant.
2 Consumer discount rates.
3 All γ_i values simultaneously (for all vehicle types).
4 Fuel prices.

The variation used is between 5% and 20%, depending on the parameters (see Tables B1–B4). The uncertainty range was chosen based on existing literature (discount rate, learning rate) or variations that we consider as reasonable (the γ_i values).

Sensitivity analysis was carried out for all the scenarios because policies constrain the direction of model evolution. Thus, one should not expect to find the same response for all scenarios.

It is important to analyze model responses to a variation of key parameters, to ensure that the model is not 'highly sensitive' to very specific values for any particular parameter. As a benchmark, if the outcome variation is less than the input variation, we assumed here that the model is not 'highly sensitive' to the particular values chosen.

Tables B1, B2 and B3 show the results for the sensitivity analysis for the four scenarios. The tables show the change of emissions or market shares (in %) as a result of change in the values of the parameters.

We conclude this analysis with the following broad findings: (1) the effect of learning rates, discount rates, γ_i values and fuel prices varies among countries and scenarios and (2) learning rates, discount rates and fuel prices have a relatively larger impact on results (changes in outcomes much larger than changes in the parameters) than γ_i values. Overall, the changes in market shares and emissions as a result of the variations in parameter are within 20%.

Table B1 Sensitivity analysis on key technological parameters in the baseline scenario

Country	*Variation of key parameters (in %)*	*Emissions (%)*	*Technology shares (in %)*					
		CO_2	*Petrol car*	*Diesel car*	*Hybrid*	*CNG*	*EV*	*Motorcycles*
China	Learning rate +5	–2.10	–2.48	–1.04	1.20	0.00	2.32	0.00
	Learning rate –5	3.90	6.10	0.12	0.00	0.00	-6.22	0.00
	Discount rate +10	1.80	1.38	0.00	–1.04	2.45	–2.80	0.00
	Discount rate –10	-3.74	-2.35	-0.82	8.13	-8.69	3.74	–0.34
	All γ values +20	2.90	2.00	0.00	0.10	–1.40	–0.70	0.00
	All γ values –20	1.40	1.20	0.00	0.00	–0.85	–0.35	0.00
	Fuel price +20	–5.90	-6.61	-0.01	3.07	3.40	–0.55	0.70
	Fuel price –20	3.78	4.98	0.02	0.80	-4.95	–0.60	–0.25
Japan	Learning rate +5	-3.45	-4.67	0.00	3.57	0.00	1.10	0.00
	Learning rate –5	0.95	2.00	0.00	-0.45	0.00	-1.55	0.00
	Discount rate +10	4.52	2.90	0.00	-2.40	0.00	–0.50	0.00
	Discount rate –10	-3.56	-3.10	0.00	2.10	0.00	1.00	0.00
	All γ values +20	-2.22	-2.37	0.00	2.39	0.00	–0.02	0.00
	All γ values –20	0.02	0.01	0.00	-0.02	0.00	0.00	0.00
	Fuel price +20	-3.22	–2.03	0.00	2.03	0.00	0.00	0.00
	Fuel price –20	3.31	3.77	0.00	-3.55	0.00	–0.22	0.00

Korea	Learning rate +5	–4.52	–5.60	0.00	4.64	0.00	0.97	0.00
	Learning rate –5	2.34	2.76	–0.30	–2.27	0.00	–0.19	0.00
	Discount rate +10	4.80	3.60	–2.00	–1.70	0.00	–0.50	0.60
	Discount rate –10	–3.20	2.92	0.00	–3.74	0.00	0.82	0.00
	All γ values +20	0.02	0.00	0.00	0.01	0.00	0.00	0.00
	All γ values –20	0.05	0.00	–0.01	0.00	0.00	0.00	0.01
	Fuel price +20	–0.31	–0.11	0.00	0.00	0.00	–0.06	0.17
	Fuel price –20	0.22	0.12	0.00	0.00	0.00	–0.06	–0.06
Taiwan	Learning rate +5	–0.02	–0.01	0.00	0.00	0.00	0.00	0.00
	Learning rate –5	0.01	0.00	0.00	0.00	0.00	0.00	0.00
	Discount rate +10	1.20	–1.10	0.00	0.00	0.00	0.00	1.10
	Discount rate –10	–0.49	–0.41	0.55	0.00	0.00	0.00	–0.14
	All γ values +20	0.00	–0.25	0.00	0.00	0.00	0.00	0.25
	All γ values –20	–0.57	0.07	0.07	0.00	0.00	0.00	–0.14
	Fuel price +20	–5.21	–6.00	0.00	0.54	0.00	1.76	3.70
	Fuel price –20	8.54	4.17	0.00	1.21	0.00	–1.61	–3.77

Note: Each number refers to a percentage change in either CO_2 emission or technology share (share of total fleet). Variations used are considered as realistic uncertainty values. Changes in rates are percentage point changes. Outcome changes on emissions are a cumulation until 2050, whereas for shares, values are for 2050.

Table B2 Sensitivity analysis on key technological parameters in Scenario 1

Country	*Variation of key parameters (in %)*	*Emissions (%)*	*Technology shares (in %)*					
		CO_2	*Petrol car*	*Diesel car*	*Hybrid*	*CNG*	*EV*	*Motorcycles*
China	Learning rate +5	–1.64	–3.16	0.00	0.16	0.00	2.99	0.00
	Learning rate –5	1.54	2.74	0.00	0.00	0.00	–2.73	0.00
	Discount rate +10	3.98	2.15	0.01	–1.62	3.81	–4.35	0.00
	Discount rate –10	–4.10	–2.08	–1.00	1.74	–2.84	4.55	–0.37
	All γ values +20	1.85	1.88	0.00	0.09	–1.32	–0.68	0.02
	All γ values –20	1.10	1.35	0.00	0.00	–0.95	–0.47	0.08
	Fuel price +20	–1.74	–1.50	0.00	0.02	0.00	1.06	0.42
	Fuel price –20	1.98	1.83	0.00	–0.02	0.00	–1.65	–0.15
Japan	Learning rate +5	–3.70	–3.99	0.00	3.05	0.00	0.94	0.00
	Learning rate –5	1.90	1.71	0.00	–0.40	0.00	–1.31	0.00
	Discount rate +10	3.80	4.20	0.00	–3.70	0.00	–0.50	0.00
	Discount rate –10	–1.42	–1.66	0.00	1.90	0.00	–0.24	0.00
	All γ values +20	–0.44	–0.38	0.00	2.12	0.00	–1.74	0.00
	All γ values –20	0.55	1.37	0.00	0.00	0.00	–1.37	0.00
	Fuel price +20	–5.86	–1.26	0.00	7.00	0.00	–5.74	0.00
	Fuel price –20	6.90	7.28	0.00	–4.20	0.00	–3.08	0.00

Korea	Learning rate +5	−1.85	−8.06	−0.21	6.53	0.00	1.83	0.00
	Learning rate −5	3.61	3.35	0.02	−2.65	0.00	−0.72	0.00
	Discount rate +10	7.45	6.42	0.41	−3.70	0.00	−3.64	0.51
	Discount rate −10	−4.33	−3.15	−1.96	5.58	0.00	−0.27	−0.20
	All γ values +20	1.33	1.64	0.00	0.08	0.00	−1.73	0.01
	All γ values −20	0.39	0.24	0.00	−2.45	0.00	2.21	0.00
	Fuel price +20	−10.50	−9.17	4.00	−1.38	0.00	6.29	0.26
	Fuel price −20	12.45	11.50	−5.02	1.73	0.00	−8.12	−0.09
Taiwan	Learning rate +5	−0.02	−0.01	0.00	0.00	0.00	0.14	−0.13
	Learning rate −5	0.40	0.10	0.00	0.00	0.00	−0.22	0.12
	Discount rate +10	1.60	0.16	0.00	−0.37	0.00	−0.86	1.07
	Discount rate −10	−0.54	−0.47	0.00	2.22	0.00	−1.61	−0.14
	All γ values +20	−0.34	−0.27	0.26	0.43	0.00	−0.48	0.06
	All γ values −20	−0.05	−0.04	0.14	−0.14	0.00	0.07	−0.03
	Fuel price +20	−7.98	−8.53	−3.31	0.54	0.00	3.21	5.22
	Fuel price −20	6.65	0.67	0.00	0.13	0.00	−4.80	4.00

Note: Each number refers to a percentage change in either CO_2 emission or technology share (share of total fleet). Variations used are considered as realistic uncertainty values. Changes in rates are percentage point changes. Outcome changes on emissions are a cumulation until 2050, whereas for shares, values are for 2050.

Table B3 Sensitivity analysis on key technological parameters in Scenario 2

Country	*Variation of key parameters (in %)*	*Emissions (%)*	*Technology shares (in %)*					
		CO_2	*Petrol car*	*Diesel car*	*Hybrid*	*CNG*	*EV*	*Motorcycles*
China	Learning rate +5	–4.80	–3.74	0.00	0.00	0.00	3.74	0.00
	Learning rate –5	3.41	2.63	0.00	0.00	0.00	–2.63	0.00
	Discount rate +10	3.10	3.20	0.00	0.04	0.00	–3.65	0.41
	Discount rate –10	–4.77	–5.35	0.00	0.00	0.00	5.09	–0.42
	All γ values +20	1.60	1.11	0.00	2.26	–2.24	–1.35	0.22
	All γ values –20	2.04	0.91	0.00	0.00	–0.67	–0.24	0.00
	Fuel price +20	–8.10	–7.80	0.01	2.10	–2.00	7.32	0.37
	Fuel price –20	4.90	3.21	–0.01	–2.60	1.33	–1.80	–0.13
Japan	Learning rate +5	–2.45	–5.65	0.00	4.32	0.00	1.33	0.00
	Learning rate –5	4.24	3.42	0.02	–2.75	0.00	–0.69	0.00
	Discount rate +10	5.21	3.43	0.00	–4.21	0.00	0.77	0.00
	Discount rate –10	–3.41	–4.27	0.00	6.10	0.00	–1.83	0.00
	All γ values+20	–0.32	–0.37	0.00	1.79	0.00	–1.42	0.00
	All γ values –20	–1.40	–0.92	0.00	–0.25	0.00	1.17	0.00
	Fuel price +20	–4.50	–4.05	0.10	6.10	0.00	–2.15	0.00
	Fuel price –20	5.96	3.83	0.09	2.11	0.00	–6.03	0.00

Korea	Learning rate +5	−2.91	−4.12	0.12	2.10	0.00	1.30	0.60
	Learning rate −5	4.28	1.86	0.01	−0.23	0.00	−1.29	−0.35
	Discount rate +10	6.45	4.29	0.98	0.35	0.00	−5.61	0.00
	Discount rate −10	−4.96	−4.19	−0.63	6.76	0.00	−0.70	−1.24
	All γ values +20	2.85	2.16	0.00	0.11	0.00	−2.29	0.02
	All γ values −20	2.80	0.32	0.00	−3.24	0.00	2.92	0.00
	Fuel price +20	−5.79	−7.00	3.00	−1.24	0.00	4.88	0.36
	Fuel price −20	12.41	11.34	0.01	−3.96	0.00	−7.26	−0.13
Taiwan	Learning rate +5	−3.04	−2.85	0.00	0.00	0.00	3.08	−0.23
	Learning rate −5	2.86	2.69	0.00	0.00	0.00	−2.90	0.21
	Discount rate +10	3.14	0.27	0.00	0.67	0.00	−1.50	0.56
	Discount rate −10	−2.53	−0.83	0.00	3.87	0.00	−2.81	−0.24
	All γ values +20	−0.34	−0.28	0.29	0.48	0.00	−0.54	0.05
	All γ values −20	−0.27	−0.05	0.16	−0.16	0.00	0.07	−0.03
	Fuel price +20	−6.55	−8.44	0.00	4.33	0.00	4.11	4.38
	Fuel price −20	9.21	7.34	0.00	−3.77	0.00	−3.58	3.36

Note: Each number refers to a percentage change in either CO_2 emission or technology share (share of total fleet). Variations used are considered as realistic uncertainty values. Changes in rates are percentage point changes. Outcome changes on emissions are a cumulation until 2050, whereas for shares, values are for 2050.

Table B4 Sensitivity analysis on key technological parameters in Scenario 3

Country	*Variation of key parameters (in %)*	*Emissions (%)*	*Technology shares (in %)*					
		CO_2	*Petrol car*	*Diesel car*	*Hybrid*	*CNG*	*EV*	*Motorcycles*
China	Learning rate +5	–6.24	–6.58	0.00	0.00	0.00	6.59	0.00
	Learning rate –5	4.43	4.41	0.00	0.00	0.00	–4.41	0.00
	Discount rate +10	4.10	3.75	0.00	0.05	0.00	–3.80	0.00
	Discount rate –10	–8.14	–4.69	0.00	0.00	0.00	5.01	0.00
	All γ values +20	0.91	0.74	0.00	0.03	0.00	–0.88	0.11
	All γ values –20	0.81	0.70	0.00	0.03	0.00	–0.73	0
	Fuel price +20	–9.11	–10.92	0.01	1.17	–2.80	12.50	0.00
	Fuel price –20	5.09	2.75	–0.01	–2.07	1.06	–1.73	0.00
Japan	Learning rate +5	–4.09	–6.85	0.00	3.87	0.00	2.98	0.00
	Learning rate –5	7.12	2.52	0.02	–1.75	0.00	–0.78	0.00
	Discount rate +10	6.47	4.12	0.00	–5.05	0.00	0.93	0.00
	Discount rate –10	–4.02	–5.10	0.00	0.20	0.00	4.90	0.00
	All γ values +20	–0.99	–0.21	0.00	0.93	0.00	–0.72	0.00
	All γ values –20	–0.26	–0.16	0.00	0.45	0.00	–0.29	0.00
	Fuel price +20	–5.34	–5.36	0.00	–1.45	0.00	6.8100	0.00
	Fuel price –20	4.58	3.41	0.08	1.88	0.00	–5.37	0.00

Korea	Learning rate +5	-3.74	-2.03	0.18	0.73	0.00	2.66	0.00
	Learning rate -5	3.66	2.46	0.02	0.25	0.00	-2.73	0.00
	Discount rate +10	3.43	4.13	0.94	-0.02	0.00	-5.41	0.00
	Discount rate -10	-4.65	-3.33	-0.50	5.37	0.00	-1.41	0.00
	All γ values +20	-0.05	-0.03	0.24	0.59	0.00	-0.80	0.00
	All γ values -20	0.34	0.04	-0.29	-0.97	0.00	0.98	0.25
	Fuel price +20	-8.57	-10.29	4.41	-1.29	0.00	6.72	0.00
	Fuel price -20	15.22	17.92	0.02	-6.25	0.00	-11.48	0.00
Taiwan	Learning rate +5	-5.20	-2.80	0.00	0.00	0.00	5.00	-2.20
	Learning rate -5	3.40	2.83	0.00	0.00	0.00	-4.63	1.80
	Discount rate +10	1.90	0.59	0.00	0.94	0.00	-1.53	0.00
	Discount rate -10	-2.54	-1.34	0.00	6.28	0.00	-3.97	0.00
	All γ values +20	-1.65	-0.52	0.59	0.89	0.00	-1.01	0.00
	All γ values -20	-0.67	-0.39	0.61	0.88	0.00	-1.06	0.00
	Fuel price +20	-4.87	-5.45	0.00	0.51	0.00	4.39	0.54
	Fuel price -20	6.07	5.72	0.00	-2.93	0.00	-2.46	-0.33

Note: Each number refers to a percentage change in either CO_2 emission or technology share (share of total fleet). Variations used are considered as realistic uncertainty values. Changes in rates are percentage point changes. Outcome changes on emissions are a cumulation until 2050, whereas for shares, values are for 2050.

Notes

1 www.statista.com/statistics/372156/china-number-of-passenger-vehicles-per-1000-people-in-selected-cities/
2 www.reuters.com/article/us-china-autos-electric-idUSKBN17R086
3 Domestic sales of hybrid cars increased from 108,000 units in 2008 to 1.385 million units in 2017 (Japan Automobile manufacturers Association, 2017).
4 www.theicct.org/blogs/staff/hybrids-break-through-japan-auto-market
5 www.theicct.org/blog/staff/hybrids-break-japanese-market-july-2015-update
6 We have purchased the annual car sales data of 2013 and 2014 from the MarkLines website, an automotive industry portal that consists of motor vehicles market data. MarkLines provides the total car sales by car model and brand for 63 countries from 2004 onwards. Hence, it is possible to know the sales for each car model in individual countries. www.marklines.com/en/vehicle_sales/index

References

Anandarajah, G., McDowall, W., & Ekins, P. (2013). Decarbonising road transport with hydrogen and electricity: Long term global technology learning scenarios. *International Journal of Hydrogen Energy*, *38*(8), 3419–3432.

Arthur, W. (1989). Competing technologies, increasing returns, and lock-in by historical events. *The Economic Journal*, *99*(394), 116–131.

Chanaron, J. (1998). Automobiles: A static technology, a "wait-and-see" industry? *International Journal of Technology Management*, *16*(7), 595–630.

China Association of Automobile Manufacturing (CAAM). (2017). *Automobile Statistics of China*. http://www.caam.org.cn/tjsj (in Chinese)

Fullerton, D., Gan, L., & Hattori, M. (2015). A model to evaluate vehicle emission incentive policies in Japan. *Environmental Economics and Policy Studies*, *17*(1), 79–108.

Gong, H., Wang, M., & Wang, H. (2013). New energy vehicles in China: Policies, demonstration, and progress. *Mitigation and Adaptation Strategies for Global Change*, *18*(2), 207–228.

Hao, H., Ou, X., Du, J., Wang, H., & Ouyang, M. (2014). China's electric vehicle subsidy scheme: Rationale and impacts. *Energy Policy*, *73*, 722–732.

Iino, F., & Lim, A. (2010). *Developing Asia's competitive advantage in green products: Learning from the Japanese experience*. The Social Science Research Network (SSRN).

The International Council on Clean Transportation (ICCT). (2017). *Light-Duty Vehicle Greenhouse Gas and Fuel Economy Standard*. http://www.theicct.org/sites/default/files/publications/2017-Global-LDV-Standards-Update_ICCT-Report_23062017_vF.pdf

IPCC. (2014). *Mitigation of climate change: Contribution of working group III to the fifth assessment report of the intergovernmental panel on climate change*. Cambridge: University of Cambridge.

Japan Automobile Manufacturers Association (JAMA). (2017). *Automobile Statistics of Japan*. http://www.jama-english.jp/publications/MIJ2017.pdf

Kemp, R., Schot, J., & Hoogma, R. (1998). Regime shifts to sustainability through processes of niche formation: The approach of strategic niche management. *Technology Analysis & Strategic Management*, *10*(2), 175–198.

Kitano, T. (2013). *Disguised protectionism? Environmental policy in the Japanese car market*. Tokyo: Research Institute of Economy, Trade and Industry.

Ko, A., Myung, C., Park, S., & Kwon, S. (2014). Scenario-based CO_2 emissions reduction potential and energy use in Republic of Korea's passenger vehicle fleet. *Transportation Research Part A: Policy and Practice*, *59*, 346–356.

Lam, A., Lee, S., Mercure, J. F., Cho, Y., Lin, C. H., Pollitt, H., . . . Billington, S. (2018). Policies and predictions for a low-carbon transition by 2050 in passenger vehicles in East Asia: Based on an analysis using the E3ME-FTT model. *Sustainability*, *10*(5), 1612.

Liao, F., Molin, E., & van Wee, B. (2017). Consumer preferences for electric vehicles: A literature review. *Transport Reviews*, *37*(3), 252–275.

Matsuhashi, K., & Ariga, T. (2016). Estimation of passenger car CO_2 emissions with urban population density scenarios for low carbon transportation in Japan. *IATSS Research*, *39*(2), 117–120.

Mercure, J., & Lam, A. (2015). The effectiveness of policy on consumer choices for private road passenger transport emissions reductions in six major economies. *Environmental Research Letters*, *10*(6), 064008.

Oshiro, K., & Masui, T. (2015). Diffusion of low emission vehicles and their impact on CO_2 emission reduction in Japan. *Energy Policy*, *81*, 215–225.

Paltsev, S., Chen, Y., Karplus, V., Kishimoto, P., Reilly, J., Löschel, A., . . . Koesler, S. (2016). Reducing CO 2 from cars in the European Union. *Transportation*, 1–23.

Rogers, E. (2010). *Diffusion of innovations*. New York, NY: Simon and Schuster.

Rutherford, D. (2015, July 28). *Hybrids break into the Japanese market* (July 2015 update). (The International Council on Clean Transportation (ICCT)). Retrieved from www.theicct.org/blog/staff/hybrids-break-japanese-market-july-2015-update

Sagar, A., & van der Zwaan, B. (2006). Technological innovation in the energy sector: R&D, deployment, and learning-by-doing. *Energy Policy*, *34*(17), 2601–2608.

Wang, H., Ou, X., & Zhang, X. (2017). Mode, technology, energy consumption, and resulting CO_2 emissions in China's transport sector up to 2050. *Energy Policy*, *109*, 719–733.

Weiss, M., Patel, M., Junginger, M., Perujo, A., Bonnel, P., & van Grootveld, G. (2012). On the electrification of road transport – Learning rates and price forecasts for hybrid-electric and battery-electric vehicles. *Energy Policy*, *48*, 374–393.

Yan, X., & Crookes, R. (2010). Energy demand and emissions from road transportation vehicles in China. *Progress in Energy and Combustion Science*, *36*(6), 651–676.

8 Policies to decarbonize household heating systems in East Asia

Florian Knobloch, Unnada Chewpreecha, Seonghee Kim, Yanmin He, Li-Chun Chen, Aileen Lam, Jean-François Mercure and Soocheol Lee

Introduction

Globally, the annual direct emissions of the residential building sector were estimated at 2.18 Gt CO_2 in 2010 (Lucon et al., 2014), equivalent to 7% of worldwide total CO_2 emissions from fossil fuel combustion and industrial processes. Assuming constant levels, these emissions would accumulate to around 185 Gt CO_2 between 2015 and 2100, potentially undermining ambitious climate change mitigation. Heating of space and water largely dominate fossil fuel use, and CO_2 emissions in residential buildings (International Energy Agency (IEA), 2013b; Ürge-Vorsatz et al., 2015). However, residential heating receives only limited attention compared with the electricity and transport sectors (IEA, 2014). It remains unclear if and how the residential sector can be decarbonized sufficiently fast to meet global CO_2 reduction targets.

There is a consensus that the global demand for heating can be fulfilled much more efficiently, which would reduce fuel use and emissions without reducing comfort (Lucon et al., 2014). Heating loads can be reduced by improved household thermal insulation, and the remaining heat demand can be serviced by renewable and energy-efficient technologies. Combining improved insulation with new heating technologies could reduce energy consumption by up to 90% compared with current standards (Urge-Vorsatz et al., 2013). Given that 50% of the current building stock will still be in use by 2050 (75% in OECD [Organization for Economic Co-operation and Development] countries) (International Energy Agency (IEA), 2013a), levels of building efficiency in the next decades will strongly depend on building shell retrofits of existing houses (Ürge-Vorsatz et al., 2012, 2015).

Aside from space heating, more than 40% of global residential heat demand is for water heating, with particularly large shares in warmer world regions. Demand for water heating is less impacted by insulation (Connolly et al., 2014), but mainly depends on available income and is, thus, likely to rise with growing income in many world regions (Daioglou et al., 2012). Ambitious decarbonization targets are, thus, unachievable as long as the remaining heat demand is not provided by renewable and efficient electricity-based technologies. The available alternatives to fossil-fuel heating systems rely on the use of biomass (traditional or in modern boilers), electricity (e.g. electric resistance or immersion heating), ambient heat (heat pumps) or solar energy (solar thermal panels) (IEA, 2014). Whereas the operation of solar and biomass systems can potentially be carbon-neutral (abstracting from life cycle considerations), heating with electricity can be a renewable technology once electricity generation is decarbonized; otherwise electricity-related emissions must be accounted for. A much more efficient use of electricity can be achieved through the use of heat pumps, which upgrade the ambient low-temperature energy of an air, water or ground source into higher-temperature heat for space and water heating, effectively achieving efficiencies of 200–400% (average ratio of heat output to electricity input) (IEA/ETSAP and IRENA, 2013).

In this chapter, we focus on the diffusion of renewable heating technologies in East Asia. Assuming reasonable improvements in building insulation, will it be possible to decarbonize the sector by 2050? Residential heat generation is overwhelmingly small scale and distributed, taking place on-site within homes. The uptake of new heating equipment depends on the individual decision-making by heterogeneous households, each with subjective preferences and perceptions, and only limited information. The sum of such decisions inevitably deviates from the least-cost optimum as it would be determined by models that assume a single, fully rational agent or social planner (Kirman, 1992). Avoiding costly policy-design failures requires an upfront simulation of policy effects, based on an analysis of people's actual behavior, and accounting for nonlinear diffusion dynamics (Mercure et al., 2016; Rai and Henry, 2016). A behavioral model of decision-making is particularly relevant for policies aiming at a premature replacement of existing systems, which will likely be necessary for deep decarbonization (Geels et al., 2017), and for which households are found to apply very strict payback thresholds (Olsthoorn et al., 2017).

Here, we take a simulation-based approach for modelling different policy scenarios, aiming at near-zero global CO_2 emissions by 2050 in the residential heating sector. Each of our scenarios focuses on different combinations of policy instruments. Specifically, we use the 'Future Technology Transformations' model FTT:Heat (Knobloch et al., 2017, 2019). As a non-equilibrium, bottom-up simulation model, FTT:Heat can analyze the dynamics behind policy-induced technology transitions, accounting for limited information and bounded rationality of consumers. Similarly to the other FTT models, FTT:Heat covers 59 global regions and is fully linked to the E3ME macroeconomic model.

The chapter is structured as follows: the next section gives some background information on the policy context. Following that, we present our model and data. Policy scenarios and results of the model simulations are presented and discussed in the subsequent section, with conclusions given in the final section.

Country profiles

China

Residential energy demand in China was around 4100 TWh in 2015 (11% of the country's total energy consumption): around 1600 TWh in urban residential buildings, 1700 TWh in rural residential buildings and 800 TWh of biomass consumption in rural buildings. Between 2001 and 2014, the country saw steady increases for all types of residential energy demand: space heating and cooling, water heating and appliance use. The total energy consumption of urban residential buildings (excluding northern urban heating) increased by around 40% during this time (Jiang et al., 2016).

In 2006, the Chinese government began to treat resource conservation as a fundamental national policy in its overall economic and social development strategy. Since then, energy conservation in the residential sector has been included as a binding indicator in China's National Economic and Social Development Outline within the Five-Year Plans. The main policies for energy conservation in the residential sector include the following:

- Energy efficiency standards for appliances, equipment and vehicle fuel efficiency have been laid down in various regulations, including the Ordinance of Civil-Building Energy Conservation and the Regulations on Energy Conservation for Public Institutions. National efficiency standards have been established for 40 energy end-use products.
- Supporting measures, such as mandatory energy efficiency assessments of projects involving new investments (those leading to the creation of new fixed assets), the inspection and monitoring of high energy-consuming equipment and mandatory energy-efficiency labeling.
- Incentive measures, such as the promotion of differential power pricing and subsidies for the installation of solar water heating systems.

In December 2017, eight ministries and commissions including the National Development and Reform Commission and the National Energy Administration jointly issued the Clean Winter Heating Plan for Regions in Northern China (2017–2021), with the aim of improving the share of clean heating and reducing emissions of air pollutants. To this end, it is planned that natural gas and renewables should rapidly replace coal boilers for heat generation. The work will focus on the '2+26' cities, accelerating the construction of supporting facilities for urban natural gas pipeline networks. In September 2006, 'Opinions on promoting application of renewable energy in buildings' and 'A tentative management method of special funds for renewable energy development' were issued by the Ministry of Housing and Urban-Rural Development, cooperating with the Ministry of Finance.

In these two documents, four of the eight technologies that are subsidized by the government are different types of ground source heat pump (GSHP) systems, such as water or seawater source heat pump systems. After that, a series of policies was established to promote GSHPs at the city and town level: at the end of 2010, 47 cities and 98 towns got funding from the central government to promote GSHPs. Each city got 50–80 million RMB (around US$9–15 million) and each town got 15–20 million RMB to promote heat pumps (Sichong and Wei, 2014). By 2021, the new floor supply area heated by GSHP technologies in northern China is planned to reach ten billion square meters. In addition, subsidies are paid for the installation of solar water heating systems.

Japan

In 2015, the residential sector accounted for 13.8% of Japan's total energy consumption. The share of energy used for space heating in residential energy demand was 22%, and 29% was used for water heating. The share of space cooling was 2%. In the 1960s, coal accounted for more than one third of household energy consumption. Then oil, mainly kerosene, replaced coal, which decreased to a share of only 6% in 1973. With the diffusion of all-electric homes, the share of electricity in residential energy demand (including all end-uses, not just heating) increased to 51% in 2015 (Agency for Natural Resources and Energy, 2017).

The government of Japan promotes energy management and the introduction of energy-efficient equipment. The Act on the Improvement of Energy Consumption Performance of Buildings was introduced in 2015. The Act stipulates mandatory compliance with energy efficiency standards for large construction projects. The compliance with energy efficiency standards will gradually become a requirement for all new construction projects by 2020.

In addition, the introduction of highly energy-efficient equipment and devices is promoted. The top runner program was established in 1998, and the number of targeted products and devices has gradually increased since then. Today, electric heat pumps for water heating are also included. The introduction of energy-efficient water heaters is subsidized by the Ministry of Economy, Trade and Industry. Local governments also support the introduction of energy-efficient water heaters, including solar water heaters and heat pump water heaters (Agency for Natural Resources and Energy, 2015).

Korea

In 2015, the residential sector accounted for approximately 9% of Korea's total energy consumption. The share of heating in total energy use in the residential sector has decreased from 77% in 2000 to 67% in 2015, partly owing to the diffusion of insulation and efficient heating technologies. At the same time, energy use for space cooling has grown rapidly. In the 1990s and 2000s, the main energy source for newly constructed towns shifted from coal and oil to natural gas and district heating systems, partly in response to high oil prices (Korea Energy Economics Institute, 2018).

The government of Korea established standards for building insulation in 1976. Since 1985, regulations for envelope insulation and energy-efficient design have been implemented for large and high energy-consuming buildings. In addition to the strengthened insulation standards, the government requires higher efficiency standards for buildings to expand their efforts in using high-efficiency lighting, boilers, freezers, etc. Also, the Energy-saving Building Design Standard aims to enforce regulations on total energy consumption of the building sector; it requires a 10% improvement every five years. The government of Korea has proceeded to lead a program to expand strategically the distribution of energy-efficient appliances. Energy efficiency standards and labelling programs were implemented in 1992.

The government of Korea has supported the introduction of electric heat pump systems and solar water heaters through subsidies. However, the progressive electricity charge scheme for households might impede the further diffusion of electric heat pumps. In addition, there have been disputes about whether electric heat pumps might increase the peak load on the electricity grid in winter.

Taiwan

In 2015, the residential sector accounted for approximately 11% of Taiwan's total energy consumption and CO_2 emissions. In response to the United Nations Framework Convention on Climate Change, the Bureau of Energy, Ministry of Economic Affairs (BOE, MOEA) has promoted research and development in renewable energy technologies, including solar thermal and heat pump systems.

Owing to the country's hot climate, commercial and residential air conditioning systems consume 13% of total energy consumption in Taiwan. Ground source heat pumps have the potential to increase the efficiency of air conditioning, thereby reducing energy demand. However, although GSHPs are used in more and more areas around the world, they are rarely seen in Taiwan. The main reason for this is the large imbalance between cooling and heating loads in Taiwanese buildings.

Introduction to the FTT:Heat model

The modelling approach

Like the other FTT models, FTT:Heat is a simulation model of technological change. It provides a realistic representation of how residential heating systems may develop until 2050, given households' individual decisions in a context of bounded rationality and limited information. A detailed description of the methodology and model is given in Knobloch et al. (2017, 2019), of which the key elements are summarized here.

Table 8.1 presents an overview of how some real-world key behavioral features are represented in the modelling, based on the categories for improving the behavioral realism of global integrated assessment models suggested by McCollum et al. (2017).

For each country, the starting point is an exogenous level of total annual demand for residential heating as an energy service, expressed in terms of useful energy demand. Individual heating technologies (e.g. gas boilers or heat pumps) compete for market shares of the total demand. At every time step Δt (set to quarter year), FTT:Heat simulates which technologies supply which share, along with the resulting level of fuel use and emissions.

Decision-making by heterogeneous households

At the core is an aggregate representation of decision-making by heterogeneous households, based on cost and decision parameters that have statistical variations. The decision-making determines the composition of new heating units purchased.

Table 8.1 Integration of behavioral realism into FTT:Heat

Behavioral feature	*Description*	*Modelling in FTT:Heat*
Heterogeneity	Differences in decision maker characteristics	Statistically distributed technology and choice parameters, resulting in a distribution of preferences and choices
Social influence	Imitation (herding, bandwagon) effects, distinction (status-seeking), or neighborhood effects	All decisions are linked to current market shares of technologies as a proxy for their visibility and trialability, assuming that households gather information from their peers, leading to inertia
Bounded rationality	Costs of searching for, and acquiring, information	Decisions on premature replacements are based on behavioral payback thresholds
Non-optimizing heuristics	Decisions in familiar, repeated contexts influenced by past experience (habit, inertia, loyalty)	
Non-monetary preferences	'Intangible' non-monetary costs and benefits	Inclusion of region-specific 'intangible' cost parameters for all technologies, estimated based on empirical diffusion trends
Non-market discount rates	Implicit discount rates estimated from market behavior	Behavioral discount rate of 9%, based on choice experiments
Contextual conditions	Behavior is influenced, constrained or determined by infrastructure, the physical environment or other contextual factors	Region-specific capacity and efficiency factors, constraints on the maximum diffusion of district heating
Political and social institutions	Institutions and culture shape decisions and behavior	Not explicitly modelled

Note: Categories and their description of FTT:Heat are adapted from McCollum et al. (2017).

At the point at which a household decides between heating systems, FTT:Heat performs a pairwise comparison of all available heating technologies based on a single quantity, the levelized cost of heating (LCOH), which is similar to the levelized costs used in the other FTT models. The LCOH is the present value cost of operating a heating system during its lifetime, including investment, maintenance and fuel costs, which themselves depend on technology – and region-specific conversion efficiencies and capacity factors, according to our model data. In addition, policies can be imposed, such as a subsidy on upfront investment costs or a carbon tax.

Of paramount importance is the diversity of households, which stems from different individual contexts and perceptions when they take a decision, and which may originate from a large set of individual characteristics (of the household, the technology or the dwelling), preferences and constraints. This diversity is represented by statistical distributions of cost parameters, which implies a heterogeneity of households' choices: a technology may be less attractive than an alternative on average, but more attractive for some households. This implies that the LCOH is not treated as a unique value but, rather, as a distribution, derived from distributed underlying cost parameters.

Many additional aspects, on which little information is available, may be valued by households, such as the perceived inconvenience of a technology (Sopha et al., 2010) or possible co-benefits (e.g. using a heat pump for cooling purposes). In FTT:Heat, these missing components are defined as intangibles that are equivalent to the γ values used in FTT:Transport. As in FTT:Transport, the intangibles are added as a constant to the LCOH, resulting in the *perceived* levelized cost of heating.

In a heterogeneous group of agents, choices are often unanimous. A representation of heterogeneous agents comparing two technologies, based on the distribution of perceived costs, implies a comparison of frequency distributions: the fraction of households preferring technology i over technology j is the fraction of households for which the perceived cost of heating with technology i is less than with technology j (i.e. the model calculates a binary logit). Performed for all possible pairs of technologies, this results in a complete order of distributed household preferences among all pairs of available options.

Diversity of choice implies a differentiation of the market: households take different decisions at different points in time for different reasons, which results in dynamics of technology uptake as described by diffusion theory (Rogers, 2010). If the perceived cost difference among technologies gradually decreases, then an increasing fraction of households will choose the alternative technology. The resulting profile of adoption is then a very gradual one, the steepness of which depends on the widths of the distributions.

Technology diffusion dynamics

As mentioned in previous chapters, the future development of technology shares is simulated based on a replicator dynamics equation (Mercure, 2015).

Combining the choice-based matrix of household preferences (F_{ij}) with current technology market shares (S_i and S_j) and the fraction of technology j that needs to be replaced (based on average technology lifetime τ_j), we can derive the flow of market shares from heating technology j to i in period Δt:

$$\Delta S_{j \to i} = S_j F_{ij} \tau_j^{-1} S_i \Delta t \tag{1}$$

Net flows from technology j to technology i are obtained by subtracting the reverse flow from technology i to j (since agents are heterogeneous, reverse decisions always take place). The overall net flow of market shares to technology i is the sum of all such pairwise comparisons over all competing technologies j, which yields the non-linear *replicator dynamics* equation of evolutionary theory (Hofbauer and Sigmund, 1998):

$$\Delta S_i = \sum_j S_i S_j \left(F_{ij} \tau_j^{-1} - F_{ji} \tau_i^{-1} \right) \Delta t \tag{2}$$

Each single flow from a technology j to an alternative technology i is determined by three interacting elements:

1 Preferences (F): which fraction of households would prefer which technology, given that they were to buy a heating system within period Δt? These preferences are determined by the decision-making core that compares perceived costs.
2 Replacement needs ($S_j \tau_j^{-1}$): how many heating systems of technology j need replacement in period Δt? This depends on the market share of technology j and the annual fraction of withdrawals within its population, which is approximated as the inverse of j's technical life expectancy, τ_j.
3 Flow restrictions (S_i): given preferences and replacement needs, which fraction of flows can be realized? The flow is restricted for two reasons: (a) restricted access to information by households and (b) limited production capacities in industry. Both restrictions can be approximated as proportional to the market share of the alternative technology i in the previous period (S_i), based on Mercure.

(2015, 2018a, 2018b)

Without flow restrictions, one would implicitly assume that (a) all households have perfect information on all technologies at all times and (b) that technologies can be obtained everywhere on demand, that is, that the industry is assumed to be able to instantaneously scale up its production of any technology, without any limits. Instead, by introducing the dynamic share restrictions, the trajectory of technology uptake resembles S-shaped diffusion curves. This is an improvement compared with exogenous growth constraints in standard optimization models, since here the constraint is fully *endogenous*. As a central implication, technology transitions in FTT: Heat become subject to inertia, as technological change cannot occur instantaneously: it possesses autocorrelation in time (i.e. it is strongly path dependent).

Additionally, we assume that households do not switch to technologies with a much lower comfort level. Coal and traditional biomass can only be chosen if at least one is the existing heating system. Furthermore, solar thermal heating is limited to the demand for water heating in each country.

Finally, the new levels of heat production per technology are obtained by multiplying the resulting shares by the (exogenous) level of a region's total heat demand in the new period, which includes potential demand increases or decreases.

Premature replacements

Households may consider replacing a functioning heating system ahead of its rated end-of-life date, based on economic considerations. For a household with perfect information and without risk aversion, this would be when the marginal running costs of operating the current system exceed the full levelized costs of buying and operating an alternative technology. In practice, households may apply much stricter criteria, and only consider a premature replacement if the potential savings exceed the initial investment in a limited period of time – the so-called *payback threshold*. While it remains debated whether such behavior is an expression of bounded rationality or of neglected economic factors (Gillingham and Palmery, 2014), it accurately describes household behavior. We here model premature replacements based on results by Olsthoorn et al. (2017), who find that the mean *payback threshold* for a premature replacement of heating systems is three ± one years.

The resulting preferences and share flows are modelled in conceptually the same way as for regular household decisions, performing pairwise comparisons among all technology pairs and, finally, applying the replicator dynamics equation. For the same reasons as described in the previous section, the *realized* flows because of premature replacements are, thus, smaller than the hypothetical ones owing to limited information and capacity constraints.

Learning by doing

Reductions in upfront investment costs are endogenously calculated based on learning curves. As in the other FTT models, the learning curves are not a function of time but of the cumulative global capacity production of a technology, based on technology-specific learning rates. We take learning rates from the literature (Henkel, 2012; Weiss et al., 2010) as between 10% (for advanced gas, oil and biomass boilers and solar thermal) and 30% (for heat pumps). These percentage values refer to the relative reduction in a technology's upfront investment costs, which are assumed to take place for every additional doubling of a technology's global cumulative capacity. For example, if the global capacity of heat pumps doubles by 2030, then heat pump investment costs in 2030 would be 30% below their current value.

Economic feedbacks

FTT:Heat is hard-linked to E3ME in a way that is similar to that of the other FTT models (Cambridge Econometrics, 2014). This allows an analysis of the wider macroeconomic effects of policies that are primarily targeted at the residential heating sector.

Data

Energy demand

Only limited data are available on the specific demand for residential heating, related fuel consumption and technology composition (IEA, 2014; Lucon et al., 2014). We have, therefore, compiled a new database with time series of final and useful energy demand by technology for all the E3ME regions, which is described in Knobloch et al. (2019).

The IEA energy statistics report final residential energy demand by fuel type, but do not differentiate by end-use application (IEA, 2017). We calculate the shares of heating based on estimates from the IEA (International Energy Agency (IEA), 2013b). Where such estimates are not available, the heating share is approximated based on heating degree days (given the average relationship in world regions with available data).

Residential heat generation by solar thermal installations for most world regions is available in the IEA energy statistics, which we amended by adding data from the IEA Solar Heating Programme (Mauthner et al., 2016). No standardized global data set exists on heat generation by heat pumps. Data on heat generation by ground-source heat pumps are taken from Lund and Boyd (2016). Data on the use of air-source heat pumps are taken from country-specific sources where available (China Heat Pump Committee of China Energy Conservation Association, 2015; EIA, 2017; Japan Refrigeration and Air Conditioning Industry Association (JRAIA), 2017; Kegel et al., 2014; Lapsa et al., 2017).

Data on final energy demand were transformed into useful energy demand according to technology-specific conversion efficiencies (see Table 8.2). The electricity demand of heat pumps is calculated based on region-specific seasonal performance factors.

Technology data

Cost and performance data for the 13 different kinds of heating technologies are summarized in Table 8.2. Mean investment costs (including installation costs) are taken from Fleiter et al. (2016) and Connolly et al. (2014), which we extrapolated to different world regions based on available household income. A standard deviation equivalent to one third of the mean cost is assumed for all technologies (based on cost ranges reported by the Danish Energy Agency, 2013, 2016; NREL, 2016). Residential fuel prices are taken from the IEA (2016), with an assumed standard deviation of 15% (NREL, 2016).

Table 8.2 Model assumptions for residential heating technologies

	Upfront cost (US\$/kW$_{th}$)	*O&M cost (US\$/kW$_{th}$ pa)*	*Efficiency (kWh$_{th}$/kWh)*	*Learning rate (%)*
Oil	539	22	0.75	–
Oil condensing	586	23	0.86	-10
Gas	447	9	0.75	–
Gas condensing	496	10	0.9	-10
Biomass stove	503	0.1	0.1–0.7	–
Biomass boiler	598	2	0.85	-10
Coal	283	6	0.75	–
District heating	303	18	0.98	–
Direct electric	615	1	1.00	–
HP – ground source	1602	16	3.50	-30
HP – air/water	858	17	2.50–2.70	-30
HP – air/air	583	58	2.50–2.70	-30
Solar thermal	884	9	Not applicable	-10

Note: Costs refer to mean values. O&M cost, operation and maintenance cost; HP, heat pump.

Sources: Fleiter et al. (2016), IEA/ETSAP (2012), Danish Energy Agency (2013)
Source: Estimated by Cambridge Econometrics for this study

Conversion efficiencies refer to the ratio of thermal energy 'leaving' the heating system, relative to the necessary energy input, covering both space and water heating. For heat pumps, efficiency values are defined as their seasonal performance factor (the annual average ratio of delivered heat to electricity input), which differs by climate region. For solar thermal, local productivity differences are expressed as region-specific capacity factors, calculated from data from the IEA Solar Heat Programme (Mauthner et al., 2016). A useful lifetime of 20 years is assumed for all technologies.

Heat demand

The demand for useful heat in each region is an exogenous parameter that can be calibrated to different assumptions. For the scenarios in this chapter, we use projections of future changes in heat demand (UE_{tot}) from the IMAGE-REMG model, following the methodology described in Isaac and van Vuuren (2009) and Daioglou et al. (2012) and resulting in the demand trends as described in Knobloch et al. (2019). Demand levels are projected for (a) a baseline scenario and (b) a mitigation scenario that involves increased efficiency of new buildings and increased retrofitting of existing houses.

IMAGE-REMG projects UE_{tot} as the sum of demand for space and water heating. For water heating, future demand per capita is modelled as a function of income, converging to a maximum saturation value that depends on the numbers of heating degree days (HDD) (Daioglou et al., 2012). For space heating, demand is modelled as a function of population, floor space per capita (m^2/cap), the number of heating degree days and the useful energy heating intensity $\left(UE/m^2/HDD\right)$ (Isaac and van Vuuren, 2009).

Future changes in population, climate and income are exogenous drivers, based on the Shared Socioeconomic Pathway (SSP) 2 (i.e. 'middle of the road') (Riahi et al., 2017). All relevant data are publicly available via the IMAGE website (PBL, 2018).

Scenario definition

We have created five model scenarios (referred to as scenarios 1–5) that aim to decarbonize residential heating by 2050. Each scenario uses a different set of policies, implemented from 2020 onwards. Scenario 1 assumes increased levels of thermal insulation for new houses, compared with the baseline trend in heat demand: we assume that space heating intensity converges to 60 kJ_{UE}/m2/HDD by 2100 (from current values in the range 50–150 kJ_{UE}/m2/HDD), consistent with the assumption that aggregate insulation efficiency increases (e.g. in reaction to more stringent building regulations) (Knobloch et al., 2019). In addition to improved insulation, Scenario 1 includes a continuation of current policies for technology uptake, the effect of which is implicitly included in the intangible parameters.

In scenarios 2–5, we explore two policy instruments and combinations thereof: a residential carbon tax and technology subsidies for renewable heating technologies, both of which are implemented in addition to the improved levels of building insulation. These policy instruments have been chosen based on their successful previous implementation in at least some countries (Connor et al., 2013) (Table 8.3).

1 The (sectoral) *carbon tax* is specified as an absolute increase in the household price of fossil fuels, relative to their respective carbon content (we do not assume an inclusion of households in emissions trading).[1] We simulate carbon taxes of (a) US\$29/tCO_2 linearly increasing to US\$114/tCO_2 in 2100 (Scenario 2), and (b) US\$57/tCO_2 linearly increasing to US\$229/t CO_2 in 2100 (Scenario 3).

2 *Technology subsidies* are defined as a relative reduction in a mean upfront investment cost of renewable heating technology. The eligible technologies are solar thermal, heat pumps and modern biomass. We simulate a subsidy rate of 25% (Scenario 4), which is assumed to remain constant from 2020 until 2030, and linearly phased out afterwards, reaching zero by 2050.

Scenarios 2–4 focus on single policy instruments, whereas Scenario 5 simulates a policy mix involving both a carbon tax (of US\$57/tCO_2) and a technology subsidy (of 25%).

For all the scenarios in this chapter, we assume constant energy prices over time, for two reasons. First, future energy prices are highly uncertain, especially in a

Table 8.3 Overview of policy assumptions in the modelled scenarios

Scenario	*Policies targeted at technology uptake*	*Insulation policies*
Baseline	No new policies	No improved insulation
S1	No new policies	Improved thermal insulation of buildings, lowering the demand for space heating to kJ_{UE}/m2/HDD by 2100
S2	Carbon tax of US\$29/tCO_2 (from 2020 onwards), linearly increasing to US\$114/tCO_2 by 2050	Improved thermal insulation (as in S1)
S3	Carbon tax of US\$57/tCO_2 (from 2020 onwards), linearly increasing to US\$229/tCO_2 by 2050	Improved thermal insulation (as in S1)
S4	Subsidy payments of 25% on upfront investment costs of modern renewables, paid from 2020–30, phased out afterwards	Improved thermal insulation (as in S1)
S5	Carbon tax of US\$57/t CO_2 and 25% subsidy	Improved thermal insulation (as in S1)

context of global deep decarbonization. Effectively, this makes constant prices as likely as any other scenario. Second, it allows for a clearer identification of policy effects, which may otherwise be convoluted with the effects of a change in energy prices. Energy prices are allowed to vary when we assess the decarbonization of the whole economy (see Chapter 5).

Indirect CO_2 emissions from electricity use are projected by FTT:Power, assuming a power sector decarbonization scenario that is consistent with limiting global warming to 2C°, as described in Chapter 5.

Results

Policies for decarbonization

The main results for policy scenarios 1–5 are illustrated in Figure 8.1 and Figure 8.3. The figures show the projected technology composition (left) and CO_2 emissions (right) in China and Japan, and Korea and Taiwan, respectively, up to 2050.

China

Of the four East Asian countries, China shows the most dynamic development in its residential heating sector – both in terms of projected changes in heat demand, and in terms of projected changes in technology composition of the heating sector.

The demand for heating is projected to continue its ongoing growth, resulting from rising incomes. Therefore, even under ambitious assumptions on improved insulation of buildings, Chinese residential heat demand in 2050 will be 38% higher than in 2014. At the same time, current trends of technology diffusion suggest that residential heating in China is undergoing a rapid technological change. Coal and traditional biomass, which are still the dominant technologies in large parts of the country, get increasingly replaced by modern, more convenient heating systems – both by fossil fuel technologies (oil and gas), and by modern renewables. The most striking development is the current growth of solar thermal heating. China is currently the world's largest market for the technology. In our model projections, solar thermal is projected to continue its ongoing growth throughout the next decades, even without further policies.

Owing to the ongoing technological change, total CO_2 emissions caused by residential heating are projected to peak around 2030 and to decrease afterwards – coincidentally, in line with China's Paris pledge. This is despite the parallel growth in heat demand. The main reason is the gradual phase-out of emission-intensive coal systems, combined with a substantial growth in renewables and district heating. This is consistent with the fact that China has recently started to regulate the burning of coal, mainly to limit emissions of PM2.5 and to minimize any health impacts related to them.

In the context of the observed growth dynamics in China, we find that the introduction of additional policies could have an impact on technology composition and emissions relatively quickly. Instead of buying oil and gas heating systems, which are projected to increase their still relatively low market shares under current trends, households could shift towards modern renewables more quickly. As both solar thermal and heat pumps are already present in the Chinese market, their growth could take place at a relatively high pace. In Figure 8.1, model simulations by FTT:Heat start in 2015 (indicated by vertical dashed lines). Horizontal dashed lines represent 2014 levels. Dashed curves show the baseline demand trends without improved insulation. Percentage values refer to the change by 2050, relative to 2014. For emissions, the first percentage value indicates the reduction in annual total CO_2 emissions (direct plus indirect); values in parentheses show the corresponding reduction in direct on-site CO_2 emissions.

As a result, CO_2 emissions could peak around 2020 in all simulated policy scenarios, and quickly decrease afterwards. Direct emissions could decrease by as much as 98% by 2050. In common with the other countries, remaining emissions would then mostly consist of indirect emissions because of the use of electricity. Given the assumed trajectory in the power sector, the reduction in total emissions would be 71% for the higher carbon tax, and 75% for the policy mix.

Japan

In Japan, the gradual decrease in total heat demand is projected to continue under baseline conditions. With improved insulation, heat demand in 2050 would decrease by 29%, relative to 2014 levels. The corresponding CO_2 emissions would decrease by more than twice that value, because of (a) an ongoing diffusion of heat pumps and (b) the parallel decarbonization of the power sector, which

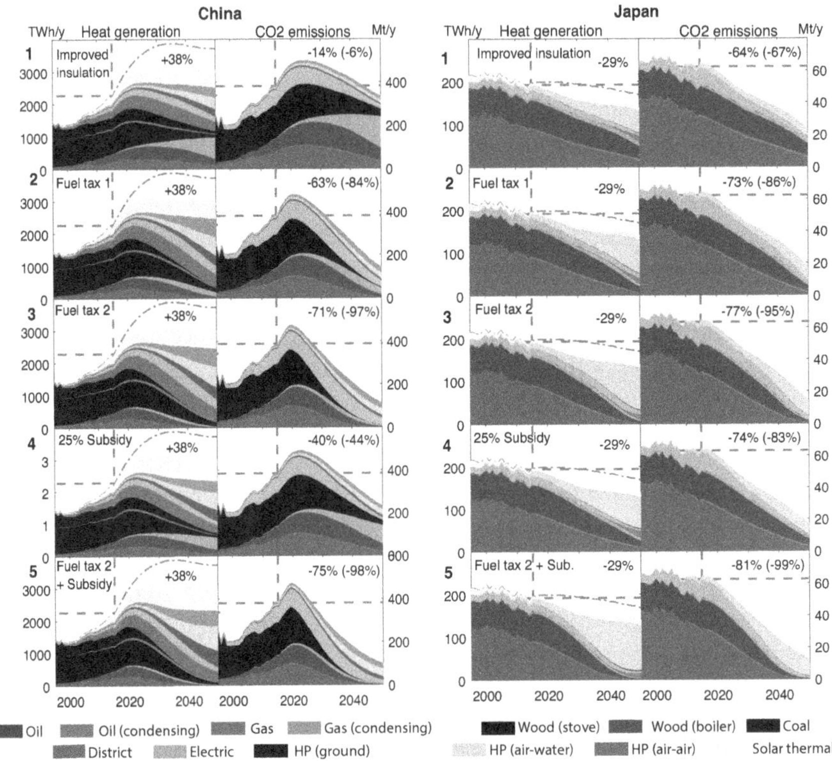

Figure 8.1 Projected technology composition and CO_2 emissions (direct on-site and indirect from electricity use) in the residential heating sectors of China (left) and Japan (right)

Source: Estimated by Cambridge Econometrics for this study

Note: Bold numbers top left of each panel) indicate improved levels of building insulation in Scenario 1 (1), and the four policy scenarios 2–5 aimed at technology uptake (2–5). Values from 1995–2014 are estimates based on historical data.

decreases indirect emissions from electricity use. As a result, total emissions in 2050 are expected to be 64% below their 2014 level, owing to a combination of improved insulation levels and gradual improvements in the technological conversion efficiencies of heating systems. However, the uptake of solar thermal systems will remain limited. As evidenced by the decrease in the technology's market share over the past 20 years, solar thermal is associated with relatively high intangible costs in Japan. Under current trends of diffusion, the technology's market share will, thus, remain relatively stable.

When policies are introduced, the current trends in technology diffusion are intensified. As heat pumps are already established in Japan, they would see the main growth in market share. In comparison, more efficient gas and oil heating systems are projected to be a less attractive alternative. Owing to the availability of heat pumps and solar thermal, households could directly switch to modern low-carbon alternatives, without choosing efficient fossil fuel technologies as an intermediate solution.

Relative to the simulated carbon taxes, the payment of upfront subsidies for renewables is projected to incentivize the uptake of more capital-intensive and efficient technologies. More households could choose heat pumps and solar thermal, which have higher initial upfront costs but lower running costs throughout their lifetime. The underlying changes in levelized costs for different heating technologies are illustrated in Figure 8.2.

In Figure 8.2, the gradual decrease regarding the cost of heat pumps and solar thermal is due to endogenous learning effects, that is, as more capacity of each one is installed over time, their upfront costs are projected to decrease. The carbon tax linearly increases the cost of fossil fuel technologies (middle panel). In the case of subsidies for renewables (right panel), the policy leads to an additional steep decrease in renewable costs by 2020. Subsidies are gradually phased out from 2030 onwards, explaining the flat profile of costs between 2030 and 2050.

In these scenarios, fewer households would opt for direct electric heating, which is not eligible for the simulated subsidies. Overall, this results in a lesser reduction of direct emissions, compared with the carbon tax scenarios. However, the higher average efficiency of adopted heating technologies reduces electricity demand and the induced indirect emissions in the power sector. Therefore, the subsidy scheme could achieve a similar reduction in total emissions.

In our simulations, we find that a combination of subsidies with a carbon tax is the most effective way to reduce emissions. The policy mix would reduce direct CO_2 emissions to almost zero by 2050. However, as long as electricity generation is not fully decarbonized, indirect emissions would remain. The volume of indirect emissions will depend on (a) the efficiency of heating equipment and (b) the carbon intensity of power generation.

In Figure 8.3, bold numbers at the top left of each panel indicate improved levels of building insulation in Scenario 1 (1), and the four policy scenarios 2–5 aimed at technology uptake (2–5). Values from 1995–2014 are estimates based on historical data. Model simulations by FTT:Heat start in 2015 (indicated by vertical dashed lines). Horizontal dashed lines represent 2014 levels. Dashed curves show the baseline demand trends without improved insulation. Percentage values refer to the change by 2050, relative to 2014. For emissions, the first percentage value indicates the reduction in annual total CO_2 emissions (direct plus indirect); values in parentheses show the corresponding reduction in direct on-site CO_2 emissions.

Korea

In Korea, heat demand is projected to grow in the baseline. When thermal insulation of houses is improved, the increase in demand could be limited to 7% by 2050, relative to 2014. In contrast to Japan, we find that, under current trends

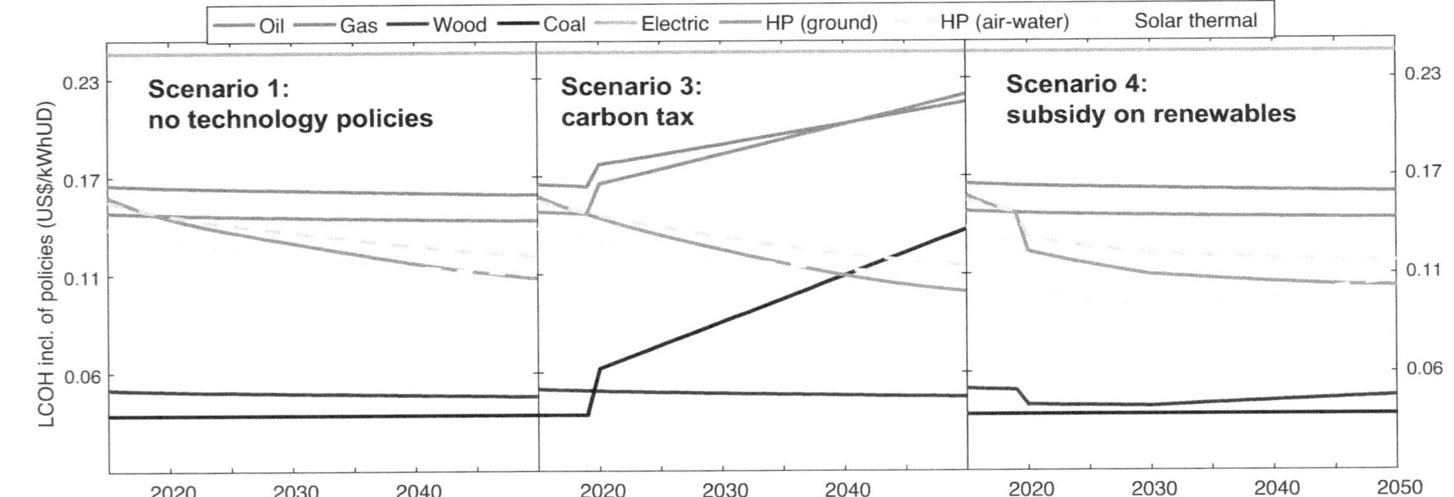

Figure 8.2 Projected levelized costs of heating (LCOH) with different technologies in Japan (2015–2050)

Source: Estimated by Cambridge Econometrics for this study

Note: Scenario 1 (without policies aimed at technology uptake), Scenario 3 (carbon tax of US$57–229/t CO_2), Scenario 4 (25% subsidy on renewable heating technologies).

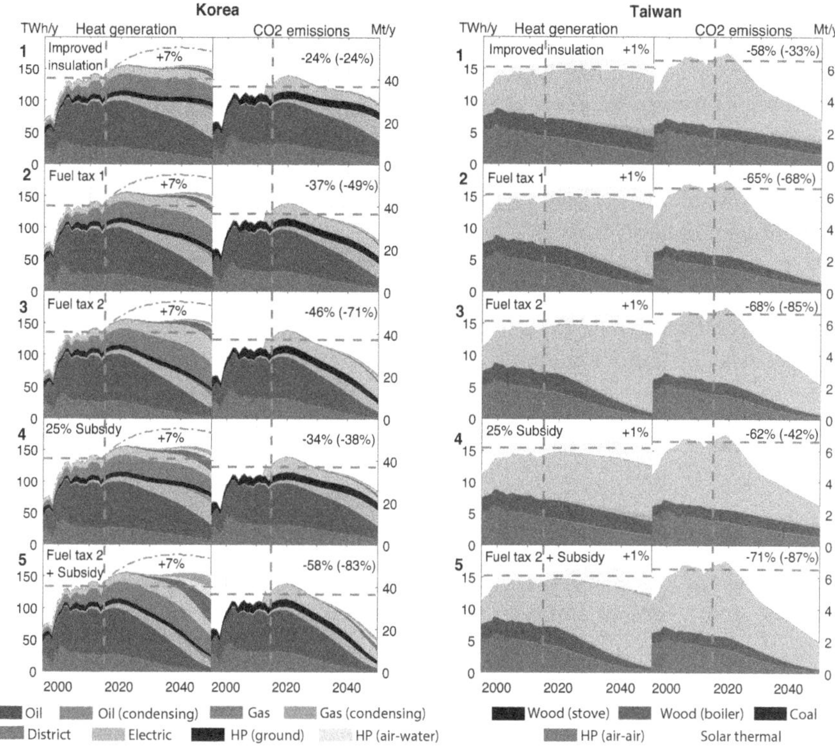

Figure 8.3 Projected technology composition and CO_2 emissions (direct on-site and indirect from electricity use) in the residential heating sectors of Korea (left) and Taiwan (right)

Source: Estimated by Cambridge Econometrics for this study

of technology diffusion, there is hardly any growth of renewable heating technologies. According to our data, the current market shares of both heat pumps and solar thermal are almost negligible. In our projections, they do not gain any significance in the country's technology mix before 2040, when no additional policies are implemented. A continued growth is projected for district heating, which has seen a steady increase over the past 20 years. Overall, the heating market is projected to remain dominated by gas and oil in the coming decades. However, despite that and the growth in demand, CO_2 emissions are projected to decrease under current diffusion trends. The main reason for the decline is a shift towards more efficient gas-heating systems. As a result, total CO_2 emissions in 2050 are projected to be 24% below their 2014 value.

When a carbon tax is introduced from 2020 onwards, the first effect would be a shift towards direct electric and district heating (the technology composition and emissions of which are not modelled here). Only after that, the policy would also induce an increased use of heat pumps. This, however, starts from a low level and, therefore, needs considerable time to gain momentum. Solar thermal, however, is both absent from the current mix and more expensive. Therefore, its role in future heating systems remains limited in our projections, at least without further policy instruments that are targeted at the uptake of this technology (such as procurement schemes or demonstration projects). Because the carbon tax would mainly lead to an electrification of residential heating, the policy's net effect on total emissions would depend on the parallel decarbonization of centralized electricity generation and heat plants.

Under a subsidy scheme, people could choose more efficient heat pumps, thereby reducing overall electricity demand as well as indirect emissions. Again, the largest effect is to be expected from a policy mix, which would reduce direct emissions by 83% in 2050 (and total emissions by 58%).

Taiwan

Owing to its warm climate, heat demand in Taiwan is relatively small, and largely attributable to water heating. The dominant technology is direct electric heating, which is a very convenient technology for low demand, in particular when it is mainly used to heat water. We estimate that the country's demand for water heating is largely saturated and will, therefore, remain flat until 2050. At the same time, demand cannot be reduced by improved insulation.

Because of the reliance on electric heating, indirect CO_2 emissions from electricity use are much larger than direct emissions from burning fossil fuels on site. Therefore, the most effective way to decarbonize residential buildings in Taiwan is to decarbonize the power sector. In addition, the climate in Taiwan is favorable for solar thermal heating and solar thermal already holds a significant market share (although without much growth dynamics).

We find that, under a carbon tax, households could shift towards direct electric heating, which is the most readily available technology. Under a subsidy, solar thermal would become relatively more attractive, and would gain considerable market share by 2050.

Overall, owing to Taiwan's significant reliance on electric heating, the effect of policies on total emissions largely relies on indirect emissions from the power sector. When the power sector is decarbonized in line with our 2°C scenario, total emissions for residential heating in 2050 would be 58% below their 2014 value, even without any policies in the heating sector.

The cost-effectiveness of policy mixes

From a public policy perspective, the decarbonization of heating could not only be beneficial for climate change mitigation but potentially also enable a more efficient provision of heat in monetary terms. Figure 8.4 shows the projected changes in levelized heating costs in scenarios 2–5 (i.e. as a result of the induced technology transitions) relative to those in Scenario 1 (i.e. improved insulation, but without technology policies). The depicted trends show the average levelized costs of heating in each country. This is calculated as the mean value of all technology-specific levelized costs in each country, weighted by their market shares at each point in time.

In all the scenarios, the projected savings from energy expenses exceed the additional costs for the purchase of new heating systems (assuming constant energy prices), leading to reductions in the 'bare' levelized cost (excluding taxes and subsidies) of heating in all four countries. The projected cost decreases are the largest in China (up to 40%), and between 5% and 20% for Korea and Japan. Importantly, the more stringent policy scenarios, that is, scenarios 3 and 5, are associated with larger cost reductions. Furthermore, the results indicate that subsidy payments for modern renewables would lead to a more efficient technology composition, leading to lower average heating costs in the medium therm. In Figure 8.4, the left-hand panels show the changes in bare levelized costs (upfront plus energy costs). The right-hand panels show the changes in levelized costs as perceived by households (including the simulated carbon taxes and subsidy payments).

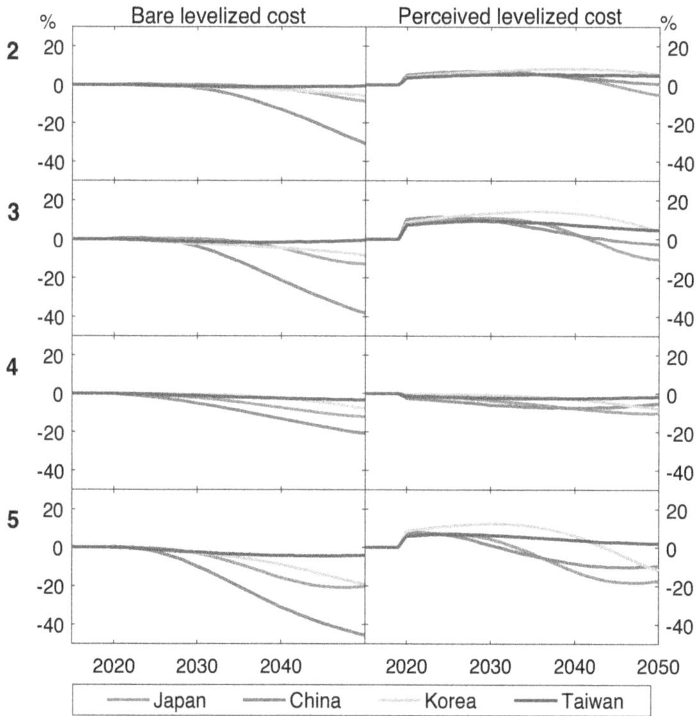

Figure 8.4 Changes in levelized costs of residential heating (in %)

Source: Estimated by Cambridge Econometrics for this study

Note: Policy scenarios 2–5 (aiming at uptake of low-carbon technologies) relative to Scenario 1 (improved insulation, without technology policies).

Table 8.4 Carbon tax revenues and subsidy payments in scenarios 2–5, cumulative from 2020–2050, in billion US$ (constant 2015 price levels)

Scenario		*Japan*	*China*	*Korea*	*Taiwan*
S2	Carbon tax revenues	54	378	56	3
	Subsidy payments	0	0	0	0
S3	Carbon tax revenues	86	469	94	5
	Subsidy payments	0	0	0	0
S4	Carbon tax revenues	0	0	0	0
	Subsidy payments	-14	-175	-3	-1
S5	Carbon tax revenues	40	292	50	2
	Subsidy payments	-16	-196	-5	-1
	Total	24	96	46	2

Source: Estimated by the authors for this study

Households, however, do not directly face the changes in bare levelized costs. They also must pay carbon taxes and, potentially, benefit from upfront subsidies. When taxes are used as the only policy instrument, tax payments would exceed the achievable savings in real costs until around 2040 in all scenarios. As a result, the perceived average levelized cost of heating would increase by 5–15% in all scenarios that involve a carbon tax. During this period, net benefits for households would then depend on the way in which tax revenues are redistributed. Table 8.4 shows the projected tax revenues and subsidy payments in each country, for scenarios 2–5. In the case of the policy mix in Scenario 5, part of the tax revenues would be recycled into purchase subsidies (equivalent to 9–67% of total tax revenues). The remaining tax revenues would be available for redistribution in other ways, for example, to decrease taxes on income (see Chapter 9).

Discussion and conclusion

Our results show that a decarbonization of residential heating in China, Japan, Korea and Taiwan is achievable in 2050, based on existing technologies and assuming improved insulation of houses. Such a decarbonization requires substantial policy efforts from 2020 onwards, involving residential carbon taxes and subsidy payments for renewables. Policy mixes are projected to be more effective than a carbon tax on its own to drive the market for new technologies, involving lower cumulative net emissions and reduced cost burdens for households. When combined with subsidies for the purchase of renewable technologies, decarbonization can be achieved with a carbon tax of US$57–229/t$CO_2$ by 2050. In all four countries, the policy-induced technology transition would initially increase the effective heating costs faced by households but would lead to net savings in the medium term (through fuel savings and induced reductions in the upfront costs of renewables).

Owing to long average lifetimes of about 20 years for heating equipment, the complete decarbonization of residential heating needs decades rather than years.

Considering the path-dependent diffusion dynamics of technology transitions, the required time scale is even longer than the average lifetime: even if policy incentives for switching to renewables are set in place from 2020 onwards, it is unrealistic that renewables could immediately gain a 100% market share in sales. It will take time for the diffusion to gain momentum. Households and installers need to learn about the existence and the performance characteristics of new technologies, and industry needs to restructure its production capacities.

The model projections demonstrate that the effectiveness of policies depends on behavioral decision-making by households. Although the net costs of the technology transition are projected to be negative in all four countries, we find that these savings would not be realized without additional policy incentives. The reason is that no household faces the system-wide cost over time. Instead, households decide from their individual perspectives, on the basis of what they know and can observe. This leads to trends of technology diffusion, which deviate from what would be considered the optimum from a societal perspective.

Other aspects of household decision-making are likely to be relevant but still remain unspecified in our modelling – such as split incentives (e.g. in case of rented property) or limited access to finance (which is one possible reason behind low required payback times). The value of 'intangibles', which we estimate from historical diffusion trends, is not necessarily constant over decades but may change over time. Furthermore, our results must be interpreted in the light of very limited data availability on energy end-use by households or on the stock of heating systems. Overall, a considerable degree of uncertainty remains regarding behavior, data and the future development of technology characteristics, under which the true long-term effect of any policy is hard to estimate a priori.

By using a detailed modelling study, we suggest that a decarbonization of residential heating in East Asia is possible by 2050, but unlikely to happen without stringent policy instruments. Whereas our modelling achieves the target with our set of assumed behavioral features, in reality, policy design must take into account as much additional behavioral knowledge as possible. Moreover, although, the evidence base is still thin, there is little time to spare and, therefore, further research will need to be carried out in conjunction with the introduction of policies.

Note

1 The specific carbon tax is only applied to the residential sector, and not assumed to be linked to other sectors, such as the power sector, which is subject to a separate set of policies.

References

Agency for Natural Resources and Energy (2015), "Top Runner Program." Agency for Natural Resources and Energy.

———. (2017), "Japan's Energy White Paper 2017." Agency for Natural Resources and Energy.

Arthur, Brian (1989), "Competing Technologies, Increasing Returns, and Lock-In by Historical Events." *The Economic Journal* 99(394): 116–131.

Cambridge Econometrics (2014), *E3ME Manual, Version 6*. Available online at www.camecon.com/wp-content/uploads/2016/09/E3ME-Manual.pdf.

China Heat Pump Committee of China Energy Conservation Association (2015), "China Heat Pump Industry Development Report 2015." China Heat Pump Committee of China Energy Conservation Association.

Connolly, David et al.(2014), "Heat Roadmap Europe: Combining District Heating With Heat Savings to Decarbonise the EU Energy System." *Energy Policy* 65: 475–489. http://dx.doi.org/10.1016/j.enpol.2013.10.035.

Connor, Peter et al.(2013), "Devising Renewable Heat Policy: Overview of Support Options." *Energy Policy* 59: 3–16.

Daioglou, Vassilis, Bas J. van Ruijven, and Detlef P. van Vuuren(2012), "Model Projections for Household Energy Use in Developing Countries." *Energy* 37(1): 601–615. http://dx.doi.org/10.1016/j.energy.2011.10.044.

Danish Energy Agency(2013), "Technology Data for Energy Plants – Individual Heating Plants and Energy Transport." Danish Energy Agency.

———. (2016), "Technology Data for Energy Plants." Danish Energy Agency.

EIA(2017), "Residential Energy Consumption Survey Data 2015." U.S. Energy Information Administration (EIA).

Fleiter, Tobias, Jan Steinbach, and Mario Ragwitz (2016), "Mapping and Analyses of the Current and Future (2020–2030) Heating/Cooling Fuel Deployment (Fossil/Renewables)." European Commission, Directorate-General for Energy.

Geels, Frank W., Benjamin K. Sovacool, Tim Schwanen, and Steve Sorrell (2017), "Sociotechnical Transitions for Deep Decarbonization." *Science* 357(6357): 1242–1244.

Gillingham, Kenneth, and Karen Palmery (2014), "Bridging the Energy Efficiency Gap: Policy Insights From Economic Theory and Empirical Evidence." *Review of Environmental Economics and Policy* 8(1): 18–38.

Henkel, Johannes (2012), "Modelling the Diffusion of Innovative Heating Systems in Germany – Decision Criteria, Influence of Policy Instruments and Vintage Path Dependencies." Berlin, Germany: TU Berlin.

Hofbauer, Josef, and Karl Sigmund (1998), "Evolutionary Games and Population Dynamics." Cambridge: Cambridge University Press.

IEA (2014), "Heating Without Global Warming: Market Developments and Policy Considerations for Renewable Heat." Paris, France: International Energy Agency.

———. 2016. "Energy Prices and Taxes, Volume 2016." Paris, France: International Energy Agency.

———. (2017), "World Energy Statistics and Balances (2017 Edition)." Paris, France: International Energy Agency.

IEA/ETSAP (2012), "Space Heating and Cooling – Technology Brief R02." Paris, France: International Energy Agency (IEA) Energy Technology Systems Analysis Program.

IEA/ETSAP and IRENA (2013), "Heat Pumps Technology Brief." Energy Technology Systems Analysis Programme (ETSAP) of the International Energy Agency (IEA) and International Renewable Energy Agency (IRENA).

International Energy Agency (IEA) (2013a), "Technology Roadmap. Energy Efficient Building Envelopes." *OECD*: 68. www.iea.org/publications/freepublications/publication/TechnologyRoadmapEnergyEfficientBuildingEnvelopes.pdf.

———. (2013b), "Transition to Sustainable Buildings: Strategies and Opportunities to 2050." Paris, France: International Energy Agency.

Isaac, Morna, and Detlef P. van Vuuren (2009), "Modeling Global Residential Sector Energy Demand for Heating and Air Conditioning in the Context of Climate Change." *Energy Policy* 37(2): 507–521.

Japan Refrigeration and Air Conditioning Industry Association (JRAIA) (2017), "Annual Shipments of Air Conditioners & Residential Heat Pump Water Heaters 1986–2016." Japan Refrigeration and Air Conditioning Industry Association.

Jiang, Yi et al. (2016), "China Building Energy Use 2016." China Building and Architecture Press. https://berc.bestchina.org/Files/CBEU2016.pdf.

Kegel, Martin, Justin Tamasauskas, Roberto Sunye, and Daniel Giguère (2014), "Heat Pumps in the Canadian Residential Sector." *IEA HPP Conference*: 19.

Kirman, A.(1992), "Whom or What Does the Representative Individual Represent." *The Journal of Economic Perspectives* 6(2): 117–136.

Knobloch, Florian et al. (2017), "A Technical Analysis of FTT: Heat – A Simulation Model for Technological Change in the Residential Heating Sector." *Technical Study on the Macroeconomics of Energy and Climate Policies (European Commission, DG Energy)*. https://ec.europa.eu/energy/sites/ener/files/documents/technical_analysis_residential_heat.pdf.

———. (2019), "Simulating the Deep Decarbonisation of Residential Heating for Limiting Global Warming to 1.5 °C." *Energy Efficiency* 12(2): 521–550. http://link.springer.com/10.1007/s12053-018-9710-0.

Korea Energy Economics Institute (2018), "Yearbook of Energy Statistics 2017." www.keei.re.kr/web_keei/d_results.nsf/0/0F00887C547033E44925812E0025B0E6/$file/OL1901.pdf.

Lapsa, M., Gannate Khowailed, Karen Sikes, and Van Baxter (2017), "Heat Pumps in North America – 2017 Regional Report." 12th IEA Heat Pump Conference (2017).

Lucon, O. et al. (2014), "Buildings." In *Climate Change 2014: Mitigation of Climate Change. Contribution of Working Group III to the Fifth Assessment Report of the Intergovernmental Panel on Climate Change*, Cambridge University Press, Cambridge, UK and New York, NY.

Lund, John W., and Tonya L. Boyd (2016), "Direct Utilization of Geothermal Energy 2015 Worldwide Review." *Geothermics* 60: 66–93.

Mauthner, Franz, Werner Weiss, and Monika Spörk-Dür (2016), "Solar Heat Worldwide: Markets and Contribution to the Energy Supply 2014." IEA Solar Heating & Cooling Programme.

McCollum, David L. et al. (2017), "Improving the Behavioral Realism of Global Integrated Assessment Models: An Application to Consumers' Vehicle Choices." *Transportation Research Part D: Transport and Environment* 55(May): 322–342. http://dx.doi.org/10.1016/j.trd.2016.04.003.

———. (2015), "An Age Structured Demographic Theory of Technological Change." *Journal of Evolutionary Economics* 25(4): 787–820.

———. (2016), "Modelling Complex Systems of Heterogeneous Agents to Better Design Sustainability Transitions Policy." *Global Environmental Change* 37: 102–115. http://dx.doi.org/10.1016/j.gloenvcha.2016.02.003.

———. (2018a), "Environmental Impact Assessment for Climate Change Policy with the Simulation-Based Integrated Assessment Model E3ME-FTT-GENIE." *Energy Strategy Reviews* 20: 195–208. https://doi.org/10.1016/j.esr.2018.03.003.

——— (2018b), "Fashion, Fads and the Popularity of Choices: Micro-Foundations for Diffusion Consumer Theory." *Structural Change and Economic Dynamics* 46: 194–207. https://doi.org/10.1016/j.strueco.2018.06.001.

NREL (2016), "Distributed Generation Renewable Energy Estimate of Costs (Updated February 2016)." National Renewable Energy Laboratory (NREL).

Olsthoorn, Mark, Joachim Schleich, Xavier Gassmann, and Corinne Faure (2017), "Free Riding and Rebates for Residential Energy Efficiency Upgrades: A Multi-Country Contingent Valuation Experiment." *Energy Economics* 68: 33–44.

PBL (2018), "User Support System IMAGE Scenarios."

Rai, Varun, and Adam Douglas Henry (2016), "Agent-Based Modelling of Consumer Energy Choices." *Nature Climate Change* 6(6): 556–562. http://dx.doi.org/10.1038/nclimate2967.

Riahi, Keywan et al. (2017), "The Shared Socioeconomic Pathways and Their Energy, Land Use, and Greenhouse Gas Emissions Implications: An Overview." *Global Environmental Change* 42: 153–168.

Rogers, Everett M. (2010), *Diffusion of Innovations.* New York: Simon and Schuster.

Sichong, Zhang, and Xu Wei (2014), "Research and Development of Large Scale Grand Source Heat Pump System." www.hptcj.or.jp/Portals/0/ahpnw/Newsletter/◎3rdAHPNWnewsletter20140925.pdf.

Sopha, Bertha Maya, Christian A. Klöckner, Geir Skjevrak, and Edgar G. Hertwich (2010), "Norwegian Households' Perception of Wood Pellet Stove Compared to Air-to-Air Heat Pump and Electric Heating." *Energy Policy* 38(7): 3744–3754.

Ürge-Vorsatz, Diana, Luisa F. Cabeza, et al. (2015), "Heating and Cooling Energy Trends and Drivers in Buildings." *Renewable and Sustainable Energy Reviews* 41: 85–98. http://dx.doi.org/10.1016/j.rser.2014.08.039.

Ürge-Vorsatz, Diana, Nick Eyre, et al. (2012), "Energy End-Use: Buildings." In *Global Energy Assessment – Toward a Sustainable Future*, 649–760.

Urge-Vorsatz, Diana, Ksenia Petrichenko, Maja Staniec, and Jiyong Eom (2013), "Energy Use in Buildings in a Long-Term Perspective." *Current Opinion in Environmental Sustainability* 5(2): 141–151. http://dx.doi.org/10.1016/j.cosust.2013.05.004.

Ürge-Vorsatz, Diana, Andras Reith, et al. (2015), "Monetary Benefits of Ambitious Building Energy Policies." Global Buildings Performance Network (GBPN).

Weiss, Martin, Martin Junginger, Martin K. Patel, and Kornelis Blok (2010), "A Review of Experience Curve Analyses for Energy Demand Technologies." *Technological Forecasting and Social Change* 77(3): 411–428. http://dx.doi.org/10.1016/j.techfore.2009.10.009.

9 Using revenues from carbon pricing measures as part of environmental tax reform in East Asia

Unnada Chewpreecha, Hector Pollitt, Park Seung-Joon and Soocheol Lee

Introduction

The concept of an environmental tax reform has been around for more than three decades. Formally, environmental tax reform (ETR) is defined as a 'reform of the national tax system where there is a shift of the burden of taxes, for example labor, to environmentally damaging activities, such as unsustainable resource use or pollution' (EEA, 2012). The concept of ETR originated in Germany, in the early 1980s (Binswanger et al., 1983), was introduced in countries of northern Europe in the early 1990s (see Andersen and Ekins, 2009) and, since then, has gradually expanded to regions across the world (World Bank Group, 2018).

In recent years, the expansion of ETR policies has lost its momentum as a result of different factors, such as an increasing popularity of other low-carbon policies, difficulty introducing new taxes after the financial crisis in 2009 and government reluctance to reduce existing tax revenues when faced with a large budget deficit. Nonetheless, the concept of ETR remains an attractive policy option among different low-carbon policies as it can generate double dividends, where benefits to the environment are realized at the same time as promoting economic growth and higher employment levels.

In Chapter 5, we explored a scenario in which a carbon-pricing instrument, a carbon tax, was used as one of the policies to meet the Nationally Determined Contributions (NDCs) and ambitious long-term 2°C target in the four East Asian economies. The modelling results in Chapter 5 suggested that, in absence of other policies, a high level of carbon tax will be required if China, Japan, Korea and Taiwan are to meet their long-term emissions reductions targets. It is not surprising that the carbon tax level turned out to be unrealistically high in this case. We then looked at three different levels of carbon tax within a mix of policies in different sectors as alternative scenarios (low, medium and ambitious). The results confirmed that a mixture of climate policies will yield better environmental and economic outcomes.

In this chapter, we use the ambitious policy-mix scenario of Chapter 5 as our starting point. This reference case includes a mixture of regulatory policies, technological support and price-based instruments to achieve the ambitious 2°C target in 2050. The main price-based instrument is a carbon tax, which generates revenues for national governments. At the same time, national governments also spend money on investments in energy efficiency and other support measures. In Chapter 5, the net revenues – that is, carbon tax minus the energy efficiency investment and other expenditures – are kept by the national government and are assumed to be used to improve public balances. We use this ambitious scenario of Chapter 5 as our reference case for this chapter.

Our analysis in this chapter comprises scenarios that are designed to have budget neutrality. In other words, there are no direct stimuli or austerity effects in the scenario. We explore different ways in which the revenues might be used through environmental tax reform (ETR). These include using the revenues to reduce existing taxes: income tax, VAT and employers' social security contributions. Additionally, we also look at a scenario in which the revenues are recycled back as a lump-sum payment – the so-called basic income or lump sum recycling – to households.

The analysis is carried out using the E3ME model. It shows that, by adopting additional ETR measures, it is possible to reduce the negative GDP impacts, or even to obtain positive GDP impacts, that is, a double dividend.

The remainder of this chapter is structured as follows: in the next section we introduce the economic literature. After that we explain the key features of E3ME-Asia, which are related to ETR analysis. The policy scenarios for the analysis are introduced next, with the results given in the subsequent section. In the final section we conclude our findings.

Existing discussions and literature

Despite there being a wide range of published papers on the topic of ETR and double dividends in Europe and North America, we have found relatively few publications regarding East Asia. The available literature mostly uses Computable General Equilibrium (CGE) models (see e.g. Park et al., 2012 for the Asia-Pacific region; Zhang and Zhang, 2013 for China; Takeda, 2007 for Japan; Kim and Kim, 2010 for Korea; Bor, 2010 for Taiwan). CGE models tend to have pessimistic results for any environmental policy owing to the supply-oriented nature and the assumption of equilibrium in all markets, including the labor market (if not explicitly designed otherwise; see the discussion in Chapter 1).

Meanwhile, macro-econometric models, such as E3ME, based on post-Keynesian economic theory, stressing market non-equilibrium and the importance of demand-side factors, can produce different results. These models can find that additional investment caused by environmental regulation (including environmental taxes) and tax reductions through revenue recycling may boost aggregate demand, thereby, triggering multiplier effects.

One of the most notable applications of the E3ME model was the COMETR research project (Andersen and Ekins, 2009), in which E3ME was used for ex-post assessment of economic and competitiveness effects of some of the first examples of ETR in Europe. The modelling results are described elsewhere (see Barker et al., 2007, 2009) and elaborated further in the context of households (see Ekins et al., 2011). They suggest that a small but strong double dividend effect is possible in Europe.

More recently, E3ME has been used widely to analyze environmental policies across the world. The model has also been repeatedly used to assess decarbonization pathways at different international levels (Barker et al., 2005, 2006, 2008; Barker and Scrieciu, 2009) and in the UK (Dagoumas and Barker, 2010). E3ME has also been applied (as described by Barker et al., 2012) to provide an economic assessment of the IEA's 450ppm scenario (IEA, 2010). In all of these studies, taxation has been a key policy input, with assumptions about revenue neutrality included in the scenarios.

In East Asia, E3ME has been applied to assess the 2020 targets of the Copenhagen agreement by China, Japan, Korea and Taiwan, and the possibility of double dividend effects through ETR (Lee et al., 2015). The findings confirm that a double dividend is possible.

In Japan, E3ME has been applied to assess the economic costs of Japan meeting its Copenhagen pledge of reducing GHG emissions to 3.8% below the levels of 2005 by 2020, and its NDC target of reducing its GHG emissions to 26% below the levels of 2013 by 2030 (see Lee et al., 2012, 2017). The model results showed this to incur a modest economic cost that could be turned into a modest benefit if efficient revenue recycling methods were used. The interaction between the share of nuclear power in Japan's energy mix and its carbon targets was discussed alongside environmental tax reform in Pollitt et al. (2014) and Lee et al. (2017).

The analysis carried out in this chapter is the first application of the E3ME model to analyze environmental tax reform in the context of long-term decarbonization targets in the East Asian countries.

The E3ME model

As the main structure of E3ME has been explained in previous chapters, the focus in this section is to outline how E3ME can be used to assess ETR. Further information regarding the E3ME model, including the full technical manual (Cambridge Econometrics, 2019) can also be found at the model website, www.e3me.com. The full list of equations is provided in Mercure et al. (2018).

The E3ME model was originally designed to assess energy and climate policy in Europe. As described in Chapter 1, E3ME is a macro-econometric simulation model based on post-Keynesian economic theory, which allows for imperfect price adjustment, market disequilibrium and limited rationality of economic actors.

Owing to detailed databases regarding taxes on income, labor, energy and so on, E3ME is well suited to analyses of ETR, as ETR comprises new or increased taxes on energy products and the recycling of its revenues by reducing other taxes. For example, a carbon tax will reduce fossil fuel consumption and CO_2 emissions because of its effect on energy prices and – in many cases – reduced economic activity levels (such as GDP or employment), while revenue recycling can boost economic activities under the right economic conditions.

Revenue recycling through the reduction of the rate of social security contributions on wages (also referred to as labor tax rates) may lead to increased labor demand. Wage rates depend on wage-bargaining functions, which are affected by overall conditions of the labor market and inflation, and will also affect employment decisions. These wage rate functions are empirically estimated for each sector and each country. However, reduced income tax rates, lump-sum payments (basic income) and reduced consumption tax rates (VAT rates) directly lead to increased consumption expenditure through the model's estimated consumption functions.

Policy scenarios and expected impacts

Our reference case for this chapter is the ambitious scenario of Chapter 5. However, it should be noted that this is different from the baseline, in which no carbon tax is introduced. In the reference case, the net revenues include carbon tax revenues, less-renewable subsidies and energy efficiency investments funded by government. In the reference case, the net revenues are used simply to improve the government budget balance. In other words, there is no revenue neutrality associated with the carbon tax. In this chapter, we further look at four different ways by which the national government can use the net carbon tax revenues for different purposes. They are as follows:

- Reductions in consumption tax (VAT)
- Reductions in income tax
- Reductions in (employers') social security contributions
- Lump-sum payment (basic income)

Owing to the budget neutrality requirement in the scenarios, there are no direct stimuli or austerity effects (when compared with baseline). The impacts in the revenue recycling scenarios are, instead, primarily driven by a reallocation of resources. Aggregate results are a combination of positive and negative effects. Environmental taxes, for example, increase costs to industries, thereby potentially impacting upon competitiveness; at the same time, however, these taxes could reduce a country's dependency on energy or material imports. Figures 9.1 and 9.2 provide examples of how a carbon or energy tax together with revenue recycling (through employers' social security contributions) affects key output indicators in E3ME.

The VAT rate in E3ME is defined as a single rate in each country, although variations of this rate are allowed for different product groups. In the VAT recycling scenario, a reduction in the VAT rate is applied equally across all consumer products, so that the same proportionate change in price is seen.

The income tax rate in E3ME is defined as a single rate in each country, which is levied on all earned wage income, regardless of the individual's total income.

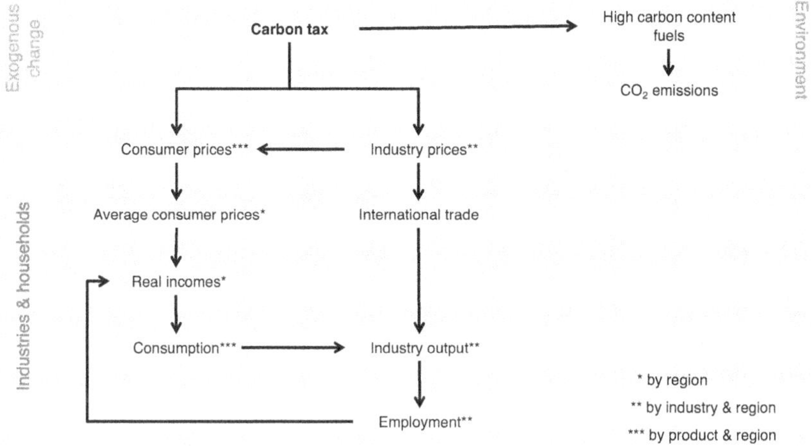

Figure 9.1 Impact of a carbon tax in E3ME

Source: Pictured by Cambridge Econometrics for this study

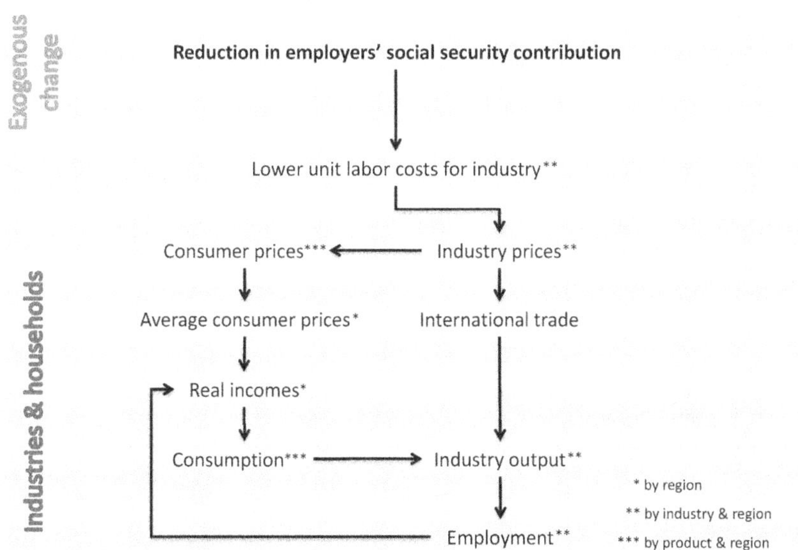

Figure 9.2 Impacts of revenue recycling through employers' social security contributions

Source: Pictured by Cambridge Econometrics for this study

Therefore, the lowest income class also pays income tax in proportion to its income. When the income tax rate is adjusted, it effectively assumes a similar proportional reduction in tax payments across all different income tax bands. The impact of a reduction in the tax rate is to increase household disposable income. There may also be a small increase in labor supply, as the reduction in income tax acts as an incentive to work.

The labor tax, also referred to in some countries as employers' social security contributions, is a tax on wages that is paid by the employer; therefore, by reducing it, the cost of labor is lowered. A single rate (as a proportion of wages) is applied for each country. The lump-sum payment is a basic payment that gets distributed indiscriminately among households. It is equivalent to the so-called basic income. In the modelling it is simply added to household income, which stimulates consumer spending.

Results and analysis

Here, we present outcomes of the four alternative scenarios, in which the revenues from carbon taxes are recycled back to the economy. The results from the reference scenario, as well as the four alternative revenue recycling scenarios, are compared against the baseline – the same as in Chapter 5 and based on current policy.

Impacts on GDP

Table 9.1 summarizes the impacts of the different recycling mechanisms on GDP in 2050, compared with the baseline and the reference without revenue recycling (carbon tax with austerity).

The E3ME results clearly show positive impacts when revenue is recycled. In all cases, impacts on GDP are positive when compared with the reference case, in which the national government keeps hold of the carbon tax revenues. In the revenue recycling scenarios, they are also positive compared to the baseline.

Table 9.1 Impacts on GDP in China, Japan, Korea and Taiwan, in 2050 (% differences from baseline in Chapter 5)

	China	*Japan*	*Korea*	*Taiwan*
Reference (carbon tax with austerity)	-0.6	1.1	1.4	-0.6
Income tax recycling	2.8	3.0	6.5	1.2
Employers' social security contributions recycling	0.3	2.0	4.4	0.4
VAT recycling	2.4	2.5	3.5	1.5
Lump-sum recycling (basic income)	2.8	2.9	6.5	1.2

Source: Estimated by Cambridge Econometrics for this study

Table 9.2 Carbon tax rate in the reference case (carbon tax with austerity) in 2050 (2018 prices, \$/tCO_2, additional to baseline)

	China	*Japan*	*Korea*	*Taiwan*
Reference case	321	178	279	131

Source: Estimated by Cambridge Econometrics for this study

The most economically beneficial methods of revenue recycling are those where revenues are directly given back to households. Our results show that income tax and lump-sum payments generate almost the same outcomes. A reduction in income tax rates increases households' after-tax income, whereas the lump-sum payment increases the amount of income directly received by households. Both methods directly boost consumers' disposable income, leading to a higher level of consumption, and creating further multiplier effects in the four East Asian economies.

Revenue recycling through reductions in consumption tax (VAT) is also an effective way to stimulate GDP. By lowering the tax on consumption, prices of goods and services become lower, and consumers respond by spending more (in real terms) as a result.

In the case of revenue recycling through employers' social security contributions, the net impacts on GDP are positive but less than following the other recycling methods. A reduction in the employers' social security contributions reduces the cost of labor to industry. These cost savings may or may not be passed on to final product prices, and the savings could, instead, be used to increase firms' profits. Consequently, the impacts on GDP in this case are lower than in cases where consumer spending is stimulated directly through revenue recycling.

The differences in the impacts on GDP between the four East Asian countries are reflected mainly in the national carbon tax rates that are applied in the reference case (Table 9.2). The carbon tax rate is higher in China and Korea and, therefore, more carbon tax revenues are available for recycling, leading to larger positive impacts.

Employment impacts

Our modelling results show that employment results can also be improved through revenue recycling, although, in contrast to GDP, the outcomes are not always positive compared to the baseline.

To achieve the best employment results, policy makers are best off by stimulating household consumption directly, as this leads to increased production and creates additional demand for labor inputs (Table 9.3). Revenue recycling through employers' social security contributions is effective in stimulating employment demand despite it producing a lower GDP impact than the other revenue recycling methods. However, this approach is still inferior to other methods of revenue recycling. The impacts of a reduction of labor costs are notable in countries

Table 9.3 Employment impacts in East Asia, in 2050 (% differences from baseline in Chapter 5)

	China	*Japan*	*Korea*	*Taiwan*
Reference (carbon tax with austerity)	-0.4	0.2	0.0	-0.6
Income tax recycling	1.5	0.9	1.9	-0.5
Employers' social security contribution recycling	-0.3	0.7	1.9	-0.1
VAT recycling	0.7	0.8	1.4	-0.2
Lump-sum recycling (basic income)	1.5	0.9	1.9	-0.5

Source: Estimated by Cambridge Econometrics for this study

where labor costs are high. In China, where labor costs are relatively low, a reduction in labor tax is less effective in stimulating employment growth.

Other macroeconomic indicators

Table 9.4 summarizes the impact of each revenue recycling method on the key components of GDP. In the reference case, higher prices resulting from the cost of climate policies result in higher inflation rates. Consumer spending in the reference case falls because of increased prices and lower disposable incomes. Remember that in the Chapter 5 baseline all regions of the world also implement climate actions to meet the 2°C target. This means that effects on competitiveness are limited. Our reference case shows a significant drop in energy imports, which might improve the trade balance of countries that import a lot of energy. Moreover, the reference case receives a stimulus from investments towards renewables and energy efficiency.

In the revenue recycling scenarios, there are clear benefits to consumers. This is the largest in the VAT case. In the case of labor tax, the boost to consumer demand is not as big. In all revenue recycling cases, higher consumer demand leads to increased imports of goods and services.

Sectoral impacts

The sectoral impacts shown in Table 9.5 demonstrate how the benefits and costs of the scenarios are distributed across the sectors of the East Asian economies. In the reference case, without revenue recycling, output in many sectors falls compared to the baseline as the costs of energy inputs increase and consumer demand falls. Construction and manufacturing may benefit even in the reference case, however, from additional renewables and efficiency investments, resulting in increases in their output (see Chapter 5 for more detail).

In all our revenue-recycling scenarios, the negative impacts from climate policies are reverted for all sectors, except those of energy extraction and utilities, both of which remain negative. However, energy extraction and utilities show slight

Table 9.4 Main macroeconomic impacts in East Asia, in 2050 (% difference from baseline in Chapter 5)

	Reference (carbon tax with austerity)	*Income tax recycling*	*Employers' social security contribution recycling*	*VAT recycling*	*Lump-sum recycling (basic income)*
China					
GDP	-0.6	2.8	0.3	2.4	2.8
Consumer spending	-4.5	4.8	-1.2	1.6	4.8
Exports	-0.4	0.3	-0.3	1.3	0.3
Imports	0.1	1.1	0.3	1.1	1.1
Investment	2.7	3.7	2.6	3.7	3.7
Inflation	2.0	1.0	1.0	-0.8	1.0
Japan					
GDP	1.1	3.0	2.0	2.5	2.9
Consumer spending	-0.8	2.1	0.7	1.5	2.1
Exports	0.0	0.7	0.3	0.4	0.7
Imports	-7.0	-4.8	-5.9	-5.2	-4.8
Investment	3.8	5.5	4.2	4.7	5.5
Inflation	1.0	0.7	0.5	-0.6	0.7
Korea					
GDP	1.4	6.5	4.4	3.5	6.5
Consumer spending	0.4	8.5	5.5	3.1	8.5
Exports	0.1	1.4	0.4	1.1	1.4
Imports	-1.4	2.4	0.5	-0.1	2.4
Investment	1.3	2.1	1.4	2.0	2.1
Inflation	2.7	0.2	0.0	-1.7	0.2
Taiwan					
GDP	-0.6	1.2	0.4	1.5	1.2
Consumer spending	-3.4	0.0	-1.1	0.8	0.0
Exports	0.4	1.3	0.5	1.1	1.3
Imports	-0.5	0.2	-0.5	-0.1	0.2
Investment	2.4	2.7	2.3	2.3	2.7
Inflation	1.9	1.7	1.0	-2.3	1.7

Source: Estimated by Cambridge Econometrics for this study

improvements as a result of the rebound in energy demand. The issue of rebounds in energy demand is discussed later in this chapter.

In the revenue-recycling scenarios, the sectors that benefit tend to be service sectors, as they are highly related to consumer sectors (and, therefore, benefit from boosts to consumption) and have relatively high labor input (and, therefore, benefit from reductions of labor costs). The manufacturing and transport sectors are relatively energy intensive so, although they benefit from the boost in demand

Table 9.5 Output in East Asia, in 2050 (% differences from baseline in Chapter 5)

	Reference (carbon tax with austerity)	*Income tax recycling*	*Employers' social security contribution recycling*	*VAT recycling*	*Lump-sum recycling (basic income)*
Agriculture	-0.9	3.3	0.4	1.9	3.3
Basic manufacturing	0.1	2.4	0.7	2.3	2.4
Advanced manufacturing	0.7	2.7	1.1	2.4	2.7
Energy extraction	-66.1	-65.8	-66.1	-65.8	-65.8
Utilities	-3.7	-3.4	-3.6	-3.5	-3.4
Construction	2.8	3.7	3	3.4	3.7
Services	-0.4	3.2	1	2.1	3.2

Source: Estimated by Cambridge Econometrics for this study

because of revenue recycling, they continue to suffer from higher energy input costs as a result of the carbon tax.

Distributional impacts

The E3ME model is capable of analyzing policy impacts for different income groups. Currently, the analysis is only available for Korea and Japan because of data limitations in China and Taiwan. The approach is based on two components: income and spending. The first part is the income side. For each income group, the impact on income comes from aggregate results from the model but the impacts on each income group depend on their share of income from wages, social security benefits and other income – minus their tax deductions (Figure 9.3). Therefore, a scenario that includes increases in benefit rates would show positive results for income groups who rely more on benefits, and a scenario with a reduction in income tax rates would benefit income groups who pay more tax as a share of their income.

The second part links survey data of household expenditure to the model results for consumer prices. This is mainly used to assess the effects of higher energy prices, because in many countries low-income households use a larger share of their income for heating. A rise in energy costs would, therefore, disproportionately reduce their real disposable income, that is, the income that is price-adjusted after tax and benefits, and adjusted for inflation.

The distributional results are summarized in Figure 9.4, and show that the carbon tax and different revenue-recycling methods unevenly affect different income groups. Impacts on the real disposable incomes of lower-income groups tend to be more negative than those for higher-income groups, mainly because of the regressive[1] price effects.

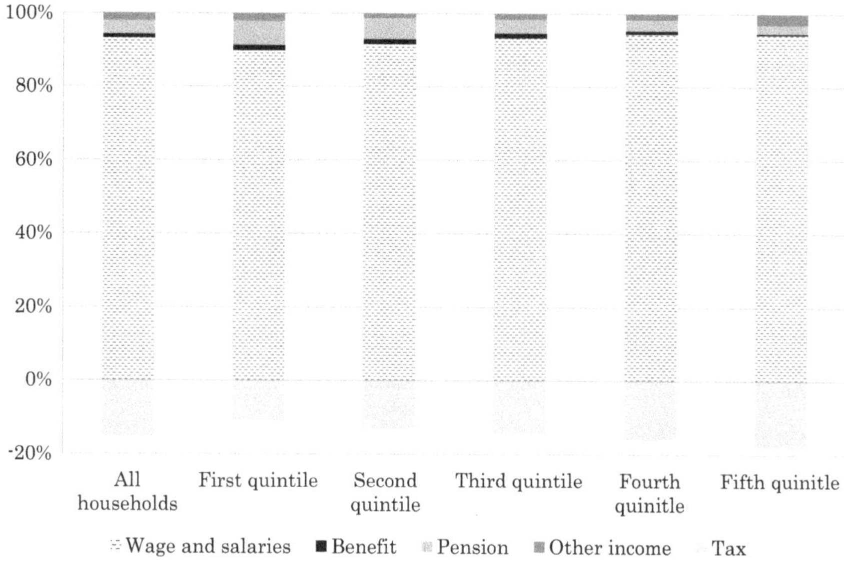

Figure 9.3 Sources of household income, Japan

Source(s): Family Income and Expenditure Survey (Statistics Japan)

In the reference case (without revenue recycling), the carbon tax negatively affects the real disposable incomes of lower-income groups more than that of higher-income groups. This is mainly because of price effects, as lower-income groups tend to spend a higher share of their income on energy, that is, necessities. However, the negative impact is limited to less than ~2%. In our revenue-recycling scenarios, the total real income effects remain regressive among all scenarios, because regressive price effects resulting from the carbon tax outweigh any progressive effects of the revenue recycling. Revenue recycling via income tax and lump-sum payment generated the most positive impact for all income classes – including the lowest – as both methods provide a direct boost to household income. This leads to higher employment, disproportionately benefiting households with a higher share of income from employment.

Even the basic income (lump-sum payment), whose direct effect is progressive on its own, cannot cancel the regressive overall effect of the carbon tax. There are some modelling limitations (because of data availability) here, however. In the E3ME model, the assumption of a single rate of income tax and no variation in the marginal propensity to consume across income groups, may understate the benefits of boosting incomes in low-income households.

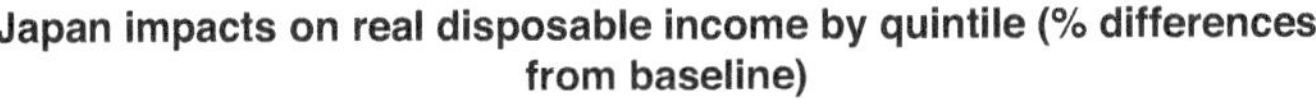

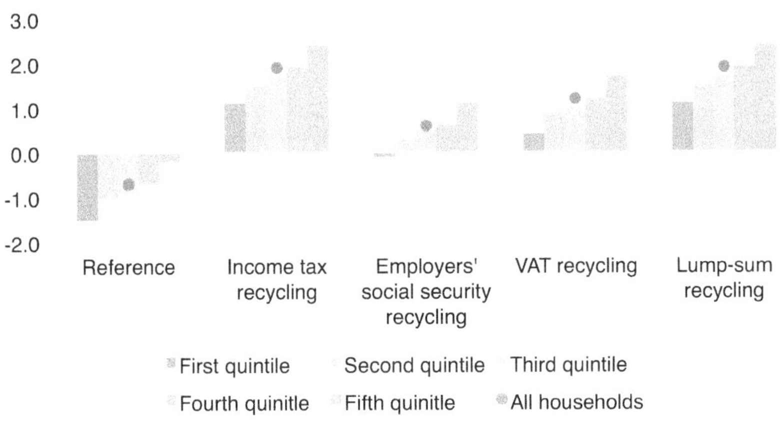

Korea impacts on real disposable income by quintile (% differences from baseline)

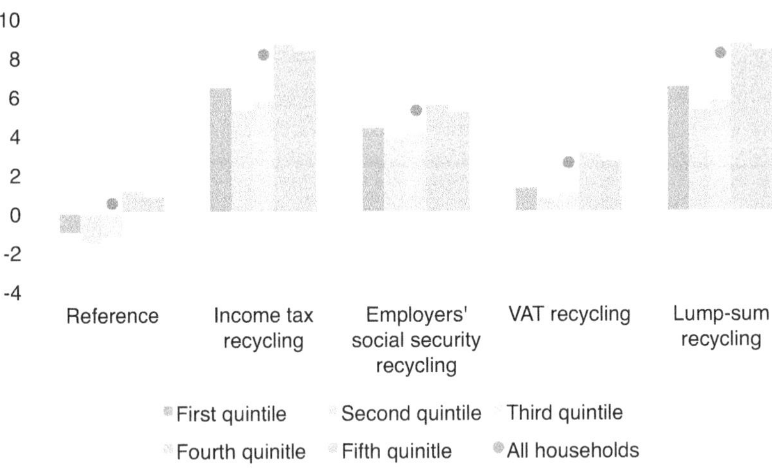

Figure 9.4 Impacts on real disposable income by quintile, Korea and Japan (% difference from baseline in Chapter 5)

Source: Estimated by Cambridge Econometrics for this study

Rebound effects

It is important to consider rebounds in energy demand as a result of higher economic activity that occurs from revenue recycling. Usually, this leads to higher emissions because higher demand for products and services requires additional

Table 9.6 CO_2 emissions in 2050 (% change from 2005)

	China	*Japan*	*Korea*	*Taiwan*
Reference	-70	-80	-80	-80
Income tax recycling	-69	-80	-80	-80
Employers' social security contribution recycling	-70	-80	-81	-80
VAT recycling	-69	-80	-81	-81
Lump-sum recycling (basic income)	-69	-80	-80	-80

Source: Estimated by Cambridge Econometrics for this study

energy inputs. However, emission results from our revenue-recycling scenarios show that this is not the case (Table 9.6). The four East Asian countries in the reference case already become low-carbon and energy-efficient economies by 2050, which means that any additional energy demand from rebounds in consumption are met by sustainable and renewable energy sources.

Conclusions

In this chapter, we have analyzed the use of carbon tax revenues to help alleviate the negative impacts that climate policies could have on the economy and jobs, and which occur in the decarbonization scenarios of Chapter 5. Overall, although there are some stimuli from efficiency and renewable investment, the costs of the carbon taxes in Chapter 5 lead to overall reductions in GDP and employment. The ambitious scenario (S3) in Chapter 5 is our reference case in this chapter.

Our results show that, by recycling revenues from the carbon tax, China, Japan, Korea and Taiwan can still meet their ambitious long-term decarbonization targets, and stimulate their economies and employment at the same time. In all the revenue-recycling scenarios, the impacts on GDP and jobs in the four countries are higher than in the reference case. The rebound effects on energy demand and emissions from additional economic activities are minimal since any additional energy demands are met with renewable sources.

The most effective methods of revenue recycling to promote GDP growth are through reductions in income tax rates and lump-sum payments, as they directly boost household income, resulting in higher spending. Using revenue recycling to reduce VAT is the second-most effective way to increase GDP, as it lowers the price of goods and services. Revenue recycling through employers' social security contributions lowers costs for firms but has limited positive impacts on GDP, as we do not expect firms to pass on all the savings to their customers. However, this method directly boosts demand for employment, as it makes labor inputs to production cheaper.

At the sectoral level our results suggest that, when designing policies, varying sectoral impacts must be taken into account. The sectors that stand to benefit from revenue-recycling measures are those that are linked to consumer spending, whereas sectors that supply energy will continue to lose out.

Income distribution must also be considered when designing climate policy. Our results show that different recycling methods can yield uneven impacts on different income groups in Japan and Korea. Our results also show that even the lump-sum payments (basic income), whose direct effect is progressive on its own (in relative terms), may not be able to cancel the regressive overall effect of the carbon tax. However, a more targeted revenue-recycling method might be required if the main policy objective is to improve the distribution of income among households.

Our main finding from this chapter is that it is possible to reverse the negative impacts that the costs of climate policy may have on the East Asian economy. We have shown that the ambitious carbon reduction target can be achieved at the same time as promoting economic growth and job creation. This is called the 'double dividend of an environmental tax reform', meaning that there are positive effects on both the environment and the economy. It is, therefore, recommended that national governments include environmental tax reform as part of their long-term climate policy portfolios.

In the next chapter we turn attention to another crucial but linked issue relating to the low-carbon transition: how to ensure that companies and households have access to the finance necessary to fund low-carbon development.

Note

1 In this chapter, 'regressive' refers to those effects that are more negative or less positive for lower-income groups and 'progressive' to those effects that are better for lower-income groups; 'proportional' means that the effect is proportional to income, so neither regressive nor progressive.

References

Andersen, MS and P Ekins (2009) *Carbon-Energy Taxation: Lessons From Europe*, Oxford, IEA.

Barker, T, A Anger, U Chewpreecha and H Pollitt (2012) 'A New Economics Approach to Modelling Policies to Achieve Global 2020 Targets for Climate Stabilisation', *International Review of Applied Economics*, special issue on 'Economic policies of the new thinking in economics', Volume 26, Number 2, pp. 205–221.

Barker, T, P Ekins, S Junankar, H Pollitt and P Summerton (2009, April) 'The Competitiveness Effects of European Environmental Tax Reforms', *European Review of Energy Markets, Energy Policy*, Volume 3, Number 1.

Barker, T, T Foxon and SS Scrieciu (2008) 'Achieving the G8 50% Target: Modelling Induced and Accelerated Technological Change Using the Macro-Econometric Model E3MG', *Climate Policy*, Special Issue on 'Modelling long-term scenarios for low-carbon societies', Volume 8, pp. S30–S45.

Barker, T, S Junankar, H Pollitt and P Summerton (2007) 'Carbon Leakage From Unilateral Environmental Tax Reforms in Europe, 1995–2005', *Energy Policy*, Volume 35, pp. 6281–6292.

Barker, T, H Pan, J Köhler, R Warren and S Winne (2005) 'Avoiding Dangerous Climate Change by Inducing Technological Progress: Scenarios Using a Large-scale

Econometric Model', chapter 38 in Schellnhuber, HJ, W Cramer, N Nakicenovic, T Wigley and G Yohe (eds) *Avoiding Dangerous Climate Change*, Cambridge, Cambridge University Press.

Barker, T, H Pan, J Köhler, R Warren and S Winne (2006) 'Decarbonizing the Global Economy With Induced Technological Change: Scenarios to 2100 Using E3MG', in Edenhofer, O, K Lessmann, K Kemfert, M Grubb and J Köhler (eds) *Induced Technological Change: Exploring its Implications for the Economics of Atmospheric Stabilization*, Energy Journal Special Issue on the International Model Comparison Project.

Barker, T and SS Scrieciu (2009) 'Unilateral Climate Change Mitigation, Carbon Leakage and Competitiveness: An Application to the European Union', *International Journal of Global Warming*, Volume 1, Number 4, pp. 405–417.

Binswanger, HC, H Frisch and HG Nutzinger (1983) 'Arbeit ohne Umweltzerstörung: Strategien einer neuen Wirtschaftspolitik', Fischer Tb. (Grün), Frankfurt, available online at https://www.booklooker.de/B%C3%BCcher/Binswanger-Frisch-Nutzinger-u-a+Arbeit-ohne-Umweltzerst%C3%B6rung/id/A01bYTmv01ZZB

Bor, YJ (2010) 'Energy Taxation and the Double Dividend Effect in Taiwan's Energy Conservation Policy – An Empirical Study Using a Computable General Equilibrium Model', *Energy Policy*, Volume 38, Number 5, pp. 2086–2100.

Cambridge Econometrics. (2019) *E3ME Manual, Version 7.0*, available online at www.e3me.com

Dagoumas, A and T Barker (2010) 'Pathways to a Low-Carbon Economy for the UK With the Macro-Econometric E3MG Model', *Energy Policy*, Volume 38, Number 6, pp. 3067–3077.

EEA (2012) *Environmental Tax Reform in Europe: Implications for Income Distribution*, EEA Technical Report No 16/2011.

Ekins, P, H Pollitt, J Barton and D Blobel (2011) 'The Implications for Households of Environmental Tax Reform (ETR) in Europe', *Ecological Economics*, Volume 70, Number 12, pp. 2472–2485, Elsevier.

IEA (2010) *World Energy Outlook 2010*, International Energy Agency, OECD.

Kim, S-R and J-Y Kim (2010) *The Design and Economic Effects of Green Fiscal Reform in Korea, Korea Institute of Public Finance*, available online at http://www.kipf.re.kr/storage/Publish/Attach/Old/pdf/634425247534577500.pdf [in Korean].

Lee, S, U Chewpreecha, H Pollitt and S Kojima (2017) 'An Economic Assessment of Carbon Tax Reform to Meet Japan's NDC Target Under Different Nuclear Assumptions Using the E3ME Model', *Environmental Economics and Policy Studies*. doi:10.1007/s10018-017-0199-0.

Lee, S, H Pollitt and SJ Park (2015) *Low-Carbon, Sustainable Future in East Asia*, New York: Routledge.

Lee, S, H Pollitt and K Ueta (2012) 'An Assessment of Japanese Carbon Tax Reform Using the E3MG Econometric Model', *The Scientific World Journal*, Volume 2012, Article ID 835917.

Mercure, J-F, H Pollitt, NR Edwards, PB Holden, U Chewpreecha, P Salas, A Lam, F Knobloch and JE Viñuales (2018, April) 'Environmental Impact Assessment for Climate Change Policy With the Simulation-based Integrated Assessment Model E3ME-FTT-GENIE', *Energy Strategy Reviews*, Volume 20, pp. 195–208.

Park, S-J, M Yamazaki and S Takeda (2012) *Environmental Tax Reform: Major Findings and Policy Implications From a Multi-Regional Economic Simulation Analysis, a Background Policy Paper for Low Carbon Green Growth Roadmap for Asia and the Pacific*, United Nations ESCAP.

Pollitt, H, S Lee, S-J Park and K Ueta (2014) 'An Economic and Environmental Assessment of Future Electricity Generation Mixes in Japan – An Assessment Using the E3MG Macro-Econometric Model', *Energy Policy*, Volume 67, pp. 243–254, Elsevier.

Takeda, S (2007, September) 'The Double Dividend From Carbon Regulations in Japan', *Journal of the Japanese and International Economies*, Volume 21, Number 3, pp. 336–364.

World Bank Group (2018, May) *State and Trends of Carbon Pricing 2018*, Washington, DC.

Zhang, J-H and W-Z Zhang (2013) 'Will Carbon Tax Yield Employment Double Dividend for China?', *International Journal of Business and Social Research*, Volume 3, Number 4, pp. 124–131.

10 Financing the low-carbon transition

Hector Pollitt and Jean-François Mercure

Introduction

In Chapter 5, we showed that it is possible for the countries in East Asia to reduce emissions to levels that are consistent with globally limiting the average temperature change to below 2°C. It may even be possible to meet this environmental goal while, at the same time, stimulating domestic economies through environmental tax reforms (ETRs) (see Chapter 9).

The model results also allude to substantial shifts in resources, for example, in the types of technology used or levels of output in different sectors within the model. It is reasonable to ask how much investment will be needed to bring about such a shift and where the financing for that investment might come from. The first question can be answered by further analyzing the model results. Table 10.1 shows the net amounts of energy-related investment that are recorded for each East Asian country under the ambitious scenario defined in Chapter 5 (S3), in addition to the baseline. It is clear that these investment flows are substantial and could influence the macroeconomic results from the modelling exercise. If, for some reason, the investment would not be provided, not only would the climate targets be in danger of not being met, but also the economic results might be quite different.

The following section discusses where the necessary finances for the investment might come from, and why the source of financing is important. This naturally

Table 10.1 Net amounts of energy-related investment for each East Asian country in Scenario 3 described in Chapter 5

	Investment (in million US$)*	*Proportion of GDP (in %)*
China	6,528.5	1.8
Japan	711.7	0.5
Korea	318.4	0.7
Taiwan	129.6	0.6

* The investment values in the table are in 2018 prices, cumulated up to 2050 (non-discounted). Chapter 5 S3 is the ambitious scenario that includes a broad range of policies across all sectors, as well as economy-wide carbon taxes.

leads into a discussion of any potential macroeconomic impacts of finance and investment; we show that the choice of modelling assumptions here is critical. Next, we reverse the relationship between finance and the 'real' economy to consider how a decarbonization scenario might impact on the financial system. The final section concludes and outlines the key questions for future research.

Potential sources of finance

Policy makers in many countries have noticed that access to finance is a crucial issue if targets for decarbonization are to be met. However, there are several complicating factors, including:

- Existing sources of finance are often not well known.
- Potential new sources of finance are even less well known.
- Lack of coordination exists between finance and environment ministries.
- Lack of knowledge transfer exists between policy makers and the financial community.

There are also substantial differences between the financing mechanisms that are used in different countries, reflecting cultural factors and regulatory divergence. Even within the European Union considerable differences exist between the sources of finance available for low-carbon development in each member state (European Commission, 2017a).

By and large, however, the main potential sources of funding for companies investing in low-carbon energy sources are:

- National governments via the public sector
- Retained savings, that is, drawing on existing wealth
- Loans provided by commercial banks
- Equity investments by pension funds and other investment funds

It should also be noted that, at the micro level, it is important to ask whether financing comes in the form of debt or equity. In some cases, only one of the options may be possible (e.g. national governments might not want to take stakes in firms; it is impossible for households to issue equity), or there may be incentives to favor one option over the other (e.g. tax relief on interest payments). At the macro level, however, this choice does not make much difference and, so, we do not discuss it further here.

The various sources of finance have quite different characteristics that make them suitable for different types of investment. We summarize each one below.

Public sector finance

The public sector will undoubtedly play a crucial role in ensuring a low-carbon transition. Broadly speaking, there is a role for the public sector in all instances in which investment will either be unprofitable for the private sector or is deemed as too risky. Notable examples include early-stage research (i.e. products that are a long way from market) or infrastructure, such as hydro or nuclear plants that are too large for individual firms to finance. However, there may also be a role for the public sector in small-scale, low-cost ventures; for example, the transaction costs in loans for household energy efficiency improvements may be prohibitive to private lenders.

Public sector finance in itself can take many different forms. For example, the government could provide subsidies, partial subsidies or loans for particular investments – or, in some cases, demand equity. The financing will usually be directed through an agency that has dedicated expertise. One important exception is investment by state-owned enterprises, for example in China. Here, the distinction between private and public financing becomes blurred; however, it may be reasonable to assume at least some implicit state backing for lending to these organizations.

Japan enacted a law on Promoting Low Carbon Investment in 2010 to encourage low-carbon investment in all parts of the country. The Green Investment Promotion Organization in Japan (comprising four big insurance companies) was established the same year in response. This organization offers long-term and low–interest rate loans to companies that develop or manufacture facilities or products, or construct low-carbon infrastructure, such as electric vehicles or hydrogen-charging facilities. The organization also offers credit to small and medium-sized companies that purchase or lease low-carbon facilities, and which do not have access to sufficient credit. In addition, it distributes Feed-in-Tariff (FIT) charge revenues (approximately 3 trillion JPY in 2018), gathered from electricity users, to renewable electricity suppliers.

There is one further important point to notice regarding public financing. For any private company or individual, high debt levels might result, ultimately, in default and bankruptcy. For the public sector, however, the amount that can be borrowed is unlimited – as long as the borrowing is in the national currency – because as long as they get the approval of the National Assembly, national governments can always instruct central banks to create additional reserves to fund debt levels.

In scenarios with high levels of additional debt, this can be an important factor to take into account. High levels of private debt have been shown to be precursors to financial instability (Keen, 2011). It is still unclear whether decarbonization scenarios could cause instability (see discussion later in this chapter) but a combination of public financing and public underwriting of private debt may, at some point, be beneficial from the perspective of financial stability.

Retained savings

The use of existing wealth to fund low-carbon developments is possible for both households and companies. For high-net-worth households or companies with large cash reserves, it may be the preferred means to finance development.

There are some important limitations, however. One is the obvious limit in magnitude, which is dictated by the size of the pool of privately held savings. There are also major restrictions in matching the demand and supply of finance, that is, cash-rich companies and wealthy households may not be the ones that need to make substantial low-carbon investments. The obvious example from the energy sector is that those companies with the largest cash reserves are fossil fuel companies, rather than companies that focus on renewable energy options. In summary, retained savings are likely to be used by both households and companies to meet some of the financing gap, but the overall contribution might be small.

Lending by commercial banks

For many companies, much of the finance required for low-carbon investment is likely to come from banks. The mechanism is fairly straightforward: if both the company and the bank can see a profitable investment, the bank will issue a loan. As described in the next section, the issuing of this loan has important macroeconomic implications.

The key requirement is that both the bank and the company expect the investment to provide a return without substantial risk. Although companies may be expected to have a reasonable idea about which investments might be profitable, knowledge in the banking sector is limited. A lack of knowledge represents a higher risk, meaning that the expected return must also be higher if the loan is to be issued.

Measures by the public sector to underwrite loans (i.e. by providing financial guarantees) could help to reduce the risk and to incentivize banks to lend. There is also an assumption that, as low-carbon investment becomes more common, knowledge of the products involved will also be spread more widely. However, there could be a role for policy makers in providing knowledge to the banking sector of some of the key technologies available.

Another impediment to the banking sector may be transaction costs. Banks are reluctant to issue small loans to households to invest in low-carbon equipment because the overheads of doing so make it less profitable. There may be a role for policy makers to assist with the creation of standardized products that would reduce transaction costs (akin to how index-tracking funds reduced the costs of investing in the stock market). Overall, however, there is a general sense that more engagement between policy makers and the banking community would be beneficial to financing low-carbon investment.

Lending from other financial institutions

Banks are not the only financial institutions that may lend money for low-carbon investment. Investment funds, including pension funds and hedge funds, could also provide finance. So far, the amounts of finance for low-carbon investment provided by these groups has been limited, as these funds typically buy existing assets rather than funding new developments. However, if the return were high enough, non-bank financial institutions might provide some of the necessary financing.

The barriers are similar to those in the banking sector and many of the same policies may apply. It is worth noticing that pension funds are typically looking to make long-term investments, which would be consistent with large-scale infrastructure but not, for example, home improvements. A final point to consider, which is described in more detail in the next section, is that the macroeconomic effects of lending from the non-bank financial sector are quite different to those from lending originating from banks.

Macroeconomic impacts of the financing

For many years, economists have debated the impact of the financing of new investments on the wider economy. The debate has become particularly focused in the context of decarbonization, which will require large amounts of additional investment (see the foregoing) as the world becomes more capital-intensive and less energy-intensive.

The economics mainstream, represented by neoclassical and new Keynesian economics, maintains that the investment will not have a positive impact on rates of economic activity and employment, because of a 'crowding out' effect. Essentially, any investment in low-carbon infrastructure will displace investment made by other sectors. This is because a fixed amount of money is within the economy and the only way to increase total investment levels is to generate a larger pool of savings from which to finance the investment. However, additional savings means lower consumption, which also detracts from GDP.

Under these assumptions, while the total aggregate of investment and consumption cannot increase in a decarbonization scenario, a new sub-optimal allocation of resources will mean that the capacity to produce is reduced. The result is lower levels of production. The Computable General Equilibrium (CGE) and Dynamic Stochastic General Equilibrium (DSGE) models that have been developed by neoclassical and New Keynesian economists reflect these assumptions. In these models it is usually not possible to obtain a 'double dividend', in which both economic and environmental outcomes improve. Any attempts to reduce greenhouse gas (GHG) emissions will, therefore, always result in economic costs – and the goal for policy makers is to minimize these costs.

The representation of finance in post-Keynesian economic models, including the E3ME model, is quite different. Most importantly, as noted in the previous section, we must make the distinction between the different types of sources of finance. For non-bank investment funds, the treatment in CGE models is appropriate, because these funds have a fixed amount of money to allocate; that is, higher investment in low-carbon activities really will mean lower investment elsewhere. Likewise, unless it increases borrowing, the public sector faces a fixed budget constraint so, again, higher low-carbon investment means that spending must be cut elsewhere.

For organizations that hold a banking license, however, the ability to lend is not linked to a fixed supply of financial resources. When a company borrows $1 million from a bank, it does not need to wait for households to deposit the same amount of money first. Instead, the bank is able to 'create' the new money that it lends out. The central bank provides the reserves to cover these operations. In the public sector, a similar process takes place. The government issues bonds, which are purchased by financial resources that would otherwise be idle. In some cases, the government may borrow directly from the central bank, which directly creates new money in response.

In post-Keynesian models, therefore, no fixed supply of money is present in the economy. Instead, the amount of money is 'endogenous', meaning it is determined by other economic factors (Pollitt and Mercure, 2017). The way the system works is that, every time a loan is advanced, there is an increase in the money supply. The company that obtains the loan can use the new money to build new capacity, which requires construction services and a range of raw materials. These products have their own supply chains, and multiplier effects can lead to additional increases in employment levels. Because there is no limit to the amount of money that may be created, there is no displacement of financial resources. The implication is that it is possible for investment in low-carbon activities to stimulate the economy and increase rates of economic growth. Therefore, a double-dividend result, in which there are simultaneous benefits for both the economy and the environment, is possible.

Crucially, the way the financial system works in the post-Keynesian world has now been recognized as the way it operates in reality. The Bank of England clarified its position in 2014 (McLeay et al., 2014) and other central banks, including the Bundesbank, have since made similar acknowledgments. From this perspective, we can view the results from E3ME, including potential double-dividend outcomes, as much more realistic than those from competing approaches.

One important point is that, although higher levels of private debt can create a short-term stimulus, these debts must be repaid in the longer term. Effectively, this puts the process of money creation into reverse, as companies use their incomes to repay debts rather than to make new purchases. This leads to a pattern of outcomes similar to that shown in the top half of Figure 10.1. Equivalent outcomes from a standard neoclassical CGE model are shown in the bottom half. Because of the strong path dependency (e.g. in the choice of technology options taken up), it is impossible to generalize whether long-term outcomes will be better in the post-Keynesian approach. Short-term trends, however, are more clear-cut; 2050 is given as an example outcome in the figure.

Discussions about money supply inevitably lead to questions of inflation and financial stability. According to monetary economists, increased money supply automatically leads to higher rates of inflation; that is, there are no real (excluding inflation) impacts. However, recent exercises in Quantitative Easing (QE), including in Japan, have shown that this is not the case.

E3ME does include equations for prices from which a measure of inflation may be derived. However, higher prices result from constraints in the real economy, rather than in the financial system. This approach points towards the limits of growth in the model, meaning if supply is unable to meet demand – that is,

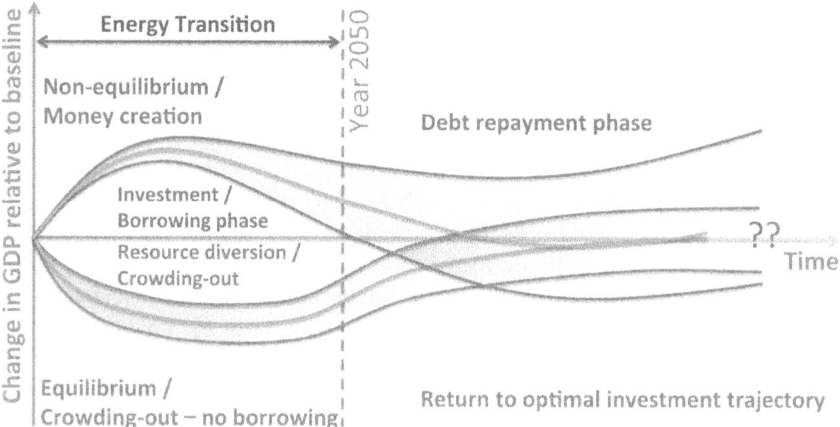

Figure 10.1 Expected economic impacts from different modelling approaches

Source: Mercure et al. (2019)

Note: Typical E3ME model results are shown above the *x* axis, while results from a standard neoclassical CGE model are below the *x* axis.

insufficient numbers of workers are available or companies reach their production capacity – any additional demand-side stimulus will result in higher prices rather than additional output. These processes are described in the E3ME model manual, specifically the descriptions of the wage and 'normal output' equations (Cambridge Econometrics, 2019).

Survey data, albeit limited, suggest that manufacturing firms typically operate at ~80% capacity (Eurostat, 2019). These findings tell us that production can be increased by the amounts proposed in the scenarios described in Chapter 5, without meeting strict capacity constraints – although firms could still increase prices in response to higher demand. Also important is that, if companies were made aware in advance of the policies promoting decarbonization, they would have a greater chance to invest in new capacity, reducing further supply-side constraints (European Commission, 2017b).

Stranded assets and potential impacts on financial stability

Another question that is often raised when discussing increases in the money supply and higher debt levels is what might happen if firms default on many of the loans that are made. In a worst-case scenario, such behavior leads to a financial crisis, like the one that the world experienced in 2008–09. Keen (2011, 2017) observed that high levels of private debt are a strong leading indicator of a forthcoming crash.

The E3ME model does not explicitly measure defaults on loans, and proper treatment of financial contagion and network effects is, generally, impossible in a macro-level model. Although large in absolute terms, low-carbon investment is unlikely to be sufficient to destabilize the financial system on its own; however, further research is needed in this area.

A more likely source of loan defaults is the existing fossil fuel sector, which will see lower demand for its products in any decarbonization scenario and, therefore, lower incomes with which to repay its debts. It seems likely that some firms will find that their fossil fuel assets become 'stranded', meaning that they are no longer economically viable within a low-carbon policy framework. Stranded assets may refer to both natural capital, that is, 'unburnable carbon', which relates to fuels that can never be used, and physical infrastructure, for example coal mines, oil rigs or pipelines. These assets are owned by a mixture of public and privately controlled enterprises. The largest values in dollar terms may be attributed to oil reserves.

The E3ME model has previously been used to estimate the potential value of stranded natural capital assets. Mercure et al. (2018a) found that US$1 trillion of assets is at risk, even on current technological trends, without any *new* policy. In scenarios like S3 in Chapter 5, this figure increases to US$4 trillion, primarily because there is a more rapid uptake of electric vehicles and less oil is consumed (Mercure et al., 2018b). If the choice of discount rate used is below the default 10% rate, even higher values of financial losses may be obtained.

It should be stressed that the countries in East Asia are not responsible for a large share of the total loss of asset value because they do not account for a large share of oil and gas reserves. However, the effects of such a loss of value on the global financial system – which could be sudden if there is panic in financial markets – are not well understood. Initial research (e.g. Battiston, 2017) has started to consider possible effects but more work is needed. It has been recognized that the potential loss of value is larger than the one that triggered the 2008–09 financial crisis (Mercure, 2018a). The crisis showed that countries in East Asia are highly dependent on international trade and may be particularly vulnerable to a sudden loss of financial confidence.

When considering financial stability, we must also make the distinction between assets owned publicly or privately. If necessary, a sovereign state that issues its own currency will always be able to cover losses of financial wealth by calling on the central bank. The risk to financial stability becomes real when it is private companies that suffer a sudden loss of value, especially when assets have been purchased using borrowed money. Such an assertion points towards a strong role of the public sector in providing finance for a low-carbon transition, such as to ensure that private debt levels do not become excessive. Alternatively, the public sector could underwrite private debt, thereby reducing the risk to the wider financial sector.

Taking this argument to its logical conclusion, a movement in the US has led the appeal for a 'Green New Deal', in which newly created public money is used to finance the low-carbon transition, by boosting employment levels at the same time (with the aim of securing full employment). The thinking draws upon 'Modern

Monetary Theory', which suggests that, as the level of government debt does not matter, social and environmental protection should instead be prioritized.

The scenarios in this book are revenue neutral for governments, meaning that they do not rely on newly created public money. Instead we see potential economic benefits from increases in private investment that is financed by commercial banks. We have, therefore, shown potential economic – and social – benefits that do not require a green new deal. However, further public stimulus is likely to increase the benefits to GDP and employment further, and a green new deal warrants further analysis in its own right.

Conclusions

In Chapter 5 we outlined a realistic policy scenario (S3) in which the countries in East Asia may reduce their GHG emissions to a level that is consistent with meeting a global temperature target of 2°C. It is clear, however, that much investment will be needed for the necessary transformations to take place.

Policy makers are correct to ask where the necessary finance for the investment might come from. There is likely to be a role for both the public and private sectors in providing finance. The public sector will need to set the framework conditions so that the private sector may provide finance where profitable to do so. It will also need to mediate in cases where there is no rationale for the private sector to act. The macroeconomic impacts of such large amounts of investment will be profound. The investment will create opportunities and jobs for companies in the construction and engineering sectors. Through multiplier effects, other parts of the economy will benefit too.

However, for impacts to be universally positive, it must be ensured that investment in low-carbon technologies does not crowd out investment in other sectors. The current literature, which is backed by central banks, suggests that this need not be the case if the financing comes from new loans that are issued by commercial banks – as long as firms do not hit capacity constraints in regard to, for example, equipment or number of workers. Likewise, public investment that is funded by additional borrowing need not lead to displacement of other investment.

Through these mechanisms, the E3ME model shows that it is possible to implement policies that lead to both a reduction in emissions and higher rates of economic growth (i.e. a double dividend). The understanding of how the financial system works is key to this outcome. Much of the economics profession still sees things differently, and positive economic results in low-carbon scenarios are very difficult to achieve while using a standard CGE model.

Finally, any scenario that predicts higher levels of private debt must also consider the possibility of large-scale defaults on those debts and the possible knock-on effects for the wider economy. There is a possibility that companies investing in renewables without the support of, for example, Feed-in-Tariffs are unable to meet loan repayments if electricity prices fall. However, the most likely defaults might be in companies that have invested in fossil fuel assets, including global oil companies. The countries in East Asia are not heavily exposed to these companies but could be affected if there were a wider recession caused by a sudden loss of value in stocks. After all, the global financial crisis in 2008–09 also affected East Asia, even though East Asian countries had a very low exposure to subprime lending in the US. There may, therefore, be grounds to build a financial support system to protect against a sudden loss of value.

The analysis in this chapter covers several issues that are critical to ensure that both the transition to a low-carbon economy and its economic benefits are realized. However, it also leaves important questions unanswered.

Perhaps most importantly is the question of how well the global financial system, including financial markets in East Asia, is equipped to manage the transition to a low-carbon economy. To carry out such an analysis requires an understanding of the complex financial networks that are involved, which goes beyond the macroeconomic representation provided by the E3ME model. Such an exercise involves a mapping of who owns the most exposed assets (e.g. firms that produce oil from expensive sources, such as the Canadian tar sands), and also who, in turn, owns the firms one step down the chain. Equity and debt levels must both be accounted for in the analysis. The paper by Battiston et al. (2017) provides an early example of such an analysis, and several authors of this book are also currently engaged in such an exercise.

This analysis may start to give an indication of whether a crisis might be triggered by a loss of value in fossil fuel assets. It cannot give a conclusive answer, however, as the global financial system is too complex to assess when using modelling alone. The most useful outcomes for such an analysis are likely to be a rough probability of whether multiple defaults can occur and an indication of where in the financial chain it might be most beneficial for policy makers to intervene. If it is possible to allocate the loss of wealth to sectors and countries, then it could be possible to assess second-order effects by using the E3ME model. Nevertheless, the high degree of uncertainty in such an exercise would need to be made clear, as to avoid giving a false sense of precision to the policy community.

References

Battiston, S, A Mandel, I Monasterolo, F Schütze and G Visentin (2017) 'A climate stress-test of the financial system', *Nature Climate Change*, Volume 7, Pages 283–288.

Cambridge Econometrics (2019) 'E3ME Manual: Version 7.0', available at www.e3me.com

European Commission (2017a) 'Assessing the European clean energy finance landscape, with implications for improved macro-energy modelling', available at https://ec.europa.eu/energy/sites/ener/files/documents/macro_eu_clean_energy_finance_final.pdf

European Commission (2017b) 'Case study – Technical analysis on capacity constraints and macroeconomic performance', available at https://ec.europa.eu/energy/sites/ener/files/documents/case_study_2_capacity_constraints_and_macro_performance.pdf

Eurostat (2019) 'Current level of capacity utilization in manufacturing industry', available at http://appsso.eurostat.ec.europa.eu/nui/show.do?dataset=teibs070&lang=en

Keen, S (2011) 'Debunking economics – Revised and expanded edition: The naked emperor dethroned?', Second Revised & Enlarged Edition, Zed books ltd.

Keen, S (2017) *Can We Avoid Another Financial Crisis? (The Future of Capitalism)*, New York: Polity Press.

McLeay, M, A Radia and R Thomas (2014) 'Money creation in the modern economy', Bank of England Quarterly Bulletin, 2014Q1.

Mercure, J-F, A Lam, S Billington and H Pollitt (November 2018b) 'Integrated assessment modelling as a positive science: Private passenger road transport policies to meet a climate target well below 2°C', *Climatic Change*, Volume 151, Issue 2, Pages 109–129.

Mercure, J-F, H Pollitt, J E Viñuales, N R Edwards, P B Holden, U Chewpreecha, P Salas, I Sognnaes, A Lam and F Knobloch (2018a) 'Macroeconomic impact of stranded fossil fuel assets', *Nature Climate Change*, Volume 8, Pages 588–593.

Mercure, J-F, F Knobloch, H Pollitt, L Paroussos, S Scrieciu and R Lewney (2019) 'Modelling innovation and the macroeconomics of low-carbon transitions: theory, perspectives and practical use', *Climate Policy*, available online.

Pollitt, H and J-F Mercure (2017) 'The role of money and the financial sector in energy-economy models used for assessing climate and energy policy', *Climate Policy*, Volume 18, Issue 2, Pages 184–197.

Part III

Wider sustainability issues

Reducing water and material consumption, and improving air quality

11 Interaction between energy and material consumption in East Asia

Hector Pollitt, Mary Goldman, Yanmin He and Soocheol Lee

Introduction

The importance of the complex interactions between material and energy consumption is increasingly recognized. The issue is related to the energy-water-food 'nexus'. The UN's Sustainable Development Goal (SDG 12, responsible consumption and production) covers the use of mineral and other inputs to production processes. The UN's overview of this theme links rises in living standards and consumption, which have been occurring in many East Asian economies, with potentially irreversible environmental damages as increases in consumption require increased use of various mineral-based resources.

First, however, we consider the relationship between energy consumption and the consumption of mineral resources. In this chapter, by 'minerals' we mean mineral-based resources that are not used for energy purposes (i.e. fossil fuels are excluded). As we present, the linkages are complex, and it is not at all clear whether reducing energy and mineral consumption are complementary or competing goals.

Most East Asian economies are net importers of raw material inputs. An over-reliance on *imported* material inputs could also become a security risk if imported products become too expensive or are made unavailable to the importing state for a range of geopolitical or economic reasons. Although SDG 12 covers biomass materials, it is often the use of minerals that gains most attention because of their harmful environmental effects. These minerals can be disaggregated to four distinct groups:

- **Construction minerals** – Non-metallic aggregates that are mainly used by the construction industry, including sand, glass and the components of cement. These are the heaviest by weight.
- **Ferrous ores** – Inputs to steelmaking, which remains a core component of industry around the world (see Chapter 6).
- **Non-ferrous ores** – Extraction of other types of metal from ores, including, for example, copper, aluminum and zinc.
- **Industrial minerals** – Minerals that are used specifically for making industrial products. These typically have much lower weight but a higher value than the other categories.

The impacts of the uses of these different minerals vary, but there are strong reasons for wanting to limit consumption of all of them:

- **Their supplies are finite** – the availability of the resources is limited and will not be replenished over time. Even in cases in which there is abundant supply, the purest or most easily available sources may become exhausted, pushing up costs. At least for the foreseeable future, there is no alternative to the naturally available supplies of many mineral resources; there is no equivalent of renewable energy that would allow continued consumption without exhausting finite stocks of resources.
- **Extraction of these resources may cause considerable damage to the natural environment** – these resources must be mined and the way they are extracted may harm local environments, either directly (e.g. through scarring landscapes, chemical seepage) or through the location of economic activities to near the sources of the minerals.
- **Means of extraction** – Some of the highest-value minerals come from countries with poor records regarding human rights and/or environmental sustainability.
- **Interaction with energy consumption** – As discussed in this chapter, the extraction, transportation and processing of minerals requires additional energy to be consumed, hindering attempts to meet long-term decarbonization targets.

Reducing mineral consumption is, therefore, regarded as a key component of the 'circular' economy, in which current production patterns based on the extraction, use and destruction of resources is replaced with a system that reuses and recycles resources. Although the circular economy lags the low-carbon economy in terms of policy attention, there is a substantial non-government organization (NGO) community that promotes its adoption.

As our aim in this book is to find a scenario of future prosperity in East Asia that is environmentally sustainable, we investigate in this chapter whether it is possible to simultaneously reduce greenhouse gas (GHG) emissions and mineral consumption. We apply a materials tax up to 2030 to encourage a reduction in minerals consumption and an increase in the material efficiency of production. The policy that we model across China, Japan, Korea and Taiwan is relatively basic, with the tax increasing over time, resulting in a 10% increase in non-energy mineral prices by 2030. The policy does not address a variety of other goals or revenue-recycling options that might enable industry to increase the resource efficiency of their production and achieve lower levels of materials consumption. We show that, while a tax may help to reduce consumption levels, further policies would be required to yield a significant reduction in material consumption levels.

The next section presents current patterns of material consumption in East Asia. The subsequent section briefly describes some of the main linkages between energy and material consumption. The modelling approach is summarized in the section after that, with results from the modelling given subsequently, before the final section presents conclusions.

Data and trends in consumption in East Asia

The available data suggest that, in general, consumption of non–fossil fuel minerals has increased year on year in the period 2005–2017 in the Asia-Pacific region (Figure 11.1, which also includes biomass consumption). By weight, by far the largest contribution comes from non-metallic minerals, which are primarily used in construction. Consumption within the region is dominated by China but Korea follows a similar trend. For Japan, consumption has been flatter, and the data are difficult to judge for Taiwan.

China

According to the United Nations Environment Programme (UNEP), from 1970 to 2008, China's per capita consumption of materials grew from one-third to more than one-and-a-half times the world's average levels (UNEP, 2013):

> Domestic consumption of natural resources per capita increased at almost twice the rate of the whole of the Asia Pacific region due to massive investments in urban infrastructure, energy systems, and manufacturing capacity. [. . .], however, some 20 per cent of the resources used in China goes towards the production of goods which are eventually consumed abroad.

In addition to being one of the most-intensive consumers of material resources, China is one of the first countries to embrace the circular economy paradigm for

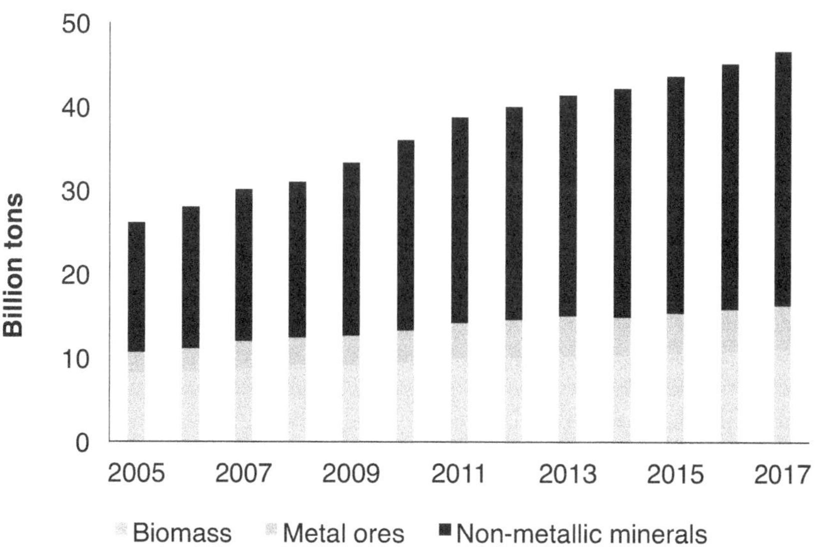

Figure 11.1 Consumption of metal ores, non-metallic minerals and biomass in the Asia Pacific Region

economic growth and development. The Chinese government has pursued several policies (including targets for energy-efficient buildings and stimulus funding for green-growth projects) aimed at strengthening the economy, and conserving energy and non-energy resources.

From 1970 to 2000, China exhibited a trend towards decreasing material intensity (tons of material use per unit of GDP). Since the year 2000, and coinciding with economic expansion in China, ongoing reductions in material intensity have plateaued (UNEP, 2013). To a certain extent, these trends reflect the types of activity that are growing within the economy; notably, investment-driven growth is likely to lead to higher volumes of materials being consumed.

Japan

In Japan, several policies have been pursued to increase resource efficiency. Japan was the first country in the world to set targets for resource productivity (European Commission, 2012). It has a set of policies articulated in the 'Fundamental Plan for Establishing a Sound Material-Cycle Society' aimed at reducing resource intensity, and decoupling material use from economic growth (Japan MOE, 2013).

Japan is one of only a handful of countries where consumption of material resources has successfully been decoupled from economic growth, even before the 2008 financial crisis (where sharp falls in investment led to lower rates of material consumption). Between 1980 and 2008, Japanese material consumption decreased by more than 20% while the economy expanded by more than 96%. However, when including unused domestic extraction and estimated indirect flows from trade, the decrease in material flow is far more modest, that is, 1% in the period 1980–2008 (OECD, 2011). In Japan, 98% of metals are recycled and, as of 2015, only 5% of waste is going to landfill. Appliance recycling laws also ensure that a majority of electrical and electronic products are recycled (Benton and Hazell, 2015).

Korea

Korea has seen intensive industrial development over the past two decades – fueled, in part, by increased consumption of an array of material inputs. In the past decade, the need to decouple continued economic expansion from materials consumption has been recognized, and a new economic development paradigm emphasizing low-carbon and green growth is being pursued (International Energy Agency, 2010).

According to analysis by the World Wildlife Foundation, Korea (2016), the equivalent of 3.3 earths would be required if global consumption patterns were comparable with those of Korea's. Resource efficiency is also recognized as a priority in Korea, albeit for a different reason: as Korea imports most of its materials, it could be vulnerable to future scarcity or limits to international trade.

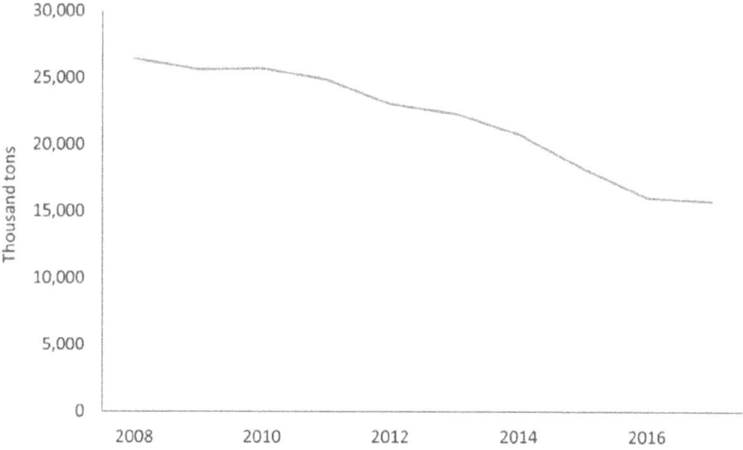

Figure 11.2 Extraction of non-metallic minerals in Taiwan from 2008 to 2017

Taiwan

Data from the Republic of China Statistical Bureau (2017) suggest that the level of extraction of non-metallic minerals declined in Taiwan over the period 2008–2017 (Figure 11.2). The current policy ambition to encourage green growth and move towards a circular economy could strengthen this trend, and might hasten long-term decreases in resource use for all main material types.

Interactions between material and energy use

Impacts of material use on energy consumption and GHG emissions

The first linkage between material and energy consumption is a more intuitive one. For each unit of mineral that is used in economic production, there is a corresponding increase in energy consumption. There may even be an increase in GHG emissions that is independent of increased energy use. To understand the relationships better, we must consider the different phases of production in which minerals are used.

Primary extraction is the first stage. A substantial amount of energy is required to remove minerals from the ground. Constructing a mine requires a lot of energy, as will operating the equipment to do the drilling. Ancillary activities, and heating and lighting for staff all require further energy consumption.

The energy-extraction sector employs the so-called Energy Return on Investment (EROI), which shows the ratio of available energy after extraction over that used in the extraction process. If the EROI is 9:1, then 10% of the energy extracted is used in the extraction process. Analyses of EROI ratios can provide information that is applicable to non-energy minerals (Guilford et al., 2011; Murphy and Hall, 2010).

Different types of extraction have different costs in terms of energy. Coal, which is most similar in nature to some of the mineral products assessed, has a low energy cost, with an EROI of up to 80:1, whereas using 10% of the available energy to extract oil is not unusual (an EROI of 9:1). The global EROI has declined substantially over time for all mineral products, as the most accessible mineral deposits have been exhausted.

According to the E3ME model database (Cambridge Econometrics, 2019), non-energy mineral extraction accounts for ~3% of total final energy consumption globally. In East Asia, non-energy mineral extraction accounts for ~6.5% of total final energy consumption. The potential for efficiency savings is relatively low so this share is expected to grow in the future.

The second linkage is transportation; that is, once minerals are extracted, they must be transported. Usually the distances involved are short and waste products are removed as much as possible but transport of materials is, inevitably, an energy-intensive process. In most cases, the energy used comes in the form of diesel, which powers either trucks or freight trains to carry the mineral products. If the minerals are transported by shipping, then they are moved by heavy fuel oil.

The third stage of energy consumption is the processing phase. Large amounts of energy are often required to separate minerals from waste materials and turn them into useful products (see, e.g. Chapter 6). The nature of the processes involved varies by mineral group but can account for a substantial share of total final energy demand:

- Ferrous metals: 6.2%
- Non-ferrous metals: 0.8%
- Non-metallic mineral products: 3.3%
- Chemicals: 9.4%

(Cambridge Econometrics, 2019)

The energy consumptions attributed here refer only to the basic manufacturing (e.g. production sheets of steel). The energy used to turn that steel into a finished product (e.g. a car) is not included in these shares.

In addition to accounting for approximately one fifth of total final energy consumption, the chemical reactions that occur in the production processes for several key minerals (including steel, cement and certain chemical products) emit CO_2. This means that, even if the production of the mineral product were to rely solely on decarbonized energy, production would still result in CO_2 emissions. Furthermore, aside from carbon capture and storage (CCS), there are few options of technology substitution that would reduce non-energy CO_2 emissions from production. Reducing consumption, thus, remains the most likely way to reduce total emissions in the future (Pollitt et al., 2019). In addition to being an articulated sustainable development goal – because of environmental degradation associated with extraction and resource security concerns – any reduction of materials consumption can also be framed in terms of achieving various climate goals.

Effects of decarbonization on material consumption

Policy aimed at decreasing material consumption is sometimes framed as being at odds with other stated goals to decarbonize the economy and achieve large-scale reductions in CO_2 emissions.

The rapid deployment of low-carbon technologies (such as solar photovoltaics [PV], offshore and onshore wind, and concentrated solar power) requires a great deal of energy and material inputs. The promotion of renewable energy comes at the cost of increased material consumption – various material inputs are required to build the physical infrastructure associated with renewable energy technologies (RETs). These materials must be extracted, transported and processed into a state at which they can be used as raw materials to implement various RETs. This entire process (as detailed earlier) is energy intensive and requires numerous energy inputs along the way. Once the physical infrastructure has been built (e.g. solar PV panels, undersea transmission cables) it must be physically moved and installed on-site in order to begin the production of renewable energy – yet another energy-intensive intermediary step.

Despite the large up-front energy and material costs of RETs, renewable energy does not require *additional* material inputs to produce electricity (beyond upkeep and maintenance) – unlike traditional non-renewable energy technologies (such as coal, gas or nuclear power).

Transition to green energy, and the material and energy outlays required to achieve it, can be framed as a temporary cost for long-term energy and materials savings. Renewable technologies require only temporary energy and material inputs. The subsequent 'inputs' for energy production for renewable technologies do not require energy, unlike those required for various carbon-intensive technologies.

This trade-off is also apparent when considering the promotion of electric vehicles. Policies to replace the existing vehicle stock with electric vehicles, necessarily, lead temporarily to more material and more energy-intensive vehicle manufacturing patterns. Various minerals, ferrous metals and non-ferrous metals would be required to construct automobile bodies and electric batteries. However, these vehicles would not require continued fossil fuel input to run and could be powered entirely by renewable energy sources (Nordelöf et al., 2014).

Modelling these interactions

Few macroeconomic models currently include physical measures of material consumption. E3ME's dynamic approach models rates of material intensity that change in response to changes in price, total output, technological innovation and other economic factors. As well as explaining past relationships that characterize patterns of materials consumption, E3ME can be used to estimate material consumption and test policy scenarios aimed at reducing material consumption, such as the consumption taxes applied in this chapter.

E3ME models material consumption at the national level and captures the following material types:

- Food
- Animal feed
- Forestry
- Construction minerals
- Industrial minerals
- Ferrous ores
- Non-ferrous ores

The tax we apply gradually increases over the period 2019–30, such that prices of raw materials increase by ~1% per year, resulting in an overall increase of 10% by 2030. Although our focus in this chapter is on non-renewable mineral resources, we also apply the tax to biomass to prevent a shift between material inputs. Biomass production requires intensive use of water, which – as discussed in the next chapter – is becoming a major issue in East Asia.

It is assumed that all material consumption meets intermediate demands, that is, materials are used as part of the production process and are not bought by households directly. A relatively small number of sectors produce the materials in question: agriculture and fishing produce food and feed; the forestry sector produces forestry; and the non-energy mining sector produces all mineral categories. Feedback is achieved through adjustments to economic input-output coefficients, which are adjusted so that the economic flows are consistent with the physical flows as described in the E3ME model manual (Cambridge Econometrics, 2019).

Impacts of the consumption tax

A tax is imposed on all materials (food, feed, forestry, construction minerals, industrial minerals, ferrous ores and non-ferrous ores) in the period 2019–30. It is increased gradually over this period to be equivalent to an ~10% increase in material price by 2030. The tax is meant to capture the effects of several potential policies that aim to reduce materials consumption and material intensity of various production processes, and also to encourage businesses and industries to be more resource efficient.

In this section, we present the results from the modelling exercise. The reference case is the ambitious decarbonization scenario (S3) described in detail in Chapter 5, that is, power sector regulations and subsidies, carbon taxes plus an industrial energy efficiency program. We assess the effects of the materials tax in addition to all policies that are aimed at reducing GHG emissions.

Macroeconomic effects

Figure 11.3 shows the impact of the materials tax on GDP for East Asia. Overall, GDP falls by between 0.1 and 0.2% compared with that of the reference case. Initially, GDP growth decreases as the tax rate increases, but growth rates largely

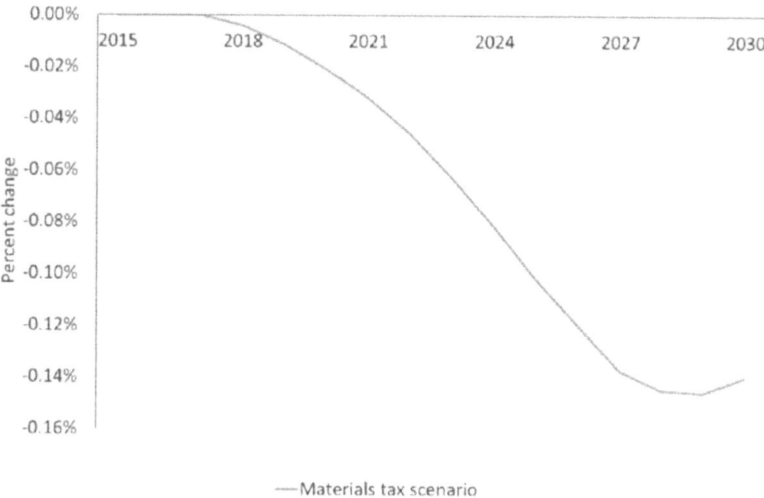

Figure 11.3 Change in GDP relative to reference scenario for China, Japan, Korea and Taiwan

return to normal by 2030. The modelling suggests that it takes some time for companies to adapt to higher material prices.

There are two important caveats to these results. First, we did not use the revenues from the materials tax to offset any other taxes (i.e. no revenue recycling; see Chapter 9). Had we done so, a double-dividend effect might have been possible, especially in countries such as Korea, where most materials are imported. Second, the level of detail in the modelling is relatively low; although improvements to resource efficiency may be modelled, the modelling approach does not account for potential increases in recycling that could boost overall activity levels. For example, Japan's reuse and recycling economy was estimated to be worth £163bn (USD326bn) as of 2007 (7.6% of GDP) and to employ more than 600,000 people (Benton and Hazell, 2015).

The observed decrease in GDP is driven largely by the effects of increased prices because of the effects of the materials tax. As summarized in Figure 11.4, regional price levels are expected to rise steadily between 2019 and 2030, as rates of inflation are slightly increased. The figure shows aggregate consumer price indices (aggregated again to a regional average), of which food is a main component. If the tax had only been applied to mineral resources, the impact would have been smaller but the overall direction of the effects would have been unchanged.

By facing increasing prices, household incomes become smaller in real terms. The result is a decrease in consumer spending across East Asia (Figure 11.5). As already noted, food accounts for a large share of household expenditure and, because it is a basic requirement, has a low price elasticity of demand. Therefore, households tend to be hit hard by increases in food prices.

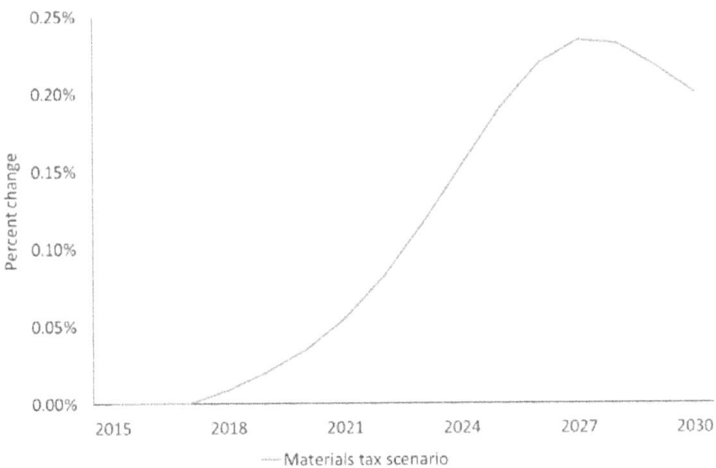

Figure 11.4 Change in prices in China, Japan, Korea and Taiwan

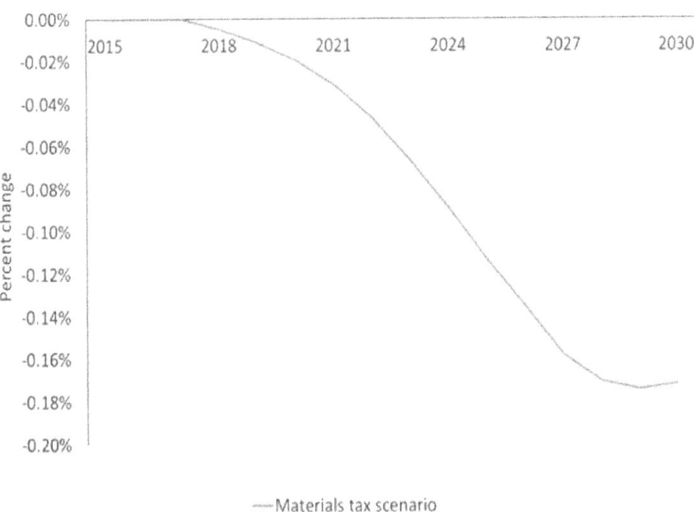

Figure 11.5 Change in consumer spending in China, Japan, Korea and Taiwan

Effects on material consumption and CO_2 emissions

For all materials, consumption (in the form of material inputs to production) is estimated to decrease steadily in 2019–30 in response to the increase in material prices over this period (Table 11.1).

Food consumption is estimated to decrease 1.3% relative to the reference scenario by 2030. It should be noted that, although consumers can shift their

Table 11.1 Change in material consumption relative to the reference scenario for China, Japan, Korea and Taiwan

	2020	*2025*	*2030*
Food	-0.4%	-0.8%	-1.3%
Animal feed	-0.1%	-0.2%	-0.2%
Forestry	-0.1%	-0.2%	-0.2%
Construction minerals	-0.5%	-2.1%	-3.7%
Industrial minerals	-0.1%	-0.4%	-0.6%
Ferrous ores	-1.5%	-3.6%	-5.3%
Non-ferrous ores	-0.1%	-0.6%	-1.5%

Source: E3ME modelling results

consumption habits to less expensive food products, there is a baseline level of necessary food consumption for continued economic activity. This is the reason why, despite the increase in prices, the materials tax on food does not lead to a significant decrease in consumption by 2030. A similar situation is seen for animal feed.

There is a slight decrease in forestry (wood) consumption. Like food and animal feed, the demand for wood is relatively price inelastic. Consumption of construction minerals is decreased 3.7% by 2030 in the four East Asian countries, as a result of the steady increase in materials costs. This suggests that the construction sector (the only consumer of construction minerals) is responsive to changes in prices and able to reduce material inputs to production, potentially seeking to recycle resources or to increase the resource efficiency of production processes. As the largest contributor to total material consumption by weight, reductions in the consumption of construction minerals tend to dominate the total change.

Industrial minerals consumption changes very little relative to the reference case by 2030, despite the 10% increase in prices. Industrial minerals often represent only a small part of the total product in which they are embedded. Consumption of ferrous ores is estimated to decrease by ~5% by 2030 relative to the reference scenario. Ferrous ores are the material most responsive to changes in material prices. This suggests that the steel sector is particularly sensitive to price increases, and that there is scope to reduce steel consumption in construction and advanced manufacturing processes (see Chapter 6). Non-ferrous ores are also responsive to price increases owing to the materials tax; its consumption is estimated to decrease by ~1.5% relative to the reference case by 2030.

Overall, these results suggest that the consumption levels of some materials are more responsive to a materials tax than others. A good policy design in East Asia, therefore, requires the identification of those materials and sectors that would be most responsive, and application of tax in a way that effectively increases resource efficiency and materials intensity. This is in contrast to the 'blanket tax' as described, which leads to mostly negative economic impacts.

Table 11.2 Change in CO_2 emissions relative to the reference scenario for China, Japan, Korea and Taiwan

	2020	*2025*	*2030*
China	0.01%	0.01%	0.01%
Japan	0.01%	0.08%	0.10%
Korea	0.0%	0.01%	0.0%
Taiwan	-0.01%	-0.02%	-0.02%

Source: E3ME modelling results

Table 11.2 summarizes changes in CO_2 emissions relative to the reference scenario for China, Japan, Korea and Taiwan.

Some Asia-Pacific regions show a slight increase in emissions after implementation of the materials tax policy. In all four counties, the change in emissions is very small, suggesting that the effects of the materials tax on total emissions is very limited. In the case of Taiwan, a slight decrease in emissions is observed after the materials tax is implemented.

Overall, we found that the materials tax effectively reduced material consumption levels in all four East Asian countries. However, because of the policy design, it also led to an increase in prices, and decreases in consumer spending and GDP. Limited impacts were observed regarding total CO_2 emissions. The following discussion considers ways in which material taxes could be implemented concomitantly with other policies (e.g. regulations) in East Asia to improve their effectiveness.

Materials taxes as a proxy policy

As noted previously, the materials tax modelled in this chapter serves as an example for a variety of policies that could be put in place in China, Japan, Korea and Taiwan. The tax on its own is a relatively blunt policy instrument, and there are other policies that could be more finely tuned to the needs of specific sectors in different countries within East Asia. These policies could enable greater resource efficiency and continued economic growth, decoupled from materials consumption.

One option relates to recycling tax revenues. In Chapter 9, we discussed issues of revenue recycling more generally, but there is scope to direct compensation either to those sectors most affected by the materials tax (e.g. agriculture, mining or construction) or to those households facing the largest cost increases (most likely low-income households that spend a large share of their income on food). The revenue recycling could be used to incentivize a shift from material-intensive production to a larger role for labor by reducing the cost of hiring additional workers by lowering employers' social costs.

Also relevant to the issue of dematerialization is the possibility to use the revenues to promote reuse or recycling of materials. For example, if demand for recycled goods exists but there are no processing facilities, then investment in recycling plants could help to stimulate both the economy and further reduce raw material consumption. However, to understand where best to initiate such interventions, more detailed analysis than is offered in this chapter is required.

In addition, the policy modelled in this chapter does not consider *how* industries could reduce the consumption of raw materials; rather, it is assumed that efficiency is improved. Regulatory measures (including information campaigns) might be a more cost-effective way than taxes to reduce material consumption. There might also be a role for voluntary agreements within industry (see Rezessy et al., 2014, for an example relating to energy consumption in Europe). In reality, a combination of all these types of instrument, alongside further technology development, might be the most effective way to reduce material consumption while still promoting economic growth.

Conclusion

The UN's Sustainable Development Goal for reducing materials consumption (and increasing responsible consumption and production) is a priority for countries in East Asia, as living standards continue to rise, the middle class in China expands rapidly, and Japan and Korea continue to expand their economies. A burgeoning middle class requires various material inputs to satisfy its consumption habits. The deleterious environmental impacts of materials consumption are well identified, and the connection between materials consumption and CO_2 emissions is evident. It is, therefore, important to recognize the issue of material consumption when it comes to meeting carbon budgets and climate goals.

It is possible, through a variety of policy interventions, to encourage increased resource efficiency and continued economic growth. Such policies are being explored in Europe through its circular policy roadmap (European Commission, 2017); they are starting to be recognized in East Asia as well.

We have shown in this chapter that – although a simple materials tax is effective to modestly reduce materials consumption – it does so with potential negative economic effects. A variety of policy options that draw on the revenues collected from materials taxes could mitigate some of these negative effects. However, as we have shown in previous chapters using the example of carbon taxes, their interaction with other policies is important as it determines the overall impact of any measures. This analysis has yet to be done for materials taxes.

References

Benton, D. and Hazell, J. (2015), *The Circular Economy in Japan*. www.the-ies.org/analysis/circular-economy-japan.

Cambridge Econometrics. (2019), *E3ME Technical Manual: Version 7*. www.e3me.com

European Commission. (2017), *Report From the Commission to the European Parliament, the Council, the European Economic and Social Committee and the Committee of the Regions on the Implementation of the Circular Economy Action Plan*. http://ec.europa.eu/environment/circular-economy/index_en.htm

European Commission, DG Environment. (2012), *Assessment of Resource Efficiency Indicators and Targets: Annex Report.* http://ec.europa.eu/environment/enveco/resource_efficiency/pdf/report.pdf

Guilford, M. C., Hall, C. E. S., O'Connor, P. and Cleveland, C. J. (2011), 'A New Long-Term Assessment of Energy Return on Investment (EROI) for U.S. Oil and Gas Discovery and Production', *Sustainability*, 3(10), pp. 1866–1887.

International Energy Agency. (2010), *Policies and Measures: Korea, Framework Act on Low Carbon, Green Growth.* www.iea.org/policiesandmeasures/pams/korea/name–38971-en.php.

Japan MOE. (2013), *Fundamental Plan for Establishing a Sound Material-Cycle Society.* https://www.env.go.jp/en/recycle/smcs/3rd-f_plan.pdf

Murphy, D. J. and Hall, C. A. S. (2010), 'Year in Review EROI or Energy Return on (Energy) Invested', *Annals of the New York Academy of Sciences*, 1185, pp. 102–118.

Nordelöf, A., Messagie, M., Tillman, A. M., Söderman, M. L. and Van Mierlo, J. (2014), Environmental Impacts of Hybrid, Plug-In Hybrid, and Battery Electric Vehicles – What Can We Learn From Life Cycle Assessment?', *The International Journal of Life Cycle Assessment*, 19(11), pp. 1866–1890.

OECD. (2011), *Resource Productivity in the G8 and the OECD.* https://www.oecd.org/env/waste/47944428.pdf

Pollitt, H., Neuhoff, K. and Lin, X. (2019), 'The Impact of Implementing a Consumption Charge on Carbon-Intensive Materials in Europe', *Climate Policy*, in press.

Republic of China Statistical Bureau. (2017), *Green National Income (Environmental-Economic Account), Minerals Depletion Account.* https://eng.stat.gov.tw/ct.asp?xItem=18741&CtNode=4942&mp=5.

Rezessy, S., Beroldi, P. and Persson, A. (2014), *Are Voluntary Agreements an Effective Energy Policy Instruments?*, Insights and Experiences From Europe.

United Nations Environment. (2013), *China Outpacing Rest of World in Natural Resource Use.* https://www.unenvironment.org/news-and-stories/press-release/china-outpacing-rest-world-natural-resource-use

World Wildlife Foundation, Korea. (2016), *Korea Ecological Footprint*, Report 2016: Measuring Korea's Impact on nature.

12 Sustainable use of water resources in East Asia

Kiyoshi Fujikawa, Hector Pollitt and Zuoyi Ye

Introduction

Globalization has rapidly advanced throughout both the developed and developing world, especially since 1980. One country's production activities, which used to be basically enclosed in a domestic market, now spread worldwide. 'Today, 70% of international trade is for production in global value chains (GVCs), where services, raw materials, parts and components are exchanged across countries before being incorporated into final products that are shipped to consumers all over the world' (OECD, 2018).

The dashed line in Figure 12.1 shows the growth of world trade volume and the dotted line shows the growth of world GDP. At least until 2010, the growth rate of world trade was generally above that of world GDP, indicating that, in comparison, trade was growing faster. Such a trend is caused by increasing cross-border transactions of intermediate goods, urged by structural changes of international division of labor within production processes.

There is ample literature related to GVCs. Some research has analyzed structural changes of vertical divisions of labor using input-output tables (e.g. Hummels et al., 2001; Koopman et al., 2008; Ye and Fujikawa, 2011). The common key phrase in these articles is 'trade in value added', which is embodied in traded goods.

Value added is created by primary inputs that include labor and natural resources. Natural resources comprise energy, land, water and air. CO_2 emissions can be considered as a proxy variable for energy inputs, but also as use – or exploitation – of air since they are the main factor of global warming. Those value-added elements are traded internationally together with goods and services, such as embodied labor, CO_2, water and land; our research in this chapter focuses on the change in water use.

The following section outlines the trend of international trade in water by using international input-output tables (WIOD). We use input-output tables that include ten countries/regions – China, Japan, Korea, Taiwan, Indonesia, India, US, Russia, the European Union (EU) and the Rest of the World (RoW). The handling of water in the E3ME model is explained after that. Then, the next section discusses using the E3ME model to simulate the change of water

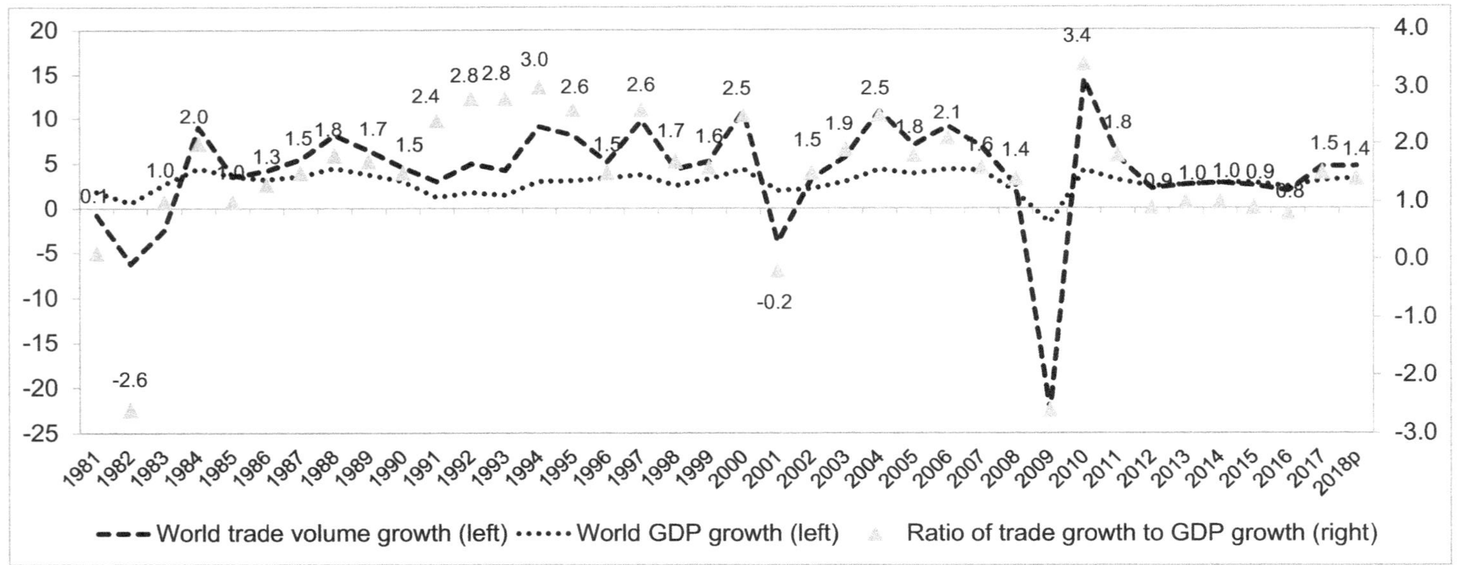

Figure 12.1 Ratio of world trade volume growth to world real GDP growth, 1981–2018

Source: WTO Press Release (2018)

consumption in Asian countries when water is taxed. The final section summarizes our findings and outlines future tasks.

International division of water

Data

We use input-output tables and data on CO_2 emissions, labor input, water use and land use by the World Input-Output Database (WIOD) (Timmer et al., 2015).

Table 12.1 shows the 40 countries (27 EU countries, four of the Americas and nine of the Asia and Pacific region) that are included in WIOD. Other countries and regions are grouped as Rest-of-the-world (RoW). RoW is treated as an endogenous sector in the WIOD. In this chapter, we aggregate the countries/regions as China (CHN), Japan (JPN), South Korea (KOR), Taiwan (TWN), Indonesia (IDN), India (IND), USA, Russia (RUS), the EU and other countries/regions (RoW). The original industry classification in WIOD is shown in Table 12.2. In this chapter, we combine three commercial industries (originally numbered 19, 20 and 21) into 'Commerce' and two service-related industries (originally numbered 34 and 35) into 'Services'.

Besides the input-output table data, WIOD provides supplementary data of social economic accounts and environmental accounts in the consistent industry classification. Table 12.3 summarizes the accounts.

Water consumption comprises three different components – green water, blue water and grey water, according to WIOD. Green water is the soil moisture from rainfall used by plants, which is part of the hydrologic cycle. Blue water is the freshwater stored in lakes, rivers, groundwater, glaciers and snow. Grey water is the drainage water resulting from human activities such as wastewater from households, manufacturing, mining and agriculture. We used the total use of green, blue and grey waters, excluding household wastewater, for the analysis of this research.

Table 12.1 Countries/regions in the WIOD

Europe			*America*	*Asia and Pacific*
Austria	Germany	Netherlands	Canada	China
Belgium	Greece	Poland	US	India
Bulgaria	Hungary	Portugal	Brazil	Japan
Cyprus	Ireland	Romania	Mexico	South Korea
Czech Republic	Italy	Slovakia		Australia
Denmark	Latvia	Slovenia		Taiwan
Estonia	Lithuania	Spain		Turkey
Finland	Luxembourg	Sweden		Indonesia
France	Malta	UK		Russia

Source: Timmer et al. (2015)

Table 12.2 Industry classifications according to WIOD as referred in this chapter

Original industry number	*Original industry description*	
01	Agriculture, hunting, forestry, fishing	
02	Mining and quarrying	
03	Food, beverages, and tobacco	
04	Textiles and textile products	
05	Leather, leather products and footwear	
06	Wood and products of wood and cork	
07	Pulp, paper, printing and publishing	
08	Coke, refined petroleum and nuclear fuel	
09	Chemicals and chemical products	
10	Rubber and plastics	
11	Other non-metallic minerals	
12	Basic metals and fabricated metals	
13	Machinery	
14	Electrical and optical equipment	
15	Transport equipment	
16	Other manufacturing and recycling	
17	Electricity, gas and water supply	
18	Construction	
19	Sale, maintenance and repair of motor vehicles and motorcycles; retail sale of fuel	
20	Wholesale trade and commission trade, except motor vehicles and motorcycles	Combined to 'Commerce'
21	Retail trade, except motor vehicles and motorcycles; repair of household goods	
22	Hotels and restaurants	
23	Inland transport	
24	Water transport	
25	Air transport	
26	Other supporting and auxiliary transport activities; activities of travel agencies	
27	Post and telecommunications	
28	Financial intermediation	
29	Real estate	
30	Renting of machinery and equipment and other business activities	
31	Public administration and defense; compulsory social security	
32	Education	
33	Health and social work	
34	Other community, social and personal services	Combined to 'Service'
35	Private households with employed persons	

Source: Timmer et al. (2015)

Table 12.3 Social economic accounts and environmental accounts according to the WIOD

Account name	*Contents of the account*
Social economic accounts	Wages and number of employees by skill and industry
Environmental accounts	CO_2 emissions modelled by sector and energy commodity
	Land, materials and water use by type and industry

Source: Timmer et al. (2015)

Model

In a one-country input-output model, the following supply-demand relation holds between final demand for domestic goods (f^d) and domestic supply (x):

$$x = A^d x + f^d \tag{1}$$

Matrix A^d is the domestic input coefficient matrix. The '*i*, *j*' element of A^d (a_{ij}) stands for the quantity of domestically produced intermediate inputs to produce one unit of output. In other words, the *j*-th column of A^d shows the input share of intermediate inputs. By solving Equation 1 for domestic output (x), the following equilibrium output determination Equation 2 is derived. Matrix B is called the 'Leontief inverse matrix'. The Leontief inverse matrix has the role of bridging final demand and production volume. More specifically, it is the linear transformation matrix to calculate the domestic total production that is required to supply a certain amount of final demand.

$$\mathbf{x} = (\mathbf{I} - \mathbf{A}^d)^{-1}\mathbf{f}^d = \mathbf{B}\mathbf{f}^d \tag{2}$$

In a two-region international input-output model, the following supply-demand relation holds between final demand and domestic supply for each region (1 and 2).

$$\begin{bmatrix} \mathbf{x}_1 \\ \mathbf{x}_2 \end{bmatrix} = \begin{bmatrix} \mathbf{A}_{11} & \mathbf{A}_{12} \\ \mathbf{A}_{21} & \mathbf{A}_{22} \end{bmatrix} \begin{bmatrix} \mathbf{x}_1 \\ \mathbf{x}_2 \end{bmatrix} + \begin{bmatrix} \mathbf{f}_{11} + \mathbf{f}_{12} \\ \mathbf{f}_{21} + \mathbf{f}_{22} \end{bmatrix} \tag{3}$$

Suffixes 1 and 2 denote regions. A_{ij} is the input coefficient where, if $i = j$, it is an intra-region input coefficient and, if $i \neq j$, it is an inter-region input coefficient for inputs in region *i* to produce goods in region *j*. A vector f_{ij} is the final demand where, if $i = j$, it is the own final demand in a region and, if $i \neq j$, it is the final demand for region *i* by region *j*.

$$\begin{bmatrix} \mathbf{x}_1 \\ \mathbf{x}_2 \end{bmatrix} = \left[\mathbf{I} - \begin{bmatrix} \mathbf{A}_{11} & \mathbf{A}_{12} \\ \mathbf{A}_{21} & \mathbf{A}_{22} \end{bmatrix} \right]^{-1} \begin{bmatrix} \mathbf{f}_{11} + \mathbf{f}_{12} \\ \mathbf{f}_{21} + \mathbf{f}_{22} \end{bmatrix} = \begin{bmatrix} \mathbf{B}_{11} & \mathbf{B}_{12} \\ \mathbf{B}_{21} & \mathbf{B}_{22} \end{bmatrix} \begin{bmatrix} \mathbf{f}_{11} + \mathbf{f}_{12} \\ \mathbf{f}_{21} + \mathbf{f}_{22} \end{bmatrix} \tag{4}$$

Assuming a vector 'a' is an input coefficient of such resources as labor, CO_2, water or land, multiplying this resource input coefficient 'a' and domestic output (x) derives the direct environmental load (E_D) based on production region.

$$\mathbf{E_D} = \begin{bmatrix} \mathbf{a}_1 & 0 \\ 0 & \mathbf{a}_2 \end{bmatrix} \left[\begin{array}{c:c} \hat{\mathbf{x}}_1 & \mathbf{0} \\ \hdashline \mathbf{0} & \hat{\mathbf{x}}_2 \end{array}\right] \tag{5}$$

Embodied environmental load (E_E) of final goods consumed by country *i* is expressed as

$$\mathbf{E_E} = \begin{bmatrix} \mathbf{a}_1 & 0 \\ 0 & \mathbf{a}_2 \end{bmatrix} \begin{bmatrix} \mathbf{B}_{11} & \mathbf{B}_{12} \\ \mathbf{B}_{21} & \mathbf{B}_{22} \end{bmatrix} \left[\begin{array}{c:c} \hat{\mathbf{f}}_{11} & \hat{\mathbf{f}}_{12} \\ \hdashline \hat{\mathbf{f}}_{21} & \hat{\mathbf{f}}_{22} \end{array}\right] \tag{6}$$

The total amount of direct load calculated by Equation 5 is equal to the total amount of embodied environmental load calculated by Equation 6. In Equation 5, it is assumed that environmental load has occurred in the area where goods and services were produced, whereas in Equation 6, it is assumed that environmental load occurred in the area where goods and services were consumed.

Water trade

Table 12.4 shows water trade as of 1995. China, India, the US and the EU are large water suppliers, as well as large users of water. China and India have a trade surplus of water, whereas the US and the EU have a trade deficit of water. Water exports to overseas countries is 10% of the total supply for China and 7% of total supply for India. The main export destinations for China are Japan, the US and the EU; the main export destinations for India are the US and the EU.

Japan, South Korea and Taiwan are water importers. Of those, Japan uses more than four times the amount of water than the amount it supplies. Although the US is known as an agricultural goods exporter, it is also a water importer; however, the water trade deficit is no more than 6% of its total use. The EU is also a large water importer, that is, more than one third of total water used is imported.

Table 12.5 shows water trade as of 2009, where total water use has increase by 37% from 1995. The most noteworthy change in this 15-year period is that China's water trade surplus has expanded even though its water use increased remarkably. The absolute value of the trade surplus has almost doubled from 103 billion tons to 203 billion tons, and the ratio to the total supply expanded by two points from 10% to 12%. On the other hand, India's water exports have not increased so much as China's, and, therefore, India's water trade surplus has almost disappeared.

Japan, South Korea and Taiwan are still water importers, and Japan's water deficit is still large though the value of the deficit has decreased. The US deficit widened sharply from 62.3 billion tons to 148.6 billion tons, and the EU water deficit also widened from 320.1 billion tons to 440.7 billion tons. The expansion

Table 12.4 Trade of water in the world in 1995 (in Bn tons)

		Water importer											
		CHN	*JPN*	*KOR*	*TWN*	*IDN*	*IND*	*US*	*RUS*	*EU*	*RoW*	*Total use*	*Balance*
Water exporter	CHN	**902.7**	37.5	5.8	2.2	2.8	1.3	32.8	2.7	30.6	32.5	1,050.9	103.5
	JPN	0.2	**51.2**	0.2	0.2	0.1	0.0	0.9	0.0	0.6	1.1	54.5	-231.3
	KOR	0.2	0.8	**15.3**	0.0	0.0	0.0	0.5	0.0	0.3	0.3	17.5	-43.1
	TWN	0.5	3.8	0.1	**35.7**	0.1	0.0	3.4	0.0	0.5	1.1	45.2	-17.0
	IDN	3.0	9.9	1.3	1.1	**255.4**	0.5	5.6	0.3	8.3	5.0	290.4	19.9
	IND	1.3	10.4	0.9	10.6	0.9	**1,002.6**	24.1	2.2	27.7	18.5	1,089.2	73.5
	US	8.4	54.7	13.2	8.3	1.8	0.8	**794.9**	2.2	34.3	68.2	986.9	-62.3
	RUS	1.6	11.5	1.3	0.4	0.3	0.7	3.3	**358.7**	17.3	7.2	402.2	12.2
	EU	1.9	5.7	1.3	1.0	0.5	0.5	10.1	4.0	**559.8**	32.2	617.0	-320.1
	RoW	27.6	100.5	21.3	12.7	8.6	9.2	173.6	19.7	257.8	**3,252.2**	3,883.2	464.7
	Total supply	947.4	285.9	60.6	62.2	270.5	1,015.8	1,049.2	390.0	937.1	3,418.4	**8,436.9**	

Source: Authors' calculation based on WIOD

Note: Rows list water exports per country/region; total supply of water per country is shown in the last row. Columns list water import per country/region; total use of water per country is shown in the penultimate column (Total used). The trade balance of water for each country is shown in the last column (Balance). Diagonal cells show the domestic use of water in bold. China, CHN; Japan, JPN; South Korea, KOR; Taiwan, TWN; Indonesia, IDN; India, IND; Russia, RUS; RoW, Rest of World.

Table 12.5 Water trade in the world in 2009 (in Bn tons)

		Water importer											
		CHN	*JPN*	*KOR*	*TWN*	*IDN*	*IND*	*US*	*RUS*	*EU*	*RoW*	*Total use*	*Balance*
Water exporter	CHN	**1,259.2**	40.6	12.6	3.5	6.6	11.7	88.1	15.1	94.0	157.4	1,688.9	202.7
	JPN	1.0	**42.9**	0.2	0.2	0.1	0.1	0.8	0.1	0.7	1.5	47.4	-173.5
	KOR	0.6	0.5	**15.5**	0.0	0.0	0.0	0.5	0.1	0.4	1.2	18.8	-46.2
	TWN	2.0	2.0	0.2	**45.1**	0.1	0.1	3.4	0.1	0.9	2.6	56.5	-9.2
	IDN	7.1	4.3	1.0	0.4	**413.0**	5.4	7.2	0.8	11.9	22.0	473.0	30.1
	IND	7.3	2.8	1.1	0.8	1.9	**1,238.0**	23.1	2.7	29.4	37.8	1,344.9	56.1
	US	37.9	33.1	7.6	4.9	3.1	2.2	**953.0**	3.5	31.7	103.5	1,180.5	-148.6
	RUS	7.8	6.2	2.4	0.2	0.4	0.9	4.5	**486.4**	13.6	20.9	543.3	-54.3
	EU	7.2	4.1	1.1	0.6	0.5	1.0	13.4	5.6	**600.2**	58.7	692.5	-440.7
	RoW	156.2	84.4	23.4	9.8	17.2	29.4	235.1	83.3	350.3	**4,500.7**	5,489.8	583.6
	Total supply	1,486.2	220.9	65.1	65.6	442.9	1,288.8	1,329.0	597.6	1,133.2	4,906.3	**11,535.6**	

Source: Authors' calculation based on WIOD

Note: Rows list water exports per country/region; total supply of water per country is shown in the last row. Columns list water import per country/region; total use of water per country is shown in the penultimate column (Total use) The trade balance of water for each country is shown in the last column (Balance). Diagonal cells show the domestic use of water in bold. China, CHN; Japan, JPN; South Korea, KOR; Taiwan, TWN; Indonesia, IDN; India, IND; Russia, RUS; RoW, Rest of World.

of deficits in the US and EU is 206 billion tons, of which half is explained by an increase in imports from China.

Estimating the consumption of water using the E3ME model

Although the E3ME model was designed to include equations that estimate the consumption of water, the model has not really been used for this purpose before. The main reason has been the difficulty in collecting the necessary data with which to estimate econometric equations, namely time series of the consumption of water by each sector in each country. The WIOD data used in the previous section provide the best information available, but the level of sectoral disaggregation is not sufficient for general use in E3ME.

Zetland (2011) lays out a range of further challenges in modelling water consumption. As noted previously, there are different types of water that have different properties and value, so it is not always easy to define the 'consumption' of water. For example, water that is used in hydroelectric power plants is returned to rivers so may be used for other purposes. Water that is used for cooling in thermal power plants may also be returned to rivers, but with a higher temperature.

For economists looking to assess the effects of pricing measures, there are further challenges. Much of the water that is used is not priced at present (especially if it is self-abstracted, as is common in agriculture), meaning that it is not possible to apply a simple price elasticity to estimate demand responses to price rises. Furthermore, at least for household use, the demand for water is highly non-linear because there is a base level of water demand that is near-essential (e.g. for drinking or cooking), but water consumption beyond that may be more responsive (i.e. elastic) to changes in prices.

The use of E3ME to estimate water demand has therefore been limited in the past, and based on assumptions to get round the limitations outlined previously. One example is presented in The Ex'Tax Project (2016, pp. 133–134). The modelling estimated that water consumption in Europe could fall by 6.3% if a 25% consumption tax was levied, using a price elasticity of –0.25. The report includes a footnote on the price elasticities in the literature and the choice that was used in the modelling:

> While there is a relatively extensive literature on the estimation of household water demand, estimates of non-household water demand are less common. Furthermore, few studies have been carried out which estimate a price elasticity of demand for water, disaggregated by user-type, using European data (European Commission, 2000). Of those studies that do, NERA (2007) estimate a price elasticity of –0.24 for non-household water demand using UK data and Reynaud (2003) estimates the price elasticity for industrial water demand in France of –0.29. European Commission (2000) cites estimates of the industrial price elasticity derived from US data ranging between –0.11 and –0.44 (although these estimates are now quite dated, having been made

> in 1991). On the basis of this limited evidence, for the purpose of this modelling experience industrial price elasticity is assumed to be -0.25.
>
> The Ex'Tax Project (2016, p. 134)

In the modelling in the next section we also use a price elasticity of –0.25.

Results from the E3ME modelling

For the reasons outlined in the previous section, it is difficult to predict by how much water consumption will increase in the baseline case. The available data from WIOD suggest a strong increase in water use in China and Taiwan up to the financial crisis in 2008–09 but a more static demand in Japan and Korea (see Figure 12.1). It seems reasonable to expect that these trends have continued since 2009, and will also continue into the future. As parts of East Asia are already facing water shortages, the need for remedial policies will grow.

If we assume a constant water consumption per unit of production for each WIOD sector, the policies described in Chapter 5 (Scenario 3, ambitious case) that meet the emission-reduction targets could slightly reduce water consumption in China and Japan, but increase consumption in Korea and Taiwan. The exact outcome depends on the impacts on different sectors but, in general, higher levels of economic activity lead to higher rates of water consumption.

However, this simple calculation misses one important point – that the power sector is an important consumer of water. A reduction in nuclear and fossil-fuel electricity generation will lead to less water consumption by the power sector (La Rovere et al., 2010), but an increase in biomass consumption will lead to more consumption of water (although this consumption may take place in other

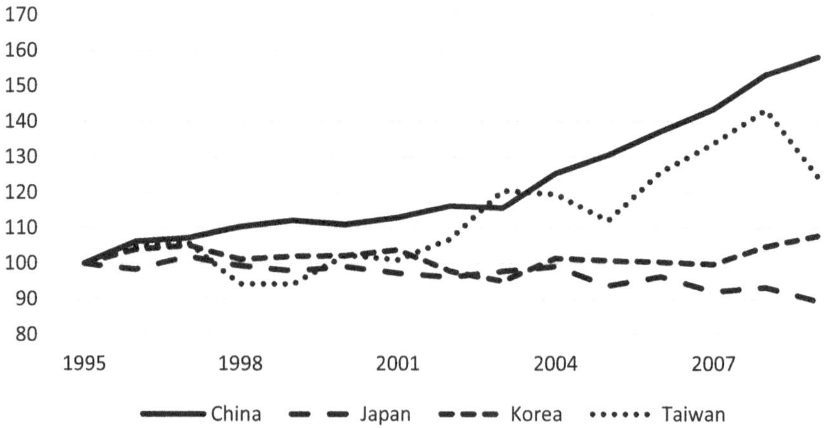

Figure 12.2 Demand for water (in 1,000 m³) for each East Asian country in 1995–2009

Source: WIOD

Note: Standardized as 1995 = 100

Table 12.6 Impacts on water consumption for each East Asian country in 2050 under Chapter 5, Scenario 3 (% from baseline)

	If we assume fixed m³ of water per unit of production in each WIOD sector	*If we also factor in changes in consumption of water by the power sector*
China	–0.4%	7.5%
Japan	–0.4%	36.0%
South Korea	0.2%	44.1%
Taiwan	0.6%	1.7%

Source: Author calculations

countries if biomass is imported). If we factor this in, we see that the increase in water consumption could be considerable in Japan and South Korea – possibly to levels that are unsustainable (Table 12.6). In reality, the increase in water consumption will not be this large, as technological improvements will reduce the amount of water required per unit of power generation. However, we can say with some certainty that our ambitious policy scenario in Chapter 5 will not lead to substantial reductions in water consumption.

There is no consensus on the level of water consumption that is 'sustainable' in each East Asian country, but a sustainable water consumption is likely to be less than current (as of 2018) use and certainly less than that shown in Table 12.6. To further improve the sustainability of our scenario from Chapter 5, we have, therefore, added a 40% tax on water consumption from the public supply, levied on all industrial sectors that use water.[1] We have run two variants of the scenario – one in which the revenues are used to reduce government debt (consistent with the scenario described in Chapter 5) and one in which the revenues are used to reduce a combination of VAT rate, income tax rate and employers' social contributions (see Chapter 9). The tax is phased in over an eight-year period, starting in 2020.

By using an elasticity of –0.25, water consumption from industry falls by 10% in each country. With the existing data, it is impossible to calculate to a high degree of accuracy the total saving of water in each country. However, annual water saving could be in the region of 200 billion m^3 in China, 5 billion m^3 in both Japan and Taiwan, and 2 billion m^3 in South Korea. For China and Taiwan, this would reduce rates of water consumption in Scenario 3 in Chapter 5 to below baseline levels.

Nevertheless, the amounts of revenue raised by the charge are not large. In China, the charge could raise \$12.6bn (2018 prices). The equivalent figures for Japan, South Korea and Taiwan are \$4.7bn, \$1.6bn and \$0.3bn, respectively. The results of this calculation, which is based on input-output coefficients, is likely to reflect the low charges for water currently (as of 2018) existing across East Asia. The economic impacts of the tax gradually increase over the period in which it is introduced and peak around 2030 (Table 12.7). Impacts then become smaller, as industries become more efficient in their use of water over time. Sectors that use water will face higher costs and may, therefore, increase prices. As a result, they may see a loss of demand both in domestic consumption and, potentially, through trade links, that is, competitiveness. Employment may fall slightly.

Overall, however, at the macroeconomic level the impacts are small, registering in the third decimal place (see Table 12.7). The impacts on employment are close to zero, and there are no major changes in sectoral production (Table 12.8). The sectors that are most affected include intensive users of water (e.g. paper and pulp) but also sectors that feature in the supply chains for these sectors and those that are particularly exposed to either consumption goods (e.g. retail in China) or investment goods (e.g. motor vehicles in Taiwan). In summary, the broader economic impacts are important for determining the sectoral impacts, although the overall size of the impacts is still less than 0.1% in any given sector. This finding reflects that water represents a small share of input costs, even for intensive users.

If the revenues from the charge on water are used to offset other taxes, it is possible to get positive economic impacts. Although still small, these impacts are

Table 12.7 Macroeconomic impacts of a water tax without revenue recycling for each East Asian country in 2030 (in %), applying the ambitious scenario described in Chapter 5 (S3)

	China	*Japan*	*South Korea*	*Taiwan*
GDP	-0.008%	-0.004%	-0.010%	-0.006%
Employment	-0.003%	0.000%	-0.003%	0.001%
Consumption	-0.017%	-0.006%	-0.008%	-0.006%
Investment	-0.007%	-0.005%	0.000%	-0.017%
Exports	-0.001%	-0.001%	-0.014%	-0.004%
Imports	-0.002%	-0.003%	-0.008%	-0.003%
Price index	0.014%	0.009%	0.014%	0.022%

Source: Author calculations

Table 12.8 Most affected sectors and their loss of output (in %) for each East Asian country, applying the ambitious scenario described in Chapter 5 (S3)

	1st		*2nd*		*3rd*	
China	Retail	-0.062%	Computer services	-0.046%	Paper and pulp	-0.039%
Japan	Textiles	-0.041%	Paper and pulp	-0.033%	Printing and publishing	-0.018%
South Korea	Paper and pulp	-0.284%	Textiles	-0.076%	Motor vehicles	-0.056%
Taiwan	Motor vehicles	-0.037%	Other transport	-0.015%	Non-metallic minerals	-0.015%

Source: Author calculations

Note: 1st, most affected sectors; 2nd, second-most affected sectors; 3rd, third-most affected sectors.

Table 12.9 Macroeconomic impacts of a water tax with revenue recycling for each East Asian country in 2030 (in %), applying the scenario described in Chapter 5

	China	*Japan*	*South Korea*	*Taiwan*
GDP	0.076%	0.070%	0.064%	0.042%
Employment	0.026%	0.031%	0.044%	0.012%
Consumption	0.245%	0.121%	0.120%	0.078%
Investment	0.007%	0.037%	0.010%	-0.013%
Exports	0.005%	0.017%	0.012%	0.017%
Imports	0.020%	0.065%	0.066%	0.005%
Price index	-0.071%	-0.066%	-0.042%	-0.043%

Source: Author calculations

larger in magnitude than the negative impacts just described. In 2030, consumers benefit from lower tax rates but companies have not yet had a chance to raise prices in response to increased water costs, so there is a stimulus effect. Over time, however, we would expect companies to raise prices and reduce this stimulus effect. By 2050, the positive impacts are ~50% of those shown in Table 12.9.

Conclusions

Currently (as in 2018), direct water consumption could be met by domestic water supply in East Asia. However, in the future it is uncertain that this will remain the case because of both growing demand and the impacts of climate change. Since 2000, droughts have increased in frequency in the northern part of China, which could affect future production patterns in China.

As shown in our analysis, China is a net exporter of 'virtual' water through its trade in intermediate and final goods. At present, the other three East Asian countries benefit from this position. However, this might become untenable if pressures on domestic consumption of water in China become too great. In several parts of East Asia, the provision of fresh water is an important issue for policy makers. In the context of sustainable development it is, therefore, important to consider rates of water consumption.

The research discussed in this chapter draws on data from the WIOD database, and we link this to previous modelling carried out with E3ME. First, however, we focus on the structural change of water trade on an international level. Water trade is measured by virtual water embodied in the trade of goods and services. The results obtained are summarized as follows:

1 In 1995, the extensive users and suppliers of virtual water were China, India, the US and the EU; all of them used ~1 trillion tons of water per year. The water trade balance showed a surplus in China and India but a deficit in the US and the EU. The water trade balance of the East Asian countries Japan, Korea and Taiwan also showed a deficit, with that of Japan being particularly large.

2 Total global water use increased by 37% from 1995 to 2009. In this period, China's water trade surplus expanded, even though its water use increased remarkably. By contrast, India's water exports did not increase as much as that of China and, therefore, India's water trade surplus almost disappeared. The water trade deficit of the US and the EU widened sharply and, although the water trade deficit decreased for Japan, its volume is comparable with that for the US. It can, therefore, be said that the EU, Japan and the US have contributed to the overconsumption of water in China.

These findings stress the need to consider ways in which water consumption can be reduced in East Asia. We note that, because of a shift to biofuels, the ambitious low-carbon scenario presented in Chapter 5 could, in fact, increase the consumption of water. Depending on where the biofuels are produced, this additional water consumption may, however, not be in East Asia. Any economic benefits from revenue recycling schemes (see Chapter 9) could also lead to increases in domestic water consumption.

We, therefore, tested the impacts of a tax on water consumption in each country. The model results should be considered as indicative because of limitations in the available data, but it seems possible that a modest reduction in water consumption could be obtained by increasing prices. Furthermore, this could come at a very limited cost to the economy and, if revenues are recycled from this tax, potentially deliver some small economic benefits.

It may be possible to further reduce water consumption through levying a larger tax, but the range of uncertainty in the model results increases with an increase of the tax rates. Other regulatory policies (e.g. restriction of any production of biofuels) could play an important role and, as we found in other chapters, policy interaction is likely to be important. However, this requires a more detailed analysis that, at this point in time, the data are unlikely to support.

In summary, there are many complexities when modelling the demand for water, and further data and analyses at both the micro- and macroeconomic levels are required. Our analysis shows that the issue of fresh-water resources in parts of East Asia is already becoming a priority and likely to become even more important in the future.

Note

1 The consumer product categories combine spending on water with rent, making it difficult to model higher charges on water. Similarly, we have not included self-abstraction (pumping from the ground directly), which usually has no price anyway.

References

European Commission. (2000), *The Application of the Polluter Pays Principle in Cohesion Fund Countries*, Publications office of the European Union.

The Ex' Tax Project. (2016), *New Era. New Plan. Europe: A Fiscal Strategy for an Inclusive, Circular Economy*, www.neweranewplan.com/wp-content/uploads/2016/12/New-Era-New-Plan-Europe-Extax-Report-DEF.compressed.pdf.

Hummels, D., Ishii, J. and Yi, K. M. (2001), 'The Nature and Growth of Vertical Specialization in World Trade', *Journal of International Economics*, 54(1), 75–96.

Koopman, R., Wang, Z. and Wei, S. (2008), *How Much of Chinese Exports Is Really Made in China? Assessing Domestic Value-Added When Processing Trade is Pervasive*, NBER Working Papers 14109.

La Rovere, E. L., Soares, J. B., Oliveira, L. B. and Lauria, T. (2010), 'Sustainable Expansion of Electricity Sector: Sustainability Indicators as an Instrument to Support Decision Making', *Renewable and Sustainable Energy Reviews*, 14(1), 422–429.

NERA. (2007), *Non-Residential Demand for Water in the Bristol Water Region*, Report for Bristol Water.

OECD. (2018), *Trade Policy Implications of Global Value Chains*, Policy Brief (Trade), December 2018, www.oecd.org/tad/trade-policy-implications-global-value-chains.pdf.

Reynaud, A. (2003), 'An Econometric Estimation of Industrial Water Demand in France', *Environmental and Resource Economics*, 25, 213–232.

Timmer, M. P., Dietzenbacher, E., Los, B., Stehrer, R. and de Vries, G. J. (2015), 'An Illustrated User Guide to the World Input – Output Database: The Case of Global Automotive Production', *Review of International Economics*, 23, 575–605.

WTO Press Release. (2018, 12 April), *Strong Trade Growth in 2018 Rests on Policy Choices*, www.wto.org/english/news_e/pres18_e/pr820_e.htm.

Ye, Z. and Fujikawa, K. (2011), 'An Analysis on Structural Change of Interregional Division of Labor in China', in H. Ji and H. Ohnishi (eds.), *China-Japan Economic Statistics Review*, Capital Economic and Trade University Publishing, 280–308.

Zetland, D. (2011), *The End of Abundance: Economic Solutions to Water Scarcity*, Aguanomics Press.

13 Transboundary PM air pollution and its impact on health in East Asia

Akihiro Chiashi, Soocheol Lee, Hector Pollitt, Unnada Chewpreecha, Pim Vercoulen, Yanmin He and Bin Xu

Introduction

In recent decades, transboundary air pollution has been a topic of debate in East Asia and has become the subject of research from both the natural and social science perspectives. As shown by the establishment of the Acid Deposition Monitoring Network in East Asia (EANET) in 1998 and the Tripartite Environment Ministers Meeting (TEMM) among China, Japan and Korea in 1999 (and the continued administration of these organizations), efforts have been made to establish schemes for international cooperation and monitoring of atmospheric contaminants, such as sulfur oxide (SOx), nitrogen oxide (NOx), particulate matter (PM10), fine particulate matter (PM2.5) and ozone across national boundaries.

Air pollution is not confined to a single political region and inevitably involves boundary transgression. Recent improvements in atmospheric monitoring systems in East Asian countries have enabled the measurement of PM10 and PM2.5[1] throughout the region. This confirmed that the pollutants affect not only individual countries but East Asia as a whole. Although now recognized as an important issue in East Asia, this has not led to the establishment of high-level legally enforceable international regimes, such as the Convention on Long-Range Transboundary Air Pollution in Europe. Even though PM air pollution has been identified as a serious health hazard in China, Korea and in parts of Japan, disputes regarding which country is responsible have become a barrier to cooperation, and no international regime in the form of a treaty or agreement has yet been established.

In this chapter, we investigate the current state, characteristics and health hazards related to transboundary PM air pollution in China, Japan and Korea, the three main actors in East Asia with respect to transboundary PM air pollution. We then explore the potential for policy coordination and the prospect for adopting policies aimed at reducing air pollution, based on an analysis using the E3ME model.

Health hazards related to transboundary PM air pollution – globally and in East Asia

Today, air pollution is a serious issue, not only in East Asia but also around the world. In May 2018, the World Health Organization issued a statement based on new data in which it estimated that nine out of ten people around the world breathe air containing fine particles comprising high levels of contaminants (both indoors and outdoors), and that this exposure causes seven million deaths per year[2] (WHO, 2018). In the same statement, the WHO pointed out that more than 90% of air pollution–related deaths occur in low- and middle-income countries, primarily in Asia and Africa.

The US-based non-profit Health Effects Institute (HEI) and Institute for Health Metrics and Evaluation (IHME) highlight the health risks of PM air pollutants, and point to research results showing that air pollution involving fine particles poses the greatest environmental risk. Moreover, exposure to PM air pollutants outdoors is the sixth-highest early-death risk factor (HEI and IHME, 2018). Specifically, PM2.5 air pollutants contain high concentrations of heavy metals such as lead, arsenic and mercury, all of which are toxic to the human body. When inhaled, they penetrate deep into the lungs, increasing the risk of developing lung cancer and other respiratory diseases, as well as circulatory system diseases.

Knowledge regarding the health effects of PM air pollutants has been accumulating since the 1990s through epidemiological research conducted in the United States and elsewhere. The health effects of PM air pollutants include both short-term effects (resulting from PM2.5 exposure lasting from several hours to several days) and long-term effects (resulting from PM2.5 exposure lasting several years or longer). Health effects on both time scales have been studied. Regarding the long-term effects of PM2.5 in PM pollutants, the United States Environmental Protection Agency (2018, US EPA) showed that mortality rates increase with increasing concentrations of PM2.5 and showed that, for every 10 $\mu g/m^3$ increase in PM2.5, the risk of mortality owing to short-term effects increases by 0.3–1.2% and the risk of death owing to long-term effects increases by 6–13%. This leads to the conclusion that both short- and long-term effects have a causal relationship to death. Recent research in Europe (Newby DE et al., 2015) also shows that a 5 $\mu g/m^3$ increase in PM2.5 increases the risk of death owing to long-term effects by 7% and the risk of death from lung cancer by 18%.

PM air pollution in Asia

Within the continent of Asia, both East and South Asia face severe air pollution. This is because China and India – countries with especially serious air pollution problems – are located within these two regions. At present, many of the cities considered to have the worst air pollution problems in the world can be found there. In 2013, the World Bank and IHME jointly issued a report indicating that, among regions of the world with the highest numbers of air pollution–related deaths, East Asia and Oceania combined for the highest (2.227 million deaths) followed by South Asia (1.797 million deaths) (World Bank and IHME, 2016).

The recent statistical survey of PM air pollution–related deaths by country (HEI and IHME, 2017) indicates that India and China had the worst air pollution in the world up to 2015 (Table 13.1). Moreover, while some improvement can be seen in China because of recent efforts by the Chinese government to

Table 13.1 PM air pollution–related number of deaths by country/region

	1990	*1995*	*2000*	*2005*	*2010*	*2015*
China	945,300	961,600	1,039,300	1,140,100	1,098,800	1,108,100
Japan	38,100	40,700	41,800	48,200	50,800	60,600
India	737,400	795,200	857,300	895,900	957,000	1,090,400
EU	329,700	302,600	269,700	244,700	240,500	257,500
Russia	133,200	162,000	157,300	157,700	138,100	136,900
US	10,600	107,200	106,200	100,000	83,400	88,400

Source: HEI and IHME (2017)

substantially strengthen air pollution control policies, air pollution in India continues to worsen. According to survey data collected in 2013 by the Ministry of Ecology and Environment of the People's Republic of China, the main sources of PM air pollutants – from largest to smallest, were coking coal (mainly for steel manufacturing), transportation, household burning of wood, non-coal minerals and ordinary charcoal (coal-fired power generation). The list for India contains many of the same sources.

In 2015, 86% of the people living in areas with a PM2.5 concentration above 75 µg/m^3 lived in China, India, Pakistan or Bangladesh (HEI and IHME, 2017). Recent efforts in China to strengthen air quality policies appear to have had some effect in reducing PM2.5. However, economic circumstances[3] substantially affect the degree of pollution. This is because – depending on economic conditions – industries, such as the steel industry (one of the largest contributors to air pollution), can choose to strengthen or relax environmental measures by, for example, increasing or decreasing production volumes.

In East Asia, not only China but also Korea is facing serious problems related to PM air pollution. By the end of March 2017, Seoul was ranked the third most polluted city in the world in terms of air pollution.,[4] just behind New Delhi (India) and Dhaka (Bangladesh).

PM air pollution and its effects on health in East Asia

Concerns regarding the health hazards of PM air pollution have increased in China, Japan and Korea in recent years, in part because of the publication of new research findings. In China, which faces especially serious air pollution, research is being conducted on the negative health effects and economic losses caused by PM air pollution. Pan et al. (2012) estimated that 2,349 deaths in Beijing in 2010 can be attributed to PM2.5 pollution and that the economic losses associated with early deaths resulting from PM2.5 in the same city were 1.86 billion CNY. The World Bank and IHME reported that welfare losses in China because of PM2.5 increased dramatically from 123 billion USD in 1990 to 1.6 trillion USD in 2013 (World Bank and IHME, 2016).

In a recent study, Chen et al. (2017) performed a nationwide time-series analysis in 272 representative Chinese cities between 2013 and 2015. This research revealed that the average annual PM2.5 concentration in each city was 56 μg/m³ – much higher than the WHO standard of 10 μg/m³. Each increase of 10 μg/m³ in the two-day moving average of PM2.5 concentration is associated with a 0.22% increase in mortality of total non-accidental deaths; of these, 0.27% are from cardiovascular diseases, 0.39% from hypertension, 0.30% from coronary heart diseases, 0.23% from stroke, 0.29% from respiratory diseases and 0.38% from chronic obstructive pulmonary disease. In addition, this nationwide investigation provided robust evidence of the association between short-term exposure to PM2.5 and increased mortality caused by various cardiopulmonary diseases. However, the magnitude of associations was lower compared with those reported for Europe and North America.

In Korea, interest in the health hazards of air pollution is also growing, as evidenced by the publication of several research articles on related topics. The reports include articles that focus on air pollution originating in Korea, as well as transboundary pollution coming from China. For example, in March 2017, an article was published in the journal *Nature* stating that more than 30,000 people died in Korea and Japan in 2017 because of effects related to yellow dust from China (Zhang et al., 2017).

In Japan, public awareness and concern regarding the health hazards of PM air pollution are below those in China and Korea, and domestic reporting on related topics has decreased in recent years. Although international concern regarding PM air pollution in China increased interest in Japan for a short period starting in early 2013, with numerous reports being filed on the negative effects and health hazards of this pollution, reporting on the issue has since waned.

PM air pollution–related measures and policies in East Asia

China

China is the leading producer of transboundary PM air pollution in East Asia because it is the largest consumer of fossil fuels (especially coal); it also releases the most emissions from industrial processes. HEI and IHME (2018) identified the burning of coal and emissions from motor vehicles as the two largest emission sources of PM2.5-related deaths in China in 2013 (Figure 13.1).

Examining this breakdown, it is apparent that, to create measures aimed at reducing the health risks of PM air pollution, not only industrial coal use, the transportation sector, coal-fired power generation and industries that do not use coal need to be targeted, but also biomass and coal burning by households as well as field burning. For the first group, it is important to integrate policies related to industry and energy sector restructuring. To address the second group, it is crucial to integrate policies related to rural agricultural communities and poverty.

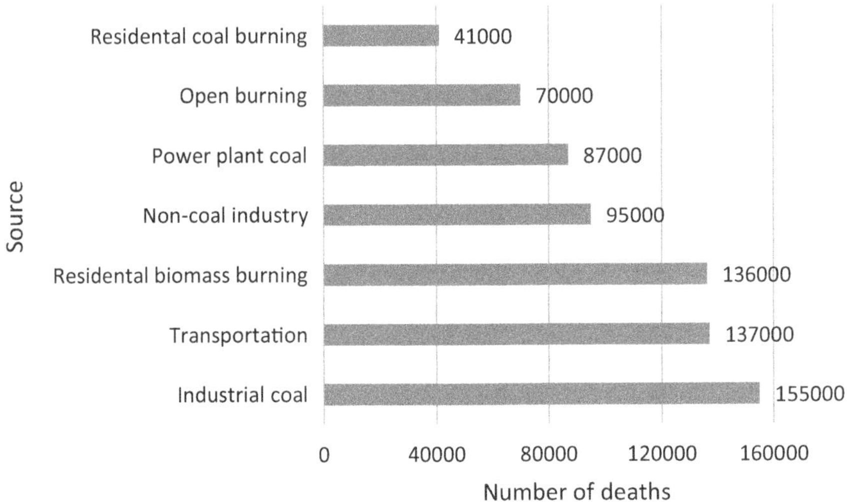

Figure 13.1 Causes (emission sources) of PM2.5-related deaths in China in 2013

Source: HEI and IHME (2018, p. 16)

Regarding the current state of PM air pollution in China, monitoring schemes have been established in various parts of the country, whose data can be easily accessed by the public, for example by using cell phone apps and other means. In addition, starting in about 2014, the government began to intensify efforts to reduce PM air pollution by heavy-handedly introducing regulations in different areas. The Air Pollution Action Plan, released in September 2013, is China's most influential environmental policy of the past five years. It helped China to make significant improvements in air quality by setting PM2.5 targets for key regions, requiring significant reductions of PM air pollutants in the Pearl River Delta (by 15%) and Beijing (by 33%) between 2013 and 2017. To combat PM air pollution in northern China, the allocation of ~1.7 trillion CNY over the five-year period starting in 2013 (and including Beijing, Tianjin and the Hebei Province) has resulted in an overall reduction of PM2.5 levels in China (Table 13.2).

In Beijing, this meant reducing PM2.5 levels by ~30% (from 89.5 $\mu g/m^3$ to 60 $\mu g/m^3$). Beijing closed its coal-fired power stations and banned people in surrounding areas from burning coal to heat homes. However, official data show that, of the 338 cities at the prefectural or higher level, 231 have not yet reached the Chinese government standard of 35 $\mu g/m^3$ PM2.5 on average (equivalent to the WHO's interim standard). July 2018 saw the release of a new three-year action plan to win the so-called battle for a blue sky. Regarded as the second phase of the original Air Pollution Action Plan, it mandates a decrease of at least 18% in PM2.5 levels based on those in 2015 in cities with prefectural or higher ranking, and where standards have not yet been met.

Table 13.2 Mean annual PM2.5 concentration in China, Beijing-Tianjin-Hebei region

	2014 (μg/m³)	*2015 (μg/m³)*	*2016 (μg/m³)*	*2017 (μg/m³)*
China (overall)	72	64	55	43
Hebei Province (including Beijing and Tianjin)	106	93	77	58
Beijing	89	86	81	62

Source: Ministry of Ecology and Environment of the People's Republic of China (2015)

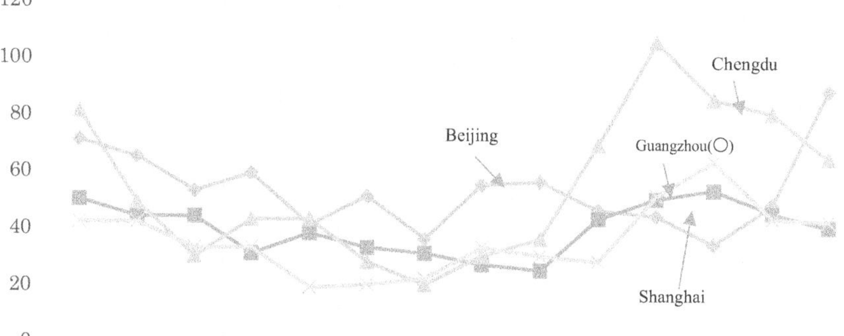

Figure 13.2 PM2.5 levels in Beijing, Shanghai, Chengdu and Guangzhou, between February 2017 and March 2018 (in μg/m³)

Source: World-wide Air Quality Monitoring Data Coverage (2018)

However, in response to concerns regarding the economic downturn stemming from trade friction between China and the United States, relevant authorities began to relax these environmental regulations in November 2018, resulting in worsening air pollution. Therefore, at least to date, the strength or weakness of environmental measures depends on the state of the economy.[5]

Seasonal concentrations of PM2.5 indicate that they are at a maximum in winter and early spring, when the use of coal heaters increases. Furthermore, PM2.5 concentrations in northern cities, such as Beijing and Chengdu, remain high, and there is the undeniable potential for concentrations to rise throughout the country, depending on the direction of the wind and other meteorological factors.

Japan

Although PM air pollution in Japan is not as severe as it is in China and Korea, there are numerous regions in and around Kyushu – which is geographically close to China and Korea – that do not meet environmental quality standards.

According to the Ministry of the Environment, 88.7% of general atmospheric monitoring stations across Japan recorded acceptable environmental quality standards of PM2.5 (i.e. up to 15 μg/m^3 annual mean and 35 μg/m^3 daily mean) in the financial year (FY) 2016. In the same FY, 88.3% of the 409 monitoring stations recorded motor vehicle exhaust gases, PM2.5, at acceptable standards (data for FY2015 were 74.5% and 58.4%, respectively) (Ministry of the Environment, 2018). The same report also noted acceptable standards in only 30–60% for some regions with low environmental-standard achievement rates (by prefecture) for general atmospheric monitoring stations, that is, northern Kyushu and parts of Shikoku facing the Seto Inland Sea (Ministry of the Environment, 2018).

Therefore, regions that do not meet PM2.5 environmental standards also exist in Japan. However, given regional differences in severity, PM air pollution is not seen as a social issue affecting the country as a whole. Consequently, surveys on health risks and other negative effects of PM air pollution on a national scale have not been conducted. However, according to the Organization for Economic Co-operation and Development (OECD), the number of air pollution (PM and ozone)–related deaths in Japan in 2010 was 65,776; the associated economic loss was 3.07 billion USD (OECD, 2014). In the same year, air pollution–related deaths or associated economic losses were 1,278,890 or 975,000 USD, respectively, for China; and 23,161 or 3.03 million USD, respectively, for Korea. Both the number of deaths and the economic losses were higher for Japan than for Korea (OECD, 2014).

Of the several studies on transboundary PM air pollution originating from China that have been conducted in Japan, a recent example is a study by the Ministry of the Environment, Environment Management Bureau (2015; Table 13.3). It estimates that 30–40% of PM air pollution in the Kanto area, 50% in the Chubu area and >60% in Kyushu originated from China. That said, considering that PM2.5 levels originating from China have been on a downwards trend since 2016, their recent impact on air pollution in Japan may be less than the estimate. However, according to an analysis by Uno (2017), recent efforts by China to reduce PM air pollution directly relate to a decline in PM levels in the Kyushu area.

Table 13.3 Estimated proportion of PM air pollution originating from China, Korea or within Japan, measured in regions of Japan

Origin of PM	*Kyushu (%)*	*Chugoku (%)*	*Shikoku (%)*	*Kinki (%)*	*Hokuriku (%)*	*Kanto (%)*
China	61	59	59	51	55	39
Korea	10	11	8	6	5	0
Japan	21	25	23	36	33	51

Source: Ministry of the Environment, Environment Management Bureau (2015)

Korea

Facing the reality of severe PM air pollution and public distrust of domestic policies, the Korean government was forced to deal with PM air pollution head on. In May 2017, President Moon directed the temporary shutdown of ten thermal power stations that had been in operation for 30 or more years, as a measure to reduce PM air pollution. Since 2018, operation of these thermal power stations has been suspended between March and June each year. However, the amount of PM reduced following this temporary cessation is estimated to represent only 1–2% of the total PM pollution.[6]

Such short-term compulsive measures have limited effect and the need for a shift to an energy structure based on renewable energy was suggested (Jung, 2017). Moreover, Korea needs to develop a comprehensive strategy to deal with air pollution, climate change and energy use, including the reduction of PM emissions from energy, industry and transportation sectors (Jung, 2017). Since a similar structural shift was suggested for China to achieve its PM2.5 reduction goals (see Ma, 2017), such restructuring is, therefore, a common goal for all East Asian countries.

As can be seen from the foregoing, regarding the state of PM air pollution, understanding of the health effect of PM air pollution has advanced particularly with respect to China. This is likely to yield more public attention to the adverse health effects of PM2.5, associated strengthening of measures that target air pollution, increased public concern and evolution of domestic responses to air pollution in general and PM2.5 pollution in particular in China. Similarly, report and identification of adverse health effects caused by PM2.5 are especially noteworthy in Korea. This reflects advances in monitoring capability and increased public awareness of serious air pollution in Korea.

International cooperation among China, Japan and Korea to reduce air pollution

Numerous schemes for international cooperation among China, Japan and Korea on environmental issues already exist (for a list of related organizations and meetings, see Park, 2019). Of these, the main schemes related to international cooperation on air pollution in East Asia are described here.

The first is EANET, which was established as a Japanese government initiative in 1998. Its main activities include the monitoring of acid rain, data collection, research, technical support and training programs in each member country.

The second scheme is TEMM, a cabinet-level meeting of Japanese, Chinese and Korean government officials to discuss environmental issues. It was established as a Korean government initiative in 1998 and has been convened each year since, marking its twenty-first anniversary in 2019. Transboundary air pollution has been an important topic of discussion since 2013, around the time when rumors about the serious PM air pollution problem in China began to circulate. At the 2017 TEMM, Korea proposed the North-East Asia Clean Air Partnership

(NEACAP) as a platform to address the issue of air pollution. NEACAP was launched in 2018.

The third scheme is the Atmosphere Action Network East Asia (AANEA),[7] established in Seoul in August 1995 as a network for private sector–level international cooperation. AANEA comprises 17 environmental NGOs in seven countries and regions (Japan, Korea, China, Taiwan, Hong Kong, Mongolia, Russian Far East) in East Asia and is the only private sector–level network in East Asia with a focus on environmental issues.

As evident by the foregoing examples, various schemes for international cooperation on air pollution in East Asia (i.e. China, Japan and Korea) exist. However, none of these schemes has gone beyond the establishment of loose frameworks[8] to exchange information and opinions on current conditions and future outlooks. They do not yet serve as regimes capable of imposing specific responses on the countries in question by, for example, identifying sources of air pollution in each country, establishing responsibilities and, thereupon, formulating common environmental policies or establishing international agreements. This state of affairs is in stark contrast to the increasing public anxiety and awareness regarding the serious health hazards posed by PM air pollution, which has become clearer with the monitoring schemes advancing throughout the region.

Meanwhile, Europe was the first region to establish a regional scheme in the form of the Convention of Long-Range Transboundary Air Pollution (CLRTAP). The long-range transboundary air pollution regime in Europe was established and developed from the 1970s to the end of the 1990s (Table 13.4). Key factors contributing to the success of the European regime include the small geographical area of individual countries and the fact that pollution problems that start out as national problems quickly evolve to be international owing to the fact that each country shares borders with multiple other countries.

According to Takahashi (2017), factors underlying the creation of the European regime include the existence of a strong belief in cause and effect, passionate actors with visions for policy (environmental NGOs and citizens' groups), motivated actors with strong political will, and political dynamics that encourage the policy shift of beneficiary actors. Consequently, regional cooperation on environmental issues began earlier there than anywhere else. Examples of such cooperation include the International Commission for the Protection of the Rhine, Convention on the Protection of the Marine Environment of the Baltic Sea Area, and the Convention for the Protection of the Mediterranean Sea against Pollution. Such activities at the regional level created a firm foundation for the establishment of a Europe-wide regime.

In East Asia, the creation of schemes calling for regulation of PM air pollution in each country would be insufficient. If we consider the movement of pollution-causing industries within East Asia and the supply chain structures that constitute trade among countries, it is evident that a new approach to policies that go beyond conventional nation-level regulations is important (Takahashi, 2017). For example, an interrelation exists among China, Japan and Korea, wherein foreign direct investment and trade from Japan and Korea into China influences air pollution

Table 13.4 Evolution of efforts in Europe, North America and East Asia to address transboundary air pollution

Europe	*North America*	*East Asia*
1960 – Damage caused by acid rain in Scandinavian countries identified by a Swedish scientist		
1972 – International monitoring program started in ten West European countries		
1977 – EMEP started		
1979 – CLRTAP convention adopted with 32 signatory countries, including the US and the USSR	**1979** – US and Canada become signatories to CLRTAP	
1983 – CLRTAP registered **1984** – EMEP protocol **1985** – Sulfur protocol **1988** – NOx protocol	**1981** – Negotiations between US and Canada reached a deadlock	
1991 – VOCs protocol **1994** – Second sulfur protocol: using computer tools **1998** – Heavy metals protocol, persistent organic pollutants protocol **1999** – Gothenburg Protocol	**1991** – US-Canada Air Quality Agreement SO_2 and NOx Annex	**1994** – EANET expert meeting (spearheaded by Japan) **1996** – LTP research project (Korean initiative: Japan-China-Korea)
	2000 – Ozone annex	**2000** – EANET intergovernmental meeting joint declaration **2001** – EANET official launch **2010** – Paper on strengthening EANET

Source: Created by the authors based on Takahashi (2017)

Note: EMEP, European Monitoring and Evaluation Programme; VOCs, volatile organic compounds; LTP, long-term persistence.

within China and transboundary pollution from China. This, in turn, affects the people of Japan and Korea (Shapiro, 2016). Given this interdependence of East Asian countries in terms of international trade and supply chains, and in addition to simply demanding that the main countries responsible for transboundary pollution address the issue themselves, transnational schemes for PM2.5 emissions trading and environmental taxes should also be explored. To this end, policies aimed at decarbonization that are currently implemented by East Asian countries and other countries around the world are expected to have impacts similar to those aimed at reducing PM air pollution.

Recent research demonstrated that integration of policies aimed at air pollution and policies that target the reduction of greenhouse gas (GHG) emissions at the regional level are cost effective and have synergistic effects (Huang et al., 2017; Sakuramoto, 2018).[9] In the next section, we consider the potential effects and impacts of various air pollution–related policy scenarios based on analysis using the E3ME model.

Analysis of PM emissions using E3ME

As just discussed, the adverse impacts of PM air pollution in East Asia are considerable, and there is an urgent need to strengthen related policies.

In this section, we estimate the level of PM emissions generated in China, Japan and Korea, using the E3ME model. We use the baseline scenario (i.e. no special limits on fossil fuel consumption) described in Chapter 5 and Scenario 1 (S1; i.e. carbon taxes only) described in Chapter 5, in which fossil fuel consumption decreases in line with the long-term decarbonization target. Although PM air pollution policies have already been implemented in China, Japan and Korea, here, we investigate the spillover effects from meeting ambitious long-term emission targets in these countries.

Fossil fuels, including coal, natural gas and gasoline, contain certain amounts of nitrogen and sulfur compounds that, upon combustion, are released to the air as SO_2 and NOx. Both are known precursor pollutants of PM that also is emitted directly by combustion fuels. When no limits are placed on fossil fuels, emissions of air pollutants are expected to increase because of increased fossil fuel consumption. When policies, such as carbon taxes, energy efficiency programs or renewable energy mandates, are implemented to discourage fossil fuel consumption, it is expected that emissions of air pollutants decrease as well.

Emissions of SO_2, NOx, CO and N_2O, and direct PM2.5 emissions for a few selected years in each scenario are shown in Table 13.5. As expected, large reductions in annual emissions or pollutants can be achieved by enacting carbon-limiting policies. Compared with those of the baseline scenario, direct PM2.5 emissions in 2050 reduced in China and Japan by 35% and 25%, respectively, in the climate change mitigation scenario S1, whereas Korea reduced direct PM2.5 emissions by 61%. The latter is important in the context of the societal issues currently caused by exposure to PM2.5 in Korea. It should be remembered that the scenario includes only policies to reduce energy-related emissions. Therefore, these results are due to changes in energy use rather than policies that directly target improvements in air quality.

The changes in emissions affect the concentration of PM2.5 and, therefore, exposure of the population downwind of the emission sources. When we connect the change of air pollutant emissions with health damage factors in humans determined in life cycle assessment studies, we can roughly estimate the change in years of life

Table 13.5 Development of annual emissions of several air pollutants at baseline scenario and scenario 1

Pollutant		*Emission at baseline (kt/y)*			*Emission at S1 (kt/y)*		*Change from Baseline (%)*	
		2010	*2030*	*2050*	*2030*	*2050*	*2030*	*2050*
Japan	*SO_2*	2,390	2,473	2,391	1,504	998	-39	-58
	NOx	2,468	2,518	2,522	1,582	1,137	-37	-55
	CO	9,859	9,146	8,724	6,944	4,493	-24	-49
	N_2O	94	97	96	82	73	-15	-23
	PM2.5	167	166	178	133	133	-20	-25
China	*SO_2*	41,367	40,499	42,970	17,384	9,279	-57	-78
	NOx	21,528	24,011	23,425	12,994	8,254	-46	-65
	CO	109,635	119,810	108,766	84,918	63,321	-29	-42
	N_2O	1,817	2,174	2,499	1,764	1,651	-19	-34
	PM2.5	12,431	13,355	12,992	10,428	8,468	-22	-35
Korea	*SO_2*	1,082	1,059	947	632	251	-40	-74
	NOx	1,414	1,593	1,946	1,138	920	-29	-53
	CO	3,411	3,602	3,753	2,895	2,203	-20	-41
	N_2O	67	71	70	61	48	-15	-31
	PM2.5	167	158	148	104	57	-34	-61

Source: E3ME model outcome

Note:
1 Baseline scenario, no fossil fuel consumption limit (as described in Chapter 5).
2 Scenario 1, carbon taxes only (as described in Chapter 5).
3 Pollutants in bold are direct PM emissions; pollutants in italics are PM2.5-precursor pollutants.

lost (YLL), that is, premature mortality, of the population between the scenarios. Van Zelm et al. (2016) calculated health damage factors of direct PM2.5 and its precursor pollutants for several regions across the world by comparing changes in PM2.5 concentration caused by changes in emission with those in the base year 2000. Note that figures produced by this and similar studies are static, and not very applicable on large timescales, because many factors are susceptible to change. Among them are demographics (affecting mortality and/or morbidity), climate change (affecting atmospheric chemistry) and annual emission profiles (affecting non-linear PM2.5 formation). In addition, the change in YLL applies to the global population because of the transboundary effects of pollutant transportation. However, since China, Japan and Korea mainly affect one another, it is justified to assume that the largest portion of adverse health effects can be attributed to the population of the East Asian countries (see Tang et al., 2018). Table 13.6 shows the change in YLL for the combined emission changes of the East Asian countries.

Highest values are obtained in China, where the adverse effects to human health are expected to increase at baseline scenario in 2030 compared with those in 2000. At the climate change mitigation scenario S1, only adverse effects resulting from

Table 13.6 YLL caused by PM2.5 exposure, as a result of precursor or direct emissions, in millions of years of life lost (applicable to the global population)

Pollutant		*YLL 2030 (mln yr)*				*YLL 2050 (mln yr)*			
		Baseline[1]	*S1*[2]	Δ[3]	*Total*[4]	*Baseline*	*S1*	Δ[3]	*Total*[4]
Japan	SO_2	−0.08	−0.23	−0.15		−0.10	−0.31	−0.21	
	NOx	−0.01	−0.05	−0.04		−0.01	−0.06	−0.05	
	PM2.5	−0.19	−0.24	−0.05		−0.17	−0.24	−0.07	
China	SO_2	5.52	−0.72	-6.24		6.19	−2.91	-9.10	
	NOx	2.78	0.13	-2.65	-14.21	2.65	−0.84	-3.49	-20.59
	PM2.5	7.00	2.02	-4.98		6.38	−1.31	-7.69	
Korea	SO_2	−0.09	−0.14	−0.05		−0.01	−0.01	0.00	
	NOx	0.00	−0.02	−0.02		0.00	0.00	0.00	
	PM2.5	−0.12	−0.16	−0.04		−0.03	0.00	0.03	

Source: Authors' own calculation, based on E3ME model results and human health characterization factors as obtained by Van Zelm et al. (2016)

Note:

1 Baseline, emissions at baseline scenario in 2030 or 2050 relative to those in 2000, multiplied by the human health characterization factor (Van Zelm et al., 2016).

2 S1, emissions at Scenario 1 in 2030 or 2050 relative to those in 2000, multiplied by the human health characterization factor (Van Zelm et al., 2016).

3 Δ, Difference of YLL between scenarios by pollutant.

4 Total, Difference in YLL between scenarios (all three pollutants and three East Asian countries combined).

direct PM2.5 are still noticeable, which implies that emission levels are close to that of the year 2000. However, the difference between the relative human health damage at baseline and S1 is a large decrease in YLL, which is even more obvious in 2050. Emission levels in Japan and Korea under baseline conditions are similar to their respective emission levels of the year 2000. When S1 climate change mitigation policies are implemented, the adverse effects to human health are reduced further, except for PM2.5 exposure attributable to direct PM2.5 emissions in Japan and Korea. However, Korea is likely to benefit greatly from the policies in China as the country is located downwind of China (see Tang et al., 2018).

Another way of expressing the effect of direct and indirect PM2.5 exposure is through monetization. A study carried out by the International Monetary Fund (IMF) has sought to quantify the costs to the economy because of adverse health effects following exposure to PM2.5 (IMF, 2014). Although monetization of adverse health effects or lives saved is not without controversy, it can provide insights to the economic benefits of reducing air pollution. Based on a willingness-to-pay metric linked to average wages in each country, the IMF established monetized air pollution damage by emission source and pollutant type for PM2.5 exposure. They distinguished impacts of emissions by pollutant and source. The sources here are emissions by coal-based power plants, gas-based power plants and mobile emissions. For this study, regional data were used that were available in

2010. An example is the number of power plants with controlling units to prevent emissions. This is susceptible to change over a long time span. In addition, the valuation of life is wage based and, especially in China, this might change in time and, thereby, change the cost impacts of emissions.

By using these data and connecting them to the E3ME outcomes, we obtained the values presented in Table 13.7. At first glance, it seems that major costs can be avoided when climate change mitigation policies are enacted (as in S1). China

Table 13.7 Amount of pollutant emissions by source type at baseline and S1, and costs avoided and its share of the projected GDP

Pollutant			*Baseline (kt/y)*		*S1 (kt/y)*		*2030*		*2050*	
			2030	*2050*	*2030*	*2050*	*Costs avoided (bn US$)*	*GDP (%)*	*Cost avoided (bn US$)*	*GDP (%)*
Japan	PG emissions	SO_2	855	1,013	291	182	23.70	0.5	34.87	0.6
		NOx	1,008	1194	343	215	16.30	0.4	23.99	0.4
		PM2.5	17	20	6	4	0.56	0.0	0.83	0.0
	TP emissions	SO_2	12	11	11	9	0.02	0.0	0.05	0.0
		NOx	475	438	457	372	0.11	0.0	0.42	0.0
		PM2.5	20	18	19	16	0.58	0.0	2.26	0.0
China	PG emissions	SO_2	23,720	29,094	6,140	3,716	418.60	4.1	604.29	3.0
		NOx	9890	12,130	2,560	1,549	117.77	1.1	170.01	0.8
		PM2.5	935	1,146	242	146	20.73	0.2	29.92	0.1
	TP emissions	SO_2	287	238	233	201	0.24	0.0	0.16	0.0
		NOx	4,862	2,883	3,672	2,434	1.09	0.0	0.41	0.0
		PM2.5	439	328	345	274	11.65	0.1	6.79	0.0
Korea	PG emissions	SO_2	377	443	102	33	9.61	0.7	14.35	0.7
		NOx	390	459	106	34	7.23	0.5	10.79	0.5
		PM2.5	49	57	13	4	1.62	0.1	2.42	0.1
	TP emissions	SO_2	20	29	18	18	0.05	0.0	0.22	0.0
		NOx	854	1,234	757	784	0.42	0.0	1.91	0.1
		PM2.5	20	28	17	18	1.22	0.1	5.58	0.3

Source: Authors' own calculation, based on E3ME model outcome and monetized damage as calculated by IMF (2014)

Note:

1 Whereas the IMF distinguishes the costs caused by emissions between those from coal-based and gas-based power plants, we combined them into one category, that is, power generation (PG), by averaging the cost impacts of both.

2 PG emissions, smokestack GHG emissions resulting from power generation.

3 TP emissions, transportation GHG emissions (e.g. by vehicles, rail, etc.).

could save roughly a little less than 500 bn US$ (deflated to year 2010; $2010) by reducing SO_2 emitted by its power plants. Relative to China's projected GDP, this is 4.1% in 2030 and 3.0% in 2050. Considering all emissions and sources, China would be able to save 5.5% in 2030 and 4.0% in 2050. Japan would be able to save 1.0% of their projected GDP in both 2030 and 2050 and for Korea this would be ~1.5% in 2030 and 1.7% in 2050.

In summary, by imposing climate mitigation policies as in S1, air pollution will be reduced and air quality improved. Moreover, adverse effects of air pollution on human health are likely to decrease substantially in the future. As a result, health care spending by governments or the private sector should decrease. In addition, a healthier population is more productive and, therefore, contributes to higher rates of economic growth.

Conclusions

East Asia faces a serious PM air pollution problem, and a wide variety of research has been conducted regarding pollution specifics and the damage caused by PM. Although not all latent adverse effects have been sufficiently identified, past research has demonstrated the enormity of health hazards as well as economic and welfare losses. Whereas several policies are being strengthened in each East Asian country, short-term measures implemented in China and Korea – such as forced temporary shutdown of power plants and industry, are insufficient. Instead, a drastic shift in energy structure is needed, that is, one in which industry relies on renewable energy types rather than fossil fuels. Moreover, such policies are expected to interact positively with the low-carbon policies discussed in previous chapters.

Coordinated efforts by China, Japan and Korea are essential to dealing with PM air pollution and other issues of transboundary pollution in East Asia. As mentioned in this chapter, transnational schemes, such as TEMM and EANET, exist. However, such schemes in East Asia have little legal basis and there is little coordination or cooperation between the various frameworks. Thus, there is no guarantee that these schemes will yield effective policies in the future.

By contrast, in Europe, progress has been made to effectively reduce acid rain, ozone and GHG emissions, and to deal with PM air pollution through multiple frameworks, such as the CLRTAP and a Europe-wide regulation of PM emissions. The creation of analogous legal arrangements in China, Japan and Korea is hindered by various factors, including weak environmental policies in East Asia overall – and China in particular, insufficient economic incentives for cooperation, language barriers, undeveloped grassroots level schemes relative to Europe and the weak problem-solving ability of the governments concerned because of their vertical structures.

In addition to overcoming the aforementioned challenges, the integration of environmental and energy policies, and the creation of schemes with a firm legal basis are essential to effectively deal with PM air pollution and other transboundary pollution issues in East Asia. To achieve this, a paradigm shift is required. This means moving away from a framework that splits the region into upstream and downstream countries, and pits perpetrators against victims. Rather, it is crucial to implement a structure that does not seek to assign unilateral blame or create unidirectional policies.

From our analysis using E3ME, we conclude that emissions of non-CO_2 air pollutants can decrease because of spillover effects from decarbonization policies. Improvement of air quality directly leads to reductions of adverse health impacts and may have further positive economic impacts by improving labor productivity. In such a scenario, government spending on health care is expected to decrease. The model-based analysis also confirms that all of East Asia stands to benefit from reductions in air pollution in China. The challenge for policy makers is, thus, to coordinate a system that provides benefits to the region as a whole.

Notes

1 Hereinafter, PM10 and PM2.5 are referred to collectively as 'PM air pollutants' or 'PM air pollution', unless specification is necessary.
2 Owing to strokes, heart disease, lung cancer, chronic obstructive pulmonary disease, respiratory infection and pneumonia
3 In China, the degree to which environmental policies are enforced tends to be left to the discretion of local governments and thus varies depending on the economic conditions and climate at the time.
4 South Korea among most polluted nations, *The Straits Times*, April 1, 2017, www.straitstimes.com/asia/east-asia/s-korea-among-most-polluted-nations, accessed on December 14, 2018
5 November 16, 2018, morning edition of the *Asahi Shimbun* (Japanese newspaper)
6 President orders shutdown of old plants, *Korea Joongang Daily*, May 16, 2017, accessed on December 14, 2018
7 AANEA, www.mie-u.ac.jp/chiiki/aanea/sub1.htm
8 Here, the term 'loose frameworks' refers to voluntary cooperation between related actors together with the not legally binding understandings, agreements and declarations created through this cooperation (Miyazaki, 2011).
9 Sakuramoto shows the effect of the energy structure shift on reducing health hazards related to PM2.5 in China.

References

References published in Japanese

Ministry of the Environment, Environment Management Bureau. (2015) *International Cooperation on Air Environment Policy*, www.env.go.jp/air/osen/pm/conf/conf02-03/mat05.pdf.

Ministry of the Environment. (2018) *State of Air Pollution in FY2016 (Report on General Atmospheric Monitoring Stations and Motor Vehicle Exhaust Monitoring Stations*, March 20, 2018, www.env.go.jp/press/105288.html, accessed on December 1, 2018.

Miyazaki, A. (2011) 'Formation of "Loose" Systems of Environmental Cooperation', *Japan Kokusai Seiji [International Politics]*, published by the Japan Association of International Relations, 166: 128–141.

Sakuramoto, H. (ed.) (2018) *Inter-Disciplinary of Environmental Protection for the Improvement Effect of Particulate Matter (PM2.5) by Energy Conversion to Control Pollution in China Based on Input-Output Analysis*, V2-solution Books.

Takahashi, W. (2017) *Comparative Politics of Transboundary Pollution: Europe, North America, and East Asia*, Chikura Publishing Company.

References published in Chinese

Ministry of Ecology and Environment of the People's Republic of China (2015) *Platform for Displaying Real-Time Air Quality of Chinese Cities*, 24-hour data, http://113.108.142.147:20035/emcpublish/.

Pan, X., Li, G. and Gao, T. (2012) *Dangerous Breathing: PM2.5 Measuring the Human Health and Economic Impacts on China's Largest Cities*, China Environmental Science Press.

References published in English

Chen, R., Yin, P., Meng, X., Liu, C., Wang, L., Xu, X., Ross, A. J., Tse, A. L., Zhou, Z., Kan, H. and Zhou, M. (2017) 'Fine Particulate Air Pollution and Daily Mortality: A Nationwide Analysis in 272 Chinese Cities', *American Journal of Respiratory and Critical Care Medicine*, 196(1): 73–81, https://doi.org/10.1164/rccm.201609-1862OC, accessed on December 14, 2018.

HEI and IHME. (2017) *State of Global Air/2017: A Special Report on Global Exposure to Air Pollution and Its Disease Burden*, www.stateofglobalair.org/archives, accessed on December 14, 2018.

HEI and IHME. (2018) *State of Global Air/2018: A Special Report on Global Exposure to Air Pollution and Its Disease Burden*, www.stateofglobalair.org/report, accessed on December 14, 2018.

Huang, C., Wang, Q., Wang, S., Ren, M., Ma, R. and He, Y. (2017) 'Air Pollution Prevention and Control Policy in China', in H. Guang (Ed.), *Ambient Air Pollution and Health Impact in China*, Springer.

IMF. (2014) *Getting Energy Prices Right: From Principle to Practice*, IMF.

Jung, W. (2017) *South Korea's Air Pollution: Gasping for Solutions*, Policy Brief, Institute for Security and Development Policy, No. 199, June 16, 2017, http://isdp.eu/publication/south-koreas-air-pollution-gasping-solutions/, accessed on November 28, 2018.

Ma, J. (2017) *The Economics of Air Pollution in China: Achieving Better and Cleaner Growth*, New York: Columbia University Press.

Newby, D. E., Mannucci, P. M., Tell, G. S. et al. (2015) 'Expert Position Paper on Air Pollution and Cardiovascular Disease', *European Heart Journal*, 36: 83–93.

OECD. (2014) *The Cost of Air Pollution: Health Impacts of Road Transport*, OECD.

Park, J. B. (2019) *Regional Environmental Politics in Northeast Asia: Conflict and Cooperation*, New York: Routledge.

Shapiro, M. (2016) *Transboundary Air Pollution in Northeast Asia: The Political Economy of Yellow Dust, Particulate Matter, and PM2.5*, KEI Academic Paper Series, KEI (Korea Economic Institute of America).

Tang, L., Nagashima, T., Hasegawa, K., Ohara, T., Sudo, K. and Itsubo, N. (2018) 'Development of Human Health Damage Factors for PM 2.5 Based on a Global

Chemical Transport Model', *The International Journal of Life Cycle Assessment*, 23(12): 2300–2310.

The United States Environmental Protection Agency. (2018) *Particulate Matter (PM) Pollution*, www.epa.gov/pm-pollution, accessed on December 1, 2018.

Uno, I., Wang, Z., Yumimoto, K., Itahashi, S., Osada, K., Irie, H., Yamamoto, S., Hayasaki, M. and Sugata, S. (2017) 'Is PM2.5 Trans-Boundary Environmental Problem in Japan Dramatically Improving?', *Journal of Japan Society for Atmospheric Environment*, 52(1): 177–184.

Van Zelm, R., Preiss, P., van Goethem, T., Van Dingenen, R. and Huijbregts, M. (2016) 'Regionalized Life Cycle Impact Assessment of Air Pollution on the Global Scale: Damage to Human Health and Vegetation', *Atmospheric Environment*, 134: 129–137.

WHO. (2018) *Nine Out of Ten People Worldwide Breathe Polluted Air, But More Countries Are Taking Action*, May 2, 2018, www.who.int/news-room/detail/02-05-2018-9-out-of-10-people-worldwide-breathe-polluted-air-but-more-countries-are-taking-action, accessed on December 1, 2018.

World Bank and IHME. (2016), *The Cost of Air Pollution: Strengthening the Economic Case for Action*, World Bank.

Zhang et al. (2017, March 29) 'Transboundary Health Impacts of Transported Global Air Pollution and International Trade', *Nature*, 543: 705–709.

Concluding remarks and future challenges

Soocheol Lee, Hector Pollitt and Kiyoshi Fujikawa

Summary and conclusions

The objective of this book was to clarify the direction in which systems related to energy, the environment and resource use in East Asia should change in order to achieve a sustainable future. Toward this end, we quantitatively analyzed the impact that environmental, energy and resource use policies aimed at achieving the 2°C goal set forth in the Paris Agreement has on the environment and the economy in the medium- and long-term up to 2050 using the E3ME global macro-econometric model and the FTT bottom-up technology choice models, and used the results as a gauge for analyzing the efficacy of various changes to relevant policies. To achieve these goals, the book was divided into three parts with the following themes.

Part 1 – building low-carbon power generation while simultaneously reducing the role of nuclear

We considered how existing policies pertaining to the power sector, including regulations on nuclear and coal power, carbon taxes and Feed-in-Tariffs will change the power mixes of East Asian countries – China, Japan, South Korea and Taiwan – and how they could be improved upon for the sustainable future of the region. We suggested a desirable policy mix for a low-carbon sustainable power sector under denuclearization and coal power regulation. The results of analyses using the E3ME and FTT: Power models led us to conclude that such policy mixes – which involve the use of carbon taxes, renewable energy subsidies and energy conservation – could enable the achievement of the power generation sector's contribution to the 2°C climate target without hindering economic prosperity.

Part 2 – innovating to reduce CO_2 emissions in industry, transport and buildings

We evaluated the impact of policy mixes including a low, politically acceptable carbon tax and various low-carbon policies on meeting the 2°C target. We also tested the impacts of these policies on macroeconomic performance, sectoral production and employment. In Part 2, we demonstrated that, when low-carbon subsidies and regulations are effectively designed, the 2°C goal and economic prosperity can simultaneously be achieved through the development and diffusion of new technologies in the industry (steel), transport and building sectors. We showed that, if a portfolio of policies is applied, CO_2 reduction targets could be met without excessively high carbon tax rates. We also showed that the revenues from carbon taxation could be used to increase economic growth rates at the same time as reducing emissions.

Part 3 – wider sustainability issues: reducing water and material consumption, and improving air quality

In Part 3, we elucidated on the need for resource taxation and other policies to reduce the environmental pressures resulting from the high consumption of water and material resources. We also considered transboundary environmental issues in East Asia, first through the movement of virtual water in trade and second through air pollution. Regarding countermeasures to transboundary pollution, we proposed new legally based governance structures (e.g. establishment of an advisory council on environmental and energy security in East Asia that is jointly chaired by the heads of state of each country) that could enable East Asian countries to closely coordinate policy.

Insights and future challenges that emerge from the investigations in this book

The investigations in this book indicate that, at the very least, close policy coordination and cooperative action by China, Japan and Korea are essential conditions for the creation of sustainable, low-carbon societies in East Asia and to ensure societies that are secure in terms of the environment and energy.

In this section, we attempt to clarify the current state of understanding and direction of policies regarding three issues – the risks of nuclear power (energy security), climate change (low-carbon societies) and PM air pollution (environmental safety and human health) – based on insights drawn from the investigations presented in this book.

First, in light of the risks posed by nuclear power, the world is moving in the direction of abandoning or gradually decreasing nuclear power generation, and this movement is centered on European countries. By contrast, nuclear power continues to be positioned as an important energy source in East Asia, and efforts are being made to build new nuclear power plants or to restart offline plants. This trend is especially evident in China, where 37 plants were in operation as of the end of 2018, and plans are in place for 100 plants to be operating by 2030. Some of the plants currently in operation in China, Japan and Korea suffer from deterioration because of age. If an accident were to occur, the impact would likely be devastating, not only to the country where the accident occurred but also to neighboring countries.

In the wake of the Fukushima Dai-ichi Nuclear Power Plant (NPP) accident, Europe, which is subject to EU directives regarding the safety of nuclear power generation, has urged member countries to conduct stress tests and has engaged in efforts to reexamine safety based on highly transparent risk assessments. Similar advances are not evident in East Asia, where even the sharing of data related to nuclear power safety is not common. A report by the U.S. Environmental Protection Agency (October 16, 2012) pointed out that efforts to create a common management system in East Asia are hindered by China, Japan and Korea having different aging and safety standards. Although there are several organizations for cooperation on nuclear power safety by China, Japan, Korea and other nations – including the Forum for Nuclear Cooperation Asia (FNCA) and the Asian Nuclear Safety Network (ANSN) – such organizations do little more than hold annual meetings and, in fact, have not taken any action even after the Fukushima Dai-ichi NPP accident. There is a long list of issues requiring immediate attention, including:

- Comparative analysis of nuclear power policies and regulations in East Asia
- Creation of systems for implementing countermeasures before and after accidents
- Training of experts in risk management
- Establishment of a common regime and governance structure for managing the risks of nuclear power covering a wide range of areas, including technological improvement and information sharing.

Regarding the issue of climate change, China, Japan and Korea account for approximately one third of global greenhouse gas (GHG) emissions (as of 2015). However, given that China and Korea use output and business-as-usual (BAU) levels as bases for emission reduction targets, the goals set by these two countries (as well as Japan) are insufficient for achieving the 2°C target set in the Paris Agreement. Furthermore, given that East Asia has no shared governance structure for reducing GHG emissions, policy coordination is lacking. In contrast, the EU has contributed substantially to GHG emission reduction in Europe through the establishment of an emissions trading system and various other joint initiatives. If East Asian countries were able to work together to develop low-carbon policy, promote technical cooperation, establish a common carbon market and expand renewable energy use, this would lead to substantial progress with respect to transitioning to a new energy structure and developing new low-carbon technologies, and would enable East Asia to become a global leader in new low-carbon economic growth.

Regarding the issue of transboundary pollution, the concentration of PM2.5, which is a representative pollutant, exceeds environmental standards in several locations in Japan and is a serious problem in China and Korea. According to air pollution dispersion models utilized by the National Institute for Environmental

Studies, in Japan, 40–45% of PM2.5 emissions in Tokyo and the Kanto region originate from outside Japan, with this figure reaching 70% in Fukuoka and the Kyushu region. In East Asia, there are multiple frameworks related to transboundary pollution, including the Acid Deposition Monitoring Network in East Asia (EANET), led by Japan, and the Joint Research Project on Long-Range Transboundary Air Pollutants in Northeast Asia (LTP), led by Korea. Reduction of PM2.5 is also recognized as an important priority by the Tripartite Environment Ministers Meeting among China, Japan and Korea (TEMM). That said, there is little coordination and cooperation among these frameworks, and it would be difficult to say that they have resulted in the adoption of effective measures. In contrast, in the EU, initiatives to effectively reduce acid rain, ozone and GHG emissions and efforts to reduce PM2.5 have been advanced through various frameworks, including the Convention on Long-Range Transboundary Air Pollution and the EU Emissions Trading System. The examples from Europe suggest that a similar approach of dealing simultaneously with multiple contaminants would also be effective in Asia.

It is clear that the use of fossil fuel energy contributes substantially to both climate change and transboundary pollution, and that reducing fossil energy use will contribute to the simultaneous resolution of climate change and transboundary pollution. At the same time, reducing the use of fossil fuel energy is directly related to medium- and long-term energy planning and the transition of energy structure. Thus, it cannot be separated from the issue of nuclear power generation. The foregoing discussions indicate that these three issues are deeply interrelated.

The preceding discussion lays bare the lack of progress in East Asia in the context of not having a foundation for common governance by all member nations like the one present in the EU. Why is it so difficult to put into practice measures with a scientific basis that are known to be effective? Is the root cause the weakness of governance in East Asia?

It should be noted here that previous studies have pointed out the potential for highly effective handling of environmental and energy-related issues if China, Japan and Korea were to act simultaneously in a coordinated manner (Lee, 2014; Lee et al., 2015). That said, the reality is that such coordinated action has not yet been observed. Environmental and energy issues affect all aspects of a nation's economy and society. The weak governance of East Asian policy cooperation makes international policy integration difficult. For example, although cooperative frameworks such as TEMM, EANET, LRT and FNCA exist, they have not yielded noteworthy results because of the weakness of governance. Furthermore, the issue of nuclear power is rarely, if ever, discussed in the context of these regional frameworks.

Recognizing that East Asia is a community with extremely complicated interrelations when it comes to the environment, economic activity and geopolitics, perhaps emphasis should be placed on developing a shared perception of issues and values. Ample experience has taught us that effective measures do not arise from frameworks that divide the region into upstream and downstream countries and pit perpetrators against victims. Those responsible for formulating policies in their respective countries must bear in mind that the critical element for ensuring environmental and energy security in East Asia is not an approach that seeks to assign unilateral responsibility or to demand implementation of policies by a single actor, but rather an integrated approach that emphasizes spillover effects, sustainable development and ecological modernization.

References

Lee, Soocheol (ed.) (2014) *Energy and Environmental Policy in East Asia-Nuclear Power/Climate Change/Air – Water Pollution*. Showado Press: Japan.

Lee, Soocheol, Hector Pollitt and Seung-Joon Park (eds.) (2015) *Low-Carbon, Sustainable Future in East Asia: Improving Energy Systems, Taxation and Policy Cooperation*. New York: Routledge.

Index

Note: Page numbers in italic indicate a figure and page numbers in bold indicate a table on the corresponding page.